John Paul II
FOR
DUMMIES®

**by Rev. John Trigilio, Jr., PhD, ThD;
Rev. Kenneth Brighenti, PhD; and
Rev. Jonathan Toborowsky, MA**

Foreword by Rev. Monsignor James Cafone, STD
Assistant Professor of Religious Studies, Seton Hall University

WILEY

Wiley Publishing, Inc.

John Paul II For Dummies®

Published by
Wiley Publishing, Inc.
111 River St.
Hoboken, NJ 07030-5774
www.wiley.com

For general information on our other products and services, please contact our Customer Care Department within the U.S. at 800-762-2974, outside the U.S. at 317-572-3993, or fax 317-572-4002.

For technical support, please visit www.wiley.com/techsupport.

Wiley also publishes its books in a variety of electronic formats. Some content that appears in print may not be available in electronic books.

Library of Congress Control Number: 2006929464

ISBN-13: 978-0-471-77382-5

ISBN-10: 0-471-77382-4

Manufactured in the United States of America

10 9 8 7 6 5 4 3 2 1

1B/QR/RS/QW/IN

WILEY

About the Authors

Rev. John Trigilio, Jr., PhD, ThD: A native of Erie, Pennsylvania, Father Trigilio serves as the pastor of Our Lady of Good Counsel (Marysville, Pennsylvania) and St. Bernadette Catholic Churches (Duncannon, Pennsylvania). He is the President of the Confraternity of Catholic Clergy and Executive Editor of its quarterly journal, *Sapientia* magazine. Father Trigilio is a co-host of two weekly TV series on the Eternal Word Television Network (EWTN): *Web of Faith* and *Crash Course in Catholicism.* He also serves as a theological consultant and online spiritual advisor for EWTN. He was listed in *Who's Who in America* in 1993 and *Who's Who in Religion* in 1999 and is a member of the Fellowship of Catholic Scholars. He was ordained a priest for the Diocese of Harrisburg (Pennsylvania) in 1988.

Rev. Kenneth Brighenti, PhD: A native of New Britain, Connecticut, Father Brighenti serves as pastor of St. Ann Catholic Church (Raritan, New Jersey). He is the Managing Editor of *Sapientia* magazine, a member of the Board of Directors for the Confraternity of Catholic Clergy, and is co-host of *Crash Course in Catholicism,* a weekly TV series on EWTN. Father Brighenti also served as a U.S. Naval Reserve Chaplain for ten years and was ordained a priest for the Diocese of Metuchen (New Jersey) in 1988. He and Father Trigilio co-authored *Catholicism For Dummies* (2003), *The Everything Bible Book* (2004), and *Women in the Bible For Dummies* (2005).

Rev. Jonathan Toborowsky, MA: A native of Port Reading, New Jersey, Father Toborowsky serves as Parochial Vicar of St. Mary Catholic Church (Alpha, New Jersey). He is the host and moderator of *Proclaim the Good News,* a weekly radio show, and an online theological advisor for Ave Maria Single Catholics Online. He was ordained a priest for the Diocese of Metuchen (New Jersey) in 1998.

Dedication

This book is dedicated in memory of His Holiness, Pope John Paul II, whom we firmly believe and trust will one day be proclaimed John Paul the Great and Doctor of the Church (the *Luminous Doctor,* just as St. Thomas Aquinas was known as the *Angelic Doctor* and St. Bonaventure as the *Seraphic Doctor*). Although his beatification and canonization are within the hands of Almighty God and the current reigning pope, like many of the faithful, we are confident that these, too, will eventually happen in time as per Divine Providence. Each one of us owes a great debt of gratitude for the example, inspiration, and model of priestly sanctity, personal piety, and pastoral love John Paul lived and expressed throughout his priesthood and pontificate. We grew up with heroes like the courageous astronauts who landed on the moon and the honest athletes who showed good sportsmanship, but when we became adults, the temptation to cynicism arose thanks to scandals, dishonor, deceit, and disgrace, which infected sports, politics, and even some within religion itself. Then, when it seemed as if a dark shadow of malaise had permeated every institution from church to state, God sent us a priest, prophet, and shepherd — a wise man from the East (at least Eastern Europe), called Karol Wojtyła. His 26-year papacy, in its zeal, its orthodoxy, and its effect, inspired many of us to follow the "fisherman" and become priests. May the Good Lord reward Pope John Paul II for his great love and service and the sacrifices he rendered to save souls and to serve Holy Mother Church as the Servant of the Servants of God. We commend him in our prayers to the bosom of Our Lady, Queen of the Clergy and Mother of the Church, so she may escort him to her Son Whom he loved and served to the best of his ability.

We also commend this work to our current pope, Benedict XVI. As (Cardinal Ratzinger) a faithful friend, loyal servant and accomplished advisor, he served Pope John Paul II to the best of his abilities. As he now brings those same gifts to the Church as Vicar of Christ himself, we believe that the good work begun by JP2 will continue and flourish under B16.

This book is also dedicated in memory of our dear friend and colleague, Father James Pilsner, a priest of the Archdiocese of New York and member of the Board of Directors of the Confraternity of Catholic Clergy as well as Treasurer of our organization, who passed away suddenly while we were writing this book. May Christ the High Priest give him eternal rest.

Authors' Acknowledgments

We wish to thank the Pope John Paul II Cultural Center (www.jp2cc.org) for their invaluable assistance and recommend that our readers visit this jewel in Washington, D.C., where you can experience the life, teachings, and papal ministry of Pope John Paul II. This facility is a resource of material and information on the most influential pope of modern times, if not since St. Peter himself. More than just an exhibit, the Pope John Paul II Cultural Center is a national treasure like the Basilica of the National Shrine of the Immaculate Conception, which is just across the street, adjacent to Catholic University of America — well worth the visit any time you're in the District of Columbia.

Finally, we would like to thank Rev. Robert J. Levis, PhD; Heather Dismore; Christopher Kaczor, PhD; Jessica Faust; Tracy Boggier; Joyce Pepple; and Elizabeth Kuball for their technical assistance.

Publisher's Acknowledgments

We're proud of this book; please send us your comments through our Dummies online registration form located at www.dummies.com/register/.

Some of the people who helped bring this book to market include the following:

Acquisitions, Editorial, and Media Development

Project Editor: Elizabeth Kuball

Acquisitions Editor: Tracy Boggier

Assistant Editor: Courtney Allen

Editorial Program Coordinator: Hanna K. Scott

Technical Editor: Christopher Kaczor, PhD

Consultant: Heather Dismore

Editorial Manager: Michelle Hacker

Editorial Supervisor and Reprint Editor: Carmen Krikorian

Editorial Assistants: Erin Calligan, Nadine Bell, David Lutton

Cover Image: © Martin Child/Photographer's Choice RF

Cartoons: Rich Tennant (www.the5thwave.com)

Composition Services

Project Coordinator: Adrienne Martinez

Layout and Graphics: Carl Byers, Andrea Dahl, Stephanie D. Jumper, Barbara Moore, Barry Offringa, Lynsey Osborn, Heather Ryan, Alicia B. South

Proofreaders: Leeann Harney, Christy Pingleton, Dwight Ramsey, Techbooks

Indexer: Techbooks

Publishing and Editorial for Consumer Dummies

    Diane Graves Steele, Vice President and Publisher, Consumer Dummies

    Joyce Pepple, Acquisitions Director, Consumer Dummies

    Kristin A. Cocks, Product Development Director, Consumer Dummies

    Michael Spring, Vice President and Publisher, Travel

    Kelly Regan, Editorial Director, Travel

Publishing for Technology Dummies

    Andy Cummings, Vice President and Publisher, Dummies Technology/General User

Composition Services

    Gerry Fahey, Vice President of Production Services

    Debbie Stailey, Director of Composition Services

Contents at a Glance

Table of Contents

Foreword

In the 20 centuries since Jesus Christ called Simon Peter to follow Him, there have been many popes. Some have been saintly and most others very ordinary men. A very few have been infamously notorious and guilty of every sin under the sun. Some of Peter's successors have imitated that humble fisherman's shame and awe in the face of his miraculous Lord and Savior. Others, filled with Peter's faith, have bravely endured anguish and martyrdom to follow their Master to the last. Some pontiffs convened Ecumenical Councils to fight heresy and clarify doctrine. Some have worked for peace and been condemned for it. Some bishops of Rome have courageously saved their flock from destruction. Others have wielded Peter's sword against the enemies of the Church. Some Holy Fathers made lasting contributions of insight and understanding to moral and doctrinal teachings. Others courageously corrected those who might have led Catholics astray. Some inspired magnificent works of art and architecture that continue to uplift the hearts of all human beings of good will.

In almost 2,000 years of popes, not many people have been so fortunate as to have lived during the papacy of one who would have a major influence on the history of the world and take his place among those who are called great even by those outside the Church. After all his dynamic pilgrimages and lucid encyclicals, his honored accomplishments in art and philosophy, his restoration of unity by strongly shepherding the manifold members of God's people, Pope John Paul II, like St. Peter, ended his earthly journey having his belt tied by others who led him where he did not want to go. At the end of all this glory, we witnessed the sagging eyes and the drooping head of one who was led by illness and pain to endure the cross that his Master had predicted.

I commend Fathers Brighenti, Toborowsky, and Trigilio for their thorough, fair, honest, and candid look into the life, times, thought, and person of Pope John Paul II. This book is not a definitive biography like George Weigel's *Witness to Hope,* but it is a wonderful introduction and appetizer to such a main course. These authors have done a terrific job in summarizing, analyzing, and explaining the man, Karol Wojtyła, and the pope, John Paul II, without resorting to myth and legend. Other books may expose some of his faults and shortcomings or actually sensationalize them by blowing them out of context. *John Paul II For Dummies* is not a sanitized or saccharin product of propaganda; rather, it is a respectful, intelligent, and sensitive journey into the life, the mind, and the heart of a man who shaped history. Too often, modern biographers feel the need to "humanize" their subject by disclosing embarrassing details, highlighting rare acts of imprudence, or imputing motives. These prolific authors, by no means naïve, present just the facts of what John Paul said and did, leaving judgment where it belongs, with God and with history.

Glory, praise, and gratitude to Almighty God for this precious gift to the Church and to the world, whom we were blessed to have known as Pope John Paul II!

Rev. Monsignor James Cafone, STD
Assistant Professor of Religious Studies
Seton Hall University
South Orange, New Jersey

Introduction

When he died on April 2, 2005, three million people came throughout the next week to pay their respects by visiting his body. Six days after his death, 4 kings, 5 queens, at least 70 presidents and prime ministers, more than 14 leaders of other religions, as well as 157 cardinals, 700 bishops, and 3,000 priests were present at the funeral Mass along with another quarter million faithful crammed into St. Peter's Square. No other person in recent history has had such a tremendous display of respect, honor, and mourning over his life and death as was given to Pope John Paul II. Not only did the more than one billion members of the Catholic Church, which he shepherded for 26 years, grieve his death, but over 200 heads of state sent representatives or went themselves to his funeral.

You don't get such a spectacular exit from this world unless you've done something during your life to merit the admiration and respect of so many. The fact that so many non-Catholics honored the man known as John Paul II attests to his effect on the world — and not just within his own religion.

Here are just few of the statistics that reinforce Pope John Paul II's popularity:

- He was the first pope in history to visit most of the nations he visited. He traveled 721,052 miles (1,160,421 km), or the equivalent of 31 consecutive trips around the globe, making pastoral trips to 129 countries and 876 cities.
- Over the course of his papacy, he received 17.6 million visitors at 1,161 general audiences in his own backyard (actually, St. Peter's Square or Pope Paul VI Hall) in Rome.
- Hundreds of thousands of young people traveled halfway around the world to see him for International World Youth Days. This guy not only got around, he was very popular.

The first non-Italian pope in 450 years and the first Polish pontiff ever, Karol Wojtyła was elected Bishop of Rome and Supreme Pastor of the Catholic Church on October 16, 1978, and took the name Pope John Paul II. He was one of the youngest popes elected, at the age of 58, and had the third longest reign (26 years) from the long list of 266 people (from St. Peter to Benedict XVI) who have held that office.

Just the fact that so many people in the world knew who he was and what he stood for, even if some of them disagreed with him or did not share his principles and convictions, is a testimony to his influence on the world. Soviet dictator Joseph Stalin once dismissively remarked, "How many divisions does the pope have?" Both Stalin and Hitler had no time for and showed no respect for Pope Pius XII during World War II, for either the man or the office. Though Pope John Paul II was not able to convert Mikhail Gorbachev or Fidel Castro, he did have the Communist leader of the U.S.S.R. visit him at the Vatican, and he was greeted by the Communist leader of Cuba when he landed in his country for a pastoral visit. Uncle Joe Stalin must have been spinning in his grave.

About This Book

This book is written for anyone and everyone, whether you are Catholic or Protestant; Christian, Jewish, or Muslim; Hindu, Buddhist, or Taoist; whether you are of the Shinto, Jainist, Sikh, Confucian, or Baha'i faiths; even if you are agnostic or atheist. Pope John Paul II may not have been the leader of your religion and you may not have agreed with every one of his positions, statements, policies, or decisions, but despite his philosophy and theology, he had an enormous impact on the entire world, and this book explains the impact he had.

Not only do you not have to be Catholic to appreciate or even just to be curious about John Paul II, you can read this book regardless of your faith affiliation or the religion you profess. We don't sanitize the life of John Paul II — as others have done in the past with other historical figures, so that their lives are more myth than reality. Nor do we sensationalize his weaknesses and shortcomings, attacking the integrity and honor of a person who is no longer alive to defend himself. Instead, we give you an objective, concise, and pertinent overview of his life and the effect he had on the world, on history, and on the church he governed for more than a quarter-century.

This book will help you appreciate the background and roots of the man born and baptized as Karol Wojtyła, as well as his personal struggles and tragedies. We look at what shaped and formed the man, what he did and said before he became pope and as Pope John Paul II — including his numerous visits to foreign nations, his frequent World Youth Days, the prolific number of saints he canonized, the multitude of documents and letters he issued, and the impact his papacy had on the world, from the dissolution of the Soviet Union to defending life in the womb, in the hospital and nursing home, in the battlefield, and even in prison.

That said, this book is a reference, which means you don't have to read it from beginning to end. You can use the table of contents and the index to find the information you're most interested in at the moment, dipping into the book as you want to over time. Of course, if you want to read the book cover to cover, that's no sin either!

Conventions Used in This Book

In this book, you'll find different names referring to the same person. Karol Wojtyła was the name given to the man about whom this book is written. He was baptized with that name as an infant. We use the proper name Karol Wojtyła to refer to him in the days before he was pope. We refer to him as Pope John Paul II, John Paul, or JP2 when we're referring to him during his pontificate, because that's how he was known at that time.

Every pope of the Catholic Church is simultaneously the Bishop of Rome. The two offices are inseparable. But to keep it simple, we just refer to John Paul as pope. We don't use his other titles — Vicar of Christ, Successor of St. Peter, Servant of the Servants of God, Patriarch of the West, Prince of the Apostles, Primate of Italy, Archbishop and Metropolitan of the Roman Province, Sovereign of Vatican City, Supreme Roman Pontiff, Supreme Pastor of the Universal Church, and His Holiness — to prevent confusion.

Catholic custom is to use the first two words of the original Latin text for any official document, whether a papal letter or a decree from an ecumenical council. We use that same convention and list Pope John Paul II's encyclical letters as they can be found on the Internet or in any library or reference book. For example, *Veritatis Splendor* is Latin for "Splendor of Truth"; it's also the name of a papal encyclical on morality and ethics. When we use these Latin titles, we usually include the English equivalent in parentheses.

Sacred Scripture and the *Bible* are synonymous terms in Catholicism, so either one refers to the same thing. We also alternate the use of adjectives like *scriptural* or *biblical,* but both mean the same thing: anything found in either the Old Testament or the New Testament.

To help you navigate through this book, we use the following conventions:

✔ We use *italics* for emphasis and to highlight new words or terms that we define in parentheses.

✔ We use `monofont` for Web addresses and e-mail addresses. Note that some Web addresses may break across two lines of text. If that happens, rest assured that we haven't put in any extra characters (such as hyphens) to indicate the break. So, when using one of these Web addresses, just type in exactly what you see in this book, pretending the line break doesn't exist.

What You're Not to Read

This book is a reference book, so as we mention earlier, you don't have to read everything. Sidebars, which are text enclosed in a shaded gray box, give you information that's interesting to know but not necessarily critical to your understanding of the chapter or section topic. You can skip them if you're pressed for time, and still get the most important information. You can also skip any text marked by a Technical Stuff icon (see "Icons Used in This Book," later in this Introduction for more information).

Foolish Assumptions

In writing this book, we made some assumptions about you:

- You're curious about this man who was pope for 26 years, who led over a billion followers, and who traveled around the world more than anyone else in human history.

- You may not be a Catholic Christian, but you're still intrigued by the faith and witness this man gave in the name of his God and for the service of his church.

- You may be a Catholic who just wants to know more details about the life, background, ministry, and impact John Paul II had on the world as well as on the Church.

- You may have no religious affiliation but you have respect and admiration for the man behind the office and want to know more about him as a person.

- Either you grew up knowing no other pope than John Paul II or you remember the papacies of other popes before JP2.

How This Book Is Organized

This book comes in six parts, consisting of 23 chapters and 2 appendixes, but you can read any one you like and not have to worry if you didn't read the previous chapters. We refer you to other parts of the book to make it easy for you to get a better appreciation and understanding, but each part and each chapter in those parts can work on its own.

Part I: Getting to Know John Paul II

In this part, we paint the landscape of Pope John Paul II — the background, context, and climate (social, political, and theological) of the place and time he lived. Before we look at the man and the pope, we examine the religious, philosophical, and historical scenery on which the portrait of the life of Karol Wojtyła would be painted. No one is born into an empty, sterile world with no past behind it; likewise, this man from Poland, who would one day become pope and leader of more than a billion Catholic Christians around the globe, was in a sense painted onto an already existing canvas we call *life in the real world.* This part gives you the origin of the man himself, especially before his ecclesiastical career as a priest, bishop, cardinal, and finally pope.

Part II: Continuing the Legacy of Others and the Traditions of the Church

Karol Wojtyła, the churchman, was unique but at the same time was like other popes, cardinals, bishops, and priests before him and after him as well. This part looks at his pontificate, as a whole, from the beginning of his vocation and seminary training to his priestly career and eventual papal ministry.

Like all popes, he was Supreme Pastor and shepherd of the Universal Church. That meant his job was to be the representative of Christ (literally, Christ's vicar on Earth) to the Church and to the world. The priestly work of sanctifying the people of God with divine grace, the prophetic work of teaching them the faith, and the kingly office of governing and providing sound leadership are expected in the person who has been chosen to this awesome task.

This part examines the role of pope as teacher and as shepherd as he maintains connection and continuity with the past, while addressing the needs and concerns of the present and looking to the promise of the future.

Part III: Putting His Unique Stamp on the Papacy

What distinguishes Pope John Paul II from other popes, like Paul VI, John XXIII, and Pius XII? This part looks at how JP2 injected his own flavor into the papacy and wore it like a tailor-made suit. We examine his unique contributions and perspectives, his policies and programs, and other aspects that made an impact on the Church and the world, specifically because of his style and his leadership during his 26-year pontificate.

Part IV: Embracing Modernity and Looking to the Future

Although his theology, philosophy, and ethics were considered mainstream and *orthodox* (that is, consistent with what the official Roman Catholic Church has taught and held for ages), some have erroneously labeled John Paul II doctrinally conservative, morally traditional, and socially progressive. This part examines his use of the modern world, not in embracing its values but in using its technology to communicate his message. A man of his era, John Paul II utilized modern media, modern travel, and modern approaches (like appealing to the younger generation) in fulfilling his role as teacher and pastor of the Universal Church. Finally, we look at his legacy and what lies ahead for his successors, the popes who follow him.

Part V: The Part of Tens

In this part, you see ten reasons that Pope John Paul II was considered the "people's pope," discover ten fascinating and fun facts about him, understand ten of his important papal encyclicals and letters, and identify ten of his notable canonizations. You see the philosopher-theologian in John Paul II show his colors when he writes to the Church around the world about issues of faith and morals. You find out about the missionary and evangelical vein in him that prompted pastoral trips around the world to see the people of his parish — which, as pope, meant the entire planet. You discover little-known facts about this famous man of history and his diverse repertoire of talents, experience, and knowledge. In this part, you get four short chapters that are long on his accomplishments and his influence.

Part VI: Appendixes

If you have a propensity for statistics, you'll enjoy the appendixes, which include a chronological timeline of pertinent events in the life of Pope John Paul II, as well as the details of his travel itinerary throughout his papacy.

Icons Used in This Book

Icons are the fancy little pictures in the margins of this book. Here's a guide to what they mean and what the icons look like:

This icon marks interesting information that helps you get the inside scoop on JP2.

This icon points out ideas that sum up and reinforce the concepts we discuss. In fact, if you're short on time and can't read an entire section, go straight to this icon. Also, if you need a refresher in a chapter for any reason, you can skim through and read these to reinforce the main points.

Think of this icon as bonus material — the info flagged by this icon gives you some background information that isn't critical. In some cases, this information gives you the brief history of a point, or more detail than is absolutely necessary. We think the information is interesting so we include it — but if you're in a time crunch, you can skip it.

Where to Go from Here

You can start right in with Chapter 1 and read to the end, or you can use the table of contents and index to find just the bit of information you're looking for.

If you want even more information on JP2, we highly recommend a visit to the Pope John Paul II Cultural Center in Washington, D.C., or a virtual trip to www.jp2cc.org, where you'll find a vast amount of material on the person and the papacy of JP2. The exhibits and displays are fantastic and are rivaled only by the Vatican Museums themselves in Rome.

If you can't make a trip to the Eternal City (otherwise known as Rome) to visit the Vatican in person, you can go to its Web site and find plenty of information on Pope John Paul II, especially his official writings. Check it out at www.vatican.va/holy_father/john_paul_ii/index.htm.

Many good biographies on Pope John Paul II are available, but we personally and highly recommend *Witness to Hope: The Biography of Pope John Paul II,* by George Wiegel. Also very informative are *John Paul the Great: Remembering a Spiritual Father,* by Peggy Noonan, and *John Paul II: A Personal Portrait of the Pope and the Man,* by Ray Flynn. Even though we don't share or agree with all their opinions, interpretations, or inferences, you may also find interesting *Pope John Paul II,* by Tad Szulc, and *His Holiness,* by Carl Bernstein and Marco Politi.

Part I
Getting to Know John Paul II

The 5th Wave   By Rich Tennant

"I'm pretty sure the Holy Father plans to reach out to other faiths. He said failing to do that just wouldn't be kosher."

In this part . . .

We look at the personal history, background, landscape, and major influences that shaped and formed the early life of Pope John Paul II. Besides his fascinating story of where, when, and how he grew up into the man called Karol Wojtyła, we also examine the cultural, historical, intellectual, and spiritual forces that contributed to his formation. This will give a glimpse into the person — the human being, the world would later know as John Paul II.

Chapter 1

John Paul II: A Man for All Seasons

Robert Bolt's play titled *A Man for All Seasons* (1960) was about the life of Sir Thomas More, Lord Chancellor of England, who remained completely faithful to his God, his church, and his conscience even to the point of death. Although fidelity is easy when things are going well, maintaining and persevering in one's faith in times of trial and tribulation is not an easy task. Thomas More was called a "man for all seasons" because he didn't allow public opinion or political pressure to infect his soul.

Karol Wojtyła, who became Pope John Paul II, can also be called a "man for all seasons," because he did not allow anything to weaken his faith. Neither the German Nazis who invaded his homeland during World War II nor the Soviet Russians who occupied Poland throughout the Cold War could discourage this man's convictions and commitment to his religion. Despite a would-be assassin's bullets and Parkinson's disease, JP2 never succumbed to discouragement.

Both Thomas More (1478–1535) and John Paul II were poets, philosophers, and men of many talents. They were truly spiritual men who loved their countries but loved their God even more than their own lives. Like More, JP2 was a man of conscience and a *Renaissance man* (someone who has a broad education and has some proficiency in the arts, humanities, and sciences).

At the movies

One of Pope John Paul II's favorite movies in English (according to anonymous sources) was the screen adaptation of Bolt's play *A Man For All Seasons* (1966), starring Paul Scofield as Sir Thomas More, Robert Shaw as King Henry VIII, and the famous Orson Welles as Cardinal Wolsey. The Academy Award–winning movie was later resurrected in a 1988 version with Charlton Heston as More and Sir John Gielgud as Wolsey. Ironically, Vanessa Redgrave was in both movies; she played Anne Boleyn (Henry VIII's second wife and mother of Elizabeth I) in the first film and played Lady Alice, Sir Thomas More's wife, in the remake.

In this chapter, you discover how Pope John Paul II was a true pioneer in the sense that he went into uncharted waters and territory. We show you how he made an impact on the world itself, how he left an indelible mark on the Catholic Church, how he injected his own style and flavor into the papacy, and how he brought his Polish culture and personal faith into his public role as leader of the world's largest religion. Groundbreaker, innovator, defender, protector, shepherd, and pastor — these are but a few of the hats Pope John Paul II wore.

Being a Groundbreaker

John Paul II came from an ancient land steeped in tradition, was raised in a 2,000-year-old religion, and would become the visible defender of traditional morality and orthodox doctrine. At the same time, JP2 was innovative, not in content but in presentation. He showed his followers how the Church and especially the papacy could — and should — adapt to the modern world.

JP2 broke the stereotype of popes being elderly Italian church bureaucrats. Unlike some of his predecessors, he was elected at the young age of 58; was the first non-Italian pope since the 16th century; and traveled more than any other pope in history. He had the third longest reigning papacy (after St. Peter and Blessed Pius IX). The non-Catholic world, however, will remember John Paul II for his groundbreaking efforts to open dialogue with members and leaders of other faiths and religions. His gestures to heal wounds between Christians and Jews and between Catholics and Protestants were sincere and profound — if not totally successful.

The first Polish pope — and the first non-Italian in 455 years

The first mold John Paul II broke was the origin of the popes. JP2 was the first non-Italian pope in 455 years. The last non-Italian was Cardinal Adrian Florensz Boeyens, a Dutchman, elected Pope Adrian VI in 1522. From the time of St. Peter (the Jewish fisherman Jesus chose to head his church, whom Catholics consider the first pope) to Benedict XVI (the current pope, as of this writing), we've had 217 popes from Italy, 17 from France, 8 from Germany, 3 from Spain, and 1 each from Africa, England, Portugal, the Netherlands, Poland, and Palestine (present-day Israel).

Why the Italian monopoly? Believe it or not, no strong-arm tactics were involved here. The practical reason was that, until the era of John Paul II, the papacy was very much involved in local concerns involving the diocese of Rome, of which the pope is the bishop, and surrounding Italian dioceses of Italy. It made sense to elect a local, an Italian, who not only spoke the language but who knew the culture and the problems the local and national churches were experiencing.

These days, the popes no longer need to worry about national defense and other domestic issues that other world leaders have to contend with every day. The small 109 acres of land that make up the Vatican are merely a home, a place of pilgrimage, and a center of ecclesiastical administration.

Since the time of Pope Paul VI (1963–1978), who was the first pontiff to visit five continents (and was called the "pilgrim pope" until the arrival of John Paul II), the universal ministry of the office became more relevant. Instead of just handling the affairs of the diocese of Rome or the Catholic Church in Italy, the papacy in the latter half of the 20th century became much more global in its perspective.

With the College of Cardinals comprising representatives from almost every nation on Earth, the unofficial Italian "monopoly" over the papacy ceased to exist. The year Pope John Paul II was elected (1978) was as good a time as any to elect a non-Italian, even if it hadn't been done for 455 years.

The last pope of the 20th century — and the first pope of the 21st

John Paul II has the unique claim of being the last pope of the 20th century and the first pope of the 21st century; he reigned from 1978 to 2005. Because of the unique time in which he was pope, a time of numerous technological advances, Pope John Paul II was able to bring the Church and the papacy into the 21st century, embracing technology instead of shunning it.

The *message* would be the same: perennial teaching of Christ as found both in Sacred Scripture (the Bible) and Sacred Tradition and as taught for two millennia by the Catholic Church. The *medium* by which the message was delivered would utilize the best the contemporary world had to offer. Pope John Paul II used modern tools to bring time-honored values and principles to a new generation.

JP2 inaugurated the Vatican Web site on Easter (March 30) 1997, and was considered the first "high-tech pope." Unlike previous popes who occasionally used modern media like radio and television, John Paul II was the first to capitalize on and utilize the full potential of high-tech communications. His weekly Wednesday audiences were broadcast by radio, television, satellite, short-wave radio, and Internet to all corners of the Earth.

Reaching out: Around the world, across religions, and to young people everywhere

John Paul II certainly broke the mold when he took the papacy on the road. Other popes had traveled, but none of his successors would cover as many miles, visit as many nations, and be seen and heard by as many people of every age, race, and background. Some old-time Vatican bureaucrats thought he traveled too much and should have stayed home more to "mind the store." But in practice, Vatican City (as an independent country) and the Holy See (as the administrative center of the one-billion-member organization) virtually run by themselves in terms of the day-to-day business and work that has to be done. The pope does not micromanage every diocese or nation. For the most part, he lets the local bishop shepherd his own flock.

Pope John Paul II's 104 pastoral trips to 129 countries around the globe were always media events, attracting reporters and journalists from every nation. He used the press to help communicate his message to the universal flock he was shepherding, even if those who covered him did not completely agree with him. He was the first pope to actually hold press conferences on airplanes during his worldwide travels.

JP2 was a true groundbreaker not only because he used modern media, but also because he was the first to make monumental advances in *ecumenism* (efforts to bring more unity and cooperation among all religions). As the first pope to visit a Jewish synagogue (in 1986) since St. Peter, he referred to all Jews as "our elder brothers." John Paul II was also the first pope ever to visit an Islamic mosque (in Damascus in 2001) and was the first pope ever to preach in a Lutheran church (in 1983).

The third longest pontificate: 26 years, 5 months, 17 days

John Paul I had one of the ten shortest papacies (33 days), but his successor, John Paul II, had the third longest. St. Peter, considered the first pope, is thought to have served 37 years, from A.D. 30 to approximately A.D. 67. This would have been, so far, the longest pontificate in history.

Blessed Pius IX (1846–1878) reigned 31 years, 7 months, and 23 days (or a total of 11,560 days, if you go in for the big numbers) and ranks number two in papal longevity. He was only 54 years old when he was elected pope, and he died at the age of 85.

John Paul II (1978–2005) ruled 26 years, 5 months, and 17 days (or a total of 9,665 days).

Four years older than Pius IX when he was elected, JP2 was an energetic and athletic 58-year-old when the cardinals chose him to be pope. Some even called him "God's athlete" due to his love of hiking, swimming, and skiing. Many doctors and physicians have speculated that, had he not been shot in 1981 and had he not contracted Parkinson's disease, this robust man could have surpassed the previous two and been the longest reigning pope in history, living well into his 90s or longer. Unfortunately, he *was* shot and he *did* get Parkinson's, but the fact that he was able to survive both until he was a month and half away from his 85th birthday is still noteworthy.

Besides his efforts to communicate with the spiritual leaders of other religions and with the political leaders of other nations — whether capitalist, socialist, or communist — JP2 was also a groundbreaker in reaching out to the youth. He was the first pope to have World Youth Day, an annual event in which young people across the globe get together with the head of the Catholic Church. Since 1986, these events have brought together anywhere from 300,000 to more than 4 million young men and women at one place and time.

Author, Author

Most people know of John Paul II's papal encyclicals (see Chapter 22) and letters. What a lot of people don't know is that he authored many books:

- *Sign of Contradiction* (1979)
- *Love and Responsibility* (1960, Polish; 1980, English translation)
- *The Way to Christ: Spiritual Exercises* (1982)
- *Crossing the Threshold of Hope* (1994)

- *Gift and Mystery: On the Fiftieth Anniversary of My Priestly Ordination* (1996)
- *The Theology of the Body: Human Love in the Divine Plan* (1997)
- *Pope John Paul II: In My Own Words* (1998)
- *Forgiveness: Thoughts for the New Millennium* (1999)
- *Get Up, Let Us Go* (2004)
- *Lessons for Living* (2004)
- *Memory and Identity: Conversations at the Dawn of a Millennium* (2005)

JP2 is best known for being the first Polish pope, and then as a theologian and philosopher in his own right, before and during his papacy. He was also a poet and playwright. Like the several languages he spoke fluently, this man was also of several talents, interests, and abilities. During Nazi occupation and then under Communist control, freedom of thought was not encouraged and freedom of speech not tolerated. Plays and poetry were two ways that patriotic citizens maintained their heritage.

Playwright

Not only did John Paul II write books, he also wrote plays. Besides plays based on biblical characters like *David, Job,* and *Jeremiah,* he also wrote plays like *Our God's Brother, The Jeweler's Shop,* and *The Radiation of Fatherhood: A Mystery,* dealing with the universal themes of faith and practicing it in day-to-day life. The last two he wrote under the pseudonym of Andrzej Jawien to avoid being caught by KGB agents in Soviet-controlled Poland.

Since the time of the Nazi occupation during World War II and throughout the Soviet control of Poland during the Cold War, resistance to Fascism and Communism took expression in the arts, especially in plays, prose, and poetry. Authors tried to keep the flames of freedom burning in the hearts of their countrymen despite the occupation and oppression. A common safeguard to avoid arrest and possible torture was to use a pseudonym whenever writing such material.

The Jeweler's Shop is a three-act play still available in English today. The setting is, as the title suggests, a jewelry shop, and the main characters are three couples who enter the store. Each couple has a different struggle, as well as a different understanding and experience of love, doubt, fear, disappointment, disillusion, and hope. The moral of the story is to not give up, which applies not just to married life, but also to religious and spiritual life and to an oppressed people whose country has been occupied or controlled by another nation.

Poet

John Paul II also wrote poetry. Through his poems, you get a glimpse into his heart and soul as a man and a human being. He wrote some poems during and after World War II, during his priesthood, during his *episcopacy* (the time spent in the government of the church as a bishop, archbishop, and a cardinal), and even during his pontificate. The poems show a tender, vulnerable, yet still very confident nature of the man who became the Bishop of Rome and head of the Catholic Church.

Here is a sample of his poetry from a poem he wrote in 1939 about his mother, Emilia, who had died tragically when Karol (John Paul's name at birth and his baptismal name) was only 9 years old.

> "Over This, Your White Grave"
>
> Over this, your white grave
> the flowers of life in white —
> so many years without you —
> how many have passed out of sight?
> Over this your white grave
> covered for years, there is a stir
> in the air, something uplifting
> and, like death, beyond comprehension.
> Over this your white grave
> oh, mother, can such loving cease?
> for all his filial adoration
> a prayer:
> Give her eternal peace —

John Paul II had a very strong devotion to the Virgin Mary, which was probably based not only on his staunch Catholic upbringing, but also on his Polish heritage and his need to be a son and have a mother he could turn to for comfort. Mary was not a substitute for his mother, Emilia, but the mother of Christ was still his spiritual mother, because Jesus, her biological son, was also his spiritual brother.

Becoming a Philosopher-Theologian

When John Paul II was still Karol Wojtyła, a teenager in high school, he was so good at public speaking that he was chosen to give the welcome address to a very special dignitary visiting the school one day. Prince Adam Stefan Stanisław Bonfatiusz Józef Sapieha (that's a mouthful), the Archbishop of

Krakow and one of the most dignified members of Polish aristocracy, came for a visit. When he heard the eloquent speech given by Wojtyła, he asked one of his teachers if the lad was headed for the seminary. His professor replied that Karol had designs on going to Jagiellonian University to study philology (linguistics). Momentarily disappointed, thinking the church was losing a potential intellectual jewel for the priesthood, the archbishop merely replied, "Too bad." Little did he know then that divine providence had another plan for Karol Wojtyła.

Loving linguistics

As an incoming freshman, Karol Wojtyła had a heavy load. He studied not only Polish grammar, phonetics, and etymology but also the Old Slavonic and Russian languages. He loved language because it conveyed to others what was in the mind and heart of the writer or speaker of that tongue.

Language is the cornerstone of civilization, because it unites individuals and ideas. Without language, or without a means of communication, no society, no community can exist. Many occupying powers impose a foreign language on a conquered nation and often outlaw the native dialect to prevent a national identity. Yet, a common language, even if foreign, would sometimes have the opposite effect and unite people of the same nation who initially spoke completely different dialects and who, beforehand, could not easily communicate with those outside their own region. John Paul II not only had a talent for learning languages, he truly loved being able to communicate with others in their native tongue. He understood the philosophy of language and showed how to communicate verbally and nonverbally throughout his pontificate. A multilingual pope who traveled the world made the *catholic* (universal) part of his job and of his church have more meaning than ever before.

Showing a keen mind for linguistics, the young Karol developed a love of theater and poetry. In both of these, language was at its best. Polish plays and poems not only showed pride in the motherland but also instilled appreciation of the culture, art, and history of the people who lived in that country. He even helped form a student theater group known as Studio 39, and it was there that he felt an attraction to the stage. Even though he was not known as a "ham" actor seeking attention and applause at every opportunity, Wojtyła nevertheless recognized the power of presence. As a linguist, he knew the importance and effect of words. As an actor, he knew the importance of how those words were spoken and even the impact of saying nothing at all, just allowing the symbols and gestures to speak for themselves.

Secretly studying philosophy

In 1942, seminaries were officially closed like the colleges and universities, so Wojtyła pursued a covert underground education. Hidden in the residence of Archbishop Sapieha of Krakow, he discovered the sublime beauty of philosophy. He learned about the great philosophers such as Plato, Aristotle, Augustine, and Aquinas.

He was ordained a priest on November 1, 1946; two weeks later, he was sent to Rome to continue his studies and earn his first doctorate. His bishop sent him to the Angelicum, a seminary run by the Dominicans (brothers and priests of a religious community who follow the spirituality of St. Dominic from the 13th century, a contemporary of St. Francis of Assisi). St. Thomas Aquinas was not only the preeminent theologian of the Catholic Church, but also one of its finest philosophers and he happened to be a Dominican. No mystery then that Father Wojtyła would be immersed in scholastic philosophy, sometimes called *Thomism,* after Thomas Aquinas.

He threw himself into understanding such complex topics as objective realism, Natural Moral Law, and the three levels of truth (scientific, philosophical, and theological). So, to Karol Wojtyła, science and faith were not at odds with each other. Instead, they were two ways of examining the same reality.

Wojtyła defended his dissertation and passed his examinations with flying colors in 1948 but could not get the degree from his alma mater, the Angelicum. He was too poor to have his doctoral dissertation printed, and the seminary required that the dissertation be printed prior to conferring the degree. When he returned to Poland, Father Wojtyła resubmitted his paper to Jagiellonian University, and it awarded him a doctorate in theology. He earned a second doctorate in theology in 1954.

Thomistic philosophy and theology and other philosophies shaped the mind of Karol Wojtyła. Whether it was abortion, euthanasia, contraception, or the death penalty; economic, political, and social justice; he was always on the same page: promoting and defending what is good for humans, individually and communally. John Paul II believed that the ultimate good was the happiness found in knowing and doing the Will of God.

Wondering about a Sign of Contradiction

The greatest *paradox* (or apparent contradiction) in Christianity is that death brought life: The death of Jesus Christ on the cross brought eternal life to the human race. Before Christians can live forever in heaven, they must first die here on Earth. It seems a contradiction that death, which is the absence of life, would somehow be the cause or catalyst for life, yet that belief is what Christianity is founded upon. The cross itself and the crucifixion — symbols of shame, guilt, crime, punishment, and death since their creation — become symbols of love, forgiveness, mercy, and eternal life. This ultimate sign of contradiction is also called the *divine paradox.*

John Paul II was also, in many ways, a paradox. He could not easily be labeled as a liberal or a conservative. When he spoke out against the death penalty and capital punishment, the press and media tried to label him a liberal. When he reiterated the Church's ban on artificial contraception, women's ordination, homosexual marriage, or abandoning the discipline of mandatory priestly celibacy in the Western Church, they called him a conservative.

Liberal theologians who promoted political activism saw John Paul II as a staunch conservative when he publicly chastised Father Ernesto Cardinal (also a member of the Marxist Sandinista government) of Nicaragua in 1983 on the tarmac at Managua Airport. JP2 saw no place in government for any member of the clergy. Instead, he believed the government was the proper environment for the *laity* (members of the Church who are not part of the clergy) to be and to witness good lay leadership.

George Weigel points out in his book *Witness to Hope* that there are not two Wojtyłas — one a traditional, fundamentalist conservative on doctrinal and moral matters, and the other a liberal, social progressive on economic and political matters. "There is only one Karol Wojtyła" whose faith is not reduced to an ideology or an agenda but is intimately connected and dependent on the living 2,000-year-old church founded by Christ, who is the same yesterday, today, and forever.

One of the ways John Paul II differed from many of his predecessors was that he was not by any means a bureaucrat. He was a shepherd, a teacher, and a priest. Although some people may have initially considered the papal road trips (see "Reaching out: Around the world, across religions, and to young people everywhere," earlier in this chapter) neither proper nor dignified for the Supreme Roman Pontiff (they preferred that others come visit him), they eventually saw this as a real evangelization, bringing the good news like the first pope St. Peter and his companion St. Paul, the missionary apostle, did when they journeyed from place to place.

Like his predecessor Pope John Paul I, JP2 chose not to be crowned with the papal tiara and replaced the coronation ceremony with an installation one. Ultraconservatives considered him liberal for not restoring many of the elaborate or detailed traditions, which had developed in the papacy over the centuries but which Pope Paul VI discarded after the close of the Second Vatican Council, also known as Vatican II (see the nearby "Vatican II" sidebar for more).

Vatican II

The Second Vatican Council, sometimes known as Vatican II, was a gathering of the Catholic bishops from around the world, which met in Rome from 1962 to 1965. There have been 21 ecumenical or general councils in Catholic Church history, from the First Council of Nicea in A.D. 325 to the Second Vatican Council attended by John Paul II, who was then Bishop Wojtyła. The first seven or eight councils met to define doctrinal points or settle theological controversies. The Council of Trent met from 1545 to 1563 to respond to the Protestant Reformation. Vatican II, unlike the previous 20 councils, was not convened to solve a problem but to address pastoral concerns of the modern era. Although no new doctrines or dogmas were defined, and no previous ones were dissolved, this council attempted to teach and explain the old faith in new language and with newer techniques.

Ultraliberals thought JP2 was an archaic, draconian traditionalist when he would not allow liturgical innovations and experimentation; when he gave permission for the old Tridentine Mass to be said in Latin, they were sure he was on the far right. At the same time, the far right considered him a "bleeding-heart liberal" when he called for wealthy nations to forgive the debts of poorer nations, when he allowed women to be altar servers, and when he added five more mysteries to the Rosary.

John Paul II however, did not see anything he did or said in terms of left or right, liberal or conservative, progressive or traditional. As Weigel put it, Karol Wojtyła was a *radical* Catholic Christian, in the original sense of the term.

Although many people might use the word *radical* to denote someone on the far left, as opposed to a *reactionary* on the far right, Weigel uses the precise dictionary definition of *radical* based on the Latin word *radix* meaning "root." *Radical Christianity* is not aligned with Communists and socialists; rather, it is Christianity taken very seriously, to the very root and core of what it means to be Christian.

John Paul II was indeed a radical Catholic in that he was thoroughly Catholic to the very core of his being. Christianity permeated everything he said or did — while he was growing up, while he was a student, while he was a worker and layman, while he was a priest and bishop, and while he was pope. For JP2, the Church was more than an institution; it was his beloved spouse. He saw himself as the Vicar of Christ, which meant that he had to love as Christ loved, to forgive as Christ forgave, to teach as Christ taught.

His Catholic Christian faith was not limited or defined by political, economic, or social theories. In many ways, he was his own man in that he did not seek to impress anyone, but he always tried to persuade and convince others.

Revisiting His Legacy

The legacy of John Paul II is still materializing and developing. The quarter-century he led the Church encouraged many vocations to the priesthood and religious life. After the confusion that followed after Vatican II — not from the documents themselves but from what many claimed to be the "spirit of Vatican II" rather than the actual and literal message of Vatican II — some priests and nuns abandoned their vows, there was a rise in the divorce rate, fewer people attended Mass, there was more dissent among theologians, and more Catholics ignored Church teaching and discipline altogether.

Paul VI had closed Vatican II in 1965, but it was under his pontificate that much of the spiritual decay had begun to infect the mystical body of Christ. Paul VI tried to preserve, protect, and repair the damage, but the sexual and cultural revolutions were simultaneously transforming the world into a place of greater instability and uncertainty. John Paul II came in 1978 and did not repeal or repudiate the Second Vatican Council; rather, he sought to fully, properly, thoroughly, and correctly implement what the Council Fathers had intended but that time and circumstance had previously prevented from happening.

JP2 did not come to set back the clock to before 1963. He came to prepare the Church and the world for the third millennium, which would come as soon as the 20th century ended and the 21st began. He sought reconciliation where possible. He defended the consistent, perennial teachings of the 2,000-year-old religion. He used modern tools — like the jet plane, the Internet, television, and radio — to spread his message. He preserved the rich heritage and patrimony of Catholicism, while at the same time he shook some of the dust off the places that had become complacent and lethargic.

John Paul II did not define any new dogmas, nor did he deny, dilute, or tamper with the revealed truths he was entrusted with as Supreme Pastor of the Universal Church. He did explain the age-old doctrines in a brighter light and with full enthusiasm and gusto. Prolific in his writings and speeches, Pope John Paul II had an important message — but as a former actor and poet, he also knew the importance of how the message was delivered.

The pope is considered by Catholics to be the head of the entire Universal Catholic Church while a local bishop is head of the diocese and the local pastor is the head of the parish church. *Universal Church* is used to refer to the Catholic Church as a whole.

JP2 could defend the tradition of priestly celibacy while extolling the virtues of married love between one man and one woman for the rest of their lives. He could defend the doctrine of a male priesthood while denouncing the exploitation of women through pornography and abortion. He spoke of the sacredness of each human person and the beauty of conjugal love open to the possibility of new life. He associated with all who suffer, because of the sufferings of his own past — losing his mother, brother, and father at an early age; living under Nazi and Communist oppression; surviving a would-be assassin's bullet; and his long battle with Parkinson's disease.

He was not able to convince all Catholics to embrace completely and totally all that the Church teaches, all the doctrines, disciplines, and sacred rituals. He could not get the Eastern Orthodox, for example, to come any closer to ecclesiastical unity, and the Protestant churches did not pack up and move to Rome.

Since 1054, the Roman Catholic and Eastern Orthodox churches have been divided. Prior to that, there was one Christian Church with several patriarchs (bishops from historical places of antiquity — for example, Jerusalem, Antioch, Alexandria, Rome, and Constantinople). The division was called the *Eastern Schism,* and the churches that separated and sought to be autonomous from Rome and the pope are called Eastern Orthodox. The patriarch of Moscow became independent in 1589. Although the Orthodox churches do not accept the primacy of jurisdiction of the pope as Supreme Pastor of the Universal Church, they do share the same theology, have the same seven sacraments, and have a strong devotion to the Virgin Mary as the Mother of God. Though very similar in substantial areas, the political and jurisdictional differences have historically prevented a formal reunion of the Eastern Orthodox and Western (Roman) Catholic churches.

The Protestant Reformation, which began in 1517 with Martin Luther then with John Calvin, John Knox, Thomas Cranmer, John Wesley, and others, broke from Rome and created the Lutheran, Calvinist, Presbyterian, Anglican, and Methodist churches. Unlike the Eastern Schism in the 11 century, the 16th-century Protestant Reformation divided Western Christendom along doctrinal and liturgical lines as well as jurisdiction.

Does the fact that JP2 wasn't able to achieve all of his goals mean he failed? Should he have even tried? Well, look at it this way: For a long time, nothing was said about the dangers of cigarette smoking. Then doctors and the surgeon general began telling everyone that smoking can cause cancer. Despite the amount of information and the scope to which it has been disseminated, there are still those who choose not to believe or to just ignore the warnings. Likewise, despite the global access John Paul II had, the 26 years he had it, and the wonderful manner he had in spreading it, not everyone paid attention. Those who did will never forget. Those who actually embraced it will never regret it. Not a waste then, after all.

A People's Pope: John Paul the Great?

Even before his death, some were calling him John Paul the Great. At his funeral and after his burial, the usage has become prolific. Only three other popes in history have had the honor of the title "the Great." Whereas only a pope can canonize a saint, it has been the prerogative of the people and posterity to bestow the title "the Great." It's an informal but rare moniker saved for those very few who surpassed their contemporaries and many of their predecessors in achievements, accomplishments, impact, and overall influence.

Many contemporary scholars believe that Karol Wojtyła will eventually inherit the title "John Paul the Great" for several reasons:

- ✔ **On the global level, he was instrumental in the dissolution of the Soviet Empire with the breakup of the Soviet Union, the unraveling of the Warsaw Pact, and the tearing down of the Berlin Wall.** Although he did not personally coordinate or participate in any of those incidents, he did make it easier for them to occur, and many people consider him the catalyst history needed at the time. He preached a nonviolent resistance to those who are denied human rights and dignity, like the freedom to worship. (Take a look at Chapter 13 for an in-depth look at JP2's role in the process.)

- ✔ **He made the papacy truly international by taking it on the road.** By visiting millions of people in hundreds of nations, he showed how universal the Catholic Church was. Speaking several languages fluently, he visited foreign lands, made many *cardinals* (the guys who advise the pope and who elect the new one when the old one dies) from almost every nation, and invited the youth of the planet to gather every year at World Youth Day. He made the papacy and the Catholic Church extremely visible during his pontificate.

- ✔ **He was the first pope in a century to revise the Code of Canon Law (which had not been done since 1917) and the first pope to revise the Catechism in 450 years.** He canonized more saints than any of his predecessors and did so from all four corners of the Earth, from every race and nation. (Chapter 14 gives you all the details on his saint-making activities.)

Being "great" does not mean John Paul II was perfect or sinless. Even the Catholic doctrine of papal infallibility does not cross that line. Designating John Paul as "the Great" is not a dogmatic or spiritual judgment on the man. It is merely a title of convention given by history to those few who influenced so many people for the good. Mistakes? Sure, he made some — and he would've been the first to admit it. He acknowledged that he was like the rest of us sinners, in need of mercy and forgiveness. And he confidently — and regularly — went to confession.

The other Greats

Here's a quick summary of the accomplishments the other "Greats" achieved:

- **Pope St. Leo the Great** (A.D. 440–461): Leo was impressive in his ability to shepherd wisely and bravely. He is personally credited with convincing Attila the Hun to spare the Eternal City (Rome) in A.D. 452. When he sent a theological treatise (called a *tome*) to the ecumenical council of Chalcedon in A.D. 451, he succinctly explained the doctrine of Christ being one divine person with two equal and distinct natures — human and divine — yet united in the one divine *hypostasis* (hence the term, the *hypostatic union*). The council fathers, upon hearing this read, proclaimed, "God has spoken to us through Peter." (Leo, like all popes, was considered the successor of St. Peter.)

- **Pope St. Gregory the Great** (A.D. 590–604): Gregory was able to keep the Church intact and even prosper spiritually after the shadow of the fall of the Roman Empire. Born a hundred years after the city of Rome fell in A.D. 476, Gregory inspired a renewal that sought to prioritize the spiritual and moral values in a world devastated by war and violence. He was instrumental in the proliferation of monasteries throughout Europe, which eventually led to the conversion and civilization of the very barbarians who had come to rape, pillage, and sack the people and lands of the old empire.

- **Pope St. Nicholas the Great** (A.D. 858–867): Nicholas, like Leo and Gregory, had to contend with a crumbling and falling empire. Whereas the previous guys dealt with the chaos of the fall of the Roman Empire and the ensuing barbarian invasions, Nicholas had to confront the dissolution of the Carolingian Empire. When Charlemagne was crowned Holy Roman Emperor on Christmas Day in A.D. 800, there was a brief period of peaceful unity in Western Europe, and it was evidenced in one rule (Holy Roman Empire) and one religion (Christianity), one emperor and one pope. There were no divisions among the churches until the Eastern Schism in 1054 and again when the Protestant Reformation took place in the 16th century. At the death of Charlemagne, however, unified Christendom began to unravel. The warring factions of Franks, Lombards, Saxons, Normans, and others would have destroyed everything had Nicholas not been able to keep some reasonable calm and order.

Not a shabby group to be part of. . . .

Poland bordered Russia and Germany, and when Polish King Mieszko I aligned himself and his nation with the West, that meant that when the Eastern Schism occurred in 1054, sides were now taken. Poland remained with the Western (Latin) Church under the authority of the Bishop of Rome (the pope) and aligned with the German King and Holy Roman Emperor, Henry III. Russia, on the other hand, joined the Eastern churches aligned with the Byzantine Emperor Constantine IX and broke from Rome and formed the Greek Orthodox Church. Later, in 1448, the independent Russian Orthodox Church, with its patriarch in Moscow, separated from the jurisdiction of the Patriarch of Constantinople, the headquarters of the Greek Orthodox Church.

So, in the 15th century, Poland was bordered on the east by Orthodox Russia and on the west by Roman Catholic Germany (the center of the Holy Roman Empire). The Roman Catholic Church and faith in Poland remained strong and steadfast, especially after the Protestant Reformation began in 1517 with Dr. Martin Luther in Germany. The Lutheran Church separated itself from the authority of the pope and, since the emperor was crowned by the Bishop of Rome, German princes who were not religiously supportive of the Reformation supported it militarily to break from imperial authority themselves. Northern and eastern Germany became primarily Protestant, and southern and western Germany stayed predominantly Catholic. Catholic Poland became a key buffer between the Russian Orthodox on its east and Protestant Germany on its west.

During the many years of religious wars and conflicts, the only resolution found was that of the Peace of Augsburg. Religion became as much a part of national identity as did language. Poland's Catholicism only strengthened when surrounded by religious and political opponents on either side of it.

Germany and Russia (and occasionally Austria and Prussia) alternated their territorial expansion and control over Poland for hundreds of years after the Polish monarchy became too weak to remain totally independent and secure. Yet, the Catholic faith remained constant as the one element that neither German nor Russian invaders could squelch.

Jozef Pilsudski, founder of the Polish Socialist Party, carried out successful raids in 1906 against Russian occupiers sent by the czar to control the nation. When World War I broke out in 1914, much of Poland was under Russian control and therefore legally it became part of the Allied Powers (Russia, France, Britain, Italy, and the United States). Sadly, significant parts of Poland had been taken over by Germany, which was part of the Central Powers (Germany, Austria-Hungary, the Ottoman Empire, and Bulgaria). This meant that many Poles were forces into military service to fight some of their own countrymen, who unfortunately were behind enemy lines due to the partitioning of Poland before the war.

The Polish people had no eagerness for Russia to win the war, because it controlled most of their territory. But there was no enthusiasm for a German victory, either. Nevertheless, the Central Powers lost, and even though Russia was one of the victorious members of the Allied Powers, the Bolshevik Revolution of 1917 forced the czar's armies to leave Poland. A year later, on November 11, 1918, Marshal Pilsudski proclaimed Polish independence and became commander-in-chief as well as head of state. On August 15, 1920, the Polish Army, under Pilsudski, successfully fought and won the Battle of Warsaw over the Red Army of the new Soviet Union.

Witnessing the end of Victorian morals after the "Great War"

When World War I ended in 1918, Europe would never be the same again. Old, traditional, time-honored values and traditions were on the endangered species list. This was due to the aftermath of the carnage, violence, terror, and death wreaked upon the peoples who survived the so-called "war to end all wars."

Roughly 15 million casualties were created by World War I, of which 9 million were military and 6 million were civilian. Poison gas, trench warfare, and the enormous destruction of life and property (on both sides) during the war made life in general miserable for most people, rich and poor alike. Many towns and villages were destroyed, and some were obliterated off the map.

When the fighting stopped and the war ended, many people wanted to forget the horrors of 1914 to 1918, so they indulged themselves into numerous pleasures and distractions. "Party hardy, dude," may not have been a familiar phrase back then, but its sentiment was certainly shared at the time.

Relieving the burdens of everyday life: Focusing on fun, humor, and fatalism

Post World War I Europe entered the Roaring Twenties with a boom. Factories that once produced weapons and ammunition now cranked out consumer goods, and people wanted to spend money on entertainment, fashion, and leisure. Because so many people endured enormous hardship during the war, after the war they wanted to compensate their former misery with contemporary fun.

The invention of "talking" movies (movies with sound) in the early 1920s and the invention of vacuum tubes for wireless radio (which allowed more radios to be produced at a lower cost and to be manufactured in smaller models) made going to the movies and listening to radio shows two popular pastimes. Although the former only cost pennies to do, the latter was free (after the initial purchase of your radio, of course), and that made it even more popular.

Partying like it's 1919: Believing life was futile

Prohibition (the outlawing of alcohol in the United States from 1920 to 1933) did not poop out the partying by any means. Though illegal, booze was still produced, shipped, and consumed during those years. Organized crime made a fortune on *bootlegging* (manufacturing and transporting illegal beverages like beer and whiskey), and Americans drank their hooch at *speakeasies* (secret locations where members had to quietly order the illegal drink) run by gangsters like Al Capone, Bugs Moran, and Lucky Luciano.

The straight-laced Victorian era (1837–1901) where manners and protocol were strictly adhered to by almost everyone in society regardless of social rank or economic status, was caricaturized, ridiculed, and repudiated in the years between World War I and World War II (1919–1939). Because many monarchies were involved in the eruption of World War I, some overreacted after the war by not only abandoning the monarchical style of government, but also the social expression of the aristocracy as well. The Victorian-era morality was seen by some people as a relic and symbol of the antidemocratic-republican system. The prim and proper demeanor of people during the reign of Queen Victoria of England (1837–1901) was now seen as being prudish or even puritanical. Whereas the older morality found it socially unacceptable to be seen in public exposing more than your face and hands, the new morality of the 1920s not only saw the hemlines of women's skirts go higher and higher, but the overall ethical behavior become more and more lax and licentious.

Whether it was drinking illegal alcohol, visiting places of public prostitution, or attending burlesque shows, the Roaring Twenties would later be considered somewhat decadent and antithetical to traditional values like marriage and family. Pride, greed, envy, lust, sloth, anger, and gluttony are not only the seven deadly or capital sins — most of them were also the hobbies, if not preoccupation, of many people after World War I when some economic prosperity and new political freedom gave them a feeling of total liberty.

Rejecting democracy and liberalism

While ancient expressions of monarchy or aristocracy were blamed for the debacle of World War I, the weak democratic-republics that replaced them were not strong enough to handle the enormous problems of a chaotic economy or of social upheaval. The emigration and immigration of millions of people after World War I meant that a larger population was being created where people thought there would be more opportunity and less oppression. Civil secular society was not adequately prepared for the mass immigrations that took place in the early 20th century. It strained the limited resources available.

Unemployment and inflation began to rise astronomically, and even war veterans who suffered so much in the so-called "Great War" were left in the cold with reduced or nonexistent benefits. Crime and violence often erupted in overcrowded cities in Europe and North America. Weak national and local governments could not address or satisfy the needs of the populace.

Believing the parliamentary process too burdensome

Some people of this era believed that the democratic process itself, whether it was a European parliament or an American Congress, was inherently inadequate to respond to the new and more profound needs of the growing masses. Republics use democratic procedures like voting and committee meetings and reports, open discussions, and civil rights as their method of government. When chaos at an economic, political, or geographical level is immanent, many people are ready and willing to suppress the parliamentary process and expeditiously allow a few to rule more efficiently.

Crowned monarchs and ancient empires had failed the general public with World War I but in the 1920s and 1930s, democracy and republicanism did no better with economic and social unrest becoming more and more dangerous and possibly uncontrollable. Radical responses from the far left (Communism) and far right (Fascism) would not only seek to eliminate the weak democracies but also to eradicate the opposition and become a single-party government.

Seeing capitalism as too chaotic and risky

Capitalism is the system of economics where a free market exists unfettered by government restrictions, and where supply and demand determine the price and cost of goods and services. Capitalism is based on the private and corporate ownership of goods. During the 1920s and 1930s, some people lost faith in the capitalist system. They saw it as too vulnerable, risky, and chaotic. Susceptible to many economic and social factors, unbridled capitalism with no supervision led to corruption, greed, and, ultimately, the collapse of the entire economic system.

The apprehension centered on the fact that human nature, while basically and substantially good, can and often does at times, succumb to the innate weaknesses present in every human being. Without checks and balances, a free-market economy can become too vulnerable to the whims of the buyers and sellers. Monopolies were born in capitalism whereby the little guy got bought out by the big guy. Big business muscled small business. The final outcome often was that competition was dissolved after a monopoly eliminated the other players. Then the price was no longer based on supply and demand, but on what the consumer was willing to pay.

Failing with the Treaty of Versailles

World War I ended in 1918 one year after the Russian Revolution deposed the czar. France, Great Britain, Italy, Belgium, Russia, and the United States as members of the Allied Forces had defeated Germany, Austria-Hungary, Turkey, and Bulgaria. There were 8.5 million casualties in the war and 21 million wounded.

The defeated Central Powers were predominated by Germany, led by Kaiser Wilhelm. The details of the treaty were not reviewed or discussed in advance, which irritated Germans in general. The surrender also stipulated:

- ✔ The surrender of all German colonies as League of Nations mandates
- ✔ German reparations of US$12 billion
- ✔ A ban on the union of Germany and Austria
- ✔ Admission of Germany's guilt in causing the war
- ✔ A provision for the trial of the former Kaiser and other war leaders
- ✔ Restriction of the German army to 100,000 men with no conscription, no tanks, no heavy artillery, no poison-gas supplies, no aircraft, and no airships
- ✔ Limitation of the German Navy to vessels under 100,000 tons, with no submarines

Although Germany signed the treaty under protest, the United States Congress refused to ratify it. There was no way Germany could fulfill the reparations assessment and the unwillingness of France or Britain to reduce the amount further angered Germans back home. The disarmament of the German military was also considered humiliating by the populace while the French, British, and Belgians saw it as justice, not as revenge.

The treaty was, in fact, more punitive than prescriptive — it did not prevent Germany from becoming a greater threat in the future. Instead, Adolf Hitler used the treaty as an excuse to rearm and rebuild the German military. Playing on national pride and the perception that the winners of World War I were seeking a vendetta against those who lost the war, the Nazi Party won many votes from disgruntled citizens.

The Allied Powers had no viable way of enforcing the treaty, either, because the League of Nations, which was called for by the same treaty, was not ratified by the U.S. Congress, and thus the United States did not participate in any way with this international group of countries. With no armed forces to persuade or coerce, the League merely made suggestions and could not implement resolutions.

Democratic President Woodrow Wilson was the creator of the League of Nations, which he had hoped would become the current equivalent of our United Nations. An international gathering to resolve disputes and to enforce and protect peace and justice is what he envisioned, but without the financial, military and moral support of the United States, the League was doomed to failure.

Experiencing a worldwide depression

When the U.S. stock market crashed on October 24, 1929, the consequences were devastating. Banks closed, and millions of people lost their jobs, their savings, their pensions, their homes, and some even their lives.

Dealing with astronomical unemployment rates

After only four years, the U.S. unemployment rate went from 3.2% when the Depression began in 1929 to a whopping 24.9% in 1933. Germany went as high as 29.9% unemployment a year earlier (1932). Great Britain hit an unemployment level of 25% by 1931. The problem was that all the veterans who had fought in World War I now needed civilian jobs, and there weren't enough to go around. Many businesses collapsed in postwar years, so the number of employers dropped, but the number of employees increased.

Feeling outrageous inflation

After World War I, in 1919, one U.S. dollar was worth four German deutschmarks. Inflation rose so high that in 1923, it took more than four *trillion* marks to equal one dollar. You'd need pretty big and deep pockets just to buy a burger and fries with that kind of inflation.

When consumer goods became more expensive than a week's, a month's, or even a year's salary, then people stopped buying as much. That resulted in fewer sales, which meant lower profits and that translated into more layoffs. Prices rose uncontrollably during inflation; people had to work longer and harder for the same goods and services they received only months before.

Losing confidence in the system

The Great Depression extinguished the hope and trust many citizens had in their local and federal governments to protect and serve them. Unemployment and inflation spiraled out of control. All those previous years of paying taxes and the blood shed by brave patriots on the battlefield, seemed wasted now as government was completely incapable of helping its citizens as it had promised to do.

Taking Advantage of the Situation: Communism and Fascism (1920–1940)

With the chaos caused by the Great Depression, the impotency of the League of Nations, and the unwillingness for individual nations to unilaterally engage another country in armed conflict out of fear of another world war, dark forces were able to secure a strong foothold in Western Europe.

Introducing the dictators

The democratic republics that disappeared under the reigns of Fascist dictators were weak, often corrupt, and incompetent in terms of addressing the needs of the people in time of crisis. Dictatorships such as those found in Germany, Italy, and Spain capitalized on popular fears and anxieties that left-wing Communists would turn their country into a puppet of the Soviet Union, the great sleeping bear waiting to overrun Europe.

In the following sections, we cover the major European dictators who played a role in the early part of John Paul II's life.

Lenin and Stalin

Vladimir Ilich Ulyanov, alias Lenin (1870–1924), embraced the radical philosophy of Karl Marx. *Marxism* is based on revolution and class struggle between the *proletariat* (the workers) and the *bourgeoisie* (the management). Basically, Marxism contends that class struggle is good and the outcome is better in the end. Marx embraced a Socialist framework, so Lenin was of course amenable to state control of the economy, manufacturing, banking, and so on.

Lenin is considered the founding father of Communism. The Communist Party became the state and the ultimate authority in Lenin's political system. When Czar Nicholas II was forced to abdicate in 1917 and was subsequently executed along with his entire immediate family, the governance of Russia fell into the hands of the Communist Party, and the Union of Soviet Socialist Republics (U.S.S.R.) was formed in 1922.

Focusing on the good of the state rather than the freedom of the individual

Extremist governments exalt the state over the individual. *Fascism* is the far-right form of government, where a very strong centralized government controls almost all political and economic activity. There is private ownership of private property, but the national government also controls the economy as well as the military. *Communism* is the far-left form of government, where there is no private ownership and a very strong centralized government controls everything. Whereas Fascism is extremely nationalistic, Communism seeks international control and domination. Both forms of government are willing to suppress, dilute, or even deny certain basic and fundamental human rights for the sake of the state (Fascism) or the political party (Communism).

Whenever economic or political turmoil ravages a nation, there is always a danger that some people will take advantage of the situation. Usurping more and more authority, these elements pretend to represent the masses while in reality they seek to rob individuals of their rights and liberties for the good of the state. Crime, chaos, terror, and other social dangers can often lure citizens to surrender their rights momentarily and give a few influential people dictatorial power.

Josef Vissarionovich Dzhugashvili, alias Stalin (1879–1953), met up with Lenin in 1905. They were fellow dissidents to the czar's policies and government in Russia. Stalin was arrested for stirring up rebellion; he was sent to Siberia from 1913 to 1917. After the Bolshevik Revolution was underway, Lenin used Stalin to be the "enforcer" of the Communist Party. Not considered an intellectual like Lenin, Stalin was content to be the muscle behind the brains until 1922, when he became chairman of the Communist Party and general secretary of the Central Committee. At this point, Stalin controlled the U.S.S.R.

History later exposed Stalin as a malevolent and evil dictator — as malevolent and evil as Adolf Hitler (see the following section). Ruthlessly, Stalin had anyone from his past executed so he could create his own myth about his origins. Brutal, merciless, and cunning, Stalin signed a nonaggression pact with Hitler in 1939, which was honored until 1941 when the Nazis invaded Russia and violated the treaty. Originally, Stalin and Hitler had agreed to divide Eastern Europe between them — that is, until the Germans broke the agreement.

After the pact was dissolved, Stalin took Eastern Europe for himself so that by the end of World War II, the Warsaw Pact nations were under Soviet control. Countries like Poland, Czechoslovakia, Hungary, Romania, Bulgaria,

Albania, and East Germany were not independent after Nazi Germany surrendered in 1945 — they were under Soviet control as satellite nations. At least 11 million victims died at the orders or under the authority of Stalin during his long reign of terror (1922–1953).

Hitler

Adolf Hitler (1889–1945) became chancellor of Germany in 1934 after the death of President Paul von Hindenburg. As head of the National Socialist German Workers' Party (the Nazis) since 1920, Hitler rose through the ranks of political power. He used the country's dissatisfaction with the Versailles Treaty and with the ruling power of the Weimar Republic to forge support for his Nazi Party. He used the Depression, unemployment, and inflation to fan anti-Semitism (by blaming the German Jews for social and economic problems, despite the lack of any credible evidence to support such racist claims).

Manipulating public opinion, Hitler was able to poison the national political climate with racist lies so much so that the infamous Nuremburg Laws would finally legalize prejudice and discrimination against all Jews in Germany. By using fear, anxiety, hatred, bigotry, and other distasteful methods, *der Fuhrer* ("the leader," as he was called in the German language) eliminated his rivals and opponents and directed a tyrannical reign of 11 years. During the Holocaust, 6 million Jews were murdered. Fifty-two million casualties were suffered in World War II (20 million from the U.S.S.R., 6.8 million from Germany, and 6.1 million from Poland). Both Hitler and Stalin used their own people to amass political power and personal grandeur. Ordinary citizens were mere pawns to these men of little or no conscience.

Mussolini

Benito Mussolini (1883–1945) was dictator of Italy (called *il dulce,* or "the leader") from 1922 to 1943. He developed and refined the Fascist agenda (in 1919) before Hitler really came to power. Like Hitler, Mussolini used the economic chaos of the Depression, high unemployment (especially among the war veterans of World War I), and hyperinflation to convince the ruling authorities to ally with his Fascist Party to restore order. Civil liberties were curtailed in Fascist Italy as they were in Nazi Germany, because the state was more important that the individual. Anti-Communist support allowed Mussolini's party to win enough seats in parliament, just as Hitler did in Germany a few years later.

Mussolini did not agree with every ambition, tactic, strategy, or goal of Hitler — but they were allies. Mussolini played to the crowds with their romantic yearning for former glory from ancient times. Though the Roman Empire fell in A.D. 476, it had endured for more than 12 centuries (since 753 B.C.). Pre–World War II Italians were mesmerized by the prospect of another imperial destiny for their homeland. Like the Third Reich, however, the Fascist rule lasted far less than the thousand years that Hitler promised.

Franco

Francisco Franco (1892–1975) was the only Fascist dictator to survive World War II. He was a Spanish General who had supported the military dictatorship of Miguel Primo de Rivera (who was forced to resign in January 1930). One year later, King Alfonso XIII abdicated and allowed free elections in 1931. The Socialists won a majority vote, and, in the 1936 election, they formed a coalition government with other left-wing parties to create the Popular Front. Franco and other military leaders and monarchists who opposed the direction that the Republic was taking formed their own coalition, the National Front. The Spanish Civil War (1936–1939) erupted between the two factions. When it was over, Franco and the right wing emerged victors.

Unlike Mussolini, Franco was not admired by Hitler. In fact, Hitler was quoted as saying that he would rather go to the dentist to have his teeth removed than have another meeting with Franco. This was because Franco wanted Spain to remain neutral during World War II and Hitler wanted him to commit troops as Fascist Italy had — but Franco refused. Like his Fascist contemporaries, Franco used an iron fist to rule. He was as vehemently anti-Communist as Mussolini or Hitler.

Spreading anti-Semitism

The plague of anti-Semitism has never been fully extinguished, and sadly its reappearance during World War II was the worst expression of it in human history. Jews were blamed and reviled by both the far right and the far left. Numerous groups mistreated the children of Abraham and often used them as a scapegoat for social and economic woes.

Working toward a "pure Aryan nation"

The Nazi Party was by far the most anti-Semitic of all the political regimes as they ultimately devised the heinous horror of the "Final Solution," the euphemism used to describe the Holocaust (which Jews call the *Shoah,* in Hebrew), in which six million Jewish men, women, and children were murdered. Hitler and his henchmen sought to "purify" Germany but getting rid of those they considered genetic inferiors. The idealized German was called an *Aryan* (a descendant of the Nordic-Teutonic tribes that ruled the land called by the Romans "Germania"). This archetype of "racial purity" was depicted in propaganda posters by young, blonde-haired, blue-eyed Germans. Ironically, Adolf Hitler and many of his closest cohorts didn't fit that cookie-cutter mold.

Though Germany had been predominantly Christian (with a Protestant Lutheran majority and a Catholic minority), there were also a significant number of German Jews who had been born and raised in the Fatherland for centuries. The Aryan myth promoted by the Nazis had nothing to do with Judeo-Christian religion. The political rallies were often peppered with ancient pagan rituals and overtones.

Introducing the Nuremberg Laws

Nazi Germany passed the notorious Nuremburg Laws (1935), which in essence legalized the confiscation of Jewish property and financial assets, the termination of Jewish employment, and the deportation of Jews to labor or to extermination camps. These totally immoral but technically legal decrees and ordinances allowed the Nazis to deny Jews living within Germany all civil and human rights.

Under the Nuremberg Laws, Jews were classified according to degrees of "Jewishness" (someone who had at least three Jewish grandparents was considered a full Jew; someone who had two Jewish grandparents was considered a mixed Jew of first degree; and someone with one Jewish grandparent was considered a mixed Jew of second degree). These distinctions determined whether or not German Jews could marry Aryan Germans.

Taking War to a New Level: World War II (1939–1945)

Hitler had convinced British Prime Minister Chamberlain that allowing Hitler to annex the Sudetenland from Czechoslovakia to Germany (under the infamous Munich Agreement of 1938) would preserve peace. History would later judge this to be a miscalculated appeasement which only spurred on further bold aggression. One year later, in 1939, Hitler violated the agreement and invaded *all* of Czechoslovakia, which quickly surrendered under the threat of total annihilation of historic cities like Prague.

It was the invasion of Poland, however, that triggered World War II. On September 1, 1939, German tanks, troops, and planes overwhelmed Polish defenses. Two days later, in compliance with previous treaties, Britain, France, Australia, and New Zealand declare war on Germany. By September 29, Poland surrendered to the German occupiers. The Nazis closed universities and seminaries and restricted public religious activities. They systematically rounded up Jews and confiscated their property. Those who were not left in horrible ghettos like those in Warsaw were deported to concentration camps or extermination camps. All six of the notorious death camps — Belzec, Chelmno, Sobibor, Treblinka, Auschwitz-Birkenau, and Majdanek — were constructed in Poland because they could easily be hidden from Allied view due to Nazi control of the country.

The United States remained neutral until the Japanese Empire bombed Pearl Harbor on December 7, 1941. Four days later, Germany declared war on the United States.

Fighting a multifront war

Disregarding Napoleon's mistake of waging a two-front war, Hitler had become overconfident in his victorious invasions of Poland, Denmark, Norway, and finally France. Though Great Britain was still a viable threat, his ego lured him into unleashing Operation Barbarossa, the military code name for the invasion of the Soviet Union. Breaking the nonaggression pact with Stalin, Hitler sent his troops into Russian territory in June 1941. Six months later, he declared war on the United States and now had a full-blown enemy allied with Britain, while the Germans continued to fight the Red Army defending their homeland. Six months later, in December 1941, Nazi troops finally breached the capital of Moscow, in the middle of the nasty Russian winter.

Allied forces eventually squeezed the German dictator when on June 6, 1944, the famous D-Day invasion took place; under the command of General Dwight D. Eisenhower, 160,000 Allied troops and 30,000 vehicles landed on the shores of Normandy in France. This officially marked the beginning of the two-front (East and West) war for Hitler and also the start of his defeat. On April 30, 1945, Hitler committed suicide as Red Army troops besieged Berlin. On May 7, 1945, Germany unconditionally surrendered to the Allied forces.

Dropping the bomb

While Europe celebrated V-E (Victory in Europe) Day on May 8, 1945, the United States was still at war with its other enemy, the Empire of Japan. Planned invasions of mainland Japan came with dire predictions of enormous civilian and military casualties as many, if not all, Japanese would be expected to fight to the death to defend their homeland. U.S. President Harry Truman decided to drop the first atomic bomb the world had ever seen on Hiroshima, Japan, on August 6, 1945. A second atomic bomb was dropped on Nagasaki, Japan, on August 9, 1945. The Japanese government unconditionally surrendered on August 14.

World War II pitted the evil of Fascist totalitarianism against human liberty and freedom. The Cold War merely changed directions, and the new enemy was atheistic Communism, which threatened to dominate the world as Hitler had tried to before. They were times of military might and ideological conflict.

Feeling the Chill of the Cold War (1947–1991)

Within two years of World War II ending, a new phenomenon was recognized as Eastern Europe went from Nazi occupation to Soviet control. Unlike the hot battles involving actual military engagements, a new war emerged. The war was known as the Cold War, because it did not involve the direct firing upon or by an enemy. After Germany and Japan surrendered, the Allies, especially the United States and Great Britain, were not eager for another war. After the troops went home and the rebuilding of Germany and Japan took place, the West thought life would go back to normal. Eastern Europe never again experienced normality after World War II — it only exchanged occupation with domination.

Under the appearance of democracy, politicians favorable to Soviet "assistance" (which in actuality meant "control") were aided in getting elected even by means of rigged elections and stuffed ballot boxes. By 1947, the Communist Party seized control of the Polish government, and the process of Stalinization began. Only too late did the Western powers of Britain, France, and the United States realize that an "Iron Curtain" had been draped around Eastern Europe.

Weary from World War II, the West had no stomach to fight the expansionist agenda of the U.S.S.R., so it adopted a policy of *containment,* which led to a division of East Germany and West Germany and a wall separating East Berlin from West Berlin. The Warsaw Pact nations were those under Soviet control and influence. The West responded with the establishment in 1949 of the North Atlantic Treaty Organization (NATO), which remains to this day an international military alliance that pledges to defend each and every member state from foreign attack or invasion. This was now the era of the Cold War.

Dropping the Iron Curtain

Prime Minister Winston Churchill, shortly after being voted out of office in Great Britain, had coined the term *Iron Curtain* to describe the forced absorption of Eastern European nations into Soviet control. (Some historians use the phrase *Bamboo Curtain* to refer to countries under the control of Communist mainland China.) Russian tanks and troops were "loaned" to these countries to prevent uprisings and rebellions against their new masters. Political, economic, and religious liberties were as absent as in the days of Nazi occupation.

Soviet controlled Poland, Hungary, Romania, Albania, Czechoslovakia and East Germany were governed by local citizens who joined the Communist Party to acquire political power. Technically, the countries still existed and had their own leaders and governments and armies, but in reality they were puppet states of Communist Russia, now the heart and soul of the Union of Soviet Socialists Republic (U.S.S.R.). As such, the Catholic Church was the biggest thorn and obstacle to complete control by the Communists. The faith had given hope and sustenance to the Polish people during the war, while Nazi Germany raped the Polish nation.

Warsaw Pact Communists had to obey their Soviet masters in Moscow and yet realized that their own people could rebel one day. Red Army troops were sent as advisers and technicians to help their native ethnic comrades defend themselves from any capitalist scheme of the West to invade. The reality was that the nations of the Warsaw Pact were being held hostage by Stalin and his successors. Moscow did not fear an invasion from NATO as much as an escape of Eastern Europeans from their Communist-controlled homeland.

Raising up the superpowers: The Soviet Union and the United States

Though Great Britain and France also developed the atomic bomb, the huge nuclear arsenal of atomic bombs and hydrogen bombs rested with two super-powers: the United States the Soviet Union. Launched from sea, land, or air, both nations engaged in an arms race that would eventually bankrupt and dissolve one of them for good.

Many people have claimed that the avoidance of World War III during the post–World War II era up until the crumbling of the Soviet Union and the fall of the Berlin Wall, was due to the mutually assured destruction (MAD) policy of nuclear deterrence, a military strategy of targeting major civilian popula-tion centers, like New York City, Boston, Los Angeles, Philadelphia, Moscow, Leningrad, and so on. The idea was that both sides were capable of and threatened to annihilate most enemy population centers if any of theirs were hit with a first nuclear attack. In this lose-lose scenario, the hope was that neither side would ever initiate a first strike because to do so would result in complete and total launch of every nuclear warhead in the arsenal. Total destruction on both sides, allegedly, would deter either one from striking first and unleashing Armageddon.

The problem was that, over time, both the Soviet Union and later the United States altered their doctrine from mutually assured destruction to tactical and precise use of limited nuclear warheads aimed at strategic military tar-gets rather than civilian targets. Development of less-dirty (less-radioactive) but more-precise missiles also led to research into antiballistic missile defen-sive systems.

The United States, helped by NATO, and the Soviet Union, helped by the Warsaw Pact and their new fledgling allies (Communist China, North Korea, and Cuba), often competed with one another in third-world politics. Countries in South America, Africa, the Middle East, and the Orient were either aligned with the West (the U.S.) or the East (the Soviet Union). Capitalism and democ-racy were being exported to other parts of the world at the same time that atheistic Communism and Soviet satellite nations were being sought by the competition.

Witnessing the space race

When Russia launched the first man-made satellite into outer space to orbit the planet on October 4, 1957 (named Sputnik), the United States held its breath. The fear was that, eventually, nuclear weapons could be launched from outer space, which meant little, if any, early detection and much more devastating effects. Satellites also paved the way for electronic spying, which until then was contingent upon land-based, old-fashioned field operatives (the James Bond secret agents) or on long-range, stealth aircraft.

American pride was also hurt because the Soviets beat them to outer space and Russian cosmonauts were preparing for the first man in space. Yuri Alekseyevich Gagarin would become the first human being to orbit the Earth in 1961. One month later, President John F. Kennedy told a joint session of Congress that "this nation should commit itself to achieving the goal, before this decade is out, of landing a man on the moon and returning him safely to the Earth." On July 21, 1969, just before the decade closed, U.S. astronauts Neil Armstrong and Buzz Aldrin became the first human beings to land and walk on the moon.

Under the presidency of Ronald Reagan, terms like *Star Wars* (not referring to the Luke Skywalker and Yoda films) appeared in the press and media to describe Reagan's plans to erect a strategic defense initiative, which would intercept incoming nuclear warheads before they hit their intended targets. Reagan also pursued strategic arms reduction talks (START) to begin the actual dismantling of nuclear missiles. Previous strategic arms limitations talks (SALT) by previous administrations (begun under President Richard Nixon) had merely sought to slow down the arms race by reducing the number of new weapon systems.

Throwing off the yoke of Communism

Prior to this move to reduce nuclear arms, Reagan had previously beefed up military spending, especially on strategic weapons, because he felt that the United States had fallen behind the Soviet Union on capability and there was an imbalance in favor of the Soviets. Some experts contend that the United States forced the Soviets to almost bankrupt their economy to keep up with the arms race and then, by reducing both sides' ability to destroy the world, indirectly added to the demise of the entire Communist system.

Mikhail Gorbachev became General Secretary of the U.S.S.R. in 1985 and governed until 1991, when the Soviet Union was dissolved and Boris Yeltsin became the first president. It was during Gorbachev's tenure that economic and political relaxation (*glasnost* and *perestroika*) were extended, to some degree, to Soviet satellite nations as well as to the main body of the U.S.S.R.

With the taste of economic and political freedom — small as it was — many political experts believe the genie was out of the bottle and what Gorbachev uncorked could not be put back. Furthermore, the enormous military spending trying to keep up with the arms race initiated by Reagan and continued by President George H.W. Bush, also contributed to the fact that the Soviet Union was beginning to unravel due to decreasing resources. Many people contend that the actual spark to ignite the fuse was the presence of Pope John Paul II, who supported human rights and Polish Solidarity.

The Polish Trade Union, Solidarity, was founded in 1980 by Lech Wałęsa, a shipyard worker from Gdańsk. A nonviolent organization, it sought to promote and protect workers' rights by the use of strikes. Staunchly anti-Communist and predominantly populated by devout Roman Catholics, this labor movement received the blessings of the newly elected Polish Pope, John Paul II, who had been chosen in 1978 as the first non-Italian pontiff in 450 years. Polish Communist leaders and their Soviet superiors feared the influence a Polish pope would have over this upstart labor union. If the Soviet control of Poland became diluted, then it would only be a matter of time before the other Warsaw Pact nations fell like dominoes.

East Germany was by far the most tightly controlled Soviet satellite. After World War II, half the nation of Germany was taken by Stalin. The capital city of Berlin was divided into four zones managed by France, Great Britain, and the United States in the western part of town and the Soviet Union in the eastern part.

A wall separating East Berlin from West Berlin was constructed in August 1961 by order of the Soviet party bosses to prevent mass defections of East Germans into West Germany. Barbed wire, landmines, armed guards, and vicious guard dogs watched the Soviet side of the wall and prevented East Berliners from crossing over to the West. The wall became an ugly symbol of Communist tyranny as many people died trying to scale the wall only to be shot or killed by the booby-traps.

The 1989 victory of Solidarity candidates over Communists in the Polish national elections and the 1990 election of Lech Wałęsa as the president was an omen of the soon-to-die Soviet Empire. The old *Breshnev Doctrine* (crush any political opposition in any Soviet satellite to prevent a domino fall of the rest) was replaced by the *"Frank Sinatra" Doctrine* (let each country do it "my way," as Old Blue Eyes used to sing) coined in October 1989 by Foreign Ministry spokesman Gennadi Gerasimov.

The Berlin Wall itself fell on November 9, 1989. Germany was finally reunited in October 1990. Almost simultaneously, in December 1989, Czechoslovakia experienced the Velvet Revolution, the first peaceful overthrow of the Communist regime. That same year, Hungary declared its independence; Hungary's independence had been denied by force since the 1956 Hungarian Uprising, which had ended with Russian tanks and troops occupying their nation. Romania had a more violent revolt from its Soviet masters in 1989 with their December revolution and the execution of former tyrant and Communist dictator, Nicolae Ceauşescu.

Looking at Other Cultural Forces of the Times

The political and military demise of the former Soviet Union and the liberation of the former Warsaw Pact coincided with an astronomical growth in technology and science since after World War II. Radio gave way to television. And personal computers, cell phones, pagers, PDAs, and the Internet were made possible as after-effects of the space program. Miniaturization was needed to get things into outer space and that same technology made life on Earth much more convenient, from remote-controlled TVs to microwave ovens.

Medical advances also helped eliminate many lethal childhood diseases or at least provide viable treatments; it also offered reasonable remission if not recovery from several adult maladies. High-tech inventions and advances have saved and extended lives. Beginning and end-of-life bioethical issues never before in existence now challenge modern human beings. Abortion, euthanasia, and in vitro fertilization now force moral judgments upon medical treatment, procedures, policies, and decisions.

The Watergate scandal (which caused President Richard Nixon to resign rather than face impeachment in 1974) and the aftermath of the Vietnam War (1965–1973) disillusioned many young people with politics. The sexual revolution of the 1960s and 1970s and the availability of the birth control pill since the 1960s; the open theological dissent to Pope Paul VI's encyclical letter *Humanae Vitae* in 1968; the legalization of abortion since *Roe v. Wade* (1973); the increase in divorce and in premarital sex as well as *cohabitation* (unmarried couples living together) — all these factors have put strains on traditional values and institutions like marriage and the family, schools, and churches.

Exposure through media to all kinds of deviation as well as open access to pornography and violent material have further complicated moral lives. Racism, anti-Semitism, abuse of women and children, drug and alcohol abuse, gambling addictions, corporate greed, unethical behavior, and even recent clergy sex scandals all came onto the playing field to battle Judeo-Christian morality as the world ended the 20th century and ushered in the 21st.

Chapter 3

Discovering the Man Who Would Be Pope

In This Chapter

▶ Starting out life in an common family

▶ Handling family crisis with grace

▶ Achieving scholarly success

▶ Considering his own mortality

Before he became the Bishop of Rome, Pope John Paul II was Karol Jozef Wojtyła. In English, his name would be Charles. He often went by his nickname of Lolek, which is akin to Charlie or Chuck. You may have a hard time thinking about a man of John Paul II's stature being called Chuck, but in many ways he was a humble man of extraordinary intellect, insight, and grace.

In this chapter, we introduce you to the life of John Paul II. We explore his younger years spent with his family in Poland. We look at how he handled the loss of his parents and siblings and how that loss shaped the man he would become. We get to know how his mind worked by taking a peek into his university career and academic and philosophical influences. And finally, we take a look at how he handled the very real threats to his own life, including an assassin, debilitating disease, and the inevitable end of his life.

Growing from Humble Roots

Karol Wojtyła was born in a little town in southern Poland, Wadowice. It was founded in the late tenth century as a trading settlement. In the 17th century, the town became a regional center of crafts and trade. Eventually, it became part of the Austrian-Hungarian Empire. After World War I and the dissolution of the monarchy, Wadowice became part of the newly reborn Poland, in which it was the county seat of government in its region.

In 1939, the town was annexed to the *Third Reich* (Nazi Germany). Polish intellectuals were targeted by the harsh Nazi racial and cultural policies. Hundreds of people from the area — including priests, teachers, and artists — were murdered in mass executions. Between 1941 and 1943, a ghetto was established in the city for Jews. (A *ghetto* in this context is a section of town where a minority, class, or race of people are forced or compelled to live separate from the majority.) Nearly all the Jewish people of the town were exterminated in the nearby Auschwitz concentration camp. Even though Germans occupied the town, the *Home Army,* a resistance movement that later became known as the Underground State, was quite active in town. The war industry declined, however, and since the election of Pope John Paul II, Wadowice has become an important tourist-pilgrimage center.

The Wojtyłas were devout Catholics and did not share in any of the anti-Semitic views of some of those in their community. Karol, Sr., married Karol's mother, Emilia, in 1906. Nine months after their wedding, Emilia, who was a schoolteacher of Lithuanian descent, gave birth to a son, Edmund. Her second child, a daughter named Olga, died as an infant. Karol, Jr. (known as Lolek by his mom) was born on May 18, 1920. (See Figure 3-1 for a photograph of a young Karol with his mother.)

Figure 3-1:
Karol with his mother, Emilia, who died when he was only 9 years old.

© Sygma/Corbis

Emilia was somewhat frail and worn out from the tough childhood she endured losing her own mother at an early age and having to help raise her younger brothers and sisters. Emilia was the one who first saw priestly qualities in young Karol. She taught him to cross himself and read Sacred Scripture with him. Yet she was often in bed suffering from illnesses related to the heart and kidney. These last two experiences were a basis of two of JP2's encyclical letters — the first on human suffering and the second on the family. Karol wrote years later that the home and parents are the first educators in the Catholic faith, something he practiced by way of example from his mother and his father.

Karol, Sr., was a retired lieutenant in the Polish Army and served in an administrative post in the Austrian-Hungarian Army. The military became his lifetime career. He was awarded the Austrian Iron Cross of Merit for bravery during Word War I. The qualities of both of his parents played a major role in young Karol's life. Bravery, piety, and devotion were the marks of the future Pope John Paul II, and they were qualities he brought to the papacy.

Karol, Sr., lived a frugal life in a one-room apartment behind the church. As a retired tailor, Karol sewed his son's clothes. He made the younger Karol study in a cold room so that he could develop his concentration, a fine example of a teaching from Karol, Sr.'s, military background.

Surviving Family Tragedy

Historians have little concrete information about Pope John Paul II's feelings about his family. JP2 himself divulged little about his relationships with his brother, mother, and father. He was fiercely private about his personal family history — not out of shame, but simply out of tradition. Many people speculate that losing his earthly family at a young age, made his connection to his heavenly family even stronger.

The loss of his mother

Karol, Jr.'s, mother died in 1929 of heart and kidney failure. This deeply affected young Karol, who was almost 9 years old. Rearing the young boy was now exclusively on the father's shoulders.

Pope John Paul II loved his mother deeply and referred to her as the soul of their home. His conspicuously absent references to her have made some speculate that JP2 then turned to the Virgin Mary as his mother-figure. But the

Wojtyła home and family had been very devout Roman Catholics for generations, in both Poland and Lithuania before his mom ever got sick. Many armchair analysts can quickly psychoanalyze Karol, Jr., and hypothesize about his reaction to losing his mother while he was still a pre-adolescent. In reality, he was just being private with his most intimate feelings and recollections.

What we do know is that Karol, Jr., wrote a very moving poem about Emilia (see Chapter 1) when he was 19 years old. Polish culture demonstrates that no matter how young a mother dies, her influence over her children is tremendous.

The loss of his brother

Karol, Jr.'s, brother, Edmund, died three years after their mother, when Karol was 12 years old. Edmund died from scarlet fever while working as a physician at the Powszechny Hospital in Bielsko. Edmund was young Karol's idol growing up; the boys were very close to one another, despite the 14-year age difference.

After Edmund's untimely death, young Karol and the elder Karol became as close as a father and son could get. Often, the young Karol would pray with his father before he left for school. It was JP2's early sufferings that brought him closer to God. His father was a model and inspiration for Karol, Jr.'s, vocation as priest. Yet, life was not all work and no play. Often, the two Karols would play soccer in the afternoons. Karol, Jr., learned from his father that prayerfulness and manliness go hand in hand. This valuable witnessing of his father had far-reaching effects in the future of Karol, Jr.

From his experience with his dad, John Paul II learned and appreciated the role of manly piety. His father was a staunch Catholic but never overbearing. When JP2 wrote his encyclical letter *Redemptoris Custos* on St. Joseph, the foster-father of Jesus and husband of the Virgin Mary, you can see that the fatherly care of his own dad helped JP2 appreciate what fatherhood was really about. Unlike some cultures, where the men often relegate religious upbringing of the children to their wives, Polish men are as involved in the spirituality of the family as are the mothers. Many biographers detect the manly strength of Karol, Sr., in the paternal style of the papacy of John Paul II. He loved his flock and gave them the same strong love, attention, and, when necessary, correction, he got from his dad while growing up.

The loss of his father

During World War II, Karol, Jr., personally witnessed death. Tragedy hit him once again at home with the death of his father in 1941. It was during this time that he began to contemplate the priesthood. He often looked to his father as an inspiration in this area. His kind, religious, and devotional father had laid the foundation for young Karol's vocation. The great religious witness of his father combined with Karol's Jewish friends, the experiences of workers in the quarry, biblical theater, and the underground resistance movement all molded the young Karol and left lasting impressions that would one day be beneficial to his vocation as pope.

Being Successful at School

By all accounts, Karol Wojtyła was a strong student. With a sharp mind, hungry for knowledge, few subjects slowed him down.

His love of theater and the classics began in high school, in which he focused on Slavic plays, concentrating especially on his native Poland. At times, he would even direct the plays; often, he played the leading character. In the theater, as an actor, he learned many valuable skills, including how to interact with people and how to maintain self-discipline. In 1938, he graduated from high school and was the class valedictorian.

Upon his high school graduation, Karol enrolled at the Jagiellonian University in Krakow, and both Karol and his father (who did not die until 1941; see the preceding section, "The loss of his father") moved to the city.

Jagiellonian University was founded by Casmir III of Poland in 1364. Throughout the history of the university, thousands of students from all over Poland, Lithuania, Russia, Slovakia, Hungary, Bohemia, Germany, and Spain have studied there, truly making it an international school. Nicholas Copernicus, the famous astronomer, was a graduate from this institution.

Karol worked as a volunteer librarian and did compulsory military training in the Academic Legion. At college, he continued with his passions as an ardent athlete, actor, and playwright. He began his learning of 11 languages.

During his university career, World War II began. The war was fought between the Axis Powers (Germany, Japan, and Italy) and the Allies (the United States, Great Britain [and its Commonwealth countries like Canada, Australia, and New Zealand], and Russia). Almost 55 million people died as a result of this war. Acts of genocide such as the Holocaust were a major influence in the future pope's writings on the dignity of man and the evils of prejudice.

Nazi Germany tried to exterminate hordes of people in the name of ethnic cleansing. The Jews of Europe were the main victims of the Holocaust, in which six million were exterminated in death camps. Other groups joined the

Jews in the death camps. The Nazi regime was threatened by these groups, which included Poles, Catholics, Russians, Slavs, gypsies, the mentally or physically disabled, homosexuals, and political dissidents. The estimated number of Holocaust victims, including men, women, and children from these other groups, totals 11 million.

Another tactic of the Nazis was to obliterate any cultural institutions in the hope of homogenizing culture. Universities such as Jagiellonian were sacked. Professors were arrested. Libraries and laboratories were ruined. This was happening all around Karol during his university years. The legitimate university had to go underground, which was quite dangerous. Professors and students risked their lives in defiance of a dictatorship. They met in private homes and apartments.

During this period, every able-bodied man had to have a job. Karol worked as a messenger for a restaurant. Because it was a light job by nature, it afforded the young Karol time to continue his studies, learn French, continue his theatrical career, and even write. In the face of adversity, he did not curse his situation — he used his time well.

For more information on the historical events of the time, take a look at Chapter 2.

Facing His Own Mortality

Pope John Paul II's deep prayer life was the center of his reign or the core of his being. His quiet holy hours in the early hours of the morning before a private Mass gave him the energy to deal with the many problems that his church was facing. His deep devotion to Mary, the Mother of God, added to his spiritual strength. This devotion began many years ago, when his father took him on a pilgrimage to the shrine of the Black Madonna; the new pope emblazoned her image and motto, *Totus Tuus* (Latin for "All Yours"), on his coat of arms.

After his mother's death, when Pope John Paul II was just a little boy, he grieved deeply over the loss of her. In mourning her passing, he also thought of his own mortality and his total dependency upon God. This led him to the style of prayer that later became his trademark position for meditating in his private chapel, in the early morning hours, before celebrating Holy Mass: lying on the floor in a crucified position. Lying in a prostrate position denotes deep humility and total abandonment to the Will of God. As a boy, he entrusted himself to God through the intercession of Mother Mary. Mary became his spiritual mother and more than once helped Karol through many difficult situations — from the death of his mother to the attempt on his life — by bringing the spiritual graces from her Son, Jesus Christ.

Surviving an assassin's bullet

One of the most poignant times in the long reign of Pope John Paul II was the attempted assassination of the Holy Father, in which he was shot and critically wounded (see Figure 3-2). Turkish gunmen entered St. Peter's Square on May 13, 1981. Mehmet Ali Agca attempted to kill the pope with a gun. The pope's wounds were quite extensive, and he needed many days of recuperation in the hospital.

The day of the attempted assassination, May 13, is also a religious day for Catholics. It is the anniversary of the apparition of the Blessed Virgin Mary to three little children — Francisco, Jacinta, and Lucia — in the small town of Fatima, Portugal. Mary conveyed to the children that the Lord wished that Russia would be consecrated to the Immaculate Heart of Mary by the pope and all the bishops of the world. In this way, Communism would be defeated. This not-so-coincidental coincidence — of JP2 being shot on the anniversary of the incident in Fatima — proved to be very important in the life of the pope and the direction the Church would take.

Figure 3-2: Pope John Paul II lies injured after being shot by Turkish gunman Mehmet Ali Agca in 1981.

© Reuters/CORBIS

The consecration to the Immaculate Heart of Mary is marked by Catholics who honor her on the first Saturday of every month. Centering on the heart is merely a technique of describing love, in this case, to Mary. This devotion came out of the Fatima apparitions when Mary asked the faithful children to honor her on the first Saturday of the month. Catholics who commemorate her Immaculate Heart on five consecutive first Saturdays by going to the Sacrament of Confession, receiving Holy Communion, and praying five decades of the Holy Rosary in reparation for sins will receive Mary's maternal intercession at the hour of death when Satan tempts the soul for the last time.

In the messages from the Blessed Mother at Fatima, she predicted that the Holy Father would suffer much. In fact, in the third message, she predicted the attempt on the Holy Father's life. It was on this feast that this all took place. Knowing much of this, Pope John Paul II did extensive research and reading on the apparitions of Fatima.

The following year, on May 12, 1982, he went to Fatima in thanksgiving for the graces received by God through the intercession of the Mother of God, Mary. He credited Mary with saving his life. The pope at the moment of the assassination stooped over to bless a girl who was wearing a badge of Our Lady of Fatima. This gesture allowed the bullet to strike the pope in the abdomen instead of his head, which was the original attempt of the assassin. As act of thanksgiving, he had the bullet mounted in the crown of the statue of our Lady of Fatima in Portugal.

Forgiving an enemy

Following his recuperation, as soon as he was released, John Paul II in a gesture of forgiveness visited the jail of his assassin (see Figure 3-3). Before the whole world, the pope gave witness to the fact that we have to forgive people — even our enemies. Papers and tabloids printed pictures of the pope embracing Mehmet.

Many questions surrounded Mehmet Ali Agca. Was he hired by the KGB to take out the pope who was considered the Soviet Union's arch nemesis? Or was he just a mad man? This event will likely be talked about and investigated for years to come.

Remember the secret of Fatima with the conversion of Russia: Because of his time of recuperation, Pope John Paul II was able to see what Our Lady actually meant. Also, he was able to discuss this with the last of the three children still alive, Sister Lucia, who was now a Carmelite Nun in Portugal. This event led to the universal consecration of Russia, by all the bishops and the pope in 1984 to the Immaculate Heart of Mary. Shortly after the historic consecration, the threads of Communism started to unravel. With the aide of President Reagan, the Iron Curtain dissipated without a bullet or a bomb.

Figure 3-3:
Pope John Paul II speaks with Mehmet Ali Agca, the man who tried to kill him.

Enduring declining health

Twenty-five years on the throne of St. Peter and two assassination attempts, one which was quite serious (see the preceding sections), resulted in severe physical injury to John Paul II. A number of cancer scares also contributed to the continued decline in his health. Later, JP2 developed Parkinson's disease complicated by arthritis; the later years of his reign were filled with pain and difficulties. He could no longer hike, swim, or ski. Yet, the motto with which he began his reign, "Be not afraid," was definitely something he believed and lived by. By continuing the arduous responsibility of the papacy, JP2 gave courage, hope, and dignity to countless people suffering in nursing homes or hospitals or confined to their beds.

Even in the last week of his life, John Paul II taught by way of example. He had issued a teaching the previous year stating that all patients, even the termi-nally ill and dying, were to be given nutrition and hydration (food and water) even if by artificial means (like a feeding tube). These steps constitute ordi-nary medical care along with making the patient comfortable and using non-lethal pain relief. (During this same time period, an American, Terri Schiavo, was being denied food and water through artificial means.)

Four days before he died, John Paul II could no longer eat and drink on his own, and doctors inserted a feeding tube. These steps attested to his professional and personal conviction that no one should be starved to death even if terminally ill. He also denounced the use of embryonic stem cell research (because it involved, in his eyes, the destruction of human life), even though some claimed it might lead to the treatment and cure of such horrible diseases like Parkinson's, which he himself had suffered from.

Throughout his whole reign as pope, John Paul II taught and witnessed the dignity of the human being as created by God from the moment of conception. He taught his followers that human beings have certain inalienable rights until natural death.

Chapter 4

Identifying Early Influences in John Paul II's Life

*E*veryday experiences shape everyone's lives, setting us up for who we will be, often without our even realizing it. In this way, Karol Wojtyła's life was no different.

In this chapter, we cover the experiences that shaped Pope John Paul II's early life and made him the man he became. We take a look at how Poland — with its traditional, Catholic values — shaped the life and times of a future pope. We examine his experiences pursuing his education despite great hardship and danger during the Nazi era. And finally, we explore the impact of the oppressive Communist system that punctuated Eastern Europe during the last half of the 20th century.

Growing Up in a Country with a Rich Heritage

In Pope John Paul II's first speech to the people gathered in St. Peter's Square following his election in 1978, he acknowledged that the world's cardinals had elected a man from a "faraway country." But he was quick to add, "Far away [in distance], but always close in communion in the faith and the Christian tradition." Like any historical figure, to understand Pope John Paul

II, we need to understand his roots. Biographer George Weigel quotes Pope John Paul II as saying, "They try to understand me from outside. But I can only be understood from inside." To identify Pope John Paul II's influences, we need to go beyond the particular friends and historical events, back to what was written into his DNA as a Pole.

Poland's Catholic roots can be traced back to the Baptism of Prince Mieszko in the year 966, perhaps inspired by the example (and the urging) of his Christian wife. But more important than the prince's Baptism was the fact that Mieszko chose to be baptized into the Latin Rite Church (associated with Western Europe and centered in Rome) and not the Greek Rite (associated with Eastern Europe and Asia Minor and centered in Constantinople). In doing so, Prince Mieszko aligned himself with the political powers of Western Europe and gained protection from people like Holy Roman Emperor Otto the Great, as well as Pope John XIII. (In those days, popes were political rulers as well as spiritual leaders.)

Although many armies and governments have come and gone in Polish history, the Catholic faith has remained a constant in the lives of the people. Their faith is what has helped them survive centuries of being the "battered child" of Europe. Because of their past, they came to understand that internal faith is more powerful than external shows of might and strength. They believe that "who runs the government" is not as important as "who we are as a people." And although other countries (France and the United States) were eager to experiment with new forms of government, Poles always felt the "old and stable" way was better than "new and shaky." The same reasoning also means that Polish Catholicism has always been very traditional; they really held on to the saying, "If it ain't broke, don't fix it."

Practicing the faith: Catholic and traditional

In Poland, traditional Catholicism can be seen even today. Numerous shrines and places of pilgrimage dot the landscape in every direction. The grand-daddy of them all is Jasna Góra (or "bright hill") in the town of Czestochowa.

Closer to Karol Wojtyła's boyhood home of Wadowice is the shrine called Kalwaria Zebrzydowska (literally, "Zebrzydowski's Calvary"). It's named for a 17th-century governor of Krakow who built a series of chapels on the side of a mountain to resemble the shrines and chapels built in Jerusalem at the places Jesus Christ walked on the way to his death on Mount Calvary. Over the years, chapels were added that took into account the traditional lore of Mary's where-abouts during her son's *Passion* (his suffering on the way to his Crucifixion).

Here at Kalwaria Zebrzydowska, young Karol's *Marian devotion* (devotion to Jesus's mother Mary) took root, as he saw the connection between Christ's sufferings and Mary's faithful resignation to her son's mission. (Check out Chapter 6 for more information about Pope John Paul II's Marian devotion.)

Meeting a mentor in the Catholic Church

The parish in Karol Wojtyła's hometown of Wadowice was the Church of the Presentation of the Blessed Virgin Mary, but was simply called St. Mary's. Here, Karol was baptized in 1920, received his First Holy Communion in 1929, and was confirmed in 1938.

The parish priest, Father Kazimierz Figlewicz, had a profound effect on Karol. The two met in 1930, when Figlewicz was assigned to St. Mary's. Figlewicz asked Karol to be an altar server for Masses, and later Karol helped Father Figlewicz organize a group of young altar servers. Figlewicz assisted Karol and his father with his priestly presence and counsel following the death of Karol's older brother, Edmund, in 1932. When Father Figlewicz was eventually transferred to Wawel Cathedral in Krakow, he invited Karol to spend Holy Week in Krakow, attending all the ceremonies at the cathedral. Years later, Pope John Paul II wrote that this experience had a "profound impact" on him.

In 1938, when the Wojtyłas moved to Krakow, their friendship with Figlewicz rekindled and deepened. Eventually, Father Figlewicz became Karol's spiritual director and the priest who regularly heard his confessions. Karol was serving Father Figlewicz's Mass on the morning of September 1, 1939, when war broke out in Poland. It was Father Figlewicz who helped Karol in his decision to become a priest himself, and who arranged a meeting between Karol and Cardinal Sapieha. Years later, in 1946, when Karol was ordained a priest and celebrated his first Masses on All Souls Day, it was Father Figlewicz who acted as his Master of Ceremonies, standing at his side and guiding the nervous and newly ordained Father Wojtyła through the parts of the Mass.

Receiving devotional lessons at home

Not enough can be said about the impact Pope John Paul II's parents had on his Catholic upbringing. (We cover part of the story in Chapter 3, but we mention it here as well because it's so important.) Both Emilia and Karol, Sr., had immeasurable impacts on their son's faith.

Although his mother's early death prevented him from remembering specifics, Pope John Paul II acknowledged that his mother made a great contribution to his religious training. Critics who thought Pope John Paul II's Marian devotion was excessive attempt to attribute it to the fact that he lost his mother early in life. But what is probably more correct is that young Karol's Catholic faith helped him to better understand and accept his mother's death.

Of the whole Wojtyła family, Pope John Paul II's father had the most profound effect on young Karol. He was a man with a strong, pious faith that made a huge impression on his son. In *Gift and Mystery* (1996), JP2's reflections on 50 years of ordained priesthood, Pope John Paul II reflected on the example of his father's faith, calling his father a "deeply religious man" whose life was filled with constant prayer. "Sometimes I would wake up during the night," Pope John Paul II wrote, "and find my father on his knees, just as I would always see him kneeling in the parish church. We never spoke about a vocation to the priesthood, but *his example was in a way my first seminary,* a kind of domestic seminary."

Living with Jewish neighbors

At the time the Wojtyłas lived there, the town of Wadowice had a population of about 10,000 people, a significant minority of which were Jewish. Karol grew up in a town that had learned to coexist without the problem of large-scale anti-Semitism. (In fact, the Wojtyłas rented their apartment in Wadowice, 2 Koscielna Street, from Chaim Blamuth, a Jewish man.)

Anti-Semitism certainly existed amongst some individuals but never culturally or with the support of discriminatory laws. Why? Wadowice is an old town whose origins go back to the 1200s; it had long been a regional center for particularly "Polish" culture and education. Perhaps the town's nationalistic spirit meant that each person was seen first as a Pole, and then as a person who happened to be either Jewish or Christian.

Karol's father, through his years in the Austro-Hungarian army, had come into contact with a good number of Jewish soldiers and had a profound respect for them. In addition, in his Christian faith he remembered the fact that Christ himself was a Jew. In later years, as Nazi discrimination forced Jewish neighbors of the Wojtyłas to leave Poland, JP2's father made a point of telling his neighbors, "Not all Poles are anti-Semitic." This point of view was reinforced at one point by a priest of St. Mary's in Wadowice, who told his congregation (among them the Wojtyłas) that anti-Semitism was "against the Gospel of Christ."

Growing up in Wadowice, Karol had many friends, both Jewish and Catholic. A key moment in his life was his meeting of Jerzy Kluger on Karol's first day of elementary school. Jerzy was the son of a lawyer who was a leader in Wadowice's Jewish community. Kluger remembers Karol as a boy who loved the outdoors: Karol and Jerzy spent their days hiking or playing soccer in the summer, and skating or playing hockey when the river froze in the winter. Karol would spend time at the Kluger home, listening to classical music with his family. Jerzy remembers visiting the Wojtyła home and listening to "the Captain" (as Karol's father was called because of his military rank) tell stories of Polish history, as well as recite Polish poetry and read passages of Polish literature.

Honoring the Jewish legacy in his homeland and abroad

In August 1991, Pope John Paul II traveled to Poland for the celebration of World Youth Day in Czestochowa. During the trip, he stopped in Wadowice, where he spoke about his Jewish friends:

> Nor can I forget that among our classmates in the school of Wadowice and in its high school there were those who belonged to the Mosaic religion; they are no longer with us, just as there is no longer the old synagogue next to the high school. When a [memorial] stone was [unveiled] in the place where the synagogue used to be, I sent a special letter through one of our classmates [Kluger]. In it we find the following words: "The Church, and in her all peoples and nations, are united with you. Certainly first of all your people feel your suffering, your destruction — here we recall how close it is to Auschwitz — then they want to speak to individuals and people, and to all of mankind, to admonish them. In your name

this warning cry is also raised by the pope, and the pope who comes from Poland has a special reason for this because, in a certain way, he experienced all this with you in our homeland. . . ."

On March 23, 2000, during his pilgrimage to the Holy Land, JP2 visited Yad Vashem, the Israeli memorial to those killed in the Holocaust. The pope was visibly moved as he prayed along with Holocaust survivors, among them Jerzy Kluger and other Jewish friends from Wadowice. During the meeting, he was greeted by Edith Tzirer. She told him she was a 14-year-old girl, exhausted and sick with tuberculosis, when she was liberated from a concentration camp in January 1945. Too weak to walk, she collapsed on the side of a road, when a stranger, "strong and tall, an athlete," gave her a piece of bread and a cup of tea and carried her for 2 miles. That man's name, Tzirer told the pope, was Karol Wojtyła! The pope didn't remember the specific incident, but he didn't doubt that it was true.

During World War II, Karol lost contact with Jerzy, and when no information could be found, he assumed Jerzy had been killed. Decades later, during the Second Vatican Council, Jerzy, then an engineer living in Rome, rediscovered his old friend while reading a newspaper article about a speech by Archbishop Wojtyła. Later, Jerzy Kluger played a key role in Vatican-Israeli dialogue, acting as a private intermediary between Pope John Paul II and Israeli diplomats in Rome. Kluger's work culminated in a 1993 document called the "Fundamental Agreement between the Holy See and the State of Israel." (For more information on the friendship between JP2 and Jerzy Kluger, take a look at Darcy O'Brien's book *The Hidden Pope*.)

Living Under Nazi Occupation

On the morning of September 1, 1939, Karol served the Mass of his friend and spiritual director, Father Figlewicz, at Wawel Cathedral as sounds of bombs exploding and planes flying overhead went on around them. The Nazis had invaded Poland and were heading toward Krakow. Following the Mass, Karol headed home, got his father, and together with thousands of others began to head east, away from the invasion to what they hoped would be safer territory.

After walking over 100 miles over a period of days and reaching Poland's eastern border with the Soviet Union, they were shocked to find out that the Soviet army was invading Poland from the east! In a secret understanding, Poland had been divided by Hitler and Stalin into what they called "spheres of influence." With no place in Poland being safe, Karol and his father headed back to their home in Krakow.

By the time they arrived back in Krakow the Nazis had moved in and taken control of the city. Soon the Wojtyłas, like many other Poles, felt the oppression of Nazi tyranny. The occupiers sought to erase the Polish nation from memory and break the spirit of the Polish people.

On a personal level, Karol, Sr.'s military pension was eliminated by the Nazis, which caused an immediate financial strain on the father and son. Like other Poles, their supply of food was suddenly cut off. While Nazis and their sympathizers could shop at exclusive, well-stocked stores, most Poles waited in line for a loaf of bread. Anything else had to be bought through the black market, which was dangerous as well as expensive. The Wojtyłas, like everyone else, made the best of it, living simply and eating whatever was available.

Outlawing higher education

Even with the occupation, Karol was set to begin his second year of studies at Jagiellonian University when the Nazis called a meeting with the university faculty on November 6, 1939. What they thought was going to be a meeting turned out to be a roundup of the faculty. Those attending members were arrested and deported to the Sachsenhausen concentration camp. Soon the Nazis closed most schools, universities, and newspapers.

Karol and his friends responded to this attempt to eliminate Polish culture by getting their hands on and reading any Polish literature, history, and poetry they could find. Eventually, the reading of the works led to discussion of the works, and from that it was a small jump to performances and dramatic readings.

Joining the underground theater as resistance to the Nazis

Pope John Paul II's love for drama and acting go back to his childhood days in Wadowice. The Wojtyłas' upstairs neighbor, Ginka Beers, was two years older than Karol and active in school plays. She spotted Karol's talent at home and got him involved in the school productions. Supposedly this acting ability also helped him do excellent imitations of his teachers, much to the amusement of the other students!

This involvement in school plays brought about his meeting with Mieczyslaw Kotlarczyk, who was a teacher at the local girls' high school and directed their productions. Occasionally, the boys and girls would collaborate on a production, and that's where the two first met. Kotlarczyk had a profound influence on Karol, both socially and personally.

Kotlarczyk and his wife had been evicted from their Wadowice home by the Nazis and headed to Krakow. At the same time that the university students were embracing Polish literary works, Kotlarczyk's "Theater of the Living Word" gave them exactly what they were looking for to put their patriotism into practice. In Kotlarczyk's mind, what was important in a performance was not the scenery or costumes, but the connection made between the actor and each audience member. Under Kotlarczyk's direction, performances had no scenery or costumes. Props were used only if they had a purpose in the dialogue. As the theater company's title reveals, what were important were the words themselves. Words were read precisely and distinctly, giving them all the purpose the author intended. Almost on a metaphysical level, the actor gave a life to the words of the play or poem, which then traveled out to every person listening. The listeners, who came with their own life experiences, took the words in and applied them to their own situations, giving them a new relevance.

These performances took place in different locations, always in secret, usually in the apartments of the actors for safety's sake. Windows had to be kept shut and covered to prevent eavesdroppers from listening in. Invitees were usually very close friends and family members, because inviting the wrong person could be dangerous for everyone. Usually the room was lit only with candlelight as the actors stood before a dark curtain hung as a backdrop and performed for the small audience.

Here, Karol discovered the power of words, both written and spoken. This newfound knowledge was extremely important for someone who would constantly be called upon to write and to preach to motivate people.

Deepening his spiritual life

While Mieczyslaw Kotlarski fed Karol's intellectual and patriotic needs, another man was to come into his life who would have a profound impact on his spirituality. Living in the Debnicki quarter of Krakow, the Wojtyłas attended church at the parish of St. Stanislaus Kostka. The parish was run by the Salesian Fathers, whose numbers had been seriously depleted when the Nazis arrested most of them. Only one elderly provincial and one parish priest, Father Jan Mazarski, remained. In February 1940, the parish organized a Lenten retreat for the young men of the parish. Following the retreat, these young men wanted to continue meeting and praying together, but the parish priest found it impossible to run these meetings himself. To organize and conduct the meetings, Father Mazarski enlisted the help of a parishioner of St. Stanislaus's named Jan Tyranowski.

Tyranowski seemed to be a man from a bygone era, both in the way he dressed and his manner of speaking. But there was something in him that spoke to the young people about God. Earlier in life, Tyranowski had a conversion that caused him to develop a deep spiritual life consisting of prayer and contemplative reading of the spiritual classics. Tyranowski turned these meetings with young people into opportunities for spiritual conversations (both with the whole group and individually) and prayerful reflection, which he called the "Living Rosary."

Every week, 15 young men (Karol Wojtyła included) would gather at Tyranowski's apartment, and each would be given a small white card with one of the mysteries of the Rosary. As the young men took turns meditating on each mystery of the Holy Rosary, they had their first experience with contemplative prayer. Tyranowski helped them see God as a living God, dwelling within each of them, even in the midst of the horrors of wartime. Eventually, as their prayer lives deepened, these young men began to strive to live Gospel values in their everyday lives. They committed themselves not only to perfecting themselves, but also to helping each other lead more perfectly Christian lives. They all kept notebooks of thoughts and experiences they had during the week, and when they met they compared notes and gave each other advice and encouragement on how to grow in virtue, all under the watchful eye of Tyranowski.

Through Jan Tyranowski, Karol was introduced to the classics of Carmelites St. John of the Cross and St. Theresa of Avila, as well as a deepening of his prayer life, not only in quantity but in quality. Eventually, Karol would bring the writings of these two saints into his theater performances, exposing the audiences to their spiritual classics.

Karol Wojtyła had a connection to Carmelite spirituality going back to the "Monastery on a Hill" just outside of Wadowice. In *Gift and Mystery,* he remembered the fact that many people paid visits to them, and in fact he credited this as the reason for the widespread use of the brown *scapular* (a Catholic devotional item made up of two pieces of cloth joined together by strings and worn like a necklace) as a devotional item by the people of Wadowice. Pope John Paul II remembered receiving the scapular when he was 10 years old, "and I still wear it," he wrote at the age of 76.

In Krakow, there was a monastery of Discalced Carmelites on Rakowicka Street. (The word *discalced* literally means "without shoes"; they were a cloistered community that never left the enclosure, so they didn't need shoes.) Karol visited them often, even making a retreat with them at one point. So intense was his love for the Carmelite way of life that he appears to have given serious thought to becoming a cloistered monk, rather than a parish priest. Apparently, he thought so much about it that he spoke to Archbishop Sapieha about it, and Sapieha advised him, "First, you finish what you have begun," referring to the decision he already made to be a priest of the Krakow archdiocese.

Working hard at other jobs

In 1940, the Nazis imposed forced labor on all Polish males between the ages of 14 and 70. Poles were required to work or else risk deportation to labor camps in Germany. Through friends, Karol was able to get a job at the Zakrzowek quarry, about 2 miles from home, which was part of the Solvay Chemical Plant. Besides keeping him from being deported, the job also gave a small income for Karol and his father, whose pension was eliminated by the Nazis.

Karol began work as a laborer: Eight hours a day in every kind of weather imaginable, the future pope hauled wheelbarrows full of crushed stones from inside the quarry to a rail car that took them to a kiln. After three months, Karol was promoted to assistant to the blaster, a man by the name of Franciszek Labus; Karol's new position meant constant exposure to the danger of high explosives used to break apart large pieces of the quarry walls. If anything good could be found in the situation, it was the fact that their supervisors were not Nazi soldiers, but Poles who treated them well (because they knew these students were being forced to work and would be no threat to their jobs after the war).

After a year, Karol was transferred from the quarry to the Solvay Chemical Works, where he worked as a maintenance man on the boilers. It was a longer walk from his home, but it was an indoor job. Karol preferred the overnight shift, because it was the least busy and allowed him time to read and to pray. As usual, his personality won him friends amongst his coworkers, who regularly kept watch so that he wasn't caught not working.

In *Gift and Mystery,* Pope John Paul II wrote that "Having worked with my hands, I knew quite well the meaning of physical labor. Every day I had been with people who did heavy work. I came to know their living situations, their families, their interests, their human worth, and their dignity." Karol Wojtyła worked at the Solvay plant until 1944, when the members of Archbishop Sapieha's underground seminary were all brought to live secretly at the archbishop's residence. Sapieha was able to get Karol's name removed from the employee roster, essentially making him disappear from existence.

On the morning of February 18, 1941, Karol made his way home from work stopping to get their midday meal to bring home for the two of them. Arriving at home, he found his father dead. He knew his father's health was not good (besides the food, Karol was also bringing home medicine), but his death was totally unexpected and devastating to Karol. He knelt at his father's bedside and wept, all the time holding his hand. Karol, Sr., was buried on February 22, 1941, with Father Figlewicz performing the burial rites.

By his early twenties, Karol Wojtyła had lost his whole family. This certainly did not cause him to flee from the world and into the priesthood, but there is no denying that Karol, Sr.'s death made his son's vocational decision easier, without an elderly father to support. In his sorrow, Karol found support amongst the friends he and his father made in Krakow. In particular, he turned to Jan Tyranowski to help him make spiritual sense out of his grief. To help Karol, Tyranowski gave him a copy of St. John of the Cross's *Dark Night of the Soul,* which deals with the interior struggles of prayer and spiritual dryness. Eventually, Karol returned to work and kept up his meetings of the Living Rosary as well as the underground theater performances.

Entering the underground seminary in 1942

Karol was torn between his love for acting and the theater and his desire to serve God. For a while, he had been able to blend both by bringing his spiritual world (represented by Tyranowski) with his secular world (represented by Kotlarczyk). In addition, he had been regularly seeing Father Figlewicz, who served as Karol's spiritual director and confessor, and no doubt Figlewicz had been helping Karol come to a decision.

What seems to have pushed Karol over the edge was the story of Adam Chmielowski (known to Poles as "Brother Albert"). Chmielowski was a Polish patriot who lost a leg fighting for Polish freedom in 1864. Eventually, he studied art in Munich and became a well-known artist with a promising career. Suddenly, he left it all to become a Third Order Franciscan who found his vocation serving the poor of Krakow. Eventually, men and women joined him in the work and two religious congregations were founded by Brother Albert. He died in 1916, and Pope John Paul II was happy to both beatify him in 1983 and canonize him in 1989.

Brother Albert was particularly important, wrote Pope John Paul II, because ". . . I found him a real spiritual support and example in leaving behind the world of art, literature, and the theater, and in making the radical choice of the priesthood."

When Karol finally made his decision to become a priest in the fall of 1942, he confided it to Father Figlewicz, who arranged a meeting between Karol and Archbishop Sapieha. When Archbishop Sapieha accepted Karol as a seminarian, he immediately sent him to meet with Father Piwowarczyk, the rector of Krakow's seminary. Father Piwowarczyk sent him, in turn, to Father Kazimierz Klosak, the seminary's Director of Philosophical Studies (because Karol never completed his studies at Jagiellonian University). The Nazis allowed the Krakow seminary to exist, but they forbade the acceptance of any new seminarians.

It was decided that Karol, along with six other men, would be accepted as seminarians, though secretly. Karol continued to live in his apartment and work at the Solvay chemical factory, all the while meeting regularly with the archbishop, seminary faculty, and the other seminarians.

On Sunday, August 6, 1944, just after the Warsaw Uprising began, the German governor of Poland ordered the arrest of all men who were seen as a threat (in all, 8,000 men and teenage boys were arrested and sent to concentration camps). Karol was home at his basement apartment at 10 Tyniecka Street when Nazi troops entered the house and went room by room. Karol was praying in the front room of the house in his normal position (on the floor, arms open so that his body looked like a giant cross) when a soldier stopped just outside of Karol's door. Almost miraculously, Karol's life was spared when the guard decided (without looking) that there was no one in the apartment and turned around.

After the roundup, Archbishop Sapieha decided it was too dangerous for his underground seminarians to live apart. Word was sent to all seminarians to make their way to the archbishop's residence. There they would live secretly, but together, under Archbishop Sapieha's roof.

The seminarians lived in the large rooms on the first floor of the residence. The rooms were furnished with metal beds, desks for reading and writing, and a few chairs. Archbishop Sapieha ordered all the seminarians to dress in cassocks, so that they might at least seem to be priests to visitors. For the first time, Karol and the other seminarians had a formal schedule to follow.

Each day they rose before 6 a.m. and washed. They prayed for half an hour and then attended daily Mass celebrated by Archbishop Sapieha (each day, two of them alternated as servers). Following breakfast and some recreation time, they spent the rest of the morning in classes. In the afternoon, they had their midday meal and then some time of adoration before the Eucharist. In the evening, they finished the day with private study time.

The important thing to remember is that, at any time, had the Nazis discovered this secret seminary, everyone from Archbishop Sapieha down to the seminarians themselves could have been arrested, sent to concentration camps, or simply shot. They lived with this fear every day, knowing that at any moment their existence could have been found. In addition, the Nazis were, for a time, searching for these suddenly missing persons. The seminarians also knew that a favorite tactic of the Nazis was to make hostages out of the missing person's family, threatening their execution if the person did not return.

Escaping Death

On February 29, 1944, Karol was walking home from the chemical plant when he turned onto Konopnicka Street. He walked on the edge of the street because there were no sidewalks. Suddenly, he was hit by a passing truck, which knocked him unconscious into a ditch as the truck kept going. An anonymous woman witnessed the accident and called an ambulance. (He never found out who this woman was.)

Karol spent several days in the hospital, before being released to recover at the home of a friend whose home was often used for secret theater performances. Eventually, he recovered, although years later some attributed Pope John Paul II's hunched posture to the accident. Shortly after he was ordained to the priesthood in 1946, the room he recuperated in was used for a party honoring the new "Father" Wojtyła!

The accident was interpreted by Karol as a confirmation of his decision to leave the world of manual labor and pursue studies for the priesthood.

Surviving Communist Oppression

In January 1945, the Russian army advanced east to the point of entering the city of Krakow. After a night of trading explosions between the Russian and German armies, the Germans fled to the east, and the Russians liberated Krakow. Karol, the other seminarians, and Archbishop Sapieha spent the night in the cellar of the residence.

At last the war was over, and the Russians were greeted as heroes and given the little food that the seminarians could offer them as hospitality. Karol made a quick trip to his old apartment to see if it was still standing; then he returned to the archbishop's residence to begin the cleanup. Slowly, life began to return to some normalcy. The seminarians reorganized the seminary library. They completed a massive cleanup of the old seminary building, which had been used by the Nazis as a headquarters. In fact, Karol won the admiration of his classmates when he and another seminarian volunteered to clean the piles of frozen solid human waste that had been left in the bathrooms by both soldiers and prisoners.

But while the war was still being fought, Poland's future had been taken out from under the people. At Allied war conferences at Teheran and Yalta, a new Poland was drawn with a significant loss of territory. At the same time, as Nazi-friendly local-government officials were eliminated, they were replaced with officials who were Soviet-friendly. The Polish government-in-exile, which had located itself in London during the war, was ignored. The Lublin Commission, Soviet-sympathetic, gave the Soviet Union complete control over maintaining law and order in Poland. As the months passed, Poles began to realize that, though one totalitarian regime had been defeated, it was replaced with another. With the support of the Soviet Union, the Polish Worker's Party was created, and Poland joined other countries "liberated" from the Nazis only to be imprisoned by atheistic Communism.

By 1946, the seminarians moved out of the archbishop's residence and into the theological seminary. Things were hardly luxurious, but they made the best of their small classrooms, and life went on. Karol's studiousness was noticed by both fellow students as well as faculty. Professor Rozycki, who taught Dogmatic Theology, suggested to Karol that he might want to begin writing a dissertation with an eye toward earning a doctorate degree. Together they determined the topic: "The theological virtue of faith in St. John of the Cross."

On February 18, 1946, Archbishop Sapieha was created a cardinal of the Roman Catholic Church by Pope Pius XII. He traveled to Rome for the *consistory* (an assembly of cardinals presided over by the pope) and received the red hat (called a *gallero*) that was the symbol of his office.

The color red is worn by cardinals to remind them that their office may mean the shedding of their blood (a concept Sapieha certainly lived with before his elevation to cardinal).

Upon returning from Rome, Cardinal Sapieha was eager to reestablish the tradition of sending priests from Poland for graduate studies in Rome, and he chose Karol Wojtyła and another seminarian for this task. At this same time, Cardinal Sapieha decided to ordain Karol to the priesthood earlier than the rest of his classmates, in order for him to go to Rome as a priest.

Karol Josef Wojtyła was ordained to the priesthood by Cardinal Sapieha on November 1, 1946, in the chapel of the cardinal's residence. I can still remember myself in that chapel," Pope John Paul II remembered in *Gift and Mystery,* "lying prostrate on the floor with arms outstretched in the form of a cross, awaiting the moment of the imposition of hands. It was a very moving experience! . . . in accepting in one's own life — like Peter — the cross of Christ and becoming with the Apostle a 'floor' for our brothers and sisters, one finds the ultimate meaning of all priestly spirituality."

Following his ordination, Father Wojtyła left Krakow on November 15, 1946, on a train bound for Paris. It was his first trip outside of Poland, and he watched with excitement as the train drove through cities he has previously only heard about. After spending the night at the Polish College in Paris, he left the next day on a train bound for Rome, arriving by the end of November.

The Polish College in Rome was full, so Karol and his classmate resided at the Belgian College. Karol was enrolled at the Pontifical University of St. Thomas Aquinas, commonly called the *Angelicum.* He had been advised by Father Kozlowski (his old seminary rector) that to study in Rome is only half of the education received. "You have to get to know Rome, too!", he was constantly advised. Rome was, and still is, a multilingual city, and because of it we can see how Pope John Paul II's *polyglot* (speaking and writing several languages) ability took shape: a Pole living in Italy, taking classes in Latin alongside fellow students from all over the world who converse in a variety of languages!

Cardinal Sapieha gave Father Wojtyła the instructions: "During your vacations, you will not return to Poland but will go to France and Belgium to study new methods of religious ministry." The *worker-priest movement,* which sought to make Christian ethics available and understandable by having priests share in the lives and labor of the working class, had begun in these countries. In France, Father Wojtyła learned the nuts and bolts of the movement from Father Henri Godin, who said, "Priests doing missionary work should not only spend time in the factory but live with the workers, share their burdens, expenses, eat with them, play with them and pray with them." When Father Wojtyła returned to Poland in 1948, he wrote of his experiences in the Catholic newspaper *Tygodnik Powszechny.* He could sum up the key to the future of humanity with five words: "God, economic and political justice."

Chapter 5

Building the Foundation of His Thinking and Reasoning

In This Chapter

▶ Looking at influences on JP2's thoughts

▶ Identifying the theology of the body

▶ Using the Bible as a teaching tool

*L*ike most great thinkers of any age, Pope John Paul II was influenced by the thoughts, writings, and teachings of many philosophers and theologians. Among other truths, he understood that reason and faith are not incompatible. He knew that the body and soul are two parts of one being. He believed that we are made in God's image. And he believed that all these things come from Jesus Christ.

In this chapter, we look at how JP2 used the philosophy of Thomas Aquinas to underscore his belief that faith and reason can peacefully coexist. We look specifically at John Paul II's theology of the body as the soul's physical manifestation here on Earth. And finally, we recognize that John Paul II's teachings and writings relied heavily on the most sacred text, the Bible.

Using Traditional Philosophy to Look at the World

John Paul II was a philosopher before he was a theologian. This progression has been the normal sequence since St. Thomas Aquinas, the Dominican intellectual giant of the 13th century known as the Angelic Doctor, who said that "philosophy is the handmaiden of theology." *Philosophy* (which means "lover of wisdom") is indispensable to *theology* (which means "study of God"), because it shows that faith and reason are not incompatible, antithetical, or hostile to one another.

Since the time of St. Augustine (4th century A.D.) who used the ancient Greek Philosophy of Plato (5th century B.C.) to explain Catholic theology, theologians have found philosophy an indispensable help. St. Thomas Aquinas (13th century A.D.) employed the philosophy of Aristotle (4th century B.C.), a student of Plato. Aquinas's influence was great throughout the Middle Ages and even to our own time.

Philosophy is based on human reason, whereas theology is based on faith. Science is based on observation and experimentation. All three (philosophy, theology, and science) give us valid truths, according to Aquinas, but each one has a different strategy. They examine the same world and universe but from separate perspectives. Science seeks to answer the questions "What is it?" and "How does it work?" Philosophy wants to know "Why is it (or why are we) here?" Theology looks at the question of "Who created it (or us)?"

Karol Wojtyła was first exposed to philosophy at the Jagiellonian University as an undergraduate student. He continued to study philosophy after his ordination to the priesthood at the Angelicum University of Rome. His keen and sharp mind fully appreciated the clean and precise thinking of St. Thomas Aquinas.

Wojtyła easily grasped the simplicity of *objective realism,* the essence of Aristotle's and Aquinas's philosophy. Objective realism teaches that the created universe is composed of *matter* and *form.* Human beings, for example, are made up of a body (matter) and a soul (form), the latter of which is *immaterial* (meaning you can't see it, touch it, smell it, and so on). Matter and form are not two ingredients — instead, according to objective realism, they are two aspects of a single unified thing. *Matter* is what something is *made of* whereas *form* is what something *is.*

Though a medieval theologian and philosopher, Aquinas was also a student of St. Albert the Great, who is considered the grandfather of modern science by many because of his work in chemistry and physics. From his mentor, Aquinas learned the reality that there are three levels of truth:

- ✔ *Empirical* **(scientific) truth:** Known by observation and experimentation, empirical truth is based on what the five senses tell us through our bodies. We know fire is hot, for instance, because we can feel the heat.

- ✔ **Philosophical truth:** Known by reason, philosophical truth is based on what our minds figure out (2 + 2 = 4, for example).

- ✔ **Theological truth:** Known by faith, theological truth is based on what God has divinely revealed, like the doctrine of the *Holy Trinity* (one God in three divine persons).

Such a system, therefore, does not see reason as an enemy of faith, nor does it consider science antithetical to religion. Science, philosophy, and theology look at the same created reality from different perspectives and use different tools and methods. But the incontrovertible truths they discover can't conflict with each other, because only one reality exists, and they are all a part of it. Faith and reason are not in competition — they're just two sides of the same coin. Opinions and tastes may vary, but there can be only one reality and one truth. Either Alexandra is alive or dead — she can't be both at the same time (unless Alexandra is a character on a soap opera, and she's also suffering from amnesia). Science, philosophy, and theology examine the same reality — life and death — but from different starting points. What each one learns is valid, but all three are necessary to know in order to have full and complete knowledge of things in and of themselves.

Karol Wojtyła taught ethics and philosophy at the Catholic University of Lublin. His *Thomistic* (the word used to describe the philosophy of Thomas Aquinas) and Aristotelian background gave him an easy way to teach morality. The Bible gave divine commandments of ethical behavior (known as the *Ten Commandments*), and reason itself could discern what the ancients called the *Natural Moral Law.* Any act involving free will is a moral act, according to Aquinas, and some moral acts are intrinsically evil, while other acts are intrinsically good. Human beings do not determine the goodness or badness of an act, but we do discover them and then must act accordingly. This is the foundation of morality and ethics for Thomas Aquinas, Karol Wojtyła, and the Catholic Church for that matter, because it is based on the Natural Moral Law.

While he was in Lublin, Wojtyła began to refine his classical philosophy with a flavor of *personalism* (the ethical philosophy that centers on the person as having intrinsic value just by being or existing). According to this philosophy, only persons have a free will and, thus, only persons can perform moral acts, which are either good or evil. Personhood is *relational,* so persons need to relate to other persons. (Or, as Barbra Streisand sang, "People . . . who need people. . . .") It's the reason we form friendships, romances, marriages, families, and societies. Theologically, this philosophy of personalism is affirmed in the doctrine of the Holy Trinity, where one God is three persons (Father, Son, and Holy Spirit). Each person of the Trinity knows and loves the other persons, and together they form a *communio* (a profound, deep, and intimate union where each person relates fully to the other persons).

JP2's belief in personalism complemented his Thomistic philosophy based on objective realism, but it also denied and opposed the radical Communism that made the person subservient to the state and to the party. JP2's philosophy also collided with extreme capitalism, which deified the individual and ignored all social responsibility. Personalism as a philosophy paralleled the Christian theology of brotherly love. Taking care of your neighbor when he's in need was not only a mandate of faith, but for John Paul II it also became an imperative of reason. Persons have to help other persons to maintain the union — otherwise, both are harmed in the end.

Wojtyła also explored a modified form of phenomenology called *realistic phenomenology. Phenomenology* is the philosophy of what is experienced and not just what is observed. Unlike *existentialism,* which only values the interior experiences, phenomenology takes into account the appearances and consequences of human actions. Instead of deteriorating into a form of ultimate subjectivism where a person decides his own reality, especially in the moral and ethical realm, realistic phenomenology and the theology of the person takes a significantly different path. Persons make moral choices that have consequences. Persons are influenced by their experiences, but they are also endowed with reason and free will — both of which compel the person to seek the true and the good with the help and assistance of other persons.

Thomistic philosophy and theology, flavored by some phenomenology and molded by personalism shaped the mind of Karol Wojtyła. Whether it was abortion, euthanasia, contraception, or the death penalty; economic, political, or social justice; he was always on the same page: promoting and defending what is good for the human person, individually and communally. Pope John Paul II believed that the ultimate good is the happiness found in knowing and doing the Will of God.

Exploring the Theology of the Body

Pope John Paul II's Thomistic philosophy enabled him to see man as an entire being — body *and* soul. The spiritual, while superior to the material, still needs and uses the material because a soul has no eyes to see, ears to hear, fingers to touch. Unlike the dualism of the ancient past, which regarded the body as evil and only the soul as good, Judeo-Christian religion saw *both* body and soul as being good, because the same good God created both. If God intended to make human beings a union of body and soul, and because God created the material as well as the spiritual world, you can't say one is evil and the other good.

The human body, especially the five senses, are absolutely necessary for the soul because it is the only source of information for the rational intellect. Thomas Aquinas said that we are born with a blank slate for an intellect. Like computer hard drives at the factory, our minds are completely clean and totally blank until information from the outside is written on it. As soon as our five senses communicate data to our brain, the intellect extrapolates information and we form ideas. If you are unable to see a chair, feel it, or even hear someone tell me about it, you have no idea what a chair is. After seeing several varieties of chairs and sitting in them, you can form the idea of *chair* so that you can distinguish between a chair and a table or a chair and a sofa. Because chairs can be made of wood or metal, can be bare or upholstered, in any size or color, the fact that one word can describe all these variations is what we call an *idea*.

John Paul II not only appreciated the human body for the value of the five senses that enable the human soul to know and to choose based on what the objective real world tells it, he also saw the body as being a holy and sacred creation of God. Some people may have overemphasized the soul in the past when they excluded or diminished the value of the body, but JP2 saw it differently. He knew that men and women were created in the image and likeness of God (Genesis 1:27). John Paul II described the body like this:

> The body, and it alone, is capable of making visible what is invisible, the spiritual and divine. It was created to transfer into the visible reality of the world, the invisible mystery hidden in God from time immemorial, and thus to be a sign of it.

These words of Pope John Paul II show his concept of the theology of the body. Like a *sacrament,* which is an outward sign of divine grace, the human body is the external manifestation of the invisible soul. The person, however, is *both* body and soul. If I intentionally pull the hair on your head or if you slap my cheek, we're insulting the person, not just causing the body pain. The dignity offended is in the person. Someone kicks your leg under the table and apologizes, saying, "Sorry, I thought it was the table," and you respond, "No, it was *me.*" The *me* or *I* is the person, and any part of your body is an extension of your personhood.

Identifying the meaning of the body in marriage

Man and woman become one flesh in marriage as well as becoming husband and wife. Without both people, there is no marriage. Just as the body cannot survive without the soul, and the soul needs the body to know what is in the real world. The body and soul are, in a sense, married to one another as a man and woman are married to one another in Matrimony.

Animals have sex by instinct when in heat and merely to reproduce. There is no love or intimacy, no commitment and no sacrifice. Practical, yes, but nothing spiritual. Human beings, however, have sex by choice. Any time the free will is used, it is considered a moral act and not just physical. Moral acts are done by persons, whereas anything — animal or mechanical — can perform a physical act. Persons engage in moral acts, which are either good or evil.

Pope John Paul II's theology of the body teaches that sexual intercourse between human persons is a holy and sacred act *only* when done for the right reasons and in the proper context. Human sex is limited to marriage because the Bible and religion designate sex outside of marriage as the sin of *fornication* (sex between unmarried persons) or the sin of *adultery* (sex with an unfaithful spouse of another person).

Understanding sexual pleasure and the theology of the body

When sexual pleasure in and of itself becomes the primary goal and object of a person's desire, it's sinful because the essence of proper sexuality resides within the permanent and faithful covenant of marriage whose union is oriented to love (unity) and life (procreation). JP2 told married couples when he was a priest and then as a bishop and finally as pope that selfish sex is sinful and harmful because it goes against the nature of human sexuality. Unlike other human functions, like eating, which can be both physically necessary and psychologically or socially desirable (dining with family or friends), human sex is necessary for the human race but not for the individual. A person *needs* to breathe, to eat, to sleep, but a person does not *need* sex. A person can have sex if he is married and if he uses it as an intimate sign of his giving of self, body and soul, to his beloved spouse. Otherwise, it becomes merely an act of self-stimulation, and there is no giving of self — instead, it's a taking of self.

Masturbation, pornography, homosexuality, fornication, artificial contraception, adultery, and the like, are lies according to John Paul II's theology of the body, because all of these do not and cannot express the complete sacrificial gift of human sexuality, which is essentially and substantially connected to marriage. The *unitive* (love) and procreative (life) elements are two lungs that work together. Isolating or separating one from the other is often a self-inflicted wound on the person. The damage may not be immediately recognizable, yet the long-term effect is no less destructive.

Opening the Scriptures: Using the Bible

John Paul II, like the popes before him, quoted the scripture, but he was second only to St. Peter himself in quoting the Bible. St. Peter was inspired to write an epistle of the New Testament. JP2 began his pontificate with the biblical words "Be not afraid." These words are the same words spoken by

- ✔ God to Abraham in Genesis 46:3
- ✔ The Archangel Gabriel to the Virgin Mary in Luke 1:30
- ✔ The Archangel Gabriel to Zechariah (father of John the Baptist) in Luke 1:13
- ✔ The angels to the shepherds at Christmas in Luke 2:10
- ✔ Christ himself in Matthew 14:27, Mark 6:50, Luke 12:4, and John 6:20

Pope John Paul II's first papal encyclical *Redemptor Hominis* (1979), on the Redeemer of Man, has 75 percent of its footnotes from the Bible. Like St. Jerome, who translated the first Christian Bible into one language (Latin) and one volume in 400 A.D., and who said "ignorance of the Scriptures is ignorance of Christ," Pope John Paul II not only peppered his papal speeches with and inserted into his myriad writings a slew of biblical quotes, he truly used the written Word of God as a starting point for discussion.

Whether in the *Code of Canon Law* in 1983, the *Catechism of the Catholic Church* in 1993, or any of JP2's numerous encyclicals, you'll find a good number of references to verses in the Bible. JP2 was not shy or timid to show the world that Catholic Christians did in fact believe in the inspired, inerrant, and revealed Word of God and that much of our theology is rooted in Sacred Scripture. Even when he added five new mysteries to the Holy Rosary, he pointed out that each one was found in the New Testament:

- ✔ Baptism of the Lord (Matthew 3:13–17)
- ✔ First Miracle of Jesus, the changing of water into wine at the wedding of Cana (John 2:1–11)
- ✔ Proclamation of the Kingdom of Heaven (Matthew 4:17–25 through Matthew 5:1–16)
- ✔ Transfiguration at Mount Tabor (Luke 9:28–36)
- ✔ Institution of the Holy Eucharist at the Last Supper (1 Corinthians 11:23–29)

John Paul II's final apostolic letter inaugurating the Year of the Eucharist is based on Luke 24:29 when the risen Jesus meets the two disciples on the road to Emmaus and they say to Him, "Stay with us Lord."

John Paul II used the Bible to teach and to inspire his followers to aspire, to seek the higher things of heaven. Catholicism regards Sacred Scripture and Sacred Tradition as two sides of the same coin, *divine revelation*. The revealed Word of God is both a written word (in the Bible) and an unwritten or spoken word (in Sacred Tradition). Both come from the same source, Jesus Christ, who himself is the fullness of revelation of the Father. Jesus is the Word made flesh who dwelt among us. JP2 cherished the written word of scripture and quoted it heavily, not just as a footnote but as a divine message from God.

Part II

Continuing the Legacy of Others and the Traditions of the Church

In this part . . .

We consider the context in which Karol Wojtyła entered and practiced his priestly vocation in the Catholic Church. A loyal son of the Church, not only was this man influenced by those who went before him, but he also built upon and drew from their collective wisdom from the past. Instead of reinventing the wheel, the future Pope John Paul II as Father Wojtyła (then as Bishop Wojtyła and later as Cardinal Wojtyła) embraced the rich history, patrimony, tradition, and continuity of a 2,000-year-old religion. Specifically, we look at his staunch defense of perennial Church teachings on doctrinal and moral issues, from abortion and contraception, to women's ordination, theological dissent, the death penalty, and the Just War Doctrine.

Chapter 6

Tracing John Paul II's Career

*J*ohn Paul II's path that would lead him to the Vatican began before he ever went to underground seminary in Krakow. It started in his home, with his parents, true faithful Catholic believers, who showed him how to worship, how to treat others, and how to live.

In this chapter, we look at many of JP2's obstacles and accomplishments that led to him becoming the 264th pope of the Roman Catholic Church. We look through his eyes to see how he viewed the world, through the filter of his devotion to the Virgin Mary and his philosophy of phenomenology. We trace his career from his ordination to the priesthood through his inauguration as pontiff, highlighting many of the challenges he faced along the way. And ultimately, we show you how he was the right man at the right time for the job of head of the Catholic Church.

A Marian Man: His Early Devotion to the Virgin Mary

Young Karol Wojtyła learned devotion to Our Lady (the Virgin Mary, Mother of God) from his father. Often, the older Karol would take his two sons on pilgrimage to the National Shrine of Our Lady of Czestochowa, known as the

Black Madonna. The Black Madonna is the most important image of the Blessed Mother in Poland. His experience visiting the Black Madonna was something that Karol would take with him throughout his life as priest, bishop, cardinal, and pope. (For more on the Black Madonna, see the nearby sidebar, "The tradition of the Black Madonna.")

Mother of God is an important title of the Virgin Mary in Catholic theology. It's a title that was given to her at the Ecumenical Council of Ephesus in 431 A.D. The term basically means that Mary's son, Jesus, was true God and true man, meaning he was fully divine and fully human. Jesus Christ is one divine person with two natures, a divine nature and a human nature. These natures are united to the second person of the Holy Trinity (God the Son). Hence, Mary's son was literally the Son of God. By way of analogy, then, Christianity has given her the title the Mother of God. It does not give her any divine attributes, and she remains as human as you and I, yet her son Jesus is considered the God-Man, the incarnate Word of God.

Through this Catholic understanding of Mary, the Mother of God, Father Karol Wojtyła turned to the Virgin Mary especially because his own mother Emilia died one month before his ninth birthday. During this time, he read the great St. Louis de Montfort, the premier expert on *Mariology* (the study of the Virgin Mary). He wrote the spiritual classic *True Devotion to Mary.* He discovered that any and all attributes to Mary come to her because of her relationship to Jesus Christ as his mother.

JP2's devotion to Mary was also evidenced by the fact that he wore a brown *scapular* (a special garment worn by members of some religious orders) all the time underneath his white papal cassock.

The scapular is worn over the shoulders and hangs down in front and in back. (Laypeople and clergy who are not in religious vows often wear an abbreviated form of the scapular that developed from the religious habits. Such a scapular is the one that Karol wore from the time he was 10 years old.) The order that Karl wore a scapular in honor of was Our Lady of Mount Carmel, from a little Carmelite monastery of nuns located outside of Wadowice, Poland. The scapular of Our Lady of Mount Carmel, also known as the brown scapular, is adapted from the scapular of the Carmelite Order and represents a special consecration to Mary. At one time, he even considered becoming a Carmelite monk, but the superior felt that Karol Wojtyła was better suited for the diocesan (parish) priesthood instead.

Pope John Paul II adopted the motto *totus tuus* from his Marian spirituality as St. Louis de Montfort taught that it was beneficial for a Christian to imitate the discipleship of the Virgin Mary. Specifically, it relates to the time when she told the Angel Gabriel (Luke 1:38) "be done unto me according to your word." As Mary surrendered herself completely to the will of God by accepting the invitation to become the mother of the Messiah, she in essence said to God, "I am totally yours." Likewise, de Montfort and JP2 saw value in embracing that same pledge of the Virgin Mary and declare *"totus tuus"* (totally yours).

This Marian spirituality then gave him the impetus to keep close to Jesus as Mary did and to be the same kind of humble and obedient servant of the Lord as Mary was. Her example inspired Karol as a young man, as a priest, as a bishop, as a cardinal, and later as pope, to give himself totally to Christ and to the Church with the same zeal, love, and intensity the Virgin Mary did when she was asked to accept the Will of God in her life.

As a young person, JP2 feared that a devotion to Mary, if excessive, might end up compromising the supremacy of worship of Christ. After reading St. Louis de Montfort, however, he realized that if the mystery of Mary is lived in Christ, such a risk does not exist. It was St. Louis who first said *totus tuus ego sum, et omnia mea tua sunt* ("I am all yours, and all that is mine is yours"). John Paul II merely borrowed those first two words and consecrated himself and later his priesthood and papacy to imitate Mary by remaining close and obedient to her Son, Jesus Christ.

The tradition of the Black Madonna

In *Catholicism For Dummies,* we note the *pious tradition* (legends, customs, or folklore that may or may not be historically verifiable or completely accurate, but are nevertheless told from one generation to the next), which maintains that St. Luke the Evangelist painted an icon of the Virgin Mary. The icon was later brought into Poland for veneration around the time the Catholic Church took root and converted the land from *paganism* (the natural religion of ancient times that believed in *polytheism* [many gods] as opposed to the *monotheism* [one god] found in Judaism, Christianity and Islam) to Catholic Christianity.

The image was not always as dark as it is today. Rather, it was desecrated years later by non-believers who tried to set fire to it; over hundreds of years, it was also subjected to the soot from candle flames (hence, the title, the *Black Madonna*).

An unknown pagan soldier in 1430 became enraged when the flames did not consume the icon. He had hoped the icon would have been destroyed by fire because he hated this image as a symbol of the Catholic faith. In his anger, he struck the image with his sword three times. As pious tradition relates, upon the third slash on Mary's face, the soldier was struck dead. Since then, the icon of the Black Madonna has been venerated as a national treasure of devotion. In Czestochowa, today, pilgrims still venerate her image darkened by fire and slashed by the soldier. Catholic Poland was saved from the marauders and continued to be saved from every invading country, ideology, or regime ever since.

Hiking and Skiing with "Uncle Lolek"

Karol Wojtyła was ordained to the priesthood in 1946. After his ordination, he was sent to Rome by his bishop for postgraduate studies. He remained in Rome until 1948, when he returned to Poland as a parish priest. His first assignment was as parochial vicar (assistant pastor) at Assumption of Our Lady Church in Niegowic, 15 miles east of Krakow. While serving in Niegowic, and in his next assignment a year later at St. Florian's in Krakow as a student chaplain, he became known as *Wujek Lolek* (Polish for "Uncle Chuck"). He acquired the nickname while on hiking and skiing trips, because he was not in his priestly garb on such occasions.

Wujek Lolek was not just a term of endearment, it was also a safety measure to protect him and the youth from the Communist Secret Police. Countries controlled by the Soviet Union typically outlawed religious outings and field trips so that the state (secular government) could indoctrinate citizens into the principles of the Communist Party.

Priests were not allowed to be seen publicly with students, so they had to dress in civilian clothing and not be called by their title, "Father" or "Reverend." "Uncle Lolek" appeared as an ordinary fellow with several nieces and nephews and their schoolmates, which was not uncommon at that time. During the time when he was sometimes called "Uncle Lolek," Wojtyła never stopped being or working as a Catholic priest. He wore his priestly vestments to celebrate Mass and other worship services in church, but he also spent time teaching and giving spiritual direction to young men and women. Skiing and hiking trips not only appeared safe to the secret police, they were also fun reasons to interest the youth to participate in these gatherings and learn the faith while enjoying themselves. (These skiing trips were a sort of precursor to the World Youth Days he held as pope.) He also organized meetings with young married couples and those preparing for marriage so they could realize they had as much a calling to holiness as did he being an ordained priest.

Ordained priest 1946

After World War II, the seminary emerged from the underground, and on November 1, 1946, on the Feast of All Saints, Karol became Father Wojtyła and was ordained a priest. The Archbishop's Chapel served as the cathedral for the ordination ceremony. It was on the Feast of All Souls, November 2, that he celebrated his first Mass of Thanksgiving. This Mass he offered for the repose of the souls of his dear mother, father, and brother. Although he is most famous for being pope, Wojtyła was first a priest, then a bishop, then a cardinal, and finally Vicar of Christ and Successor of St. Peter (titles of the pope). Being a priest was his first and true love. Taking care of souls and serving the spiritual needs of his parishioners gave him the satisfaction a father would find in the health, education, and welfare of his children.

Even after being promoted to the office of bishop and cardinal, JP2 never ceased being a priest in that he still celebrated daily Mass, anointed the sick, heard confessions, baptized babies, and officiated at weddings. Teaching philosophy or theology or even the administration of a diocese as bishop never diluted his zeal and passion for doing priestly work, especially preaching and celebrating the sacraments.

Working with youth

Niegowic, his first priestly assignment, was also a place of solace, where he continued to develop his prayer life and mysticism by reading the writings of St. John of the Cross. He also continued his other passion — sports and the outdoors — and, in this way, he won over many of the parish's young people. Together, they played soccer or volleyball or went hiking and built bonfires. During these outings, Father Wojtyła shared his faith and theology with the parish's young people.

Niegowic was also where Father Wojtyła experienced the clandestine activity of the Stalinists. The secret police tried to infiltrate and plant moles in order to break up the Catholic youth groups; they also used blackmail and torture.

Karol's time in this tiny village was brief. In 1949, the Cardinal Archbishop of Krakow recalled Father Wojtyła to the city and transferred him to a university parish, St. Florian's Church, where he met many young people in various levels of study. It was a center of Catholic intellectual activity — a perfect environment for a young cleric eager to share his experience of school and international society and aid in forming the young minds of the future citizens of Poland.

Father Wojtyła formed study groups among the young college students, where topics from the great theological works of St. Thomas Aquinas were discussed. The *Summa Theologica* is a classic collection of philosophy and theology explained by St. Thomas Aquinas, a 13th-century theologian. Even today, the Catholic Church regards the *Summa* as a basis for all theological understanding. Karol's study groups prove to be invaluable to the Catholic Church, especially as the Communists started to clamp down on Catholic institutions. In the early 1950s, a series of laws were enacted to close many Catholic schools and other charitable organizations in an attempt to distance the people from religion.

Besides the study groups, the young cleric formed *scola cantorums* ("little choirs"), which preserved the beauty of Gregorian chant. Small study groups of young students were formed to learn about the beauty of the *liturgy* (the official prayer of the Church). The Holy Sacrifice of the Mass is a primary example of part of the liturgy. However, liturgy also includes the recitation of the divine office and celebration of benediction. Young people were attracted to Father Wojtyła like a magnet to metal with all his zeal. During this period of Communist persecution, the students gathered a deeper insight into the awesome mystery of the Mass.

Father Wojtyła began the very first marriage preparation programs in the archdiocese. These programs, in which couples are prepared for the vocation of marriage, are mandatory all over the world today. For Karol, marriage was much more than a piece of paper or a contract — it was a *covenant* (a permanent and sacred agreement that can never be dissolved) between two people. To educate young couples in this idea, Father Karol found it necessary to meet with couples several times. Sometimes he met with them informally, hiking or rowing with them.

In a very important way, Father Wojtyła had a lasting influence on the young people he came into contact with. He conveyed his beliefs that marriage was a *vocation* (a calling) and that human sexuality was a gift from God that either can be consecrated in perpetual virginity or expressed between husband and wife. Finally, he instilled in young people a sense of true devotion and respect for the official *work of the Church* (the Sacred Liturgy). In this way, he fought Communism through the future lawyers, physicists, and doctors. In these centers of learning that he formed, many students found their future spouses or discovered a vocation to the priesthood or religious life.

Serving as a parish priest

Poland didn't fare well under the Communists while Father Wojtyła was away in Rome. Like the Nazis before them, the Russians were eager to stamp out the culture and the academics of the region. Communism is based on atheism; Communists found religion a threat to their empire and, therefore, thought they needed to destroy religion. In many of the satellite countries of Eastern Europe, the Communists were quite successful in controlling the Church. In Hungary, seminaries were underground. Ordaining men to the priesthood was illegal. Despite Communist oppression, in Poland the Church managed to survive and be a source of inspiration for those aspiring to defend and respect the dignity of every human being. It was to this atmosphere that the young cleric returned from Rome.

Father Wojtyła was assigned to a small parish in the country to give him pastoral experience, in a little town called Niegowic. Here, the young priest celebrated Mass, absolved sins, baptized babies, married couples, and buried the dead. The place was quite impoverished, with no running water or electricity.

In addition to his pastoral duties, the young priest often helped neighbors with farm work in order to get to know the people he was serving and preaching to.

Becoming a Philosopher

After his ordination, the Cardinal Archbishop of Krakow recognized the intellectual character of the young priest Father Wojtyła. The archbishop assigned Karol further studies in Rome and concentrated his academics in the philosophy of St. Thomas Aquinas and the Spanish mystics like St. John of the Cross and St. Theresa of Avila. In the summer of 1948, Father Wojtyła returned to Poland.

Karol's academic career in Rome was much more than the classroom and library. He had the chance to see historic churches, catacombs, and shrines, and meet hosts of other students from all over the world. Rome, with its Catholic universities, was a center of international activity. It was here that the future pope received a valuable education in the fine art of Roman diplomacy. With clergy, bishops, ambassadors, professors, students, and cardinals from all over the world, Father Wojtyła was able to practice the many languages he knew from his younger days. These interactions served as a basis for the future pope, who, some would argue, was the most diplomatic pontiff the Holy See ever had.

During this period, Father Wojtyła still wrote poetry, prose, and plays. His most famous drama was *Brother of Our God.* This play, in a theatrical way, outlined his beliefs in the social doctrines of the Church. Later these theological ideas would become more concise and articulate in the various encyclicals that he wrote and addressed to the Universal Church.

Receiving doctoral degrees

At the conclusion of his postgraduate studies, Father Wojtyła had defended his thesis on "evaluation of the possibility of founding a Christian ethic on the ethical system of Max Scheler." This he did at his alma mater, Jagiellonian University. His was the last doctoral defense before the Communists closed the institution. All the while, Father Karol continued his work with young students, choirs, study groups, and retreats. He earned a doctorate in philosophy in 1948 from the Roman University of the Angelicum and a doctorate in sacred theology in 1953 from the Jagiellonian University in Krakow, Poland.

In 1951, Father Wojtyła took another sabbatical in which he continued to study philosophy and theology. At this time, he began to develop his philosophy of man. Along with help from such greats as Dietrich von Hildebrand and Edith Stein (20th-century philosophers who taught in Germany and Austria before World War II — Stein was born a Jew, converted to Catholicism, and became a Carmelite nun before being sent to a Nazi death camp, and von Hildebrand escaped to New York City in 1940), Father Wojtyła started a new school of thought that became known as Christian *phenomenology* (a method of inquiry based on the premise that reality consists of objects and events as they are perceived or understood in human consciousness and not anything independent of human consciousness).

Becoming a professor and faculty member

Later, Father Wojtyła became professor of moral philosophy and social ethics at a seminary in Krakow and a professor of philosophy at the Catholic University of Lublin. He assumed the Chair of Ethics and lectured for 25 years before his election as pope in 1978. He became a commuter, shuttling between Lublin and Krakow on the overnight train to teach and counsel in one city and study in the other.

In Lublin, Father Wojtyła endured the harshness of the Communist regime. The government had already arrested the university's *rector* (equivalent to chancellor or president) and nine priests on the faculty. As during World War II and the Nazi occupation, which lead to underground movements, Father Wojtyła joined professors who met secretly and became a nucleus of academics who sought ways to undermine Communism peacefully and philosophically.

During this period, Father Wojtyła continued his work on marriage preparation. He composed his thoughts into a book titled *Love and Responsibility*. This book was not merely a set of instructions for marriage, but a study on the vocation of marriage and sexual love that marriage entails. By explaining marital love and chastity, it also proved to be a valuable tool to counter the sexual revolution that plagued the West after World War II. In his book, Father Wojtyła explained that human sexuality was good because sexual desire leads men and women into marriage. Chastity was explained as a virtue to love others as persons, not objects. These personal concepts helped to pave the way for his general teachings on man and woman as persons and not as impersonal objects, a view that was adopted by secular society as a whole in the 20th century.

Being a Shepherd (Bishop)

On July 4, 1958, Father Wojtyła became Bishop Wojtyła. Pope Pius XII named him auxiliary bishop of Krakow. The circumstances surrounding the announcement of Father Wojtyła becoming bishop is classic Karol. He was an ardent sportsman and worker with the young. Naturally, the two converged in the summer with outings in the country. One such outing took place in July 1958. Father Wojtyła and friends went on a kayak and camping trip. It was in the midst of this camping trip that he received word to return to the cathedral in Krakow. Karol docked his boat, changed his clothes, went to the bishop's residence, and was informed of his elevation to the *episcopacy* (the office of bishop). Later, he returned to his boat, changed his clothes, and went back to camping, boating, and soccer, saying nothing to his companions, because he did not want to overshadow their planned holiday. Such humility had been a hallmark of Karol ever since he was a young boy.

Karol Wojtyła was consecrated 11 days before Pope Pius XII died. This pope was the one he had met years before in Rome while doing his graduate work, and he was the same Holy Father who wrote extensively on Mary and the liturgy, two loves of Pope John Paul II. The next pope, John XXIII, would prove to be very important in the life of the young bishop when he convened the Second Vatican Council in Rome.

During these early years as auxiliary bishop of Krakow, Karol preached on a host of different occasions such as retreats, recollections, and symposia. He developed a theme of renewal, a theme that Pope John XXIII would also reiterate to the Universal Church at the new council he would convene.

Besides writing his theological treatise on marriage, chastity, and marital sexual love, called *Love and Responsibility,* Karol also wrote a play titled *In Front of the Jeweler's Shop.* The overall theme of the play is moral and inspirational. The play is about wedding rings, a symbol of the sanctity of marriage, the central theme of the play. The play highlights Bishop Karol's views on the equality of partners in marriage. The second act deals with a troubled marriage, and the third act deals with a couple who gets engaged after the war. The son is the product of the couple from the first act, and the daughter is the product of the couple from the second act. The play is a modern commentary on the challenges, responsibilities, and benefits of modern Catholic marriage.

Participating in the Second Vatican Council

The Second Vatican Council convened in 1962, and Bishop Wojtyła took part. The Council was monumental. It was an *ecumenical council,* which means it was a meeting of bishops of the whole Church to discuss and settle matters of Church doctrine and practice. Pope John XXIII invited other Christian churches to send observers to the Council. There was a great, historic meeting between Catholics, Orthodox, and major Protestant denominations.

The First Vatican Council was held only a century before and came to an end with the unification of Italy and the dissolution of the Papal States. As a result, the First Council was truncated, only dealing with the papacy. Another council would have to be convened in order to finish what the first could not, especially in areas of pastoral and dogmatic issues concerning the whole Church. (For more on the details of the Second Vatican Council, take a look at Chapter 7.)

A typical day for Bishop Karol at the Council began with Mass at 6:45 a.m. at the Polish Institute, where he was staying. Then he made the short, ten-minute walk to St. Peter's. He attended another Mass at St Peter's Basilica at 9 a.m., with all the bishops in attendance. All the sessions of the Council took place here. Imagine the magnitude of the event, with the attendance of 108 cardinals, 9 primates, 5 patriarchs, 543 archbishops, 2,171 bishops, 128 major superiors of men's religious orders, and 93 abbots. Sessions included deliberations and speeches by the various clergy in attendance. (Indeed, Bishop Karol addressed the Council for the first time in November 1962.) In the afternoon, Bishop Karol returned to his residency. He would then go over the documents discussed during the day. In the evening, he would attend meetings of Council commissions and subcommittees to which he belonged.

Finding inspiration in the Council

The universality of the Second Vatican Council inspired Bishop Wojtyła. At the Council, he met bishops from all over the world. The Polish bishops became the authorities on life behind the Iron Curtain. Bishop Wojtyła became the representative of this constituency. Poland was also anticipating its 1,000th anniversary in 1966 of the country's Catholicism; the hope was that the council would aide in this celebration in direct contrast to Communism.

The Vatican Council was a major step for Bishop Wojtyła on his way to the papacy. There, he met Archbishop Krol, a Polish-American from Cleveland, Ohio, who would later become cardinal of Philadelphia and a major supporter of Wojtyła becoming pope. Bishop Wojtyła addressed the council seven times. He delivered his speeches concerning the various sessions with clarity, theological insight, and academic excellence.

As pope, he changed forever the College of Cardinals by adding many men from the third world, so that the College expressed the universality of the Church in a more complete way — reflecting a universality he experienced firsthand at the Second Vatican Council. Before his changes, the College of Cardinals was basically a European membership, with the most members coming from Italy. As a result, for over 400 years, there had been an Italian on the Throne of St. Peter. Under Pope John Paul II, the membership expanded to reflect the populations of Catholics from all over the world. Because of JP2's efforts to diversify the College of Cardinals, we may see a pope coming from a third-world nation in the future.

Speaking for Poland and the Church

During the Second Vatican Council, Wojtyła became the spokesman for Poland. Wyszyński, who was the primate of Poland and therefore the most appropriate person to be spokesman, relinquished this honor to Bishop Wojtyła for many reasons:

- ✔ Bishop Wojtyła, who was an outstanding theologian, was more articulate in this area.

- ✔ Because of his theater background, Bishop Wojtyła was a more animated speaker and could convey what the Polish Church wanted to say or needed.

- ✔ Wyszyński was preoccupied with the needs of Eastern Europe under the Communist bloc and also his own native Poland's planned millennium celebration of Catholicism in 1966.

By Bishop Wojtyła becoming the spokesman, his talent as a world-class leader, diplomat, and theologian was visible to the various Council attendees who would one day elect him pope.

It was at the Second Vatican Council that Wojtyła met the future Pope Paul VI. Cardinal Montini worked under the secretary of state under Pope Pius XII. In 1953, he became archbishop of Milan and later a cardinal. Upon the death of John XXIII, Montini became Pope Paul VI, who eventually saw to the conclusion of the Second Vatican Council that John XXIII had convened. At the sessions of the Council, Montini became impressed with the young bishop from Poland.

The celebration of the millennium of Catholicism in Poland was the next major event in the life of the young bishop. The Polish clergy hoped that Pope Paul VI would grace the country at the celebration, but the Communists would not permit this to occur. Therefore, the primate of Poland, in an unprecedented way, permitted Bishop Wojtyła to deliver the major homily at the Shrine of the Black Madonna. It was here that he gave the pontifical blessings of Paul VI. For the next year, Wojtyła would celebrate and deliver over 50 Masses throughout Poland. To commemorate the event, he even wrote poems for the celebration, titled "Conversation with God," "Conversation with Man," and "Invocation to a Man Who Became the Body of History."

Implementing reforms in the diocese

One of the first things Bishop Wojtyła did when he returned to Poland after attending the Second Vatican Council was to mobilize the *laity* (everyone in the Church except the clergy). Because they shared in the common priesthood by virtue of Baptism, the lay faithful, as well as the clergy and religious, were all called to a life of holiness. Teaching the faith, called *catechesis,* was the duty of all the baptized.

Because the Communists outlawed teaching religion in schools, Bishop Wojtyła got nuns and laity to teach in private homes, church social halls, and other places not under control of the civil authorities. He also formed a diocesan synod and Priests' Council to get input from his clergy and to give them direction and guidance as they sought to serve the spiritual needs of their parishioners. He challenged all the faithful to get involved in their religion, from the personal level (daily prayer, weekly Mass, and monthly confession) to the communal level (study groups to learn more about the faith, Bible study, and social action, like feeding the hungry, sheltering the homeless, visiting the sick, and so on).

An educated Catholic is one who is more active in his Church, so the message of Christ truly becomes liberating, not only from oppressive political regimes, but also from sin and ignorance itself.

Moving Up the Ranks

Karol Wojtyła was a remarkable man, with his athletic bearing, flare for public speaking, command of languages, and sincere faithfulness. He impressed his parishioners, superiors, and fellow clergy. He was afforded opportunities to speak the faith on the world stage and made the most of them. He rose through the ranks of the Catholic Church with uncommon speed, which culminated in an uncommon papacy.

Becoming the archbishop of Krakow

Pope Paul VI appointed Wojtyła archbishop of Krakow in 1964, during the Second Vatican Council. This important and prestigious promotion was not automatic, even though Wojtyła had been an auxiliary bishop of the same archdiocese. In giving Wojtyła this assignment, the pope showed his confidence in Wojtyła's abilities to be a spiritual leader and shepherd of souls.

Receiving the red hat: Cardinal Wojtyła

Historically, the archbishop of Krakow would also be elevated to the rank of *cardinal* (a senior ecclesiastical official of the Catholic Church, ranking just below the pope), and Archbishop Wojtyła was no different in this regard: He was made a cardinal in 1967.

Cardinals wear a red hat known as a *biretta.* The color of this ecclesiastical headgear, a precursor to the academic mortarboard, indicates the hierarchal rank of the cleric: Priests wear a black biretta; monsignors wear a black one with a purple pom-pom on top; bishops wear a violet biretta. So when a cardinal is elected, we say he received the red hat. (For more on the College of Cardinals, see Chapter 19.)

Over the next 11 years — before the College of Cardinals elected him pope — Cardinal Wojtyła had to deal with the Communists and his poor people who were persecuted by them. Religious education at all levels was a primary focus in his administration. (This theme was one he would pick up again when he issued a new *Catechism of the Catholic Church* in 1994.) Banned from public schools, Cardinal Wojtyła standardized alternative programs to continue to educate his flock, including the following:

- ✔ **Youth ministry:** Wojtyła used outdoor activities with young people — such as hiking, skiing, and camping — to share and teach the faith while having wholesome fun.

- ✔ **Works of charity:** Wojtyła got volunteers to help the poor in soup kitchens, homeless shelters, health clinics, orphanages, and other outreach programs. Part of their training and work was to be exposed to the teachings of the Church, because he was thoroughly convinced that good works only have value when motivated out of love of God and love of neighbor.

Head of the Church or head of state?

The pope is not only head of the Catholic Church but also the head of state for a country, so he has the title of *sovereign*. Vatican City is the last vestige of the old Papal States, and the pope was considered its political ruler as well as its religious head. Most of the Papal States, which were a region from central Italy to the north, were lost in the unification of Italy in 1870. The Papal States bordered the Kingdom of the Two Sicilies in the south and the Austrian-Hungarian Empire and France to the north.

In 1929, under the dictatorship of Prime Minister Benito Mussolini, a formal treaty was signed between the sovereign nations of Italy and the Vatican. Cardinal Gasparri signed in the name of Pope Pius XI, and Mussolini signed in the name of King Victor Emmanuel III. This agreement became the standard legal definition of Vatican City as an independent and sovereign country, just as the Papal States had been in the previous centuries. From 1870 to 1929, the status

of the pope as the head of state and leader of an independent country was left an unanswered, open question.

Since the Lateran Treaty of 1929, however, the pope has been recognized by the world not only as the spiritual leader of one billion Catholic believers around the globe, but also as the temporal ruler of the smallest nation on Earth. The legal recognition of Vatican City as a distinct country, independent from Italy, means that diplomatic relations exist with other nations, like the United States, Canada, and the United Kingdom, and that ambassadors are sent and embassies erected just as other nations do with each other. Diplomatic relations have no religious consequence, so an atheist, agnostic, or non-Catholic nation can still sign a treaty with Vatican City merely as one country to another, without violating any separation-of-church-and-state principles.

Electing a new pope: John Paul 1

In August 1978, following Pope Paul VI's death, Cardinal Wojtyła voted in his first papal conclave since being made a cardinal. There were many possible contenders to the Throne of St. Peter. Yet the conclave elected an Italian from Venice, Albino Luciani, who was 65 years old. He broke with tradition and was the first pope to take two names, John Paul I to honor his two immediate predecessors, John XXIII and Paul VI. Luciani reigned as pope and as sovereign of Vatican City State from August 26, 1978, to September 28 of the same year. His one-month papacy is one of the shortest in history.

Wearing the Shoes of the Fisherman: Being Elected Pope

The Second Vatican Council had only been over for 13 years when John Paul I was elected, and many of its implications were still being worked out. He took the name to alert the Universal Church that he would continue the reforms of the two previous pontiffs. Sadly, Pope John Paul I lived only 33 days. This plunged the Church into another conclave. This period of the Church would be referred to by historians as the "Year of the Three Popes" (Paul VI, John Paul I, and John Paul II).

Upon the death of the pope, the period is known as the *sede vacante* (meaning empty chair, the symbol of authority since the time of the Roman Empire) or as the *interregnum* period. This period lasts between the pope's death and the election of his successor. Cardinal Wojtyła, who had returned to Poland after the election of Pope John Paul I, once again boarded a plane back to Rome to vote for the next pope. Little did he know that he would be elected the 264th pope of the Roman Catholic Church and the first non-Italian pope in over 400 years.

At the second papal conclave, two strong candidates allegedly emerged, Cardinal Siri of Genoa and the Archbishop of Florence, Cardinal Benelli. (No one knows for sure, because the cardinals take a solemn oath to keep the deliberations of a conclave absolutely confidential before they even enter the Sistine Chapel.) Cardinal Wojtyła was supposedly considered the compromise candidate because Siri was thought too conservative or traditional while Benelli was considered too liberal or progressive by many of their brother cardinals.

Cardinal Wojtyła, on the other hand, was seen as a centrist in that he was a true son of the Second Vatican Council (meaning, he participated in the Second Vatican Council and vigorously worked to properly implement the reforms). At the same time, as a bishop behind the Iron Curtain, he was a staunch defender of *orthodoxy* (the official teachings of the Church on faith and morals) against the old enemy of atheistic Communism. Yet, this so-called compromise candidate was who the College of Cardinals wanted to

lead the Church in the 20th century — a church that was fighting
Communism on all levels. Who better a candidate to fight against atheism
and Marxism than a cardinal who had suffered under its evil regime?

At the age of 58, Cardinal Wojtyła was one of the youngest popes. He chose
the name Pope John Paul II in order to continue the reforms of the Second
Vatican Council. As part of his reforms, he got rid of the traditional *papal
coronation* (a long ceremony in which a new pope was crowned head of the
Roman Catholic Church and sovereign of the Vatican City State) and instead
was installed pope at a pontifical Mass.

During the traditional papal coronations, the pope was crowned with the
three-tiered papal tiara to show that he was the chief priest, prophet, and
king of the Church. The last coronation was that of Paul VI. His tiara, which
was a gift from the Archdiocese of Milan, is now on display at the National
Shrine in Washington, D.C.

Instead of the traditional papal coronation, Pope John Paul II chose a simple
papal inauguration. At the new ceremony, the pope received a *pallium,* which is
a narrow band of wool. It's worn over the *chasuble* (which is the long sleeveless
vestment worn by a priest over other garments) at Mass. The pallium symbol-
izes the early image of Christ, who is the Good Shepherd and carries the lamb
on his shoulders. The pallium is decorated with three jeweled lances to symbolize the nails driven into Christ at his crucifixion. (See Figure 6-1 for a photograph of JP2 receiving his pallium in 1978.) Next, the pope received the ring of
the fisherman, which is decorated with a relief of St. Peter fishing and is worn
by the Sovereign Pontiff until his death, when it is ceremoniously crushed.

Figure 6-1:
Pope John
Paul II
receives the
pallium from
Cardinal
Deacon
Pericle
Felici (right)
during his
investiture
ceremony in
St. Peter's
Square.

© Bettmann/CORBIS

Upon his election as the 264th pope, the theme of his pontificate was "Be Not Afraid." These words ring true in many areas, from religious to political, economic, and even social freedom. "Be not afraid," for the Holy Spirit will guide you to the truth and to witness to it, he would tell young people at World Youth Day, so that they could recognize that old people were being killed by euthanasia.

The new pope was a beacon of light who would clarify the teachings of the Second Vatican Council in a church that was suffering from internal dissent and abusive experimentation. Everything from the Sacred Liturgy to the *Code of Canon Law* would see an imprint from the third longest reigning pope in the history of the Catholic Church. He would earn, we believe, the title of "the Great."

At the same time he was also a world leader. Pope John Paul II became a loud voice for social justice in rich and poor nations. He touched the hearts of many in his numerous trips to various countries. He was known as the most traveled pope in the history of the Church. And he used the media and technology to benefit the Church in spreading the message of the gospel.

Chapter 7

Continuing the Council: Understanding Vatican II

Most people know there was an *Apollo XIII* not because they know the 12 lunar missions that came before it or the 4 that followed but because *Apollo XIII* was the most famous. Likewise, most people — Catholics and non-Catholics alike — know Vatican II not for the 20 ecumenical councils that preceded it, but because this was the most famous. Hollywood and Tom Hanks made *Apollo XIII* more legendary, especially the phrase "Houston, we have a problem. . . ." Similarly, the word *aggiornamento* (Italian for "update" or "to open the windows") spoken by Pope John XXIII when he inaugurated the Second Vatican Council is quoted just as often among the Catholic community.

In this chapter, we explore Vatican II and its effect on the rising star, Bishop Karol Wojtyła, the soon-to-be Pope John Paul II. We look at his specific involvement in the Council. And finally, we see how he took the message from the Council and brought it home.

What Was Vatican II?

The Second Vatican Council, or Vatican II as it is often called, is the most recent of the 21 gatherings of Catholic bishops over the past two millennia. Pope John XXIII opened it in 1962 and Pope Paul VI closed it in 1965. Throughout the 2,000-year history of the Church, there have been 266 popes (from St. Peter through Benedict XVI) but only 21 ecumenical councils.

Settling disputes

The idea of getting the world's bishops together originated in the Bible. After the Crucifixion, death, Resurrection, and Ascension of Jesus into heaven, the early church was shepherded and governed by religious leaders chosen by the Founder, Jesus himself. Christ chose 12 men to be his Apostles; after one of them, Judas, hanged himself (he betrayed Jesus for 30 pieces of silver), the 11 who were left selected someone to replace the one who went bad. The Acts of the Apostles (1:15–26) tells us that Matthias was designated to take the place of Judas Iscariot, as an Apostle. Soon afterward, a controversy arose among the early Christians regarding the question of gentile converts. The Apostles, like Jesus himself, were all Jews, and that meant they were circumcised and followed the Hebrew dietary laws (like not eating pork).

The first Christians then were practicing Jews until Judaism and Christianity parted company as separate religions. Before that happened, a large and growing number of converts to Christianity were coming from *gentile* ancestry (Greek, Roman, and other pagan cultures) not Jewish. The issue became whether or not a gentile convert to Christianity should first embrace the *Mosaic Law* (the Jewish laws that came from Moses, which demanded male circumcision). Acts 15 related how the problem was resolved. A council was convened among the Apostles and their successors, the bishops.

Three centuries later, after surviving the Roman persecutions, the Christian church, once outlawed and now legally recognized (by the Edict of Milan issued by Emperor Constantine in 313 A.D.) by the Roman Empire, encountered another theological controversy. Arius (a priest-theologian of the fourth century A.D. who lived in Alexandria, Egypt) denied the divinity of Christ and claimed that even though Jesus was the Son of God, Jesus was only similar to but not equal to God.

Alexander (the Bishop of Alexandria) and others maintained that Christ was indeed divine and human, and in his divinity, he shared the same substance with God, so that the Father and the Son and also the Holy Spirit were all equally divine.

Fighting ensued, and it was so intense the Emperor (now a Christian) insisted the Church leaders settle the dispute once and for all. Remembering the Council of Jerusalem in Acts 15, an ecumenical council was convened for all the bishops of the world, and they met in the imperial city of Nicea in 325 A.D. The pope in Rome (Sylvester) was too old and sick to attend but sent two papal legates to represent him. At that council, Arius was condemned a heretic, and the Nicene Creed was formulated, which is recited to this very day at Mass on Sundays and holy days.

After Nicea, 20 more ecumenical councils followed. They primarily dealt with theological-doctrinal controversies over the centuries. The second most famous of these is the Council of Trent, which met in the 16th century to address the doctrinal errors of the Protestant reformers (like Martin Luther, John Calvin, and Ulrich Zwingli) and to initiate necessary reforms among the clergy to prevent the abuses that precipitated the Reformation.

Until 1054, when the Eastern Schism divided the Catholic Church and the Greek Orthodox broke from Rome, only one Christian church existed. So, both the Roman Catholic and Eastern Orthodox churches mutually recognize the first seven ecumenical councils. After the *schism* (division), the remaining councils were held in the west, only attended by bishops of the west and only accepted by the west. Catholic Christianity regards all 21 councils as authoritative.

A brief history of the Second Vatican Council

Pope Pius XII laid the groundwork for change in the 1950s, a whole decade before the Second Vatican Council. His encyclical *Mediator Dei* (1947) paved the way for the first document of Vatican II, *Sacrosanctum Concilium* (Constitution on the Sacred Liturgy), in 1963. In *Mediator Dei,* Pius XII encouraged and exhorted Catholics not to be mere bystanders and not to just sit as a passive audience when at Mass or any sacred celebration of the sacraments. Even when the liturgy was exclusively in Latin, the goal was to foster participation by having the congregation verbally respond to prayers from the priest, join together in singing hymns, and make the same external gestures (like kneeling, standing, and sitting) with one another. These external signs of participation were to be combined with an interior, internal, and spiritual participation of uniting heart, mind, and soul to what was happening in the sanctuary and on the altar.

Vatican II took place in the 20th century, almost a hundred years after its predecessor, Vatican I, which defined the dogma of *papal infallibility* (the Catholic teaching that the pope is prevented by the Holy Spirit from teaching an erroneous doctrine on faith and morals when speaking to the Universal Church). The Franco-German war abruptly ended the First Vatican Council (1869–1870), which was supposed to discuss other issues besides papal infallibility, such as Church law and discipline, missionary work, the sociopolitical world, and the issue of the Oriental (Eastern) Christian churches.

Unlike the previous 20 councils, Vatican II was not a *doctrinal council* (a council convened to resolve theological controversy); instead, it was called to be a *pastoral council* (one that did not define any new doctrines and instead focused on the pastoral and spiritual welfare of the Church).

When Angelo Roncalli was elected Pope John XXIII in 1958, he wanted to revise the then archaic 1917 *Code of Canon Law.* This body of ecclesiastical laws governed the Universal Church, from the Vatican all the way down to the local bishop and diocese to the local pastor and parish. Pope John XXIII and his immediate successor, Pope Paul VI, wanted to update the Catholic Church. They weren't interested in changing the content of teaching or the substance and essence of worship — they wanted to change the way and manner in which the doctrine was explained and the liturgy was celebrated.

It was clear from day one that the pope did not intend in any way, shape, or form to alter, revise, change, remove, or add to the ancient deposit of faith. The content of faith (in other words, doctrine) and the celebration of faith (sacraments) would remain intact, while the mode and manner in which they are explained and conducted would adapt to modern expressions and experiences. The *what* would remain the same, but the *how* would be another matter.

Pope John XXIII died in 1963, soon after he convened Vatican II in 1962. The Council was suspended until the College of Cardinals elected a successor, Giovanni Montini, who took the name Paul VI. Pope Paul VI reconvened the Council and later implemented many of its recommendations and resolutions. Some of those proposals included

- Allowing greater use of the vernacular (until then religious ceremonies were celebrated in the Latin language)
- Restoring the order of permanent deacon
- Promoting Christian unity (ecumenism) among the various denominations and religions (Protestant, Roman Catholic, and Eastern Orthodox)
- Respecting Christianity's Jewish origins and roots
- Using modern technology and contemporary perspectives to explain the faith

The Sacred Liturgy was the first area of discussion and dealt with the public worship of the Church. The entire Mass (or Eucharistic liturgy) was revamped, not in substance but in appearance. The common language of the local people replaced the universal ecclesiastical tongue of Latin. The priest was allowed to face the people as he celebrated from the altar. Larger selections from the Bible were incorporated so that, in a three-year period, nearly all of the scripture would be read and heard in church by the faithful.

Byzantine (Eastern) Catholics had already been accustomed to vernacular as well as liturgical Greek, Old Slavonic, Aramaic, Arabic, and Syriac in their Divine Liturgies, and they always had a permanent diaconate and married clergy. Latin (Western) Catholics, however, thanks to Vatican II, experienced some of these modernizations for the first time. The purpose of the changes was to foster and promote full, active, and conscious participation of the faithful in sacred worship and public liturgy.

According to Vatican II, worship shouldn't be seen as the exclusive work of the clergy. Vatican II allowed for lay involvement, such as reading the scriptures, serving at the altar, and, when necessary, assisting with distribution of Holy Communion as extraordinary ministers. The hierarchy was still very much alive and maintained teaching authority and governance over Church matters. But the wisdom, experience, and counsel of the laity were to be solicited and valued. Parishioners would be invited to join pastoral councils and finance committees, which have consultative though not deliberative authority to guide the pastor with his pastoral leadership.

Marriage and the single life were respected and honored as equal vocations from God along with Holy Orders (deacon, priest, and bishop) and religious life (nuns, monks, brothers, and sisters). Laity were encouraged to use their role in the world to enter political, economic, and social life and make it better by using the values and principles of their religious convictions.

Vatican II was not only pastoral and practical but truly *catholic* (universal) in the sense that 489 bishops from South America, 404 from North America, 374 from Asia, 84 from Central America, and 75 from Oceania participated and many non-Catholics (Eastern Orthodox, Protestants, and Muslims, for example) were also invited as guests. Nearly 3,000 people attended the Council in some fashion in the years it was convened, from 1963 to 1965.

Identifying the effects of the Council

Two main effects came from the Second Vatican Council. The first effect was the true intent of the Council, which sought neither to remake the Church nor to redefine the Church's teachings, but to speak and use the language of the time to communicate, explain, and defend what had been believed and taught for 2,000 years. This segment (the hierarchy) of the Church included the pope and most of the bishops who attended Vatican II. Their goal was not to "modernize" Catholicism as much as it was to use modern expressions and perspectives to present the ancient religion to a modern world.

The other effect was the elite group of "professional" theologians, journalists, liturgists, and ecclesiastical bureaucrats who attempted to hijack the Council in the claim of defending the "spirit of Vatican II." Although the bishops still met in Rome during the sessions of discussions, the spin-masters of their day distorted principles and propositions of the Council Fathers and proliferated them around the world. Liturgical experimentation, innovation, and alteration without any papal or Episcopal sanction rampaged Europe and the United States while Vatican II was being held. Aberrations and violations of liturgical regulations and *rubrics* (rules that govern how sacraments are celebrated) before, during, and after the sessions of the Second Vatican Council confused many of the laity and discouraged many of the older clergy who had only known one way of doing things. *Dissident theology,* which contradicted the official dogmas and doctrines of the *Magisterium* (the official teaching authority of the Church), were spread in numerous Catholic classrooms, colleges, universities, and seminaries.

At the same time that this distorted version of Vatican II was being followed, the bishops, priests, deacons, religious, and lay faithful loyal to the authentic "spirit of Vatican II" found their guidance in the "letter of Vatican II," or in the actual documents of the Council. Greater exposure to, reflection on, meditation on, and interpretation of the Bible by Catholic teachers and students did not conflict with official and ancient teachings and disciplines; instead, it gave them new meaning and enthusiasm. One of the greatest consequences of the authentic interpretation of Vatican II had nothing to do with power and authority in the Church, which remained hierarchical with the pope and bishops in control, but focused on the "universal call to holiness."

Almost 20 centuries had passed since Jesus walked the Earth and founded his church on the rock of Peter (Matthew 16:18). During that time, an unofficial notion crept into the common mind, not intended by the Church but never aggressively addressed, either. The idea arose among the regular laity that *sanctity* (holiness or saintliness) was only possible for professional religious people (like priests, monks, and nuns) — someone in Holy Orders or religious vows who wore a *habit* (religious garb), took vows (of poverty, chastity, and obedience), and lived in community (a monastery, friary, convent, abbey, or rectory). The clergy and religious only composed at most 5 to 10 percent of the Church at any one time in Church history, yet many people erroneously thought only the religious or clerical life could make a person holy. And without holiness, you can't go to heaven. Yet, it is erroneous to think that only clergy and religious have access to holiness. All the baptized are offered the same grace and same opportunity to live holy lives.

This false idea came about because, years ago, the clergy and religious spent a good quarter to a third of their day in formal prayer, while most if not all the lay faithful spent 99 percent of their time laboring and working for lords and ladies who owned the property and allowed the peasants to work them for survival. The amount of time spent in prayer at a chapel, oratory, church, or cathedral in many people's minds meant everything. A common person didn't have the time or the opportunity to spend quality time praying in sacred space.

Vatican II reminded the faithful that everyone who is baptized is called to live a life of holiness. The common priesthood of the laity was not an attempt to clericalize the laity or to laicize the clergy. The idea was simply that Baptism enables anyone and everyone to worship God and to practice the *corporal* (of the body) and spiritual works of mercy regardless of their state in life (vocation, career, or job). (For more on the corporal and spiritual works of mercy, see the nearby sidebar.)

Works of mercy

Vatican II clarified that all baptized Christians (both clergy and laity) are called to practice works of mercy. The corporal works of mercy are feeding the hungry, giving drink to the thirsty, clothing the naked, welcoming the stranger, visiting the sick and imprisoned, and burying the dead. The spiritual works of mercy are counseling the doubtful, instructing the ignorant, admonishing the sinner, comforting the sorrowful, bearing wrongs patiently, and praying for the living and the dead.

Reading the Bible, doing mental prayer, saying the Rosary, and other devotions are not the exclusive activity of the clergy. Any baptized person since Vatican II is encouraged to pray, study, and get involved with teaching the faith (or *catechesis*) and living the faith (like the *apostolate* — a ministry suited to the individual believer — and practicing works of mercy). The brainstorm of Vatican II was that any vocation could help achieve holiness and sanctity and, thus, help someone get to heaven, because all vocations are considered ultimately from God. So, a single man or woman working in the office, store, factory, or classroom, the average husband and wife, mother and father, all had the same chance and opportunity of growing and receiving *divine grace* (the supernatural gift from God that makes you holy) as the priests, nuns, and monks had.

Religion, faith, piety, devotion — these were no longer considered the restricted tools of the ordained and consecrated religious. Being a good, devout, and practicing Catholic Christian as a husband or wife, mother or father, single man or woman was not only a possibility, but also a necessity. Doing a good job at work, home, or school; obeying the Ten Commandments and Natural Moral Law; reading the Bible, the Lives of the Saints, papal encyclicals, and other religious works; and cultivating a daily prayer life, a regular sacramental life (weekly Mass and frequent confession), and an active *apostolate* (works of mercy) were seen as duties and obligations of everyone by virtue of their Baptism. Church authority was not what conferred sanctity — divine grace did that. And grace is made available to everyone — clergy and laity alike.

The proper implementation of Vatican II made official Church worship more participatory, not in terms of geographic location (sanctuary or pews), but in terms of external and internal involvement of body (gestures and verbal responses) and soul (intellect and will). Listening to the revealed Word of God (as proclaimed at Sunday Mass) and feeding on the word (made flesh in Holy Communion) empowers the lay and ordained faithful to seek lives of holiness (in other words, doing the Will of God in everything that is said or done — words and deeds).

Although some people improperly used Vatican II to promote their own agendas or portray it as some wild revolution against ancient doctrine and traditional discipline, the sons of Vatican II (the bishops like JP2 who actually attended and participated in it) understood the real spirit of the Council, namely to *renew* instead of *reform* the Church.

Speaking to the Council Fathers

Bishop Wojtyła (the man who would become Pope John Paul II) and his brother bishops did not give speeches but made *interventions* at the Second Vatican Council. These documents would often be submitted to a theological expert (these clergy were proficient in dogma, morality, or scripture) for suggested improvements and proper Latin translations in the cases where the bishop himself was not fluent in the tongue of Holy Mother Church (many American bishops were inadequately proficient in Latin, unlike their European counterparts).

Some of the known involvement of Karol Wojtyła during Vatican II centered on issues such as divine revelation, Sacred Liturgy, the Virgin Mary, the laity, and religious freedom. His most extensive influence was on the document *Gaudium et Spes* (Pastoral Constitution on the Church in the Modern World).

Weighing in on divine revelation

Wojtyła (who was fluent in Latin, the language spoken at the Council) entered the debate of the first session of the Second Vatican Council, which dealt with the topic of revelation, namely, how does God reveal himself? The axiom of Protestant Christianity since its birth at the Reformation has been *sola scriptura* (scripture alone). Catholic Christianity, on the other hand, saw both Sacred Scripture (the Bible) and Sacred Tradition as authentic sources of divine revelation.

Wojtyła was a staunch adherent to orthodox Catholic doctrine, so he did not dispute that commonly held Catholic belief, but he did seek to explain the doctrine in a different manner. Instead of making it a one-source proposition (the Bible only) or a two-source proposition (scripture and tradition), JP2 preferred the innovative concept of explaining God as the one source of divine revelation. God reveals Himself in scripture *and* in tradition, but He alone is the one source of revelation. This makes revelation the disclosure or unveiling of the Word of God, which is both the written word (Bible or Sacred Scripture) and unwritten or spoken word (Sacred Tradition).

Understanding the Catholic Church as a perfect society and Catholics as a pilgrim people

Bishop Wojtyła suggested that the revised rite of Baptism include some instruction to the parents and godparents to teach the faith to the child by word and example. He and other Polish bishops wanted a separate document on the Blessed Virgin Mary, instead of including a chapter on her in a larger document on the Church, but it went the other way. *Lumen Gentium* (the Dogmatic Constitution on the Church) finally included a last chapter titled, "The Blessed Virgin Mary, Mother of God in the Mystery of Christ and of the Church," which supports the notion of Mary as "Mother of the Church" — this makes sense because she is the mother of Jesus Christ and the Church is the Mystical Body of Christ, therefore the Mother of Christ must be the Mother of the Church.

He also supported the use of the phrase *people of God* in that same document to explain the Church. Previously, the Church was described in precise philosophical terminology, as in the case of *societas perfecta* (perfect society). Properly understood, *societas perfecta* does not mean that members of the Church, or the Church's leaders, are perfect, but that as an organization, the Church perfectly provides for all the spiritual needs of its members. It would be like going to a grocery store that had every conceivable kind of food (dry goods, fresh fruits and vegetables, cooked food, ready to cook, meat, fish, poultry, dairy, bakery, and so on) so that you would not have to go to any other store. Everything you need is under one roof. That same store would not have every piece of electrical equipment, stationery, or clothing you may need, because that's not the store's purpose. But if it had everything you needed in terms of food, it would be a perfect grocery store. The manager and workers would not be perfect, but they would try their best to provide you access to everything you need. Similarly, the Church is seen as a perfect society insofar as every spiritual need is provided. Physical needs, such as clothing, food, shelter, health, education, and defense are not provided by the Church; instead, those are provided by the other two natural institutions (the family and the state, either local or national).

This model has been misunderstood and misinterpreted by some to infer that membership in the Catholic Church makes you better than others or that those who belong are perfect while those who do not belong are imperfect. That view is a distorted one, but Karol Wojtyła, philosopher that he was, realized a theological rather than philosophical description was now needed.

The term *people of God* is both doctrinal and biblical. The Old Testament tells the story of the covenant between God and the *chosen people* (the Hebrews), and the New Testament tells of the new covenant between Jesus Christ and his bride, the Church. A *covenant* (also called a *testament*) is a sacred agreement between God and a person (like Abraham or Moses) or a group of people (like the Jews or Christians). The focus is on the people or the members more than on the institution itself. Although the Church has a definite hierarchical structure, the root of the Church is found in the Greek term used by Christ himself in the Gospel: *ekklesia* (*ecclesia* in Latin, where we get the word *ecclesiastical*), which is the assembly of believers that includes the structure but is not limited to it alone.

A "pilgrim people of God" is described by Vatican II; bishops like Wojtyła endorsed it wholeheartedly. A *pilgrimage* is a journey to a special, sacred place or location. Arriving at the destination is the most important thing, but the trip itself is no less significant. Imperfect, sinful humankind is born, lives, and dies on this Earth — but for the believer, this is only half the story. The other half is that life is a journey or pilgrimage from Earth to, hopefully, heaven. The destination is achieved by paying attention to the journey itself. Like driving on a long trip, you have to keep an eye on the road and observe what the map says and what the road signs tell you — otherwise, you won't get to where you want to go.

The Church is the pilgrim people of God in that all the believers want to go to the same place (heaven). Revelation is the road map; divine grace is the food and fuel to keep us going; Church teaching and doctrine are the road signs that tell us what is ahead; the sacraments are the vehicles, which get us to where we want to go; and believers are the drivers who need to pay attention to all of the above.

Expanding the responsibilities of the laity

Wojtyła also intervened with discussions on the apostolic role of the laity. Baptism makes a person a child of God and a member of the Church. It also empowers the man or woman to be a *disciple of the Lord,* which means the person has a right and obligation to share the faith, to teach by word and example. Practicing the corporal and spiritual works of mercy are not a privilege of religious nuns and monks in the monasteries — they're a mandate of every baptized Christian (see the earlier sidebar, "Works of mercy," for more information). *Evangelization* (spreading the faith) is the mission of all believers. Some do it formally as a priest, deacon, or religious; others do it informally as Christian husbands and wives, mothers and fathers.

Religious is a noun referring to men and women who take vows of poverty, chastity, and obedience. They can be sisters, brothers, nuns, monks, friars, and so on. Religious are distinct from clergy in that they are not ordained bishops, priests, or deacons but neither are they laypeople, because they live in community and follow a religious rule of life.

JP2 and Vatican II did not want to make the laity into quasi- or semi-clerics. Jesus said to the people, "You are the salt of the earth" (Matthew 5:13) and "You are the light of the world" (Matthew 5:14). He also told them that a lamp is not hidden under a bushel basket but is placed where everyone can see it. These words were spoken as part of His Sermon on the Mount and were addressed to everyone — not just his Apostles and disciples. The commission to be "salt" and "light" is not restricted to ordained ministry or formal religious life alone, but to all believers by virtue of their Baptism.

At the same time, the Council did not laicize the clergy or make the religious redundant. The laity were called to sanctify the world because they lived and worked in the world, whereas the clergy and religious lived and worked in the Church, and their job was to help sanctify the people of God.

Exploring religious freedom

Bishop Wojtyła's pivotal contribution was to the document *Dignitatis Humanae* (Declaration of Religious Freedom). Philosophically, error itself has no rights, because only the truth is what people seek and need. But human persons who are *in* error never lose their human rights. Wojtyła recognized, as did the Second Vatican Council, that freedom is not the same as license — in other words, we are not free to do whatever we want, but we are free to do what we *ought* to do. Animals act out of instinct and computers run by programming, but men and women can freely and consciously choose to do the right deed for the right reason. That distinction makes it a moral act, an act that involves the rational intellect and free will. Only actions that are consciously and freely committed are considered moral acts.

Some Council bishops feared that religious indifference would occur where people made religion a matter of opinion and taste instead of a search for eternal and revealed truths. Religious liberty did not mean that all faiths and religions were equal. The Catholic Church still firmly believed it was the true Church founded by Christ, but the old notion that "we're right, and they're wrong" was not the perspective Wojtyła and others wanted to continue. Instead, they chose to present the Catholic faith as having the fullness of grace and fullness of truth, because it had all seven sacraments and embraced both Sacred Scripture and Sacred Tradition. Other Christian denominations had two of the seven sacraments (Baptism and Eucharist) and believed in *sola scriptura* (the Bible alone), so they have some grace and some truth but not the fullness of the Catholic Church, because some of the sources of grace and truth were left out. That was JP2's understanding and the understanding of the Council. Seeing, recognizing, and affirming the presence of truth and grace — albeit not the fullness but some of it anyway in various degrees — in other faiths and religions paved the way for religious freedom.

Living under Nazi then Communist oppression, Wojtyła saw the evils of religious persecution. Catholics and Protestants, Christians, Jews, and Muslims all can at least agree on basic truths and necessities like the right to life, health, food, shelter, education, and freedom to worship. When the state denies physical and spiritual needs of the citizens, then that government has no right to govern. The authority to govern comes neither from the people nor from any social contract, nor even from any constitution, but from God. Whether a monarchy, republic, democracy, or other government, the state exists to provide and protect the people with security and assistance when needed.

Freedom was not seen by JP2 or Vatican II as the license to act or think irresponsibly, because freedom and responsibility go hand in hand. I am free to do good because I choose to do so and when I see what ought to be done, I am responsible for the good I either do or fail to do. Freedom is not an option or diversity of opinion, but the ability to act without being forced to do so. Hence, if the government passed a law that mandated citizens go to church on Sundays, that would violate religious freedom as much as if the government did the opposite and made going to church illegal. Civil law should provide the opportunity to practice religion, such as making legal holidays coincide with religious holy days to enable people to freely practice their faith.

Gaudium et Spes (Pastoral Constitution on the Church in the Modern World) was Wojtyła's masterpiece in that he was involved in that more than any other document. Some churchmen had seen the secular world as the ancient enemy of the Church, going back to a dichotomy described in the Gospel of John. St. Augustine and others would also speak of the two cities — the earthly Babylon and the heavenly Jerusalem — when referring to the world and the Church, respectively.

Bishop Wojtyła and others, however, recalled that God made the world. It was not made by the devil. If the world was abused or misused, it was not by divine design. Genesis tells us that God created the world and saw that it was good. Jesus founded the Church not to be an opponent or adversary to the world but to help *save* the world. The world was redeemable and so the Redeemer and Savior came to do just that. Just as JP2 would later show in his papal encyclical *Fides et Ratio* (Faith and Reason) that religion and science are not inherently or innately enemies, so, too, church and state or religion and government are not intrinsically hostile opponents of one another.

Optimally, the world provides material (physical) necessities for people while the church (religion) provides spiritual necessities for those same individuals. The pagans developed a notion that the world was inherently evil because they thought anything of the material world was bad and only the immaterial and spiritual realities were beneficial. This philosophy was known as *Manichaeism* or *dualism*. The Judeo-Christian religion, on the other hand, taught of God, the good creator, making the world, and man and the devil being the ones who misused and abused it.

This shift would mean more open and broader dialogue with the secular world, which had numerous problems of its own. Yet, the Church saw its mission to sanctify not condemn the world; to bring the good news of revelation and, thus, bring light to a world immersed in darkness. Instead of cursing and retreating from the world, *Gaudium et Spes* challenged clergy and lay faithful alike to change or convert the world much as the early Christians did with the pagan Roman world of their day. Thus, the Church saw its mission to encourage secular governments to work for peace and justice, eliminate poverty, protect human life in all its stages, provide adequate health care and education for all citizens, and basically help the progress of the human person rather than the glorification of the state. By helping its citizens to realize their full potential to be and to do good, the secular world and secular governments would provide stability, security, and safety. When the state ignores human dignity of the person, of the family, and of the church, then chaos, instability, violence, and war result.

Implementing the Reforms

When he returned to Poland after the Second Vatican Council ended, Bishop Wojtyła enthusiastically sought to implement the decrees and reforms called for by the pope and bishops who participated in that historical event. He broadcast on radio while in Rome and after he returned home and tried to use the press to make headway to reconcile old wounds. The Polish bishops were preparing for the millennium of Christianity in Poland in 1966 by reaching out to those who suffered during World War II. Before and after the war, some territories of Poland and Germany had been in different possessions. Instead of escalating the debate, the bishops sought reconciliation by admitting that both Polish and German officials in government and in the Church made mistakes of prudential judgment over the course of history. The Soviet-controlled Communists in Poland refused to let such talk be printed in local newspapers.

Bishop Wojtyła brought the perspective of Vatican II home with him and initiated reforms in his diocese and in the parishes. He consulted regularly with neighboring bishops of his country and listened to the needs and concerns of his pastors who shepherded the individual parishes. He encouraged his priests to be apolitical themselves and instead promote interest among the lay faithful to get involved in social concerns, from politics to economics, from social action to social justice.

The seeds of Solidarity were being sewn. It would not be the Church that confronted and toppled the Soviet Union and the Warsaw Pact, but the ordinary people of the Church who put their faith into practice and demanded change from their secular leaders. The Church was a vital and necessary catalyst, but the work itself would be done by the laity, because the secular world was its sphere of influence.

Bishop Wojtyła inaugurated *diocesan synods,* which are like mini ecumenical councils limited to the territory of a diocese as opposed to the whole world. This step was neither a duplication of what Vatican II did nor a reinvention of the wheel, but an implementation of the world council through means of a diocesan synod. It was a gathering of all the pastors, priests, deacons, religious, and lay faithful to study and put into effect the documents of the Second Vatican Council. He did not abdicate his authority as bishop, nor did he ask pastors to do likewise in the parishes. Wojtyła did want the clergy, religious, and laity, however, to know that they needed to work together on some projects for the common good.

He encouraged dialogue and cooperation with Jews and Protestants within Poland, not to dilute Catholic doctrine or to assimilate into some generic ideology, but to build bridges based on shared concerns and mutual interests. Never compromising on faith and morals, Wojtyła saw the benefit of working together to oppose atheistic Communism, to defend justice for all citizens, to help the sick and poor, to serve the common good. He challenged the laity to not only seek personal piety and holiness but to also live fully the Gospel call to serve others, especially one's neighbor in need. Catholic faith would not be sold out, but Christians and Jews could work together to fight poverty, sickness, and injustice, as well as to help build a fairer and safer society.

The Communist Party members feared this spiritual renaissance because it threatened to unite religious and moral people against the tyranny of state-controlled and state-manipulated life. Religion was not to be a merely private affair nor just a one-day-a-week involvement. It had to permeate one's entire life and perspective on life, 24/7. Politics and economics were not immune from religious and moral scrutiny any more than all human behavior, whether in church, at home, at school, or at work. The iron grip of the Iron Curtain was beginning to rust — it was just too early to tell how fast the rust would spread.

Chapter 8

Holding the Line: Reinforcing Church Values, Teachings, and Traditions

. . . .

In This Chapter

▶ Upholding traditional values

▶ Reinforcing Church teachings

▶ Requiring conformity among the clergy

▶ Looking at modern dilemmas through the filter of the Catholic faith

. . . .

*E*very pope of the Catholic Church is regarded as the *Vicar* (a personal representative, similar to an ambassador) of Christ on Earth and, as such, is expected to continue the threefold mission of the Founder (Jesus) to be priest, prophet, and king. The *priestly* mission is to sanctify the laity, the *prophetic* mission is to teach the Church, and the *kingly* mission is to shepherd and govern the flock. Pope John Paul II took all these roles seriously, filling them with diligence and enthusiasm.

In this chapter, we discuss the prophetic mission (of teaching and defending the faith) and the kingly (leadership) mission of governing the Church. JP2 was a participant and adherent of the Second Vatican Council, so no one could accuse him of being an ultraconservative reactionary. Nevertheless, he was also a faithful and loyal son of the Church, which meant he was no ultra-liberal radical, either.

Here, we show you how — and why — he upheld the teachings of the Church based on both Divine Law and Natural Moral Law. We explain how he wrestled with issues of Church doctrine and how he censured those who did not live up to their vows. Finally, we examine how JP2 applied the sacred texts, traditions, and teachings to the new frontiers of the modern world.

Reaffirming Traditional Morality

Although *canon law* (ecclesiastical law that governs the Church) and the *catechism* (the teachings of the Church) declare that every pope has full, supreme, immediate, and universal authority as the leader of the Catholic Church, the pope's jurisdiction is still limited: He can't change or alter Divine Law or Natural Moral Law. The pope's supreme authority is restricted to human or man-made laws and traditions. So, no pope can ever repeal any of the Ten Commandments ("Eh, what the heck — go ahead and steal"), nor could he substantially change a defined doctrine on faith and morals.

Understanding papal infallibility

The concept of *papal infallibility* doesn't mean that the pope has the power to change what God has already revealed or decreed (Divine Law and Natural Moral Law). Instead, Catholics believe that the Holy Spirit protects the pope and the Church from teaching error in matters of faith and morals.

Unlike divine inspiration, which is limited to the sacred authors of the Bible, papal infallibility does not involve God influencing the words used by the pope. The Gospel writers (Matthew, Mark, Luke, and John), for instance, were divinely inspired, which means that every word they wrote in Sacred Scripture is considered to have been revealed by God.

Infallibility is different from divine inspiration in that infallibility is merely a *protection* and not a *catalyst* (as inspiration is). Papal infallibility does not mean that each word and sentence the pope writes is guided by the Holy Spirit (which would be inspiration). Instead, it means that God would intervene if a pope attempted to solemnly teach a moral or doctrinal error to the Universal Church. We don't know how or what kind of divine intervention would take place — just that the pope would somehow be prevented from teaching a moral or doctrinal *heresy* (false teaching).

So Catholic Christians believe that the pope and the bishops don't possess absolute authority because they can't change what has already been divinely inspired and revealed, nor can any pope or bishop change any precept of Divine Law or Natural Moral Law. Yet, Catholicism teaches that the Church was commissioned by God to authentically interpret, define, defend, and explain what is contained in revelation to prevent confusion and ambiguity through the teaching authority of the pope and bishops. It's within this context that Pope John Paul II, like all his predecessors and successors, functions as the highest teaching authority in the Church.

Officially defined doctrines on faith and morals cannot and will not be changed — but they can, have, and will be explained in different terminology, context, and perspective. Substantially, the Natural Moral Law and defined doctrines are unchangeable. How they are *described* and *applied* in particular instances can be modified to suit the spiritual needs of the time and era.

Labeling any pope as morally or doctrinally "traditional," "progressive," "conservative," or "liberal" doesn't work. These adjectives are political, not theological, and they're inappropriate for describing Church teaching. It's more accurate to describe the personal tastes, opinions, and style of a papacy as being either "conventional" or "contemporary." John Paul II upheld what previous popes and ecumenical councils have consistently taught on such issues as divorce, remarriage, contraception, sex and reproduction, the ordination of women, married clergy, and so on. But JP2 had his own flavor in his papacy — the manner in which he taught and spread the message was uniquely his. Likewise, Benedict XVI will personalize his approach and delivery. But the content of the message will always be the same — whether the pope was Pius XII or John XXIII (from years past) or any pope of the future.

The best analogy for how the message changes is looking at how math education has changed over time. Your great-great-grandfather may have attended a one-room schoolhouse and only gone as far as the sixth grade. You may be a post-graduate student at M.I.T. But both of you learned the same basic truth, $2 + 2 = 4$. Time and space don't change the equation — what is true now was true back then and will be true for centuries to come. Moral and doctrinal truths are no less true than mathematical or scientific truths. Water will always be H_2O, just as the teachings contained in the catechism will remain perennially the same.

Discussing divorce and annulment

John Paul II upheld Church doctrine on the permanence of marriage while he pastorally reached out to those Catholics who found themselves in broken relationships. On the one hand, he could not change the teaching that the sacrament of Christian marriage is a permanent, faithful, and, God willing, fruitful union between one man and one woman. This position has been the doctrine of the Catholic Church since day one.

JP2 reminded his followers that Jesus Himself said in the Gospel: "Anyone who divorces his wife and marries another woman, commits adultery, and if she divorces her husband and marries another man, she commits adultery" (Mark 10:11–12, Matthew 19:9). This doctrine is based on the idea that a valid marriage is permanent — or, as the wedding vows state, "until death do us part" as well as the statement of Christ in Matthew 19:6 that "what God has joined together, let no man put asunder." Both Matthew and Mark show Jesus being asked by others about divorce and remarriage, because Moses allowed for it in the Old Testament. Jesus says that Moses allowed for divorce and remarriage because of his "hardness of heart" (his obstinacy or stubbornness). God's intent, however, as found in Genesis 2:24 is that a man and woman become "one flesh" in marriage, and Jesus's teaching is that a marital union is permanent (unto death).

Understanding annulment

So if marriage is permanent, you may be wondering, then how can any Christian be divorced or how can Catholics have their marriages annulled? The exception or, more accurately, the clarification, lies in Matthew 19:9 where Jesus says that a man can't divorce his wife "except for fornication" and marry another woman, or else he commits adultery.

The Greek word originally used by Matthew is *porneia,* which is translated as an "illicit" or "unnatural" union.

So the so-called exception, allowing a marriage to be annulled, would be if a man attempted to marry his sister (incest), or if he attempted to marry another man (or a woman attempted to marry another woman), or if someone attempted to marry the spouse of another (bigamy).

Moicheia is the Greek word for adultery, and Christ or Matthew does not use that word, so we can't interpret from the text that marital infidelity alone is reason to dissolve a marriage. Though sinful, wrong, and immoral, adultery does not break the bond of marriage.

Unlike a divorce, which is a legal decree stating that the rights and obligations of marriage no longer bind this man and woman, an annulment says that no valid marriage existed to begin with — so the rights and obligations are nonexistent, and the couple is free to marry someone else. Divorce does not make a judgment on the validity of the first marriage; an annulment does.

Although some Catholics and non-Catholics alike erroneously claim that Church annulments are nothing more than sanctioned divorces, in reality, they're completely different. Divorce is a secular creation of civil law that merely involves the civil obligations and duties of a married couple. Annulment is a Church decision that, despite all the good intentions, this particular marriage was never a valid sacramental union unto death. The basis for that decision is explicitly stated in canon law. The *tribunal* (Church court) examines what the bride and groom intended on the wedding day at the moment they exchanged vows.

Both the man and the woman may have had the best of intentions. They may have even loved each other completely. But if something was substantially missing or deficient, then their union was incomplete and nonbinding. Here are some examples:

- ✔ If a man and a woman marry each other but later discover that they're actually half-brother and half-sister, they aren't validly married.

- ✔ If one or both spouses did not intend to enter a *permanent*, *faithful,* or *fruitful* union, then the marriage is invalid.

- ✔ If either partner is totally incapable of fulfilling the duties and obligations of marriage, or is grossly incompetent to appreciate and understand what those duties and obligations are, then the marriage is invalid.

A bride and groom must know, accept, and be willing to fulfill the obligations of marriage and intend to enter a permanent, faithful, and fruitful union in order for a valid marriage to exist. If a bride or groom intends to be unfaithful during the marriage, or if a bride or groom intends not to have children (as opposed to someone who physically, through no fault of his or her own, cannot reproduce), or if the bride or groom intends this to be a temporary relationship, then that person's consent is deficient, and it invalidates the marriage in the eyes of the Catholic Church.

Certain psychological conditions can sometimes be so serious and dangerous to the physical and emotional safety and well-being of the other spouse that they, too, can invalidate the consent despite all the good intentions. For example, if someone has had a mental illness that was not recognized or diagnosed until after the wedding, often several or more years into the marriage, and if that illness has been present from day one, then it invalidates the marriage.

Being out of communion with the Church

Pope John Paul II upheld the doctrine of the *indissolubility of marriage* (no divorce and remarriage) as well as the discipline of withholding Holy Communion and the other sacraments from Catholics who did divorce and remarry (and are invalidly married — in other words, married after a divorce, rather than an annulment).

The restriction that says priests must withhold the sacraments from those who've divorced and remarried is not meant to add insult to injury or pour salt in the wound, as some have claimed. A person must be *in* communion in order to *receive* Communion. Someone who doesn't accept Church teaching, who rejects certain doctrines, or who refuses to submit to the official authority of the pope and bishops is as much *not* in communion as is someone who's in an invalid marriage.

Pastorally, JP2 realized that a good number of Catholics entered their first marriages in good faith and with good intentions and, perhaps through no deliberate fault of their own, their marriages fell apart. Why and how the marriage ended may remove the blame from one or both parties, but it is in the deliberate choice and act of getting *remarried* where a person can get himself or herself into a sacramental quagmire, so to speak. Technically speaking, a divorced Catholic who never remarries is still allowed to receive Holy Communion as well as confession, Anointing of the Sick, and other sacraments. It's only when a divorced Catholic attempts a second civil marriage that the person places himself or herself in a predicament where he or she can't receive the sacraments (because the invalid marriage moves the person out of the state of being in communion with the Church and the Church's laws and teachings).

JP2 did extend a hand of compassion in 1997 when he addressed the Pontifical Council for the Family and said:

> . . . however, there are many appropriate pastoral ways to help these people. The Church sees their suffering and the serious difficulties in which they live, and in her motherly love is concerned for them as well as for the children of their previous marriage.

Divorced and remarried Catholics are not considered excommunicated, but they are unable to receive the sacraments. *Excommunication* is a penalty imposed on someone for committing a crime in canon law, such as having an abortion, desecrating Holy Communion, breaking the seal of confidentiality in the confession, physically attacking the pope, and so on.

Restricting Communion and the other sacraments is not so much a punishment as it is response to the disruption or lack of full communion. A non-Catholic baptized Christian is not allowed to receive Holy Communion in the Catholic Church, but this isn't a moral judgment on the character of the person — the Church isn't saying he's unworthy. Instead, it's a response to the fact that the person is not in full communion, which itself is a prerequisite to receive Communion.

One must be *in* communion in order to *receive* Communion. The public act of taking Communion is a sign that the person is in communion with all Church doctrine, discipline, and worship. Taking Communion when someone is not completely in communion of mind and heart would be disingenuous and a false message.

Divorced and remarried Catholics cannot be godparents for Baptism or sponsors for Confirmation, but they can and are encouraged to continue to come to Mass every Sunday and worship God. Although they cannot receive Holy Communion, they can still listen to the words of scripture being proclaimed and the homily preached afterward, join in the singing and responses, and make all the proper gestures, and the like. They can internally participate with their minds and hearts even though they cannot sacramentally participate.

The hope is that the awkward situation will encourage them to rectify the situation.

JP2 was very concerned about the children of broken marriages and consistently reminded parents that every child deserves both a mother and father who are simultaneously husband and wife to each other. The family and marriage are as intimately connected as are Holy Orders and the Holy Eucharist. Nevertheless, the human reality is that, often, people are left as victims (abandoned or abused spouses), and the Church never insists that people endanger themselves or their offspring. Not living as husband and wife because of such tragedies is not a sin — but deliberately attempting to enter a second and invalid marriage does injure the person's relationship to the Church and, thus, makes the person ineligible to receive the sacraments.

Counseling against artificial contraception

Just as Pope John Paul II maintained the official teaching on the permanence and indissolubility of marriage, he continued the ban on the use of artificial contraception. Even though many Catholics relate Pope Paul VI and his 1968 encyclical *Humanae Vitae* in which the ban on contraception is mentioned with the doctrine, the teaching is not new.

Since the time of Genesis (38:9), when Onan avoided impregnating his deceased brother's wife though he was duty-bound by Mosaic law, most religions frowned upon, forbade, or condemned artificial birth control until 1930. At that time, the Church of England (Anglican) had a bishops' conference in Lambeth, which publicly changed the prohibition for their members. The Lutheran, Methodist, and Presbyterian churches along with the Catholic Church, publicly rejected the Anglican decision. Gradually, however, the other denominations switched sides, and the advent of the birth control pill in 1960 changed things overnight.

By 1968, the Catholic Church was the only mainstream religion that opposed artificial birth control. Contrary to common myth, Catholicism never taught, required, or asked that married women have as many children as is medically possible. Although large families were always considered a blessing, no one was ever told to have as many children as she could produce — instead, it was left to the prudential judgment of the husband and wife as father and mother to decide for themselves how many children they believed they were able to have, raise, and support. *Natural Family Planning* (using knowledge of the physiological cycles of the woman to ascertain her natural times of fertility and infertility) has always been a component of Catholic teaching. As long as natural means are employed, parents can space the number and frequency of children, always being open to the possibility that God might have other plans and bless them with a child sooner than they originally planned.

Often confused with the unreliable *rhythm method* (predicting current fertility based on past cycles), Natural Family Planning (NFP) is much more scientific and reliable because it tracks a woman's current reproductive cycle. When used properly, it is 98 percent effective — equal to or greater than any artificial means. JP2 urged followers to use NFP, as opposed to chemical or mechanical contraceptives, because it involves both the husband and the wife. Both must cooperate and assist in the process, just as both must cooperate to make the marriage work. It involves short periods of monthly abstinence, which is another advantage for the marriage, because it reminds both husband and wife that some things and some people are worth a sacrifice and certainly worth enduring an inconvenience for.

Pope John Paul II's theology of the body is based on the same premise as Pope Paul's injunction on artificial contraception. The marital act of sexual intercourse is a sacred and holy thing only when performed within marriage and with the right intention. Husband and wife intimately and physically express their mutual love in the sex act as long as they both see it as a means to an end and not as an end itself. If they have sex just for the sake of having sex, then they're treating each other as sex objects. If they see sex as a symbol of their union and to promote love (unity) and life (procreation), then it is a blessing for both of them. The sexual pleasure they experience must be a by-product of their married love rather than something they think that they deserve and must have whenever they want it. Self-sacrificing love means that the individual spouse seeks to show love and affection and, hopefully, pleasure to and for the other. When a person is looking for self-gratification before mutual satisfaction, then it becomes a selfish act and not an act of love.

When John Paul II was Father Wojtyła the parish priest, he counseled newly married couples about Natural Family Planning and responsible parenthood. He wrote a book titled *Love and Responsibility,* which is about sexual ethics. Demands of the flesh are de facto ontological demands, because the object of sex acts is always the human person, not just the physical body. Sex acts must therefore always be worthy of the mystery and dignity of the human person as a person and not as a mere object of desire.

Finally, John Paul II often warned about the danger of many so-called pharmaceutical contraceptives actually working as an *abortifacient* (instead of preventing conception — fertilization of the egg by a sperm — some of these drugs induce an embryo to be ejected before implantation in the wall of the uterus), which is a physiological abortion caused by the medication.

Simplifying sex and reproduction

Because married sexuality is "for the other" and "for the couple," it is a mutual good. That is why *love* and *life* (*unity* and *procreation*) are in a sense married to each other as well. According to the Catholic Church, contraceptive sex is selfish because it divides the love and life and isolates the intimate, unitive aspect of marriage from the procreative aspects. Likewise, artificial conception (in vitro fertilization, embryo transfer, donor sperm or eggs, surrogate motherhood, and so on) is equally immoral because it also separates the procreative aspect from the unitive aspect of married intimacy.

Couples having trouble conceiving children or who may be infertile have a heavy cross to bear, and Pope John Paul II understood that as a parish priest, as a bishop, and as pope. He was not immune from compassion for these husbands and wives desperate to have a family and wanting to give birth to their own children. Yet, as in all moral matters, the ends never justify the means, and that fundamental principle of the Natural Moral Law was just as operative here as in all ethical questions.

In 1987, Cardinal Ratzinger (now Pope Benedict XVI) issued a letter titled *Donum Vitae* (Gift of Life), which was personally sanctioned by Pope John Paul II as official teaching. It best summarizes JP2's theology and the Church's position as well:

> Contraception deliberately deprives the conjugal act of its openness to procreation and in this way brings about a voluntary dissociation of the ends of marriage. Homologous artificial fertilization, in seeking a procreation which is not the fruit of a specific act of conjugal union, objectively effects an analogous separation between the goods and the meanings of marriage.

Besides the moral evil of destroying unwanted or "extra" embryos (which the Church considers to be a human person at the moment of conception) in the in vitro process, artificial conception and artificial contraception both have immoral means despite the good intentions and ends they achieve for well-meaning couples. John Paul II urged women to continue their unplanned or unwanted pregnancies, and if necessary put their children up for adoption, instead of aborting the children; adoption would prevent an evil act (killing the unborn) and would provide an infertile couple a viable alternative.

The Catholic Church is not opposed to medication that increases the probability of conception. As long as the fertility drug doesn't isolate and separate love (unitive) and life (procreative), the Church does not prohibit it. *Donum Vitae* (1987) from the Congregation for the Doctrine of the Faith said morally licit fertilization and conception are the result of a "conjugal act, which is per se suitable for the generation of children to which marriage is ordered by its nature and by which the spouses become one flesh." Fertility drugs *themselves* are not prohibited as long as the process or procedure does not involve the termination of any embryos.

Reiterating Church Doctrine

Not only was Pope John Paul II famous for maintaining the consistent moral teachings of the Catholic Church on controversial topics like abortion and contraception, he also staunchly defended the official theological doctrines of that religion. Just as no one expected Stephen Hawking to deny or contradict established laws of physics discovered by his predecessors (like Newton or Einstein), JP2 did not overturn defined doctrines of *his* predecessors, whether Paul VI, John XXIII, or Pius XII. Scientific theories (unlike laws) are open for modification, adaptation, or replacement; so, too, Church *discipline* (unlike doctrine) is subject to change and modification. At a 1987 meeting with U.S. bishops in Los Angeles, Pope John Paul II said it was a "'grave error' to think a person could dissent from Church teachings and remain a good Catholic."

Rejecting the ordination of women

Although the overwhelming majority of Protestant Christian churches now have many female ministers and pastors (and now even bishops), Catholicism and Orthodoxy do not and will not. John Paul II was not being "traditional" or "conservative" when he issued a papal declaration *Ordinatio Sacerdotalis* (On the Ordination of Priests) in 1994 stating that no pope could ordain women, now or ever:

> Wherefore, in order that all doubt may be removed regarding a matter of great importance, a matter which pertains to the Church's divine constitution itself, in virtue of my ministry of confirming the brethren I declare that the Church has no authority whatsoever to confer priestly ordination on women and that this judgment is to be definitively held by all the Church's faithful.

Then-Cardinal Ratzinger as Prefect of the Congregation for the Doctrine of the Faith immediately issued a statement saying the content of the declaration is considered infallible teaching — in other words, that no one could argue with what JP2 said.

JP2 not only said the question was not open for discussion or debate, but also closed it once and for all. He said that even the Church itself cannot change what is the substance of a sacrament because each one was instituted by Christ himself, and not by the Church. Sacraments are of divine origin, not human or ecclesiastical, even though the theological names and explanations come from the Church over the centuries.

Proponents of women's ordination see it as a matter of justice that both genders be allowed to serve God as ordained ministers. John Paul II did not look at it from a political or sociological perspective, but from a doctrinal/theological one. For example, Baptism requires the use of water, either by total immersion or *infusion* (pouring over the head). Even in case of necessity, nothing other than water can be used — otherwise it's an invalid sacrament. Similarly, only wheat bread and grape wine can be used for the Holy Eucharist. Rice cakes and grape juice are invalid matter and, if used, invalidate the sacrament. The Church has no authority whatsoever to change the substance of what is used and necessary for any of the seven sacraments, be it water for Baptism, olive oil for Confirmation and Anointing of the Sick, bread and wine for the Holy Eucharist, a man and a woman for Matrimony, or a baptized male for Holy Orders.

JP2 previously addressed the issue of women's ordination in his apostolic letter *Mulieris Dignitatem* (1988):

> In calling only men as his Apostles, Christ acted in a completely free and sovereign manner. In doing so, he exercised the same freedom with which, in all his behavior, he emphasized the dignity and the vocation of women, without conforming to the prevailing customs and to the traditions sanctioned by the legislation of the time.

According to Catholic theology, a vocation to Holy Orders (as a deacon, priest, or bishop) is not an innate right of every believer, the way Baptism, Penance, Confirmation, or Communion are. Scripture shows that Jesus only chose 12 men as his Apostles and 72 men as his disciples. Although some people believe that was merely custom, Christ was not constrained by custom when he spoke and interacted with gentiles, Samaritans, or women as evidenced in the Bible. He cured on the Sabbath, which was considered taboo by many of the Jewish religious leaders of that time. If Jesus was not afraid to break with those customs, John Paul II maintained, then it was not a respect for custom that prevented Jesus from calling women to be his Apostles.

Another fact is that the Virgin Mary, the mother of Jesus, was not chosen to be one of the 12, either by her son or by the Apostles after Judas hanged himself and they needed a replacement. Sacred Scripture and Sacred Tradition have no instance of any women being ordained or exercising priestly ministry in the Christian church during what is called the *apostolic era* (the time of the Apostles).

Pope John Paul II also described the ordained priest as the *alter Christus* (another Christ), terminology from the Council of Trent in the 16th century A.D. Using the analogy of St. Paul that Christ loves the Church as a groom loves his bride, Catholic Christianity has always referred to the Church as being the *Bride of Christ.* The priest, JP2 remarked in *Pastores Dabo Vobis* (1992), is the groom because he acts *in persona Christi* (in the person of Christ) as an *alter-Christus,* and the Church, the People of God, are the bride. A female priest could not "image" the groom, who is covenanted to *his* bride, the Church, because the Church does not recognize same-sex marriages.

The possibility and likelihood of ordaining women in the Catholic Church is the same as it is for the Eastern Orthodox Church: nil. Although women are excluded from Holy Orders, they are not excluded from the Church or its mission. Pope John Paul II issued the 1983 *Code of Canon Law,* which allows for women to be appointed as chancellors of the diocese, judges of tribunals, notaries, auditors, and defenders of the bond, as well as take on other roles; these positions are open to any qualified layperson, regardless of gender. Women can serve on parish councils and finance committees in parishes. JP2 even selected some women to represent the Holy See at international conferences.

Weighing in on married clergy

Celibate priesthood is not a *doctrine* but a *discipline* (which means it's current policy, but subject to change). And it's been a discipline since 1074 A.D. — it is, indeed, an ancient tradition. Even though celibacy is not doctrine, it can't be casually abandoned, either.

Pope John Paul II never made celibacy a doctrine, but he did continue the ancient discipline for the Latin (Western) Church. Many people ask, if celibacy is only a discipline (unlike the male priesthood, which is a doctrine), then why mandate celibacy when priestly vocations are on the decline? JP2 did not want to abandon an ancient discipline merely to increase numbers. Nor did he want to diminish the gift celibacy has been to the Catholic Church in the West. Even in Christian traditions, where ordained ministry is open to both men and women, married and single, there has been a statistical decline in vocations across the board — and not just among celibate male Catholics. A clergy shortage is evident among Evangelical Lutheran, United Methodist, and Presbyterian churches in the United States, so eliminating mandatory celibacy is not the answer some contend it would be.

Certainly, the greatest promotion for celibacy is Jesus himself, who despite the bizarre allegations of a secret romance/marriage with Mary Magdalene in some fiction writings, actually never married. Sacred Scripture, Sacred Tradition, and secular history verify his marital status: single. Yet, St. Peter, the first pope, was married — the Gospels speak of his "mother-in-law" and there's only one way to get one of those. Ironically, though, even when Simon Peter's mother-in-law is sick and then miraculously cured by Christ, no mention is ever made of her daughter, Peter's wife. Many historians speculate she was probably deceased, and Peter was a widower who inherited his wife's mother to care for in her old age. Who knows for sure?

Why celibacy, besides the tradition and pragmatic reasons (like having more time for the parish because there is no wife and family to care for)? Again, John Paul II, in *Pastores Dabo Vobis,* allegorizes the celibate priesthood as being married not to an individual flesh and human woman, but to the Church as a whole and the parish in particular. He asked celibate priests to love their parishioners as a husband would love his wife. Don't see or treat them as customers, clients, or stockholders. JP2 asked priests to love the members of the congregation and parish as a beloved spouse for whom they are willing to make sacrifices, seeking nothing in return.

Enforcing Discipline within the Clergy

As Supreme Pastor of the Church, the pope sometimes has to be the policeman who enforces discipline. John Paul II never seemed comfortable in that role, because his first experience as a young priest was to teach, and the job of governing went to those in authority, like the pastor or the bishop. As bishop and then as pope, he first tried the tactic of letting the logic of his argument convince the person who was being disobedient or dissident to see the error of his ways and voluntarily recant. Unfortunately, reason alone doesn't always work and the Church has some serious measures to remedy insubordinate rebels — such as censure, suspension, and the ultimate punishment, excommunication.

Chastising priests in politics

According to the canon law, *clerics* (deacons, priests, and bishops) "are not to have an active part in political parties and in governing labor unions unless, in the judgment of competent ecclesiastical authority, the protection of the rights of the Church or the promotion of the common good requires it." They "are forbidden to assume public offices which entail a participation in the exercise of civil power."

Pope John Paul II, following the canon law that he himself consolidated and spread (see Chapter 10), didn't want priests in politics, and he definitely didn't allow them to hold office in government. Nothing but trouble follows when church and state are blended together, especially whenever clergy hold public office. Jesus said: "No servant can serve two masters; for either he will hate the one and love the other, or else he will be devoted to one and despise the other" (Luke 16:13). JP2 strongly felt that priests would have divided loyalties if they held public office or got heavily involved in politics. The laity has the competence and right to run for and hold office and exercise political authority, whereas the clergy have the right to service and jurisdiction within the Church.

When visiting Managua, Nicaragua, in 1983, Pope John Paul II openly and demonstrably chastised Jesuit Father Ernesto Cardenal who at the time was Minister of Culture for the Marxist Sandinista government, and later was suspended for not complying with canon law. JP2 also ordered Representative Father Robert Drinan, a Jesuit priest and a Democratic congressman from Massachusetts, to give up his seat in 1980.

Reprimanding dissident theologians

The Catholic Church doesn't require people to suppress their ideas, feelings, and emotions. However, to be part of the Church, you must accept its teachings. The Church also holds its representatives to an even higher standard. Being a representative of the Church requires representing the true doctrines and teachings of the Church. If a priest doesn't follow the rules or doesn't teach the true teachings, the Church and the pope take steps to bring the priest back in line with the doctrine of the Church.

Pope John Paul II censured Father Hans Küng, of Switzerland, for rejecting papal infallibility, and Father Leonardo Boff, of Brazil, for promoting liberation theology. Father Charles Curran was forced out of Catholic University of America in 1986 for his dissident theology on contraception. And in 1990, JP2 issued *Ex Corde Ecclesiae,* which demands that every Catholic theologian receive a *manadtum* (license) from the local bishop, or resign his post just as a doctor who looses his or her license is no longer allowed to practice medicine.

Father Hans Küng of Switzerland

Father Hans Küng was a Swiss professor of Catholic theology at the University of Tübingen, Germany. He was outspoken as a dissident theologian, one who openly disagreed with and rejected certain teachings of the Catholic faith. Particularly, he could not accept the doctrine of papal infallibility as solemnly defined by the First Vatican Council in 1870.

The problem was that, not only did Father Küng publicly question the veracity of this dogma, but he was also certified as a Catholic theologian. His dissent had the same repercussions as would a modern, 21st-century professor of astrophysics in a prestigious university publicly declaring and teaching in his classroom that the world was flat and not round. Such a "scientist" would lose his credentials and, in essence, so did Hans Küng. JP2 had his license *(mandatum)* pulled in December 1979 for disputing papal infallibility.

Father Leonardo Boff of Brazil

Leonardo Boff was a Franciscan priest in Brazil who was the poster-child for *liberation theology* in South America (an attempt to morph Catholicism with Marxism, especially in a political manner). What got him into trouble was his insistence on morphing Marxism with Christianity. Specifically, Marxism advocated the use of violent revolution — albeit for lofty reasons, like the liberation of the poor and the powerless — and Boff would not reject that. The Soviet Union's Iron Curtain was erected through violent revolution, which claimed to seek the welfare of the poor and lower classes. Boff's book *Church: Charism and Power* rejects the doctrine that Christ intended to found an institutional church built on the hierarchy of the Apostles and their successors. Boff's theories (including his efforts to get women ordained) were declared to be antithetical to orthodox doctrine, so he was censured in 1985. In 1992, he voluntarily left the priesthood.

Father Charles Curran of Catholic University of America

Curran was a priest who taught moral theology at Catholic University of America in Washington, D.C. He was the first college professor to openly criticize and renounce the papal teaching of Pope Paul VI in the pope's encyclical *Humanae Vitae* (1968). Not only did Curran question, challenge, and finally reject magisterial teachings on abortion, euthanasia, homosexuality, premarital sex, and divorce and remarriage, he claimed the Church had no authority or right to interfere with his right to teach what his conscience believed.

Like Küng (see the earlier section), Curran was stripped of his license to teach as an official Catholic theologian. The Vatican never said he could not espouse his personal opinions, just that he could not do so and claim they were in conformity with authentic Church teaching. Curran's morality was so different from official Catholic teaching that JP2 instructed Catholic University to dissolve his contract as a professor. This consequence is no different than if Harvard Law School were to remove a faculty member who taught that the U.S. Constitution was an insignificant document and modern laws need not conform to it. Charles Curran is currently teaching in a Methodist school.

Excommunicating a bishop

Despite his reputation by some to be a "conservative," Pope John Paul II did excommunicate the ultraconservative Archbishop Marcel Lefebvre in 1988 when Lefebvre illicitly ordained and consecrated five bishops without prior papal approval. Lefebvre was a French bishop who balked at the Second Vatican Council and its changes to the Sacred Liturgy. He refused to celebrate the *Novus Ordo,* the new Mass of Paul VI in the vernacular language. Lefebvre insisted on celebrating the old Latin Tridentine Mass. He was suspended in 1976 when he disobeyed a Vatican order not to ordain any more priests for his Society of St. Pius X, which he formed in 1970 as a reaction to some of the illicit liturgical abuses committed in the aftermath of Vatican II.

Pope John Paul II tried to reconcile the archbishop, as well as the Society of St. Pius X, with the Church by allowing them to continue to celebrate the Latin Tridentine Mass as it was before the Second Vatican Council, as long as they publicly professed their allegiance to the pope and accepted the validity of the vernacular *Novus Ordo* Mass of Paul VI.

The reconciliation failed when on June 30, 1988, Lefebvre along with Bishop Antonio de Castro Mayer, bishop emeritus of Campos, Brazil, consecrated four priests as bishops. The very next day, they were all excommunicated as required by canon 1382 of the 1983 *Code of Canon Law:*

> Both the Bishop who, without a pontifical mandate, consecrates a person a Bishop, and the one who receives the consecration from him, incur a *latae sententiae* excommunication reserved to the Apostolic See.

On July 2, 1988, JP2 issued a papal letter titled *Ecclesia Dei,* which confirmed the excommunications and defined the state of schism to anyone who publicly supported the Society of St. Pius X. A pontifical commission, Ecclesia Dei, was also erected so that any priest or seminarian from the Society of St. Pius X could abandon his schism and come back into full communion with Rome while still being able to celebrate the Tridentine Mass.

Meeting New Challenges to the Faith

The 20th century saw unprecedented technological advancements. Our daily lives are vastly different from those of even two generations ago. But Natural Moral Law, Divine Law, the *Code of Canon Law,* the *Catechism of the Catholic Church,* and our sacred texts, including the Bible, are as relevant today, as they were when they were originally created. They give us a blueprint for handling all the situations that come along. With them, Catholics have a rulebook, so to speak, for how to handle all problems that they face and all situations that arise. It's within that context that John Paul II speaks on new challenges to the faith.

Believing in organ donation

John Paul II and his theology of the body had no problem whatsoever in organ transplantation or donation as long as the donor was not terminated to harvest the organ needed. Intentionally ending or terminating the life of a patient just to acquire the patient's heart, liver, or kidneys is gravely immoral. According to JP2, ordinary means (nutrition and hydration) and normal medical care must be given to all patients regardless of their age or medical condition — otherwise, it's no more than a form of euthanasia. But when done properly, after natural death, organ donation is "a genuine act of love" according to the late pontiff. The decision on who should get organs first can be based only on medical factors, not on any other criteria like gender, age, race, religion, or social or financial status.

Weighing in on stem-cell research

Pope John Paul II said in an address in 2000:

> I am thinking in particular of attempts at human cloning with a view to obtaining organs for transplants: These techniques, insofar as they involve the manipulation and destruction of human embryos, are not morally acceptable, even when their proposed goal is good in itself.

Cloning and embryonic stem-cell research are equally immoral, because they destroy human life at its most vulnerable stage. According to Catholicism, the human person exists from the moment of conception. Therefore, the experimentation and exploitation of human embryos is no different than trafficking in children or adults for similar purposes. Human beings, even at the embryonic stage, are not guinea pigs. Because the ends can never justify the means, no alleged hope of scientific and medical breakthroughs to combat deadly disease can ever excuse the willful destruction of human embryos.

Scientists have recently found more promise in using adult stem cells (which are obtained morally and can be morally used for research) than from the embryonic stem cells (which can only be obtained by killing innocent life).

Facing the U.S. clergy sex-abuse scandal

Some critics claim that JP2 did not speak out soon enough or loudly enough during the recent clergy sex-abuse scandal.

When the story broke in 2002, John Paul II's health was on the decline with Parkinson's disease. Until then, most of the details of how many priests and bishops and how many victims were involved were not known. Because each bishop runs his own diocese, the Vatican was unaware of which priests were involved, which ones were guilty, and which were merely transferred rather than removed from office. Likewise, some cardinals and bishops in the United States did not hide or withhold information from the Vatican as much as they ineptly handled it themselves while only reporting a minimum of details at sporadic intervals.

Canon law has always had procedures and penalties to identify and punish clerics guilty of moral misbehavior even though some bishops in the past made the horrible decision to merely transfer these "problem" priests instead. John Paul II was not negligent in his duties as Supreme Pastor of the Universal Church when it came to the heinous sex abuse of children and minors by Catholic clergy — he was simply unaware of how badly the tragedy had been handled in the past by individual bishops in their respective dioceses. The solution was not to create more and newer laws; rather, the solution was to fully, equitably, and fairly implement the laws that were already on the books.

Canon law has an entire *tribunal* (court) system to determine guilt or innocence and to determine appropriate penal *sanctions* (punishment). Like civil court, ecclesiastical court presumes innocence until the contrary is proven. Besides the evil of sexual abuse of children and minors, any and all acts of sexual misconduct and other immoral behavior (alcohol or drug abuses, gambling addiction, embezzlement, corruption, and the like), as well as deliberate acts of public disobedience to Church authority or public dissent from official doctrine, are liable to this process. Any member of the clergy has the right to due process to protect his good name and reputation — but he can also be investigated for any credible allegation as well.

Pope John Paul II was grieved and offended that members of the clergy — from priests to bishops — had abused children and minors. His heart went out to the victims. He convened a special meeting of all 13 cardinals from the United States in 2002 and sternly admonished the national hierarchy of the United States to get more involved with seminary formation. The corporate business model of administration, which had been informally assimilated by Church bureaucrats in the United States, did not accurately recognize nor readily respond to the crisis in the beginning. JP2 reminded all the bishops when they came for their *ad limina visit* (the mandatory trip a bishop must take to Rome every five years) to become more pastoral in getting to know their priests and people, their seminarians and seminaries. He also urged them to use their governing authority to discipline when needed. Credible allegations of abuse are now investigated by both church and state, and guilty clergy are properly punished and removed from any and all access to children.

Chapter 9

Defending a Civilization of Life versus a Culture of Death

Pope John Paul II was known not only for his numerous pastoral visits around the globe and the multitude of saints he canonized during his 26-year pontificate, but also for his very vocal, consistent, and uncompromising teaching and defending of the doctrines of the Catholic Church. As pope, he enjoyed the fullness of teaching authority (called the *Magisterium*) on matters of faith and morals as well as having the fullness of jurisdictional authority as Supreme Pastor.

In this chapter, we look at John Paul II's position on some of the controversial topics that have plagued humanity since its beginning, including abortion, euthanasia, capital punishment, and warfare. We explore his thoughts, his words, and his writings to understand how he addressed these topics and gave guidance to his flock and the rest of the world.

For more information on the official position of the Catholic Church, see *Catholicism For Dummies* (Wiley).

Abhorring Abortion

Catholic morality is based on the Divine Positive Law revealed in Sacred Scripture, namely, the Ten Commandments and the Gospel of Jesus Christ. And, maybe more importantly, it's based on the Natural Moral Law known by everyone regardless of religion, because it's learned by human reason. JP2 was particularly known for his adamant abhorrence and condemnation of any and all abortions.

Although the Bible does not explicitly mention it by name, abortion does fall under the umbrella of immoral killing, which is found in the commandment "Thou shall not kill" (Exodus 20:13 and Deuteronomy 5:17). In fact, the literal translation should be "Thou shall not *murder,*" because the words used in scripture are *ratsach* in Hebrew, *phoneuo* in Greek, or *occidere* in Latin, which specify a particular kind of killing, namely murder, which is unjust killing of an innocent life.

JP2's encyclical *Evangelium Vitae* (Gospel of Life) states in #57: "I confirm that the direct and voluntary killing of an innocent human being is always gravely immoral."

To read the full text of this powerful encyclical, take a look at the online version at the Vatican Web site (www.vatican.va/edocs/ENG0141/_INDEX.HTM).

Scripture does not single out abortion; it merely condemns all forms of unjust killing of innocent human life. But abortion is mentioned in other important documents:

- ✔ The first-century Christians spelled it out in the *Didache* (an ancient document believed by some to be the early teachings of the 12 Apostles to gentiles): "You shall not murder by abortion or infanticide."

- ✔ The ancient Hippocratic Oath taken by doctors and physicians for centuries since the fourth century B.C. included a prohibition in assisting or inducing euthanasia, suicide, or abortion.

- ✔ Holy Communion has been withheld from anyone who had an abortion since the fourth century with the Council of Eliberis (306 A.D.).

- ✔ The Sixth Ecumenical Council of Constantinople III (678 A.D.) explicitly condemned all abortions as murder.

- ✔ In 1588 A.D., Pope Sixtus V issued the bull *Effraenatam,* which imposed an excommunication for anyone who procured an abortion and that was reaffirmed by Pope Blessed Pius IX in *Apostolicae Sedis* (1869 A.D.) and finally codified in the 1917 *Code of Canon Law* (canon 1140).

- ✔ The Second Vatican Council taught in the Pastoral Constitution on the Church in the Modern World, *Gaudium et Spes,* #27: "whatever is opposed to life itself, such as any type of murder, genocide, abortion, euthanasia or willful self-destruction, . . . poison human society, but they do more harm to those who practice them than those who suffer from the injury. Moreover, they are supreme dishonor to the Creator." Vatican II went on to say in #51: "Therefore from the moment of its conception life must be guarded with the greatest care while abortion and infanticide are unspeakable crimes."

- ✔ The World Medical Association issued a Declaration of Geneva in September 1948: "I will maintain the utmost respect for human life, from the time of conception; even under threat I will not use my medical knowledge contrary to the laws of humanity."

> ✔ The International Code of Medical Ethics in October 1969 said, "A doctor must always bear in mind the importance of preserving human life from the time of conception until death."

> ✔ The World Medical Association reaffirmed its position by way of the Declaration of Oslo (1970): "The first moral imposed upon the doctor is respect for human life as expressed in the Declaration of Geneva: 'I will maintain the utmost respect for human life from the first moment of conception.'"

These positions laid the groundwork for Pope John Paul II's beliefs well before he was pope. Having grown up Catholic and having been trained as a priest and served as a bishop before being made cardinal and eventually elected pope, he knew no other perspective. Abortion was wrong, immoral, sinful, and evil. He could and did have compassion and mercy on the women who were deceived into thinking certain circumstances and situations could make exceptions to the ban. But the ends can never justify the means, so JP2 saw no instance where any abortion would be permitted.

This position did not mean he had no sympathy for women who had been raped or whose lives may have been endangered by their pregnancy. John Paul II saw that only an absolute adherence to the principle that evil can never be directly intended or committed no matter what good comes from it (Romans 3:8) can protect the integrity of every man, woman, and child. Here is JP2 in his own words, from *Evangelium Vitae* #99, addressed to women who have had abortions:

> I would now like to say a special word to women who have had an abortion. The Church is aware of the many factors which may have influenced your decision, and she does not doubt that in many cases it was a painful and even shattering decision. The wound in your heart may not yet have healed. Certainly what happened was and remains terribly wrong. But do not give in to discouragement and do not lose hope. Try rather to understand what happened and face it honestly. If you have not already done so, give yourselves over with humility and trust to repentance.

In the following sections, we clarify JP2's position and explain the impact he had on the abortion movement worldwide.

Identifying his position

Pope Paul VI issued his famous encyclical *Humanae Vitae* in 1968. In it, he explicitly stated that "directly willed and procured abortion, even if for therapeutic reasons, are to be absolutely excluded as licit means of regulating birth." This statement was simply a continuation of what the Catholic Church had taught before. It was Pope John Paul II, however, who put the issue in a modern context. This point of view (that abortion can never be used as a means of birth control) was not merely a difference of opinion between pro-choice/

pro-abortion advocates and pro-life/anti-abortion proponents. JP2 extended the debate from a political and moral realm into a cultural one.

JP2 coined the phrase *culture of death* during his pastoral visit to the United States in 1993 during World Youth Day. Two years later, he elaborated on the battle between the "culture of death" and the Gospel of Life. Because every human being is a person, each person is endowed with inalienable rights, and the primary right is the right to life. Constitutions can and ought to recognize and defend these rights, but they do not *create* or *give* them, because the rights come from human nature itself, which according to the believer, is created in the image and likeness of God.

A culture of death involves a "conspiracy against life," according to JP2. It is waged against the most innocent and defenseless, from the unborn child in the womb to the terminally ill to the very old. Human life is precious at each and every stage of development, because it always remains human, from conception to natural death. A human embryo or fetus has human DNA and is uniquely different from the human father or mother so that it can be classified as another human being. That DNA does not change as the person grows and develops — instead, it is precisely because of the human DNA at conception that the embryo will not become a chicken, a dog, or a cat. Human DNA directs the process of growth so that a human being is alive and growing before being born and afterward as well. The DNA is not the mother's but is distinct from hers — two separate lives within one body, so to speak, for at least nine months, that is.

Pope John Paul II asked the young people at World Youth Day in Denver to "celebrate life" and to defend it. Not only are the unborn in jeopardy by the "culture of death," but so, too, are the disabled, the poor, the homeless, the unemployed, the immigrant, and the refugee. Anyone not strong enough or powerful enough to defend himself is at risk. A society that evaluates a person's worth based on what he produces rather than on what he *is* (a human being) can easily discredit and discount those who are vulnerable or weak, those who have special needs, or those who have no economic or political clout.

In *Evangelium Vitae* #58, John Paul II wrote:

> Among all the crimes which can be committed against life, procured abortion has characteristics making it particularly serious and deplorable. The Second Vatican Council defines abortion, together with infanticide, as an "unspeakable crime". . . . The moral gravity of procured abortion is apparent in all its truth if we recognize that we are dealing with murder and, in particular, when we consider the specific elements involved. The one eliminated is a human being at the very beginning of life. No one more absolutely innocent could be imagined.

Although strongly denouncing all abortion as the murder of innocent life, JP2 also acknowledged that abortion is often tragic and painful for the mother — so abortion has two victims. He even recognized that many women make the decision to abort their unborn children for purely selfish reasons or mere convenience. John Paul II did not demonize every woman who had an abortion, because some of them did it out of misguided and distorted compassion (for example, the baby would be born into poverty, with a terrible disease or disability, or into an unhealthy family situation). Despite the painful circumstances some women find themselves in when pregnant, JP2 firmly and staunchly held to a prime directive of the Natural Moral Law: "The ends never justify the means." In other words, you can never intentionally commit an evil no matter what or how much good may come from it. There is no justification for the deliberate killing of an innocent human being.

An unwanted or unplanned pregnancy may not be the result of a selfish desire to avoid the inconvenience of labor and delivery nor even avoidance of having to act and live as a responsible parent for the first time. A mother may feel serious economic, emotional, psychological, or physiological pressures that may make the abortion seem inevitable or at least palatable, but abortion is still the intentional taking of an innocent life.

John Paul II urged society, governments, churches, and individuals to aggressively find and promote viable alternatives to abortion, like adoption or crisis pregnancy assistance. Getting employment, housing, education, and security for mothers and fathers who may be tempted to abort their unborn children may add to the stability and health of the couple. Eliminating the temptations to consider abortion as a possible solution or option was JP2's goal, as well as raising the standard of living, securing economic and political sovereignty, and eroding the wall of hatred and prejudice. At the same time, he vigorously spoke out on behalf of those who had no voice, the unborn, the most innocent and most vulnerable victims of this controversy.

Unlike the U.S. Supreme Court in *Roe v. Wade* (1973), which legalized abortion and made it a "privacy issue," Pope John Paul II never saw the issue as a "right to choose." Being "pro-choice" is not always a good thing because, according to the Natural Moral Law, human beings are free to do what we *ought* to do, not whatever we *want* or *choose* to do. Criminals make a choice to kill or steal, yet society does not protect their decision from the consequences of their actions. "Freedom of choice" is not a metaphysical priority — we don't choose our parents, our genes, our DNA, our IQ, or most of what happens to us, when, and how. Because we have free will, however, we can knowingly, intentionally, deliberately, and freely do something. As JP2 stated in the *Catechism* #1750, the *object* chosen, the end in view or the *intention,* and the *circumstances* of the action all determine the morality of an act — either good or evil. All three must be operative — one or two are insufficient.

Understanding his impact

John Paul II attracted many young men and women into vocations as priests and nuns and as faithful, loyal Catholic laity — more than any other pope in history. His influence on them is tremendous in that they share his deep passion for human rights, staunchly pro-life and pro-family. This devout generation (sometimes called Generation Y) is the offspring of the lost generations (sometimes called Generation X and the Baby Boomers). Whereas the children of the Depression, World War II, and the Korean War remember long lines every Saturday afternoon for confessions and large numbers of regular Mass attendees every Sunday, their Cold War and Vietnam War–era children (also known as post–Vatican II) had a totally different experience.

The sexual and gender revolution, birth control pills, burning of draft cards, and Watergate all contributed to the upheaval that accompanied a dramatic decrease in Mass attendance, increase of divorce and remarriage, fewer religious vocations, and a dearth of doctrinal knowledge. Inadequate catechetical materials produced religions books with plenty of secular symbolism (butterflies and balloons) and little theological substance. Children in parochial schools or in *CCD* (religion classes held once a week for public-school children) did not learn their faith as well as did their parents before them.

People born between 1950 and 1980 witnessed the legalization of abortion. Although the civil rights movement showed the need and success of opposing unjust and immoral laws, a reluctance grew to fight city hall, so to speak, when it came to overturning a Supreme Court decision like *Roe v. Wade,* which legalized abortion. Not all Catholics jumped on the bandwagon (to politically oppose abortion and oppose politicians who support it) — but enough did, especially those in politics, law, academia, and medicine.

John Paul II was elected in 1978 and by the mid-1980s, he inspired a new generation to aspire to get things changed. Under his papacy, larger crowds attended the annual Right to Life Rally and March, many of them young and old (with a significant section of middle-agers conspicuously absent). The pro-life effort strengthened dramatically under JP2. Yet, when a few militant fanatics crossed the line from legal protest and minor civil disobedience into the realm of violence against abortion clinics and those who staffed them, John Paul II denounced such atrocities, saying, "Violence and religion can never go together."

Consistency was John Paul II's legacy even if some on the far left or far right disagreed. The same absolute adherence to the Natural Moral Law that the ends never justify the means, was translated into a refusal and rejection of violent response to doctors who perform abortions or politicians. Bombings and shootings were not justified, no matter how many innocent children were being killed by abortion. JP2 never advocated violence during the struggle between Solidarity and the Soviet-controlled Communist regime in Poland. Likewise, he disavowed violence directed toward those who supported abortion. Yet, he challenged Catholic voters to urge their elected leaders to protect and defend the unborn. He did not shy away from denouncing abortion in his public speeches, even when being welcomed by presidents, congressmen, or governors who openly proclaimed themselves to be pro-choice/pro-abortion.

Insisting Against Euthanasia

From conception to natural death by old age, JP2 saw both the unborn and the aged infirm as being the most defenseless. Whether the issue concerned the beginning of life or the end of life, John Paul II was adamant about seeing dignity in all human beings, all over the world. Euthanasia was as evil as abortion because it involved the unjust taking of innocent life.

Identifying his position

The same document that succinctly delineates his vigorous opposition to abortion *(Evangelium Vitae)* also rejects euthanasia. In *Evangelium Vitae* #15, he wrote:

> Euthanasia is sometimes justified by the utilitarian motive of avoiding costs which bring no return and which weigh heavily on society. Thus it is proposed to eliminate malformed babies, the severely handicapped, the disabled, the elderly, especially when they are not self-sufficient, and the terminally ill.

Pope John Paul II also denounced the practice of prematurely harvesting body parts for organ transplantation before natural death has occurred. Equally reprehensible, according to JP2, is the practice of advocating euthanasia not so much to alleviate the pain and suffering of the patient, but as a response to insurance company directives or to an inability to pay hospital bills. Economic and financial concerns should never affect the administration of normal care and ordinary means of treatment to a dying or seriously ill patient. Only experimental, extraordinary, and unreliable treatment should be evaluated on cost ratio.

After Parkinson's disease ravaged his body, JP2 did not eliminate his public appearances. He allowed the world and especially the Church around the world to see his health deteriorate. Suggestions and hints of retirement and resignation abounded, but the Polish pope would have none of it. Earlier in his papacy, while in robust health, he hiked, swam, and kept an active schedule. Later, when old age and illness weakened him, he nonetheless wanted his people to see him hunched over to one side, slurring his words occasionally, and even drooling from time to time. Why? To remove the social stigma attached to many disabilities, especially the late stages of terminal conditions. He wanted those who were battling the final phases of muscular dystrophy, multiple sclerosis, Parkinson's, Alzheimer's, and the like, to know that they need not be confined inside and out of sight just because their physical appearance may be unsettling to those who are physically more healthy.

Ironically, a year before his own death, John Paul II issued a papal directive on euthanasia while speaking to the International Congress sponsored by the World Federation of Catholic Medical Associations and the Pontifical Academy of Life in March 2004. He denounced terms like *vegetable* to describe disabled persons, because the terms are degrading and dehumanizing. Arguments based on the "quality of life" should never be dictated by "psychological, social, and economic pressures."

JP2 went so far as to state that every sick person, whether terminally ill or otherwise, is entitled out of justice to "normal care" like pain medication (as long as the dosage itself is not the direct cause of death), "nutrition [food], hydration [water], cleanliness, and warmth." The withdrawal or withholding of a feeding tube while life is still viable (the body is still able to digest the food and drink) is morally forbidden and is gravely evil. He said, "In particular, I want to emphasize that the administration of water and food . . . always represents a natural means of preservation of life, not a medical treatment." He continued, "Its employment is therefore to be considered, in principle, proportionate and ordinary, and as such morally obligatory."

One year later, Terri Schiavo, a Florida woman and a victim of brain damage, was starved to death when the feeding tube was removed by court order and all food (nutrition) and water (hydration) were withheld. Her husband and others contended that she was in a persistent vegetative state and, therefore, should be able to die with dignity. JP2 never denied that all human beings should be able to die with dignity because dignity comes from being a person. The Natural Moral Law is what restricts human actions, however. Making someone comfortable with pain medication is always permitted as long as the dosage or the medication itself does not directly cause death. Similarly, extraordinary means and heroic measures can be refused by patients and family members if the person is in the dying process or has a terminal illness. Ordinary means, however, like nutrition and hydration, must be given unless the body is incapable, as is the case when a person's stomach stops working — placing a feeding tube into a nonworking stomach is redundant and unnecessary.

Allowing people to die is different from being the cause of their death. But both can be wrong:

- *Passive euthanasia* is when necessary treatment is withheld and the person dies as a result. Specifically, any life-saving medical procedure that is considered ordinary means that is deliberately not done so as to intentionally cause death is passive euthanasia.

- *Active euthanasia* is when a procedure or medication is given that directly causes death, like an overdose of painkillers.

Natural Moral Law forbids both active and passive euthanasia. Only experimental treatment, unreliable treatment, or treatment that is more painful than the illness or injury are considered extraordinary. Allowing the dying process to take its natural course while administering ordinary means and normal care has been part of Christian health practice. Pope John Paul II's closing remarks to doctors, surgeons, and physicians is noteworthy:

> I exhort you, as men and women of science, responsible for the dignity of the medical profession, to guard jealously the principle according to which the true task of medicine is: to cure if possible, always to care.

Understanding his impact

The Catholic Bishops of Pennsylvania issued moral norms for the care of the terminally ill and dying, which fully reflect the papal decree of JP2, insisting that all normal care and ordinary means, including nutrition and hydration, must always be given. (The Pennsylvania bishops were the first to issue this statement, but it applies everywhere.) Catholic hospitals and nursing homes will now have to reflect these refinements (previously, some institutions held to the policy of withholding or withdrawing the feeding tube from persons in a persistent vegetative state). The Catholic Church does not consider physician-assisted suicide "mercy killing." No one may willingly and knowingly assist anyone in taking his or her own life. Doctors are obligated to give normal care and use ordinary means to alleviate as much pain as possible without that treatment being the direct cause of death.

JP2 endured his Parkinson's disease for many years and had an emergency tracheotomy done before a feeding tube was given to him in his final days and weeks on Earth. He showed that *when* we die and *how* we die are irrelevant to our human dignity, which is an intrinsic part of who we are as human beings. The real question for the believer is, "Where am I going to go after I die?" That question is easily answered by the answer to the question, "How well did I live my life?" The manner of death or the lifespan of a person have no bearing on their destiny. What kind of life have we lived — one of goodness, mercy, justice, love, and forgiveness to others *or* one of selfishness, greed, hatred, immorality, and revenge? A life devoted to the love of God and the love of neighbor as expressed in thoughts, words, and deeds — that is what mattered more to John Paul II than whether you or I die by disease, accident, disaster, terrorism, or just old age.

Seeing No Reason for Capital Punishment

JP2 made a key distinction, unlike some others, between taking innocent life (abortion and euthanasia) and capital punishment (also known as the death penalty). In the case of abortion and euthanasia, an innocent victim has his life taken from him. In the case of capital punishment, it is the perpetrator himself who is being punished for a crime that a judge or jury has determined that he is guilty of committing. John Paul II affirmed the ancient tradition of Christianity that recognized that the secular state had the right to execute certain prisoners. But JP2 refined the parameters of that right, which was historically never absolute or arbitrary in theory (though many tyrants acted to the contrary).

Identifying his position

In his monumental encyclical *Evangelium Vitae,* Pope John Paul II clearly and succinctly taught his position on the death penalty. Unlike abortion and euthanasia, which are intrinsically evil, sinful, and immoral and can never be justified, capital punishment is *theoretically* permissible, but *practically* unenforceable because modern society has developed means of incarceration that render the imminent threat to others negligible.

It's an *absolute* right that every innocent human life is inviolable, but the state's right to execute dangerous prisoners is *not* absolute. Executing dangerous prisoners is a last resort, to be used only when the person poses an imminent threat to others, perhaps even to fellow inmates, and only when there are no other means to protect society. Mere deterrence isn't enough of a reason for the death penalty — the very existence of a death penalty does not deter criminals from committing crimes that warrant capital punishment.

The *Catechism* (#2267) and *Evangelium Vitae* (both from Pope John Paul II) clearly teach the following:

> . . . if bloodless means are sufficient to defend human lives against an aggressor and to protect public order and the safety of persons, public

authority must limit itself to such means, because they better correspond to the concrete conditions of the common good and are more in conformity to the dignity of the human person.

At the same time, both documents also reaffirm that public authority may impose the death penalty but it is rarely, if ever, obligated to do so. Because the death penalty is not an absolute right, there are definite restrictions and moral parameters the state must comply with — or else risk committing another evil.

Capital punishment is morally permissible only when *all* these conditions are met:

✔ It is absolutely necessary to protect the common good of all or most citizens.

✔ No reasonable hope exists that prison will achieve the same goal.

✔ There is incontrovertible evidence (more than circumstantial) and proof of guilt.

✔ The criminal acted in deliberate and calculating intent to commit the crime (premeditation by a sane person).

✔ The crime committed was heinous and violent enough to warrant serious and strong deterrence from others doing the same.

✔ The penalty of execution is applied equally, fairly, and uniformly across the board regardless of race, class, or geographic location.

What JP2 found to be unjust was that only certain countries (76) still imposed the death penalty while 86 nations ended it decades ago. That would mean the country where the murder took place is more important than who did it, to whom, why, and how. Justice demands that punishment be fairly applied regardless of location. Even within the United States, which still has capital punishment, 38 states have the death penalty, and 12 (plus the District of Columbia) do not — so again, it appears that where the murder took place is more important than who was killed or in what manner. A further inequity besides location is the disparity between rich and poor. Wealthy defendants can afford expensive lawyers to make appeals and suppress evidence, while poor people have public defenders assigned to them.

Today, because there are means such as life imprisonment without parole, high-security correctional facilities, and high-tech surveillance and monitoring of released prisoners, Pope John Paul II concluded that, despite the very limited right of the state to execute certain prisoners, "the cases in which the execution of the offender is an absolute necessity are very rare, if not practically nonexistent."

Understanding his impact

The move to ban all public executions and to end the death penalty, especially by civilized nations, picked up momentum with Pope John Paul II's condemnation of capital punishment in general. Because it's not an absolute ban (as it is with abortion and euthanasia), theoretically, a nation could impose this last resort if done properly, equitably, humanely, and without unnecessary delays (years on end), particularly if it involved fanatical terrorists or serial killers who vowed to kill again if they were ever released or ever escaped.

On one occasion (January 1999, during a pastoral visit to the United States), Pope John Paul II successfully convinced a governor (Mel Carnahan of Missouri) to commute the death sentence of a convicted murderer, Darrell J. Mease, and reduce it to life imprisonment without parole.

Hating War

John Paul II did not deny the possibility of a just war — the doctrine has been part of Catholic morality since the time of St. Augustine all the way to Vatican II and the *Catechism of the Catholic Church*. JP2's opposition to recent acts of war or military campaigns or particular applications of military engagements are prudential decisions and not generic principles.

In other words, JP2 did not condemn each and every act of warfare because, unlike abortion and euthanasia, the direct object or goal is not the unjust killing of innocent lives. Like the death penalty, which is directed at the unjust aggressor, war is aimed at the hostile enemy who wants to inflict pain, misery, and death upon the citizens of a sovereign nation.

Identifying his position

The Just War Doctrine as taught by the Catholic Church from the time of St. Augustine through St. Thomas Aquinas to Pope John Paul II clearly states the position JP2 supported.

According to the Just War Doctrine, before going to war, a leader must ensure that the following conditions (the so called *ius ad bello* conditions) are met:

- **Just cause:** There are reasons for going to war.
- **Competent authority:** The war is authorized by legal rulers.
- **Right intention:** The hoped outcome of the war is a good one.

✔ **Probability of success:** The war is winnable.

✔ **Proportionality:** More evil, pain, suffering, and death will be prevented by going to war than would occur if the war did not take place.

✔ **Last resort:** All other options (diplomatic, economic, and so on) have failed.

During a war, a leader must ensure these doctrines are followed:

✔ **Proper means:** Strategic weapons and tactics are used to reduce collateral damage; only the minimum use of deadly force necessary is used.

✔ **Discrimination of noncombatants:** Only military targets are fired at.

If all these criteria are fulfilled before war is declared and while war is being waged, then it is considered a just war. Obviously, abuses can occur at any point and must be dealt with individually.

In Iraq, John Paul II did not believe all viable alternatives had been explored or employed, so he questioned whether the Gulf War of 1991 and the Iraq War of 2003 had exhausted all diplomatic or economic solutions before resorting to military action. Without knowing exactly, precisely, and completely all the intelligence being given to the president of the United States at the time, not even Pope John Paul II could have metaphysical or even moral certitude that there was not a just cause or that this was not the last resort. There may have been secret negotiations that were not successful but that showed that no more diplomatic avenues existed. There may have been classified reports about imminent and highly probable activity by Saddam Hussein not known by the Vatican.

Unlike the bombing of Pearl Harbor in 1941, which was a public act of war by the Japanese Empire on the United States, in both the Gulf War and the Iraqi War, there was public information and there was classified information. Although the only nation attacked was Kuwait in the Gulf War and only Iraq was hit with a first strike in the following war, the ambiguities today of modern, high-tech intelligence and the interpretation of it, makes modern warfare much more complicated.

In the case of Iraq, here are just a few of the complicated issues:

✔ Did weapons of mass destruction (WMDs) exist?

✔ Did more than one sovereign nation have the serious, credible belief that Iraq did, in fact, possess WMDs and was prepared to use or sell them to terrorist groups like Al Qaeda?

The reasons for going to war must be morally acceptable and, therefore, must involve repelling or resisting an unjust aggressor or preventing an otherwise imminent, serious, and deadly attack from the same. Fear and suspicion are not enough.

During the Gulf War and the Iraqi War, JP2 was not kept in the loop as he was in the past. During the two terms of President Reagan, an informal relationship (as well as formal diplomatic ones) developed between the Vatican and the White House vis-à-vis the intentions and activities of the Soviet Union. Both Reagan and JP2 were committed to breaking the tyranny that atheistic Communism had forced upon Eastern Europe after World War II. Although there is no solid evidence that Pope John Paul II and President Ronald Reagan personally spoke or even coordinated efforts, ideologically they were on the same page when it came to opposing the unjust occupation and control of the nations engulfed by the Iron Curtain. Their subordinates knew this and worked together only in terms of sharing pertinent information that each side was able to acquire. This arrangement between the president and the Vatican ended when the first George Bush became president, and it has never repeated itself.

Before engaging in war, if facts were not verified, testimony not corroborated, or evidence not substantiated, then the decision to go to war was unjust. If every reasonable and probable alternative had been exhausted or proven useless and the perceived imminent threat was grave enough, some would conclude that to be just cause. Others claim that preemptive or preventive strikes are immoral, because the enemy has not yet committed a violent attack. Still others contend it's immoral to allow a known enemy to launch an unjust attack if it could have been prevented.

The Just War Doctrine is clear enough on its principles, but determining whether each and every condition has been met sadly has to wait for the judgment of history when (we can only hope) all the facts, as they really were and as they were perceived to be, come to light. While in wartime, classified information and national security often prevent non-decision-makers from knowing what the leaders know (or at least have been led to believe).

JP2 never formally declared either the Gulf War or the Iraqi War to be an unjust or immoral war. He did oppose both wars and, from the information he had and knew, he felt the world was too hasty in resorting to military and deadly force instead of trying every plausible alternative. Although he was not a pacifist, John Paul II wasn't a war hawk either. He did not take sides in either war.

What some of JP2's critics do not realize is that even just wars can sometimes be avoided or prevented with better results as long as someone keeps trying to use every possible, reasonable, and plausible alternative. That also does not mean that just wars are not sometimes premature or that they may begin with just cause, motive, and intention but could deteriorate into unjust means being used after war has begun. The fact that JP2 tried to avert any particular war shouldn't be misinterpreted as his having judged the entire war as being unjust or immoral. His role as pope was to do as much as and whatever he could to prevent unnecessary and/or unjust wars and to make sure viable options before war were seriously considered and attempted — even though he had no way to enforce or implement this job.

The prudential judgment as to whether or not to go to war rests with the legitimate authority, the lawful leaders of government. Yet, all citizens as individuals and the pope as a world leader and icon of peace never lose their obligation to inquire before and after a war whether it was done justly, properly, prudently, and necessarily.

Pope John Paul II never denied the right of the state to wage war — but like the death penalty, war is not an absolute right. It must be a last resort and all the consequences of going to war and the aftermath of war as well as the consequences of not going to war need to be weighed and examined carefully, thoughtfully, and objectively because innocent lives will unintentionally but inevitably be lost in any war.

Understanding his impact

Opponents and protesters of both the Gulf War and the Iraqi War saw Pope John Paul II as a visible and vocal ally in this one specific area. Because he was not a pacifist, he did not oppose each and every war, but he admitted that there were times when war was inevitable — as a last resort — and hopefully would be waged in a moral fashion. Unlike abortion and euthanasia, where there can be no compromise because they involve the unjust deaths of innocent people, JP2 realized that there could be room for valid difference of professional opinion on the particulars of war, like the strategic and tactical use of some weapons in addition to the planning, deployment of troops, and timetable used.

Vatican City is a neutral country — it enters into no war treaty with any nation. The pope is the head of state and as such can send ambassadors to some countries that the United States, Canada, and Great Britain are unable or unwilling to establish relations with. As a religious and spiritual leader, John Paul II was able to persuade many followers who were able to influence world leaders themselves. Public pressure to postpone, avoid, or end an unpopular war has been known to be somewhat effective. If nothing else, JP2 gave world leaders and the world itself a moral compass to look to even if they willingly chose to ignore the direction in which they were headed.

Part III
Putting His Unique Stamp on the Papacy

The 5th Wave   By Rich Tennant

"Oh, he's the 'people's Pope' all right. It's just that when there's a good soccer game on the big screen he sort of becomes the 'pretzels and popcorn Pope'."

In this part . . .

We highlight the unique personal stamp John Paul II put on the papacy. This part looks at his innovations, adaptations, and changes to the style and the direction that the papacy and the Vatican would take as it left the 20th century and entered the third millennium. We will see the global, universal and "catholic" perspective and experience of the John Paul II papacy.

Chapter 10

Keeping Up to Date: Moving the Catholic Church into the Modern Era

*P*ope John Paul II was known by everyone — Catholic and non-Catholic alike — to be a faithful son of the Church. He staunchly defended, upheld, and maintained the moral and doctrinal teachings of his religion, without compromise, apology, or hesitation. His liberal critics may have labeled him conservative for this, but he himself would have preferred the term *orthodox* (from the Greek *orthodoxos* meaning "correct teaching"), because JP2 did not consider himself either liberal or conservative.

Although some of his detractors thought JP2 was too traditional in discipline and exercise of authority, others thought he was too progressive in his social teachings on war, capital punishment, and economics. Regardless, John Paul II cannot be pigeonholed by political or cultural adjectives. He sought to preserve the best of the past and to take advantage of the best of the present while having hope for the future.

In this chapter, we look at some of the best examples of Pope John Paul II's philosophy, as well as the major accomplishments he made in regards to internal reform of the Church. In addition to his highly visible successes like World Youth Day, JP2 also left the Catholic Church two invaluable legacies: the *Code of Canon Law* and the *Catechism of the Catholic Church.* Together with the reforms he made in the Roman Curia, they can be considered the estate he entrusted to his faithful bride, the Church herself.

Understanding the Pope as Lawmaker, Teacher, and Judge

One of the oldest symbols of the pope and the papacy is the triple tiara, or the three-level crown. The coronation of a king usually involved a single crown; the emperor was given a double crown (as a symbol of the emperor's fuller authority over all kings in his empire). The pope alone was crowned with the triple crown, to symbolize his threefold authority as priest, prophet, and king based on his role as the Vicar of Christ on Earth.

Priests offer sacrifice and sanctify or bless; prophets teach and preach; kings govern and rule. Catholic Christians believe the pope (who is always simultaneously the Bishop of Rome) has the threefold mission to sanctify, teach, and govern the Universal Church. He also has the fullness of authority in the executive, legislative, and judicial realms of the Church.

Making the law

As Supreme Lawmaker, any pope can make new laws and abolish or amend old laws. The pope has the final word in interpreting laws as well. His legal authority, however, is limited to man-made (human) legislation. So the pope has no authority to change, modify, or repeal any of the Ten Commandments or any divine command found in Sacred Scripture or Sacred Tradition — because those come from God. The pope can only make ecclesiastical laws that apply to the Church and to members of the Church.

The pope does not interfere with *civic laws* (international, national, federal, state, municipal, or local) unless they conflict with or contradict the laws of God or impede the religious rights and liberties of the Church. Papal laws or Vatican regulations are not the only aspect of Church law, however, because local bishops shepherd their dioceses with local ecclesiastical law. Bishops have jurisdiction, though, only in their own diocese and only over their own clergy — whereas the pope has universal jurisdiction all over the world. He appoints and can remove bishops anywhere in the world and not just in the diocese of Rome.

Teaching the flock

As Supreme Teacher, the pope enjoys the *charism* (gift of the Holy Spirit) of *papal infallibility,* which means that, when the pope teaches a particular doctrine to the Universal Church on a matter of faith and morals, he is protected from imposing a false or erroneous teaching (theologically called a *heresy*) on the faithful.

The pope's personal opinions or beliefs in theology, philosophy, science, history, art, politics, or economics are not part of papal infallibility. His private thoughts and opinions are like everyone else's. Only when he formally teaches a specific matter on faith and morals and intends it for and addresses it to the Church around the world does he enjoy infallibility. He can still make math mistakes, pick the wrong team to win the World Series or the World Cup, commit a personal sin (the inability to sin is called *impeccability,* and no pope has never had or claimed to have had this), or make bad decisions.

Only the Bible has *inerrancy* (the lack of any errors whatsoever). The pope is infallible only on matters of faith and morals and when he speaks officially to the Universal Church.

Acting as judge

Not only is the pope the chief teacher and lawmaker, but he is also the chief justice as well. This means he is the Supreme Judge and, therefore, any Catholic has the right to appeal to the pope to hear her case if she feels a lower ecclesiastical court has not given her satisfactory justice. Often throughout history, popes have been approached to settle disputes between religious orders or between bishops/dioceses or between Christian monarchs because there was no higher court or authority in Catholicism.

Revising the Code of Canon Law (1983)

Canon law is another term for Church or ecclesiastical law. The word *canon* comes from the Greek word *kanon,* which is a "measuring reed." When used to describe a body of laws and procedures for adjudication, *canon law* refers specifically to the regulations applying to all the Catholic faithful, both clergy and laity alike, all over the world. Unlike *Divine Positive Law* (commands directly from God as found in divine revelation) and *Natural Moral Law* (ethical mandates known by anyone and everyone who is rational), canon law is considered "human law" just as is civil law in secular society. As such, canon law can and has changed over the centuries, while Divine Positive Law and Natural Moral Law are eternally the same and binding at all times on all people. Before JP2, the last time the entire *Code of Canon Law* had been revamped was in 1917 — so by 1983, it was necessary to overhaul the system once again.

Creating the body of canon law

Gradually throughout the early history of the Catholic Church, laws were written by popes and bishops to help keep the Church running smoothly, especially when disputes arose or in cases where crimes had taken place and penal laws were enacted to stop abuses, punish the guilty, and protect the common good.

In the 12th century, a canon lawyer from Bologna named Gratian compiled a collection of canon laws for easier study and usage. His *Concordantia Discordantium Canonum* (Concordance of Discordant Canons), published in 1140 A.D., was the first compilation of Roman law, biblical law, papal decrees, *conciliar* (ecumenical council) decrees, and local ecclesiastical legislation in one body of written work.

Pre-Reformation Europe relied heavily on canon law because it not only governed the activity of the Church as an institution and its members, especially the clergy and religious, but also governed the Church at a social level. Here are a few specific instances in which canon law was necessary:

✔ **Providing annulments:** Nations in which Catholicism was the state religion had no civil decrees of divorce, so the only way to reconcile bad marriages was to initiate an annulment process to determine whether the sacramental union was invalid from day one.

✔ **Administrating institutions:** The hospitals and universities were founded, owned, and operated by religious orders, and canon law governed their activities.

✔ **Checking the clergy:** Clerics were exempt from civil law and could only be tried in a canonical court until the modern era. Even property disputes were taken to court by canon law when it involved the Church, the clergy, or the religious.

✔ **Establishing the rule of law:** In the aftermath of the fall of Rome and the advent of the so-called Dark Ages, the barbarians gradually abandoned their tribal customs and embraced the rule of law, Roman law, as continued in the canon law of the Catholic Church, which governed the monks and their monasteries throughout Christendom.

✔ **Checking the aristocrats:** Even kings, noblemen, and the aristocracy were affected by canon law because an excommunication would result in their loss of obedience and *fealty* (oath to serve someone of higher rank) from their subordinates. The faithful were bound to avoid, ignore, and disobey any excommunicated ruler, be it a duke, a lord, a baron, a prince, a king, or even an emperor.

Identifying the changes

In 1959, Pope John XXIII (1958–1963) announced his desire to revise the *Code of Canon Law,* which had become slightly archaic in only 40 years. Before beginning the work of updating the laws of the Church, the pope saw the need to first summon and convene an ecumenical council. The

Second Vatican Council met from 1962 through 1965 and issued 16 documents. (Take a look at Chapter 7 for details on John Paul II's role in the Second Vatican Council.)

It would take three more popes and another 20 years before the *Code of Canon Law* would finally be revised. After John XXIII came Paul VI (1963–1978), then John Paul I, who reigned for only a month and was succeeded by John Paul II in 1978.

Because reforms of Vatican II were well under way (including performing services in the common language of the congregation, ecumenical dialogue, and involvement of the laity) the canon laws of the Church needed to reflect not only the legal realities but the philosophy and theology that were behind them. The spirit of the law and the letter of the law needed to coincide and be known and applied by everyone.

Here's a summary of the changes made to the *Code of Canon Law* by the Second Vatican Council:

- **A reduction in the number of laws:** There are 1,752 canons in the 1983 *Code of Canon Law,* compared to the 1917 *Code of Canon Law,* which had 2,414 canons.

- **A shift in the "spirit" of the law:** Whereas both codes are legalistic in the sense that they contain official and binding legislation on the Universal Church, in the revised (1983) code, the purpose of Church law keeps coming across again and again. It is best summarized in the last canon (canon 1752), which has a concluding phrase: *"salute animarum . . . in Ecclesia . . . suprema semper lex . . ."* (the salvation of souls is always the supreme law in the Church).

- **An enhancement of theological context:** Both the 1917 and the 1983 codes contain a lot of legal jargon and stuff that concerns canon lawyers more than the average Catholic in the pew. Nonetheless, the revised code gives theological context within legal parameters, unlike the older code before it.

- **A reaffirmation of the equality of all Christians:** Though still very much a hierarchy — with the pope as supreme head, the bishop as leader of the diocese, and the pastor as leader of the parish — the 1983 *Code of Canon Law* affirms the union of exercising jurisdiction with the ordained ministry (bishop, priest, and deacon). At the same time, however, the revised code also reiterates Vatican II, *Lumen Gentium* #32 in canon 208, when it declares the equality of all the Christian faithful by virtue of their Baptism.

Holy Orders do make a man a cleric and, as such, he can exercise ecclesi-astical authority and jurisdiction, but the dignity and importance of a person derives not from his vocation, but from his Baptism, which makes him a child of God. This principle of radical equality means that each and every single individual in the Church — pope, layperson, ordained, mar-ried, single, consecrated religious — has the same destiny and same opportunity. All the baptized — not just the priests and nuns — are called to holiness. Although the ordained have authority in the Church, they do not have a monopoly on grace and sanctity, which is equally given to all the baptized.

The 1983 *Code of Canon Law* reflects the mind of Vatican II in that the essen-tials and substance of the faith have been retained, while the way in which they are explained, communicated, and experienced have been adapted to modern times. Just as the Second Vatican Council did not deny or modify any dogmas or doctrines, or deviate from previous councils and popes on substantive elements of faith and morals, so, too, the revised code did not change the mechanism of ecclesiastical law. Roman law and not English common law, remains the foundation of the canonical system (specifically, the search for truth and the decision made by a judge rather than a jury).

The rights and obligations of all the Christian faithful

The following rights are written in the 1983 *Code of Canon Law:*

✔ The right and freedom to cooperate in the building up of the Body of Christ based on the fundamental equality of all Christians due to their Baptism (canon 208).

✔ The right to evangelize so that the divine message of salvation may, more and more, reach all people of all times and all places (canon 211).

✔ The right to make known their needs, espe-cially their spiritual needs, and their wishes to pastors and bishops of the Church (canon 212/2).

✔ The right to manifest to their pastors and bishops their views on matters that concern the good of the Church. They have the right also to make their views known to others of Christ's faithful, taking into account the common good and always respecting the integrity of faith and morals (canon 212/3).

✔ The right to receive the spiritual riches of the Church, especially the Word of God and the Sacraments from their pastors (canon 213).

✔ The right to worship God according to the provisions of their own approved liturgical rite (canon 214).

✔ The right to follow their own form of spiritu-ality if in accord with Church teaching (canon 214).

✔ The right to freely establish and direct asso-ciations that serve charitable or pious pur-poses or that foster the Christian vocation (canon 215).

✔ The right to hold meetings (assembly) to pursue the same purpose as to associate (canon 215).

✔ The right to promote the apostolate by their own initiative, undertaken according to their state and condition (canon 216).

✔ The right to a Christian education (canon 217).

✔ The right to research matters in which they are expert and to express themselves prudently concerning them, with due allegiance to the Magisterium of the Church (canon 218).

✔ The right to immunity from any kind of coercion in choosing a state in life (canon 218).

✔ The right to keep and preserve their good name and reputation (canon 220).

✔ The right to protect their own privacy (canon 220).

✔ The right to lawfully vindicate and defend the rights they enjoy in the Church, before the competent ecclesiastical court (canon 221/1).

✔ The right to be judged with due process (canon 221/2).

✔ The right that no penalties be inflicted upon them except in accordance with the law (canon 221/3).

The following obligations are written in the 1983 *Code of Canon Law:*

✔ The duty to preserve their communion with the Church at all times, even in their external actions (canon 209).

✔ The duty to lead a holy life, and to promote the growth of the Church (canon 210).

✔ The duty to evangelize so that the divine message of salvation may more and more reach all people of all times and all places (canon 211).

✔ The duty to obey the teaching and disciplinary authority of the Church (canon 212).

✔ The duty to manifest to their pastors and bishops their views on matters that concern the good of the Church (canon 212/3).

✔ The duty and most serious obligation of parents as primary educators of their children to provide Catholic education for them (parochial school, CCD, or home schooling) (canon 226/2).

✔ The duty to promote social justice (canon 222/2).

✔ The duty to help the poor from their own resources (canon 222/2).

✔ The duty to provide for the needs of the Church (time, talent and treasure — that is, financial support and volunteering) (canon 222/1).

At the same time, the adversarial goal of protecting and balancing rights emerges in the 1983 *Code of Canon Law* when the rights and obligations of all the Christian faithful, as well as specific rights of the laity and of the clergy, are spelled out and a means to defend, protect, and remedy their violation is guaranteed in law.

Structural similarities and differences between the 1917 and 1983 codes are as follows:

✔ Both introduce themselves with general norms and principles in section one.

✔ Section two of the revised code is titled "The People of God," which is directly taken from Vatican II. The former code called that section "On Persons."

> ✔ The new code starts with a list (bill) of rights of all the Christian faithful, which one receives by virtue of Baptism (see the nearby sidebar, "The rights and obligations of all the Christian faithful"), and then delineates further into subsections on the laity, the clergy, the religious, and so on. The 1917 *Code of Canon Law* dealt with the laity last; the 1983 *Code of Law* deals with them first.

Understanding the impact

The 1983 *Code of Canon Law* settled disputes that some parishes and dioceses had encountered since the end of the Second Vatican Council. Some places experimented with having First Holy Communion followed by First Penance (confession), yet pious tradition and now the universal law of the Church said otherwise. Canons 777 and 914 insist that First Penance precede First Communion. The faithful who have easy access to the *Code of Canon Law* know when their priests are acting properly, when their behavior conforms to the laws (canons) of the Church.

Previously, the 1917 code was only written in Latin, and no vernacular translations were permitted, only commentaries. Because the 1983 code is a product of the post-conciliar Church, the code itself is translated and made available to everyone in every language.

Even the individual laws are no longer seen as *Pharisaical technicalities* (or rituals that have no rhyme or reason, like those preformed by the Pharisees in the Old Testament). Instead, they readily reveal the sublime wisdom of the Church to both teach and govern, to instruct as well as to correct and protect.

Revising the Catechism of the Catholic Church (1992)

Catechesis is the process of handing on (teaching and explaining) the faith to others. A *catechism* is a book containing all the necessary teachings for believers of a religion to know and accept. The previous catechism was the first universal catechism for the entire church, and it came about as a result of the Council of Trent (1545–1563). That ecumenical council was convened to address the abuses that precipitated the Protestant Reformation and the subsequent doctrinal errors that developed from them. The Roman Catechism was the name given to the Catechism of the Council of Trent.

To *evangelize* is to enthusiastically share your faith with others, usually by giving witness and telling others about the faith, especially by introducing them to what is contained in the gospels of the Bible. To *catechize* on the other hand, is to teach and give further explanation and meaning to what was initially shared by evangelization. Catechesis and evangelism go hand in hand. A catechism contains the content of faith and the context from which the doctrines were derived.

Catechisms are not unique to Catholicism. Protestant Christianity uses this technique and tool as evidenced by the Lutheran Catechism, the Anglican Catechism (found in the *Book of Common Prayer*), and the Westminster Catechism (for Presbyterian and Reformed churches). A major difference would be that Catholic Christianity believes Sacred Tradition is as valid a source of divine revelation as Sacred Scripture (the Bible), whereas Protestant Christianity regards the Bible alone as the source of doctrinal authority. Catholicism uses both the Bible and the Catechism of the Catholic Church, and neither one is in competition with the other, because 80 percent of the footnotes and quotations in the catechism are from Sacred Scripture. The Catholic Church regards the catechism as the summary of all authentic and official teachings (dogmas and doctrines), which every Catholic is morally bound to accept and believe. Within that catechism (101–141) is the premise that the Bible is the inspired, inerrant, and revealed written Word of God.

Identifying the changes

The revised *Catechism of the Catholic Church* (1992) teaches the same 2,000-year-old religion and preserves the same defined dogmas and official doctrines of the previous Catechism of the Council of Trent (1566), also called the Roman Catechism. There are no new teachings any more than there were in the documents of Vatican II, yet in both there is a new way of explaining and understanding those ancient truths of Catholicism.

The JP2 catechism (or the Catechism of the Second Vatican Council) is composed of four pillars of faith: the Creed, the Seven Sacraments, the Ten Commandments, and the Lord's Prayer. Each of these represents and encapsulates a major component of Catholic Christianity including:

- ✔ **Doctrine:** What Catholics believe
- ✔ **Liturgy:** How Catholics worship God
- ✔ **Morality:** How Catholics behave
- ✔ **Prayer:** Catholics' relationship with God

Each pillar can be examined and subdivided into smaller elements, which together form an organic whole. All four pillars maintain the foundation of Catholicism. No one pillar alone represents the totality of the religion — all four work together and are interrelated with one another like various organs within the same body. The previous catechism was also based on these four divisions as an outline to explain the faith.

The Profession of Faith: The Creed (Doctrine)

Articles 1 through 1065 of the *Catechism of the Catholic Church* focus on the Apostles' Creed and the Nicene Creed. A *creed* is a formal statement of religious belief that summarizes the essential tenets and doctrines of a religion. The Apostles' Creed (also known as *Symbolum Apostolorum*) was not necessarily formulated by the original 12 Apostles but originates in what is called the apostolic era (first century A.D.). Later, in 325, the ecumenical council of Nicea further elaborated on the articles of that creed in response to the heresy of Arianism, which denied the divinity of Christ. That Nicene Creed is now recited every Sunday and Holy Day in the Catholic Church. See Table 10-1 to examine how the creed developed.

Table 10-1 Comparing the Apostles' Creed and the Nicene Creed	
The Apostles' Creed	**The Nicene Creed**
I believe *in God, the Father* almighty, creator of heaven and earth.	We believe *in* one *God, the Father,* the Almighty, maker of heaven and earth, and of all that is, seen and unseen.
I believe *in Jesus Christ,* his only *Son,* our Lord.	We believe *in* one Lord, *Jesus Christ,* the only *Son* of God, eternally begotten of the Father, God from God, Light from Light, true God from true God, begotten, not made, one in Being with the Father. Through him all things were made. For us men and for our salvation, he came down from heaven:
He was conceived by the power of the Holy Spirit and born of the Virgin Mary.	by the power of the Holy Spirit he was born of the Virgin Mary, and became man.

The Apostles' Creed	The Nicene Creed
He suffered under Pontius Pilate, was crucified, died, and was buried. He descended into hell.	For our sake he was crucified under Pontius Pilate; he suffered, died and was buried.
On the third day he rose again.	On the third day he rose again in fulfillment of the Scriptures;
He ascended into heaven and is seated at the right hand of the Father. He will come again to judge the living and the dead.	he ascended into heaven and is seated at the right hand of the Father. He will come again in glory to judge the living and the dead, and his kingdom will have no end.
I believe *in the Holy Spirit,* the holy Catholic Church, the communion of saints, the forgiveness of sins, the resurrection of the body, and the life everlasting. Amen.	We believe *in the Holy Spirit,* the Lord the giver of life, who proceeds from the Father and the Son. With the Father and the Son he is worshipped and glorified. He has spoken through the Prophets. We believe in one holy Catholic and apostolic Church. We acknowledge one baptism for the forgiveness of sins. We look for the resurrection of the dead, and the life of the world to come. Amen.

The creed is subdivided into sections. Conveniently, there are 12 parts, which correspond to the number of Apostles (hence, the reason that the name Apostles' Creed became so popular). Before the printing press and when many of the faithful were still illiterate, the only way to teach the faith was to have them memorize the creed. After knowing it by heart, a catechist would later explain and flesh out the fuller meaning of each article contained in the creed.

The primary doctrine of Christianity — be it Catholic, Protestant, or Eastern Orthodox — is the mystery of the Holy Trinity (namely, that there is only one God but three Divine Persons). Like the other monotheistic religions (Judaism and Islam), Christianity also firmly believes in one God. The difference, however, is that Christianity's God is *triune* (God the Father, God the Son, and God the Holy Spirit). The four marks of the Church (One, Holy, Catholic and Apostolic) as listed in the creed are elaborated so that you can appreciate why they are mentioned in the first place.

The older catechism quoted Sacred Scripture but not as extensively as the newer catechism. Pope John Paul II made sure that doctrinal content was also presented in a biblical context. This way, the reader not only learns *what* the Church teaches but *why* as well. Doctrines such as the Holy Trinity, Creation, Original Sin and the Fall, the Incarnation, Virgin Birth, Immaculate Conception, Founding the Church, Institution of the Sacraments, Resurrection of the Dead, Communion of Saints, and so on, are cited and explained in the catechism.

The Celebration of Faith: the Seven Sacraments (Liturgy)

Articles 1066 through 1690 of the *Catechism of the Catholic Church* cover the public worship of the believers (called *liturgy*) as celebrated in the official rituals and ceremonies known as the seven sacraments. Baptism, Holy Eucharist, and Confirmation compose the sacraments of initiation into the Church. Penance (also called confession or reconciliation) and Anointing of the Sick are sacraments of healing. And Matrimony and Holy Orders are sacraments of community.

The *Catechism of the Catholic Church* underscores the biblical foundation for each sacrament and the concept that Christ instituted them. Sacraments are Sacred Rites, which are entrusted to the care of the Church. Each one of them has one or more components, which are perceptible to one or more of the five senses (for example, using water in Baptism or olive oil in Anointing the Sick, and so on). The supernatural grace from God, which is invisible, is symbolized by the tangible element that is necessary for the sacrament to be valid. The *Catechism of the Catholic Church* makes it clear that divine grace is not limited to the sacraments. It is not by necessity — but by divine choice — that God uses these spiritual vehicles to give humankind this special gift. It was God who made men and women a combination of body and soul, so it would make sense that the same God would use things of the created world to symbolize the invisible reality of divine grace.

The zenith and apex of Catholic worship is the Holy Eucharist, and the catechism details how it is considered the real, true, and substantial Body and Blood, Soul and Divinity of Christ. Wheat bread and grape wine are used just as Jesus did at the Last Supper and as are done by faithful Jews around the world for Passover at the Seder meal. Catholicism believes that only an ordained priest can change the bread and wine into the Precious Body and Blood of Christ, as it remains until completely consumed to the last drop and last crumb.

The doctrine of *transubstantiation* describes how the change takes place. Physical and chemical properties and the material appearances of bread and wine are changed into what Catholicism calls the *Real Presence*. Other Christian religions consider the Communion service to be a symbolic or mystical presence of Christ, whereas Catholics and Eastern Orthodox view it as the most intimate union between the divine and the human.

The Living of Faith: The Ten Commandments (Morality)

Articles 1691 through 2557 of the Catechism of the Catholic Church look at all Ten Commandments as the springboard for moral teaching and ethical behavior for the believer. There is a difference in numbering between the Ten Commandments cited by the Catholics and Lutherans and the ones cited by the other Protestant traditions. The Bible itself never assigns a number to any one of the Ten Commandments. They are listed twice in scripture, in Exodus 20:2–17 and Deuteronomy 5:6–21.

If the Bible does not number the commandments, who did and how? *Remember:* It was not until 1205 A.D. that Stephen Langton, Archbishop of Canterbury, divided the books of the Bible into chapter numbers, and it was another 350 years (in 1555 A.D.) before Robert Stephanus divided the Bible chapters into verses. The original texts of scripture were written with no chapter, no verse, and no punctuation.

St. Augustine (354–430 A.D.), Bishop of Hippo, was the first to assign numbers to the Ten Commandments. Because idolatry is the worship of false gods, he presumed Exodus 20:4/Deuteronomy 5:8 ("Thou shalt not make unto thee any graven image") was just a continuation of Exodus 20:3/Deuteronomy 5:7 ("Thou shalt have no other gods before me."). In other words, they belong in the same paragraph.

Origen and some Greek Fathers of the Church saw the injunction against graven images and idols a separate commandment from the one forbidding worship of other gods. This point of view would become the position of the Anglican, Calvinist, and Presbyterian churches. Hence, both systems count the same first commandment as the same (no false gods) but the Catholic-Lutheran numbering (thanks to Augustine) counts as number two "Thou shalt not take the name of the Lord thy God in vain," whereas the other system numbers that commandment as being number three. And it goes on, each one being one number different from the other until the very end. Then it is catch-up time. The Catholic-Lutheran system divides Deuteronomy 5:21/Exodus 20:17 into two separate commandments, number nine being "Thou shalt not covet thy neighbor's wife" and number ten being "Thou shalt not covet thy neighbor's goods." The Anglican-Calvinist system keeps them together as number ten. Table 10-2 spells it all out.

Table 10-2	Comparative Versions of the Ten Commandments
Protestant Version (Anglican-Calvinist)	**Augustinian Version (Catholic-Lutheran)**
1. Thou shalt have no other gods before me.	1. Thou shalt have no other gods before me.
2. Thou shalt not make unto thee any graven image.	2. Thou shalt not take the name of the Lord thy God in vain.

(continued)

Table 10-2 *(continued)*

Protestant Version (Anglican-Calvinist)	Augustinian Version (Catholic-Lutheran)
3. Thou shalt not take the name of the Lord thy God in vain.	3. Keep holy the Sabbath day.
4. Remember the Sabbath day to keep it holy.	4. Honor thy father and mother.
5. Honor thy father and thy mother.	5. Thou shalt not kill.
6. Thou shalt not kill.	6. Thou shalt not commit adultery.
7. Thou shalt not commit adultery.	7. Thou shalt not steal.
8. Thou shalt not steal.	8. Thou shalt not bear false witness.
9. Thou shalt not bear false witness.	9. Thou shalt not covet thy neighbor's wife.
10. Thou shalt not covet *thy neighbor's wife, nor his goods, nor* anything that is thy neighbor's.	10. Thou shalt not covet thy neighbor's goods.

In addition to covering the Ten Commandments in depth, showing how many sins can actually be traced back to breaking one or more of these divine laws, the Catechism also highlights the beatitudes from Jesus's Sermon on the Mount (Matthew 5:3–12) and expounds on the moral virtues (prudence, justice, temperance, and fortitude) and the theological virtues (faith, hope, and love). The moral and ethical life of a Christian is not limited to just avoiding sin by not breaking a commandment but also demands a conscious effort to practice virtue and do good for others.

The *Catechism of the Catholic Church* also explains the complete adherence to the Natural Moral Law, which is the principle that any and every sane and rational human being can, does, and is expected to know innately a modicum of basic morality regardless of his or her religion or lack thereof. The Nazis who were put on trial in Nuremburg for war crimes after the end of World War II could not use the defense that they were merely obeying orders, or that it was legal, or that they had no religion so how could they be held accountable to the commandments? As human beings, they were answerable to the Natural Moral Law that informs anyone with reason that genocide, murder, rape, racism, and anti-Semitism are evil.

The Praying of Faith: The Lord's Prayer (Spirituality)

Articles 2558 through 2865 of the catechism conclude the book with the Our Father (or Lord's Prayer). This whole section is on prayer and uses what Christians call the perfect prayer (because it was given by Christ Himself) as the launching pad to discover other forms of prayer.

Prayer is seen as communication with God but it is a two-way dialogue. God gives us insights and grace, and we offer adoration (praise), petition (intercession), gratitude (thanksgiving), or contrition (sorrow). These are the traditional four types of prayer a human being offers to God. We can adore and praise him; we can thank him; we can express regret and sorrow for offending him; and we can ask him for help, for ourselves or others.

The *Catechism of the Catholic Church* also delineates vocal and mental prayer, formal and spontaneous and other varieties of communicating with the Divine. Reading the Bible is as much a prayer as quietly meditating in a church or chapel. *Intercessory prayer,* where someone asks God's help for someone else, is not only encouraged but also used to explain the Catholic custom of praying to the saints. The First Commandment forbids giving worship or adoration to anyone or anything other than God himself.

Yet, adoration is only one form of prayer. There is also intercession or petition, where someone asks for help. There is no worship being done, just a request being made. Because living people have no trouble asking each other for prayers, like "I'm having surgery tomorrow. Could you pray for me?" no one objects or interprets it as if the person making the request is circumventing Christ as sole Mediator. Even the Gospels have other people making intercession on behalf of others. When the daughter of Jairus, a synagogue official, is deathly ill, her dad goes to Jesus and makes intercession on her behalf that she be healed (Luke 8:40–56). His request is granted, and Jesus heals the little girl even though she has died. Likewise, when the Roman centurion approached Jesus in Matthew 8:5–13, he also made a prayer of intercession (petition) on behalf of another, his servant, that he, too, be healed. That request was equally granted.

The catechism then points out that the saints in heaven, including the Virgin Mary, the Mother of Christ, can intercede for the living on Earth with their prayers just as you and I can do for each other. Praying to the saints is not adoration or worship, merely asking for their intercession that they pray to the one Mediator, Christ, on our behalf. The connection between the living on Earth, the saints in heaven, and the deceased souls is called the Communion of Saints.

Understanding the impact

Pope John Paul II will forever be remembered, honored, and appreciated for giving the Universal Church the *Catechism of the Catholic Church.* Shortly after Vatican II had ended, many distortions, misunderstandings, and inaccuracies were intentionally or accidentally proliferated in many areas of the Church around the world. Some erroneously said that Vatican II abolished some doctrines or disciplines that it had not. Purgatory was and is still a doctrine (and is in the catechism), but limbo, which never was (it only existed as a theological conclusion but never as an article of faith), is completely absent in the catechism. The *Catechism of the Catholic Church* is the totality of Catholic doctrine and dogma in one volume just as the *Code of Canon Law* is the singular source for universal discipline in the Church around the world. As important as the code, as spectacular the World Youth Days with millions attending, as memorable the papal visits across the globe, of all these the *Catechism of the Catholic Church* will endure as the most influential and pivotal legacy of Pope John Paul II.

Thanks to the catechism, Catholics and non-Catholics alike can look up in one book what the Church teaches and why. If it is not in the catechism, then it is not official doctrine or dogma. If it is in the catechism, then Catholic Christians are obliged to know and believe it, even if they do not yet fully understand it. The catechism is the fruit of the official Magisterium and, unlike opinions from private theologians, it is to be treated as the truth by all who profess membership in the Catholic religion.

Reforming the Roman Curia (1984–1988)

The *Roman Curia* is the bureaucratic and organizational infrastructure of the Vatican that implements the policies and decisions of the pope, gives him advice and counsel, and oversees the many departments that take care of the day-to-day business and operating of Vatican City as an independent nation and as the spiritual and authoritative head of the one-billion-member Roman Catholic Church.

When the Papal States existed, the pope was a temporal ruler of an earthly kingdom, which comprised the middle section of Italy. The Curia operated much like the cabinet does for the president of the United States or prime minister of Great Britain.

The term *Curia* goes back to the days of the Roman Empire, when the Curia was the area (offices) where the senators would advise and counsel Caesar.

Identifying the changes

Pope Paul VI made some reforms in the Curia in 1967 to reflect the mind of the Second Vatican Council. Pope John Paul II made further reforms in 1988 with his letter *Pastor Bonus,* which had 193 articles. That document strengthened the centralized "government" of the Holy See without interfering with the regular and ordinary, day-to-day business of the local diocese and parish. Bishops and pastors were not considered employees of the Vatican with cardinals being seen as corporate executives and vice presidents. Yet, the Catholic Church is still a hierarchy and still has an external structure to its organization. The Curia are not middle management between the pope and the bishops of the world. The Curia is his staff, cabinet, and administration to help him shepherd the Universal Church.

Understanding the impact

Most of the restructuring of the Roman Curia by JP2 was designed to streamline, where possible, by eliminating duplication and redundancy while at the same time centralizing authority. He did not take any authority or prerogatives from the local diocesan bishops; instead, he reorganized the Holy See so that the cardinals who ran the congregations, commissions, councils, and committees were not semiautonomous entities. John Paul saw the Vatican *dicasteries* (or departments) as part of his "administration" and "cabinet" of sorts. Although he was no micromanager, he did want to let the bureaucracy know that the pope was still very much in charge and his staff was to represent him and his agenda, not their own.

Pope Paul VI had previously done some major overhauling of the dicasteries in 1965 and 1967 as a consequence of the Second Vatican Council. Pope John Paul II's efforts were more a process of fine-tuning than substantial change. Still, in a place where things change by centuries and not by years, any time the dust flies, a little hoopla results. JP2 did not necessarily downsize, but he did centralize a little more so that everyone at the Vatican could be on the same page.

The average Catholic in the pew or the priest in the parish is not directly affected by this reorganization. The only impact on bishops, archbishops, and cardinals and their respective dioceses and archdioceses has to do with which department they direct their concerns to. Rome is where the changes took place — mostly behind the scenes, because the changes involve the internal workings of the Vatican administration and governance.

Chapter 11

Internationalizing the Church: Making It "Catholic"

As pope, John Paul II tried to make the Universal Church truly global.

One of the four identifying characteristic of the Catholic Church is the adjective *universal,* which means it cannot be limited to being a national or ethnic church. (The other three identifying characteristics of the Catholic Church are one, holy, and apostolic.) The word *Catholic* comes from the Greek *katholikos,* which means "universal."

In this chapter, we look at the tangible ways that Pope John Paul II sought to include everyone in the world into the Catholic Church. We look at his international travel, his search for saints in every corner of the globe, and his appointments of cardinals from every part of the global Catholic community.

Visiting Other Nations

John Paul traveled, literally, around the world, and in several instances his visits changed history. Not only did he inspire and encourage the faithful of his own religion, but he also greatly influenced local and national politics just by his mere presence in those countries.

From the day of his election as Bishop of Rome, JP2 had a vision that he had to fulfill the command of Christ to preach to all nations. Through these trips, the pope felt rejuvenated by the people he came to visit and, in turn, they felt encouraged by his leadership.

John Paul II traveled to some areas that had terrible suffering, including war, poverty, and famine. By traveling to both first- and third-world countries, he demonstrated that the message of salvation was for all people, rich and poor alike. The pope saw these trips in line with St. Peter and St. Paul and the tremendous missionary work those saints did. A modern-day pope must continue, according to the mandate of Christ in John's Gospel, to feed his sheep and lambs. In contemporary terms, this means to bring Christ and his Church to the people.

The central theme of JP2's papacy was to bring Jesus Christ to the world, to all its many countries, to the variety of expressions of cultures, and to each person. His pastoral visits did not exclude anyone. Although his primary purpose was to meet the Catholic community, he reached out to Christians, Jews, and people of other religions.

John Paul II promoted a new evangelizing spirit to the Catholic Church. He was eager to promote the spreading of the Gospel to those who have not yet had the opportunity to hear it, as well as to re-evangelize the Catholic Church itself. He recognized early on that many of the local churches were going through a grave crisis, especially in the industrial first world that is often referred to by the media as a "post-Christian" society. His apostolic visits were a response to the internal difficulties these churches were facing; he boosted the morale of the faithful and gave clear Catholic teaching.

As head of state, JP2 visited countries within the context of civil communities by seeking to bring the Church's dealings with states as a diplomatic emissary. To state leaders, he always underlined humanity's tie to God and his belief that society needs to construct its community life on the *Natural Moral Law* (morality that is known intuitively by all human beings).

In the following sections, we show you how JP2 showed the universality of the Church by visiting many nations, canonizing saints from many countries and bringing into the College of Cardinals the most diverse and international group. See Chapter 16 for more details on Pope John Paul's record-setting travels.

Canonizing Saints from All Over the World

While visiting a country, John Paul II often beatified or canonized men and women outstanding in faith. Many of the people he beatified or canonized were martyrs for the faith who lost their lives as recently as the 20th century, either as a result of the world wars or oppressive regimes, whether Nazi, Communist, or anti-Catholic.

The Congregation for the Causes of Saints proposed and John Paul II approved 1,339 men and women for beatification and another 483 for canonization, which is more than the four previous centuries combined. He personally placed many causes on the fast track, because one of his fundamental objectives was to give greater value to universal holiness. (Take a look at Chapter 14 for more details on changes JP2 made to the canonization process.)

Pope John Paul II attributed great importance to beatification and canonization, because it shows that sanctity isn't a rarity. The common men and women whom he recognized propose real models of holiness that challenge society itself.

JP2 continued a long tradition of canonizing men and women outstanding in faith. In 1183, popes became directly involved in the process. After the Council of Trent, the Vatican began requiring scrupulous proof of a candidate's ability to call on God to work miracles. Because the process usually took ten or more years from start to finish (and usually didn't begin until 25 to 50 years after the alleged saint died), most of the popes since 1592 didn't live long enough to canonize anyone. Only 17 did name saints, and their number only tallied 296. Most were priests or men or women from religious orders (monks and nuns).

Although, in the past, the majority of the canonized and beatified were from Europe, JP2 greatly expanded canonization to around the world to emphasize the global and Universal ("catholic") Church. For example, he canonized 120 Chinese martyrs. His message: Holiness is not limited by geography or borders. Holiness can flower anywhere. It is universal.

Some have unfairly criticized Pope John Paul II's number of canonizations as being inflated. Yet, the pope believed that saints are not "determined by computers or statistics but are the fruit of God's abundant graces." Catholic Christianity firmly believes that each and every human person not only has the potential of sainthood but also is given the divine mandate to live a virtuous and holy life, whether married or single, clergy, religious, or laity. The "universal call to holiness" spoken of by the Second Vatican Council is no option but a vocation for any and all the baptized. Mother Angelica of the Eternal World Television News (EWTN) has often remarked, "We're all called to become great saints. Don't miss the opportunity." JP2 felt more canonized saints would convince more people that they, too, had the possibility and destiny to become God's holy saints.

Like no other pope before him, John Paul II unveiled the diversity of heaven. He canonized men and women from almost every country, culture, and class, from priests to nuns, peasants to duchesses. His first canonizations, in 1982, set the tone. He named along with a monk and two nuns from 300 years ago, a Polish Franciscan priest, St. Maximilian Kolbe, who was sent to the concentration camp at Auschwitz for opposing the Nazis; he died when he exchanged his life for that of a condemned married man. In 1983, John Paul II streamlined the canonization process so that martyrs could be beatified without the requirement of a postmortem miracle.

TECHNICAL STUFF

JP2's recognition of martyrs

Pope John Paul II placed a great importance on *martyrs* (people who have been killed because of their faith). The history of the Catholic Church is a history of martyrs. Martyrs are a treasure for the Church. Their courage is not explainable in natural terms, but supernatural. Martyrs witness that life is not a matter of pleasure, but of living supernatural values.

The pope raised many martyrs to the altars, and the record of those to come is longer still. The following list of martyrs recognized by Pope John Paul II who are awaiting canonization is categorized by countries.

✓ **Spanish martyrs (1936–1939):** After the Spanish Civil War broke out in 1936, the Church suffered one of the fiercest persecutions of its history. The number of Catholic victims under the Spanish Republic included 13 bishops, 4,184 priests, 2,365 male religious, 283 nuns, and thousands of laypeople. Pope John Paul II beatified the first Spanish martyrs, three Carmelite nuns from Guadalajara, in 1987. In the following years, another 231 Spanish martyrs were raised to the altars by JP2.

✓ **Mexican martyrs (1926–1930):** The story of Catholic persecution in Mexico in the mid-1920s is almost never told in history books. In spite of its peaceful stance, the Church suffered heavy losses. Hundreds of priests were killed, 90 percent of Catholic pastors

were removed from their parishes and went into hiding, and thousands of Catholics perished. The president of Mexico made every effort to abolish the Catholic Church in Mexico and to eliminate all Catholic thought in Mexican society. In honor of the Mexican victims, JP2 beatified a first group of martyrs in 1992 — 22 priests and 28 laypersons of the "Catholic Action" movement.

✓ **Brazilian martyrs (1645):** In March 2000, 30 Brazilian martyrs were beatified. Their story is related to the 17th-century religious wars in Europe between Spanish and Portuguese Catholics and Dutch Calvinists, and it continued in the New World. The martyrdoms took place as a result of two different episodes only a few months apart: (1) June 1645, when Dutch troops entered a church and massacred Father de Soveral and all the worshippers inside, and (2) October 1645, when Father Ferro and his parishioners were tortured and murdered.

✓ **Nowogrodek sisters (1943):** During World War II, Nowogrodek, Poland, was occupied by the Soviets and then the Nazis. Communities of nuns, the Congregation of the Sacred Family of Nazareth, which served the Church and educated the children, were massacred after they killed all the Jews in the town. In July 1943, 120 Catholics were selected for execution, and the nuns, led by their Superior, Mother Maria Stella, offered to exchange their lives for those Catholics with families. When the life of the local priest was threatened, the nuns renewed their offer. On August 1, 1943, 12 nuns from the Congregation of the Sacred Family of Nazareth were taken to be shot in the woods outside the city. The nuns were beatified along with the Brazilian martyrs in 2000.

✔ **Irish martyrs (16th to 17th centuries):** On September 27, 1992, JP2 beatified 17 Irish clergy and laity who were violently persecuted by the Protestant English who controlled their country at the time.

✔ **Chinese martyrs and missionaries (17th to 18th centuries):** On October 1, 2000, Pope John Paul II canonized 120 martyrs — 87 Chinese and 33 missionaries — and called them examples of courage and coherence for the Universal Church and an honor for the noble Chinese nation. This proved to be very important to the local church, which is currently suppressed by the Communist government in China.

John Paul II definitely left his mark on the Church by the many men and women he beatified or canonized. He established them as authoritative figures for all time to come. By deciding who qualifies as authoritative, JP2's ideas and perspectives remain authoritative for all time to come as well.

The beatification and canonization became part of JP2's new evangelizing theme. The pope wanted to evangelize by means of the saints and the blessed — that is, by means of Christians who lived their faith and the Gospel both heroically and radically. Here are just a few of the ways the saints and the blessed evangelize:

✔ They are the models of Christian life in the different human conditions that we are born into.

✔ The saints enable us to see how Christ continues to make Himself present to the world, and how his Gospel is extending in time and space.

✔ They are valuable examples for the Church. They show practical ways to holiness. The pope presents their holiness and witness to the new generation and the times to come. They become part of our heritage, but they also show us what we need to do.

The pope also canonized many *laypeople* (men and women who are not in vows or ordained to the priesthood). Ninety-eight percent of the Church is made of the laity, so the canonization of laypeople reaffirms the Second Vatican Council's call to holiness. Lay witnesses to the faith become necessary illustrations on how Catholics should live in the world. They serve as role models who live as ordinary people in society, but in an extraordinary way. These examples of sanctity exemplify to the believer that all are called by Baptism to be saints.

Expanding the College of Cardinals

The pope selects new men to be cardinals at a *consistory* (a formal meeting of the Sacred College of Cardinals of the Church). These meetings are held in Vatican City for the purpose of taking care of the business of the College, which advises the pope on important matters concerning the Church, including the selection of new cardinals.

The identities of the cardinals-elect are announced in advance, but only at the time of the consistory does the elevation to the cardinalate take effect, because that is when the pope formally publishes the decree of elevation.

The first consistory for Pope John Paul II was in June 1979. It took place only nine months after he ascended the throne of St. Peter. But it wasn't until the 1983 and 1985 consistories that we saw Pope John Paul II putting his own stamp on the College of Cardinals. The appointments reflected the diversity that John Paul II wanted to bring to the Church.

In subsequent consistories, JP2 continued to change the direction of the College of Cardinals to reflect the fact that the Church is universal, not just in Europe and specifically in Italy. By the time of his death, he had appointed almost every cardinal, and only two remained from his predecessor, Paul VI — Cardinal Sin of the Philippines and Cardinal Ratzinger of the Congregation of the Doctrine of the Faith, the latter of whom later became elected the 266th pope following the death of John Paul II and took the name Benedict XVI.

Naming new cardinals from 24 countries, JP2 carried on his predecessor's policy of internationalizing the College of Cardinals. John Paul II understood that the Catholic population was significantly high in third-world countries. Therefore, his appointments reflected this shift.

After the 1994 consistory, the United States, Latin America, Africa, Asia, and Eastern Europe made up 60 percent of the College of Cardinals who could vote for the new pope at the time of a conclave.

For a complete list of the cardinals, see www.catholic-pages.com/ hierarchy/cardinals_list.asp.

Chapter 12

Building Bridges: Reaching Out to Other Religions

Among the titles that popes have been given over the course of the centuries, one of the oldest is *Pontifex Maximus,* literally "the great bridge-builder," a title given to Pope Damasus I (366–384) by the Roman Emperor Gratian. Though rooted in paganism, by the 11th century the title had taken on a deeper, spiritual meaning. Pope John Paul II came to the papacy understanding the need for a "bridge-builder" between God and humanity. Having experienced firsthand the dehumanizing effects of Nazism and Marxism, he took very seriously the need to be the one to reach out, on behalf of the world's Catholics, to other people in the world (whom he believed were created by the same God in God's image and likeness).

In this chapter, we explore JP2's work to bring Catholics and Jews together, acknowledging their place in history as Abraham's people. We look at his work designed to undo the centuries of hard feelings between Catholics and Protestants since the Protestant Reformation. We look at the progress he made in encouraging a climate of understanding with Muslims. We examine the slow healing process between the Eastern Orthodox Christian Church and the Catholics. And finally, we review JP2's unprecedented peace offering to the religions of the world.

Mending Millennial Fences: Catholics and Jews

Without a doubt, Pope John Paul II came to the papacy with knowledge of Jews and Judaism that no predecessor shared (except maybe St. Peter and the first few popes). The pope's father, Karol Wojtyła, Sr., served in the military with a number of Jewish soldiers, whom he respected and who respected him; no anti-Semitic remarks were tolerated in the Wojtyła home. Pope John Paul II's hometown of Wadowice had a large Jewish population, and the Jewish and Catholic citizens of Wadowice learned to peacefully coexist, seeing each other — first and foremost — as sons and daughters of Poland. Yes, there were occasional, isolated incidents of anti-Semitism, but these unfortunate events were understood by both Jews and Catholics to be the thoughts of *individuals* and not groups.

Perhaps the most important factor in Pope John Paul II's understanding of Judaism was his childhood friendship with Jerzy Kluger, from the day the two began elementary school in September 1926. Kluger, the son of a prominent Wadowice lawyer active in the Jewish community, remained the pope's oldest and most trusted informal "advisor" on Judaism. Years later, after Pope John Paul II's election, Kluger played a role in the establishment of diplomatic relations between the Vatican and the State of Israel.

During World War II, Karol Wojtyła's involvement with the Rhapsodic Theater also put him into contact with UNIA, the Polish resistance union that provided hiding places, false identity papers, and financial assistance to Polish Jews.

As a bishop, Wojtyła participated in all the sessions of the Second Vatican Council (1962–1965), which produced the landmark document *Nostra Aetate,* the document on the relation of the Catholic Church to non-Christian religions. In that document, the council fathers remembered "the spiritual ties which link the people of the New Covenant to the stock of Abraham" and "deplores all hatreds, persecutions, displays of anti-Semitism leveled at any time or from any source against the Jews." Later, as Archbishop of Krakow, Cardinal Wojtyła tried to educate Polish youth born after the Holocaust about their fraternal connection to Jews by asking Catholic youth groups to care for the Jewish cemeteries in communities that literally had no one left amongst themselves to care for the grounds.

From the time of his 1978 election, Pope John Paul II showed an openness to Judaism that reflected his past experiences. In March 1979, he received a delegation of Rome's Jewish community at the Vatican. This began a series of audiences with Jewish leaders that ran throughout his 27-year pontificate. On January 31, 1981, he appointed Bishop Jean-Marie Lustiger, a convert from Judaism, as Archbishop of Paris. Though he faced criticism at the time from Catholics and Jews alike, JP2's decision was a good one, proven by the fact that, at the time of the pontiff's death, Cardinal Lustiger was often mentioned in the press as *papabile* (a possible successor as pope). In 1985, Pope John Paul II actively participated in several events in Rome and at the Vatican marking the 20th anniversary of the issue of *Nostra Aetate*.

April 13, 1986, marks the date when Pope John Paul II visited the synagogue of the City of Rome. During the visit, the pope participated in a prayer service presided over jointly by himself and Rome's Chief Rabbi Elio Toaff. Aware of the power of "visuals," he saw this visit as an outward sign of the Catholic Church's new understanding of the Church's relationship with Jews, which began during the Second Vatican Council.

Establishing diplomatic relations with Israel

Pope John Paul II knew that in order to improve the relationship between Catholics and Jews, the Vatican had to recognize the State of Israel and establish full diplomatic ties. This step presented another problem, because two separate relational dynamics were going on: On one level, the spiritual conversation between Roman Catholics and Jews, and on the other level the diplomatic relationship between the sovereign nations of the Vatican and the State of Israel.

As early in his pontificate as October 5, 1980, Pope John Paul II publicly spoke of the "State of Israel" in a homily, becoming the first pope to do so. At the same time, he asked his childhood friend Jerzy Kluger (who lived in Rome at the time) to begin speaking informally to Israeli diplomats in Rome about the pope's desire to eventually establish diplomatic relations between the Holy See and Israel. Small gestures continued to pave the way as well, such as the telegram sent by Pope John Paul II to the President of Israel on the occasion of the Jewish New Year in October 1981.

In April 1990, Pope John Paul II named Archbishop Andrea Cordero Lanza di Montezemolo as apostolic delegate to Jerusalem. In 1992, Montezemolo, together with Franciscan Father David-Marie Jaeger (the first native Israeli Catholic priest), led the first Vatican delegation visit to Israel, to begin talks about establishing diplomatic ties. Finally, on December 30, 1993, the Holy See and the State of Israel signed a fundamental agreement that would eventually establish full diplomatic relations.

What's in a name?

Don't look for titles of Church documents to always give you a hint as to the content of the document. Documents officially issued by the Catholic Church, whether they come directly from the pope or (in the case of *Nostra Aetate*) from an ecumenical council of the bishops of the world, are named by the first few words of the document in Latin, which is still the official language of the Church. Thus, while *Pastores Dabo Vobis,* Latin for "I will give you shepherds," easily identifies Pope John Paul II's 1992 apostolic exhortation on priestly formation, *Nostra Aetate* literally means "in our age," and gives no clue as to the document's content.

Looking at bumps in the road

Things have not always gone smoothly. In 1984, a monastery of cloistered Carmelite nuns was established on the outskirts of the Auschwitz-Birkenau concentration camp in Poland. Jews protested the nuns' presence, saying that there should be no established presence of any particular religious denomination on the site, and for a while it became a point of contention between Jews and Catholics. Eventually it took the direct intervention of Pope John Paul II to get the sisters to relocate in 1993.

A 1987 visit to the Vatican by Austrian President Kurt Waldheim created another source of tension. At the time, Waldheim's past as a member of the German army during World War II was becoming better known, and U.S. Jewish leaders who were scheduled to meet with Pope John Paul II in one of his upcoming visits to the United States were threatening to cancel the meeting. Regardless of his past, Waldheim was the elected president of a predominantly Catholic country and had to be received by the pope. In the end, the delegation of Jewish leaders from the United States were received by the pope to voice their protest, and in receiving them, the pope defused the situation.

During the Jubilee Year of 2000, Pope John Paul II was able to, at last, visit the Holy Land. In his 1994 apostolic letter *Tertio Millenio Adveniente,* the pope hinted about a visit, writing that

> attention is being given to finding ways of arranging historic meetings in places of exceptional symbolic importance like Bethlehem, Jerusalem, and Mount Sinai as a means of furthering dialogue with Jews. . . .

The visit took place from March 21 to March 26, 2000, with the pope visiting Bethlehem, Jerusalem (including such places as the site of the Last Supper, the Holocaust Memorial at Yad Vashem, the Garden of Gethsemane, as well as his famous visit to the Wailing Wall), the Mount of Beatitudes, Capernaum, and Nazareth.

When Pope John Paul II died in April 2005, his funeral was attended by the President of Israel, Moshe Katsav; by the Israeli Minister of Foreign Affairs; and by other Israeli leaders. Representatives of Judaism also in attendance were the Chief Rabbi of Rome, Riccardo Di Segni, along with his predecessor Elio Toaff; the Grand Rabbi of Haifa, Israel; the General Director of the Grand Rabbinate of Israel; and the President of the World Jewish Congress. The Anti-Defamation League, an organization committed to fighting anti-Semitism, has written that "throughout his lifetime, the Pontiff has defended the Jewish people, both as a priest in his native Poland and for all the years of his Pontificate." (See Figure 12-1 for a photograph of JP2's lying in state at the Vatican.)

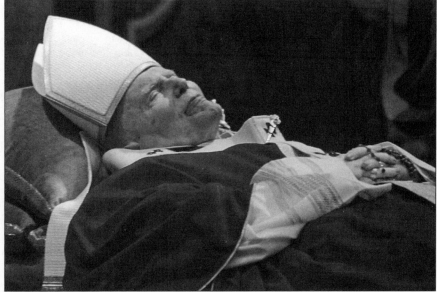

Figure 12-1: The body of Pope John Paul II lies in state at the Vatican.

© POOL/Reuters/Corbis

Taking Care of Family Business: Catholics and Protestants

The story is told about Pope John XXIII meeting a delegation of members of the U.S. Congress at the Vatican. Caught up in the moment and perhaps a little nervous about what to say, one member could only blurt out the words, "I'm a Baptist!", to which Pope John XXIII replied, "What a coincidence, I'm John!"

Protestant Reformation

The Protestant Reformation was begun by Martin Luther (1483–1546), an Augustinian priest and lecturer at the University of Wittenberg. The Catholic Church of the 16th century had problems on several levels: political and economic changes in Europe, and plenty of scandalous examples of *nepotism* (the choosing of family members to fill positions regardless of their actual qualifications) and *simony* (the buying of Church offices and Church "things," such as sacraments and relics of saints).

The straw that broke the camel's back for Martin Luther came over the ability to receive an *indulgence* (spiritual remission of all temporal punishment due to sin — for more on indulgences, see *Catholicism For Dummies*) in exchange for a donation toward the rebuilding of St. Peter's Basilica in Rome. Some unscrupulous clerics — priests and bishops alike — abused and distorted the concept of indulgences in order to get lucrative donations for their Church projects. This was always a sinful practice (simony is the selling of spiritual graces) but not always, vigorously, and universally condemned by some Church leaders as it should have been.

For a while, Luther had a long struggle over the diminished notion of personal accountability for sin. Now, with what appeared to be Rome's sanctioning of the belief that a person could "buy" his way into heaven, Luther could not

take it any more. On October 31, 1517, Luther issued 95 *theses* (statements) for debate and discussion over the issues of faith, salvation, sin, and reconciliation. His theses were met with silence; no one would debate him. Though written in Latin, the theses were quickly translated into German, and Luther soon became the unofficial leader of anyone with a gripe against the Church. Luther never intended to gain a following, and he tried to explain himself in a letter to the pope. A theologian, John Eck, was sent to debate Luther, and in the debate Luther questioned papal primacy. A battle back and forth ensued between Luther and Rome, and in 1521, Martin Luther was excommunicated. But his struggle made him famous, and his following gave rise to Lutheranism.

In questioning centralized authority, Luther also showed the lack of any need for it. This stance opened the door for anyone who disagreed with anyone else to simply split off, rather than try to decide "Who's right?" And so by 1520, Ulrich Zwingli began a reform movement in Switzerland separate from Lutheranism (he felt Luther didn't go far enough). These breaks grew exponentially as groups broke off from other groups (who had themselves broken off from other groups!). From these breaks come the thousands of Protestant (from the word *protest)* denominations that exist today.

From his days as Archbishop of Krakow, Pope John Paul II reached out to Protestants in Poland, following the example set by the Second Vatican Council. He certainly didn't do this for publicity in his native Poland, where non-Catholic Christians are in an extreme minority. As a Council Father of the Second Vatican Council, he embraced the teachings put forth in *Lumen Gentium,* the Dogmatic Constitution on the Church, including paragraph 8, which says that "many elements of sanctification and of truth are found out-side [the Catholic Church's] visible confines. Since these are gifts belonging to the Church of Christ, they are forces impelling towards Catholic unity."

Anglicans

Pope John Paul II had good relationships with each of the three Anglican Archbishops of Canterbury who served during his pontificate. In 1982, JP2 became the first pope to set foot on British soil since Henry VIII made a series of moves establishing himself as Supreme Head of the English Church in the 1530s. The multicity visit was a success, with a Buckingham Palace meeting with Queen Elizabeth II, and an ecumenical prayer service with the Archbishop of Canterbury, Robert Runcie. The visit came at a time of great tension between England and Argentina, who were fighting over possession of the Falkland Islands off the Argentine coast. Pope John Paul II, not wanting anyone to mistake his papal visit for support of England over extremely Catholic Argentina, followed his trip to England with a trip to Argentina, all the while working for peace using both British and Argentine bishops.

In the early years of Pope John Paul II's pontificate, the rift with the Anglicans seemed to be the one that would be the easiest to mend, because it flowed from a political split and not a theological one. But a severe (and some would say irreversible) blow was dealt with the widespread ordination of women as Anglican priests. Pope John Paul II's ecumenical outreach had the consistent theme of "what's past is past," but this move and the subsequent move in some of the Anglican Communion to recognize homosexual marriage and to ordain practicing homosexuals, which took hold and flourished during JP2's pontificate have continued to make reconciliation with the Anglican Communion more and more unlikely.

The most impressive show of the healing of centuries of animosity between the Church of England and the Roman Catholic Church came at Pope John Paul II's funeral. In attendance were not only British Prime Minister Tony Blair and his wife (a Catholic) representing the government, but the Archbishop of Canterbury, Dr. Rowan Williams, representing the Anglican Communion, and Prince Charles, the Prince of Wales and heir to the British throne.

Lutherans

On October 31, 1983, Pope John Paul II wrote a letter to a cardinal of the Secretariat for Promoting Christian Unity on the occasion of the 500th anniversary of Martin Luther's birth (though technically these letters are addressed to a specific person, they're meant for public distribution). Early on in his pontificate, JP2 hoped that the Catholic Church and the Lutherans could focus on the things they hold in common (the teachings of early Church councils, love for Sacred Scripture, and the like), instead of focusing solely on the events of the past that caused the division. This letter was followed by the pope's visit to Rome's Lutheran church during Advent of 1983, at which he preached at a Liturgy of the Word.

With the year 2000 on the horizon, Pope John Paul II hoped for some great breakthrough in Christian unity (not just with Lutherans, but among all Christians) in time for the Jubilee. He took the initiative to write an encyclical on the topic, called *Ut Unum Sint* (That They May Be One, from the prayer of Christ at the Last Supper), issued on May 25, 1995. In the encyclical, he reached out to Protestants and Orthodox alike, asking them to help him to understand how the pope (as the successor to St. Peter) could unify Christians around the world.

The high-water mark between Lutherans and Catholics of Pope John Paul II's pontificate was the June 25, 1998, Joint Declaration on the Doctrine of Justification. (In Christian theology, the term *justification* means "eternal salvation" — in other words, getting to heaven. Lutherans believe a person is saved solely through faith in Jesus Christ, while Roman Catholics believe that faith must be accompanied by good works.) Although the document was meant to be a declaration on the basic truths shared by both Catholics and Lutherans, some sought to make more out of it, and soon there was a need to reiterate the items that Catholics and Lutherans *disagreed* upon. Lutherans were offended at this, and Catholics were offended that the Lutherans were offended. In the end, another declaration came out from both parties saying that nothing included in the original declaration had disagreed with past doctrine.

Representatives from the World Lutheran Federation attended Pope John Paul II's funeral, and since then they have met with Pope Benedict XVI. The International Lutheran–Roman Catholic Commission on Unity continues to meet and discuss the theological questions that are sources of division.

Creating an Atmosphere for Dialog: Catholics and Muslims

Vatican II's *Nostra Aetate* speaks about Muslims, saying, "The Church has . . . a high regard for the Muslims." The paragraph praises Islam's monotheism, and the respect shown to biblical figures such as Abraham, the Blessed Virgin

Mary, and even Jesus Christ himself (whom Muslims regard as a prophet, rather than God). Though the Council Fathers acknowledge that, "Over the centuries many quarrels and dissensions have arisen between Christians and Muslims," the paragraph concludes with a plea for both sides to "forget the past, and urges that a sincere effort be made to achieve mutual understanding," and to "together preserve and promote peace, liberty, social justice, and moral values."

Pope John Paul II's first outreach to Islam happened during his 1981 trip to the Far East. On the way to the Philippines, the pope's plane made a "technical stopover" in predominantly Muslim Pakistan. But this was not your normal stop for gas and snacks. During the four-hour stop, the pope celebrated an outdoor Mass for 100,000 Pakistani Catholics.

Reaching out to Muslims of the world

Pope John Paul II's great moment of outreach to Islam took place on August 19, 1985, when, at the invitation of King Hassan II of Morocco, the Holy Father spoke to 80,000 young Muslims at a stadium in Casablanca. (The United Nations had declared 1985 as the International Year of Youth.)

At the meeting, the pope spoke to the young people about their common faith in one God and their common reverence for Abraham as a model of faith. He spoke to them about human values based upon this faith in God as the Creator of all things and all people: "The dialogue between Christians and Muslims today is more necessary than ever." He told them,

> Young people can construct a better future if they first of all place their faith in God and if they are engaged to build up this new world according to the plan of God, with wisdom and confidence.

He urged them to allow their understanding of God's goodness to also include openness to God-given liberties, especially religious liberties in a place where Christians are in the minority. (This theme would become constant in Pope John Paul II's messages and foreign visits.)

The young people's response to the pope was overwhelmingly positive, causing one Vatican official to quip that the pope got a better response from Muslim youths than he gets from some Roman Catholics! Reflecting on the visit in his 1994 book *Crossing the Threshold of Hope*, Pope John Paul II was clearly pleased with the meeting, describing it as "unforgettable," "striking," and an "unprecedented event."

Kissing the Koran

May 1999 brought Pope John Paul II another moment of controversy surrounding Islam. The month began well, with his usual catechetical address at the Wednesday Audience of May 5, focusing on inter-religious dialogue between Christians and Muslims. "We Christians joyfully recognize the religious values we have in common with Islam," the pope said.

Working toward his hope to visit Iraq in order to begin his Jubilee pilgrimage in the land of the Jewish patriarch Abraham, JP2 met with the Patriarch of Chaldean Christians as well as representatives of Muslim Shiite and Sunni factions. At the audience, gifts were exchanged (a normal occurrence), and the pope received a copy of the Koran and, upon accepting it, kissed it.

The photograph of that moment sent shockwaves around the Catholic world! Had the pope equated Islam with Christianity? He kisses the Sacred Scriptures at Mass — did he just do the same thing to the Koran? The answer is simple: Same lips, different reason. The pope had been advised that in the Near Eastern culture, when a gift is received, it is normally kissed as a sign of respect to the gift's giver. The pope would have kissed *whatever* gift was given to him, whether it was the Koran or commemorative coins (which is actually what the pope usually gives to visiting guests).

Visiting a mosque

On May 6, 2001, while on his apostolic visits to Greece, Syria, and Malta, Pope John Paul II became the first pope to visit a mosque. While in Damascus after celebrating a Mass for 30,000 Christians, JP2 visited the Omayyad Mosque, a former church that traditionally contains the tomb of St. John the Baptist. Though hardliner Muslims were able to prevent common prayer from taking place at the mosque, in his address the pope said that "Christians and Muslims agree that the encounter with God in prayer is the necessary nourishment of our souls." He said he hoped that both "Christian and Muslim religious leaders and teachers will present our two great religious communities as communities in respectful dialogue, never more as communities in conflict."

Amongst the religious delegations attending Pope John Paul II's funeral were 17 Muslims, among them the General Secretary and Imam of Rome's Islamic Cultural Center, and Muslim spiritual leaders from Israel, Albania, London, and Libya. Add to that the official delegations from countries such as Afghanistan, Iran, Iraq, Jordan, Lebanon, Morocco, the National Palestinian Authority, and others, and you see the extent that Pope John Paul II was held in respect by the Islamic world.

Trying to Heal the East-West Split: Catholicism and Orthodoxy

Pope John Paul II came to the papacy with an understanding of Eastern Orthodoxy that none of his immediate predecessors enjoyed. Having grown up a Pole, he had extensive experience with the Orthodox Church. Even his native language of Polish has its roots in Old Slavonic, which remains the liturgical language of the Orthodox (just as Latin technically remains for the Catholic Church). Following the teachings of the Second Vatican Council's Dogmatic Constitution on the Church (*Lumen Gentium* 8), JP2 chose to focus on the elements of truth that did exist in these denominations, rather than the causes of division, whether theological, historical, or political.

If Pope John Paul II could communicate to us whether he left this Earth with any regrets, he would probably tell us he wished that he'd been able to reconcile the Orthodox churches of the east with the Roman Catholic Church of the west. Certainly, he would have recognized the fact that he brought a unique perspective to the papacy, thanks to his upbringing. Looking at the time in history that he was elected, with the year 2000 looming before him on the horizon, perhaps he also saw the hand of God gently but deliberately pushing him into the direction of reunification with the Orthodox. Regardless of the fact that it didn't happen, no one can say it was because he never tried.

Visiting Turkey

Shortly after his election, Pope John Paul II indicated he wanted to visit Istanbul as soon as possible, intending on being there for the Feast of St. Andrew personally, rather than sending a delegation as usual. From November 28 through November 30, 1979, the Holy Father visited Turkey, visiting Armenian Catholics and Orthodox, and attending the Orthodox Divine Liturgy on the Feast of St. Andrew. Although the pope was not the main celebrant of the Orthodox Divine Liturgy, during the ceremony the pope and Patriarch Demetrios publicly exchanged the kiss of peace, and at the conclusion both imparted the final blessing. It was a good start to Pope John Paul II's pontificate.

More success followed. In 1983, Pope John Paul II called a special Holy Year to commemorate 1,950 years since the redeeming death of Jesus Christ. During the Holy Year, delegations from the different Orthodox churches made visits to Rome, among them the Greek and Syrian Orthodox. In December 1987, Patriarch Demetrios of Constantinople made a five-day visit to Rome. At the end of the visit, he and Pope John Paul II signed a joint declaration agreeing to continue the dialogue between the two churches with the goal toward the reestablishment of full communion. On October 2, 1991, Patriarch Demetrios died, and on November 2, 1991, Patriarch Bartholomew I, who had previously been Patriarch of Chalcedon, succeeded him.

Orthodox churches

For the first 1,000 years after Christ, there were no Greek "eastern" or Latin "western" churches, there was only "Christendom." Yes, separate traditions and rites had evolved (no big shock in the days before easy communication), but in spite of the differences, the commonly held understanding was that Christianity was one large entity.

How did the break start? It began as a political split within the Roman Empire and evolved into a theological split. The worst of it occurred on July 16, 1054, when a monk named Humbert, acting as an emissary in the name of Pope Leo IX, excommunicated the Patriarch of Constantinople, Michael I Cerularius. Cerularius returned the favor by excommunicating Leo. Push came to shove in this "sibling rivalry" in the Fourth Crusade, when in 1204 the city of Constantinople was sacked by Latin Christians. (In 2004, Pope John Paul II formally apologized for this to Patriarch Bartholomew on behalf of the Catholic Church.)

That's where things stood until 1964, when Pope Paul VI and Patriarch Athenagoras I of Constantinople mutually lifted the excommunications their predecessors had imposed. Since then, the two Churches honored each other by reciprocating visits of delegations on the feast days of their apostolic founders: the Orthodox visiting Rome on June 29 (the Feast of St. Peter and St. Paul) and the Catholics visiting Istanbul on November 30 (the Feast of St. Andrew).

Today the Orthodox churches are centered on the cities where Christ's Apostles established Christian communities: Istanbul, Turkey; Alexandria, Egypt; Antioch, Syria; and Jerusalem, Israel. From these first foundations came Orthodox churches in Russia, Greece, Serbia, Bulgaria, Romania, Sinai, and other places. Denying the idea that Christ established a papacy, the patriarchs of these churches have autonomous authority in their churches. Yet within orthodoxy, they see themselves as equals with each other, with the Patriarch of Constantinople being the "first amongst equals."

The Catholic and Orthodox churches can best be described metaphorically, as twins separated at birth: The genetic base material that makes them up is almost identical, even though centuries of separate lives have caused differences that make them seem distinct.

Today, the Orthodox churches have a membership of about 250 million people.

Capitalizing on the collapse of Communism

With the collapse of Communism in the late 1980s and early 1990s, the pastoral care of Catholics in the former Soviet republics became something to examine seriously. An October 1, 1990, law signed by Mikhail Gorbachev allowed for religious freedom in the Soviet Union, and Pope John Paul II responded to the window of opportunity.

On April 13, 1991, the Vatican announced that three apostolic administrations had been established in Russia — Moscow, Novosibirsk (Siberia), and

Karaganda (Kazakstan), with bishops appointed to the positions of apostolic administrator in each. The Russian Orthodox Church protested angrily, complaining that it wasn't even warned of the decision during a visit by Metropolitan Kyril (head of the Russian Orthodox Church's office of external affairs) to Rome just weeks before. The early 1990s may have seen the end of the political cold war, but at that time the ecclesial war was still going strong.

Striving for one church

The 1995 encyclical *Ut Unum Sint* made it clear that Pope John Paul II still had a strong commitment to ecumenical dialogue with the Orthodox churches, whom he referred to as "sisters." Rather than a return to the initial ecumenical zeal of the Second Vatican Council, JP2 wanted to go way back — to the first thousand years of Christendom, when there was a unity despite local customs and traditions.

Ut Unum Sint was followed by the proposition of a meeting between Pope John Paul II and Russian Orthodox Patriarch Aleksy in June 1997. The European Orthodox Church was holding an assembly, and Pope John Paul II was willing to travel to Austria, the site of the assembly, to meet with the patriarch. News of the proposed meeting leaked out before Patriarch Aleksy officially agreed to it, and Patriarch Bartholomew (the "first among equals" in the Orthodox churches) insisted that he be included in the meetings. The meeting never took place.

Pope John Paul II's last great hope to visit Moscow was in July 2004 and revolved around an image of the Blessed Virgin Mary. The 13th-century image of Our Lady of Kazan is an ancient icon belonging to the Russian Orthodox Church; the icon was lost during the 1917 Russian Revolution but ended up at the Vatican. The pope hoped that, from a historical art perspective, Russian President Vladimir Putin would override Patriarch Aleksy's opposition to a papal visit. Patriarch Aleksy maintained that it was not the original, but merely a copy, and so this was no great gesture. On August 28, 2004, a Vatican delegation traveled to Moscow and presented the image at the Orthodox cathedral.

A most impressive show of Christian unity came at Pope John Paul II's funeral itself. In attendance were Ecumenical Patriarch Bartholomew, along with patriarchs, metropolitans, and other representatives from 23 different Orthodox churches.

Asking for Forgiveness for Sins of the Past

On March 12, 2000, the first Sunday in the Catholic Church's penitential season of Lent, Pope John Paul II led a prayer service in St. Peter's Basilica unlike any other that people were used to witnessing: a Day of Pardon. The Holy Father wanted to take time within the festivities of the Jubilee Year not just to rejoice and celebrate, but also to ask God for forgiveness of the sins committed by the members of the Church in the past, as well as to ask God to forgive those sins that were committed against members of the Church by others.

This time of contrition had been an intention of Pope John Paul II's from the time he wrote of his plans for the Church's celebration of the Jubilee Year of 2000 in the 1994 apostolic letter *Tertio Millennio Adveniente*. JP2 understood that a Jubilee year was primarily a time of joy, and part of that would be the "joy of conversion" based on the forgiveness of sins. "Acknowledging the weaknesses of the past," the pope wrote in the letter, "is an act of honesty and courage which helps us to strengthen our faith, which alerts us to face today's temptations and challenges and prepares us to meet them."

The pope began the service praying before Michelangelo's *Pietà,* the marble sculpture depicting Mary holding in her arms Jesus's body after he had been taken down from the cross. Like Mary, Pope John Paul II felt, the Church needed to "embrace the crucified Savior, to take responsibility for the past of her children and to implore the Father's forgiveness." As the procession made its way to the altar, the Litany of the Saints was sung, asking those whom the Church holds up as examples of holiness to pray for us before God, in whose presence they now exist.

Upon reaching the altar, following the pope's homily, seven members of the Vatican curia prayed prayers of intercession before lighting oil lamps in front of the 15th-century crucifix from the Church of San Marcello al Corso, which is traditionally brought to St. Peter's Basilica during Holy Years for the veneration of pilgrims. The prayers asked for

- An "authentic purification of memory" and the grace for true conversion
- Pardon for defending the truth using methods not in keeping with the Gospel
- Pardon for wounds against fraternal charity that have prevented Christian unity
- Pardon for sins committed against Jews

✔ Pardon for sins committed against society's weakest and members of other religions

✔ Pardon for sins against women and the unity of the human race

✔ Pardon for sins that deny the dignity of every person

As each of the lamps was lit, the choir chanted the Greek prayer of petition, *Kyrie, eleison* (Lord, have mercy). The ceremony concluded with Pope John Paul II embracing the crucifix and asking that the forgiveness asked for in the prayer service become a moment for the Church and all its members to recommit themselves to fidelity to the Gospel.

In remarks from the window of the papal apartments to the crowd below, Pope John Paul II asked, "For all believers may the fruit of this Jubilee Day be forgiveness reciprocally given and received!" He continued, "Forgiven and ready to forgive, Christians enter the third millennium as more credible witnesses to hope."

The reaction from the world ranged from those who thought it a publicity stunt to those who thought it meant the Roman Catholic Church was apologizing for its teachings. It is interesting to note, though, that following the Day of Pardon in 2000, no other leader of a major religious denomination followed suit and asked for pardon for sins committed by their own members through the course of history.

In the end, the Day of Pardon was not meant to get good headlines or to appease the world. Nor was it specifically done as a peace offering to other religions. It was John Paul II, the Vicar of Christ, leading the flock entrusted to him in a giant act of contrition before God. He was being a good *pontifex,* a good bridge-builder, making sure his work was properly maintained and cared for.

Chapter 13

Slaying the Dragon: Helping to Defeat the Evil Empire

....

In This Chapter

▶ Figuring out how popes worked with Communist regimes

▶ Traveling to Poland

▶ Working with Solidarity to effect change

....

After World War II, many countries turned to the hope that Communism would help cure what ailed them. As we know now, that system was ill-fated and short-lived. But at the time, the outlook was often very bleak for those who lived under the Communist regimes. One of those people was Karol Wojtyła. (Take a look at Chapter 2 for information on what historic events shaped his life and times.)

In this chapter, we show you how popes historically interacted with the Communist governments. Then we show you how Pope John Paul II used his visits and encouragement to give the Polish people support and hope. Finally, we explore his involvement with the infamous labor union, Solidarity.

Recognizing How JP2 Dealt with the Communist Bloc

Each pope had his own way of dealing with the Communist bloc (see the nearby sidebar for more on how other popes handled it). In the following sections, we give you a look at how John Paul II interacted with Communists.

The popes versus Communism: Rounds 1, 2, and 3

In the years following World War II, popes dealt with the Communist bloc according to their own style as opposed to following any official Vatican policy on the subject.

Pope Pius XII (1939–1958) had a policy of not dealing directly with Communists, so no real exchanges took place during his pontificate.

Pope John XXIII (1958–1963) devoted much of his brief pontificate to the preparations for the Second Vatican Council, which he called for in January 1959. He did, however, write the encyclical *Pacem in Terris* (issued on April 11, 1963, dealing with the topic of world peace), which was received well in public responses by the countries under Soviet control.

Pope Paul VI (1963–1978) hoped to build upon the good will generated by John XXIII's encyclical. Pope Paul VI had a special place in his heart for Poland; in 1923, as a young priest in the Vatican diplomatic service, his first assignment had been to the *nunciature* (embassy) in Warsaw. The year 1966 marked the 1,000-year anniversary of the arrival of Christianity in Poland, and Pope Paul VI hoped to visit Poland to mark the celebration. The government of Poland (with the advice of the Soviet Union) never actually "refused" the trip, but it made negotiations so difficult that eventually it was the Vatican that decided against the pope's visit.

Working within the communist system

Although politically aligned with the Soviet Union after 1945, Poland's historical alliance with western Europe and the Latin-Rite Church (see Chapter 4) meant that there would be a built-in strain in relations. Tensions always existed between the Holy See and the Polish authorities, but the Vatican knew that, in order for the Church to survive, the people would need priests to make the sacraments of the Church available for them. In order to have these priests, the Vatican knew they needed the government's acceptance of Rome's naming of bishops, who alone had the sacramental power to ordain men to the priesthood.

The Polish communists actually encouraged Rome to name new bishops, hoping that it would water down the power and influence of the Primate of Poland, Stefan Cardinal Wyszyński, who was a constant thorn in the side of the Polish government. In 1967, then-Archbishop Karol Wojtyła was named a Cardinal of the Roman Catholic Church, and the Communist regime was actually happy that there would now be another cardinal in Poland besides Wyszyński. The fact that Cardinal Wojtyła was not from a noble family fed nicely into the Communist philosophy. Besides, internal investigations into Wojtyła reported that he was actually seen by the government as more of a moderate and someone who could be reasoned with.

Wojtyła, for his part, made sure that he never played into the hands of the government. He made sure, even as a cardinal of the Catholic Church, to remain respectful and publicly deferential to Cardinal Wyszyński. (This wasn't a hard thing to do, as Wyszyński was a living legend.)

Instead of becoming two opposing sides, as the Communists had hoped, Wyszyński and Wojtyła complemented each other in the fight against totalitarianism. Wojtyła represented the advent of the intellectuals into the fight for the soul of Poland. Cardinal Wojtyła attacked Communism on intellectual grounds, besides serving as the liaison between Wyszyński and the Polish academics. By the time Pope Paul VI died on August 6, 1978, Polish authorities had regretted their earlier stand and had grown to fear Wojtyła more than Wyszyński. (Supposedly, following the news of Wojtyła's election as pope, KGB head Yuri Andropov angrily questioned his subordinate in Warsaw, asking, "How could you allow this to happen?")

Waiting for the Polish government's reaction to his election

The election of Cardinal Wojtyła as Pope John Paul II on October 16, 1978, was met with several hours of official silence in Poland, while government authorities struggled to come up with an "official" government response! When they did respond with a congratulatory telegram, they ignored the religious dimension and praised his election as a "triumph for the Polish nation." Pope John Paul II reminded them of the religious implications of the election of a Pole by mentioning Poland's thousand-year loyalty to the Catholic Church. Bowing to public pressure, Polish television (under government control) agreed to air three hours of Pope John Paul II's installation on October 22. JP2, with an actor's sense of the importance of timing, made sure his installation took exactly three hours, thus preventing government commentators from subjecting the massive audience to Communist Party propaganda.

On October 23, the day after his installation, Pope John Paul II held an audience for Polish pilgrims who had been able to come to Rome and the Vatican. As the Poles left behind one of their own, it was an emotional farewell. Pope John Paul II had written two letters, which he sent back to Poland by way of the Polish bishops who were in Rome for the festivities: The first letter was for all of Poland, explaining his sadness on leaving his homeland and crediting the witness of the Polish Church under Nazism and Marxism as the reason a Polish pope was elected. The second letter was a more personal goodbye to his Archdiocese of Krakow.

Having a unique understanding of the system

Pope John Paul II's experience in Poland meant he was the first pope to deal with Communism "from the inside." But when he became pope, he did not set out to "tear down the Iron Curtain" as part of some vendetta (he knew he was a spiritual leader, not a political leader).

JP2's years of pastoral work as a priest and bishop gave him valuable insight into the minds of those who lived day-to-day under Communist rule. Furthermore, his natural curiosity as an intellect meant that he had studied Marxism and knew where the weakness lied. He certainly wanted to further the cause of fundamental human rights, among them being the right to freely practice religion and organize labor unions to promote better living conditions.

But in working to bring hope and moral support to his fellow Poles to further those goals (especially by his 1979 visit), he revealed the "weak underbelly" of the Communist bloc: If citizens decide not to submit to the state, without doing so in a violent way, the state has no way of functioning or maintaining control. This premise quickly spread to the other countries under Soviet control in the late 1980s and early 1990s, at the same time that the Soviet Union was being financially stretched by constantly competing with the United States. In the end, the Soviet Union wasn't "destroyed" from the outside as much as "imploded" from within, and it all began with Poland.

The Soviets did their own investigation and made their own predictions of Pope John Paul II's pontificate, and feared that he would work specifically for religious freedom in the countries of Eastern Europe. They were also particularly worried about his influence in Poland, whose geographic location made it vital in the support (and possible defense) of East Germany. They also feared his influence amongst Latin-rite Catholics in places like Czechoslovakia, Hungary, Lithuania, and the Ukraine.

JP2 avoided direct challenges to the Soviets. But like a termite, he began to attack Communism from the inside, going after its claim to be the true "liberator" of the people. The Church, according to Pope John Paul II, has the right to speak out to the world's governments as an advocate for human rights and the dignity of every human being as a creation of God. (Soviet Marxism stressed the dignity of the state over the dignity of its people.)

At the same time JP2 was attacking Communism from within, he named Archbishop Agostino Casaroli, a veteran diplomat from the Pope Paul VI years of negotiating with the Soviets, as the Vatican Secretary of State. In this move, JP2 blocked any charge by the Soviet Union that he was making a radical change in the way the Soviets and the Vatican had previously done business.

JP2's experience rooted in Polish tradition taught Pope John Paul II that the most effective way of fighting oppressive governments was to promote the culture and history of the people. Pope John Paul II's homily during his installation (aired nationwide in Poland) sent the message home to "be not afraid," reiterating, "Open wide the doors for Christ." In other words, do not be afraid of displays of power; allow Christ into your lives, your homes, and your social interactions, and you can be stronger than the shows of might.

In addition, Pope John Paul II made use of his own knowledge of Polish culture by sending home a Christmas letter to the Archdiocese of Krakow, reminding them of the example of St. Stanislaus (1030–1079), the Polish Bishop of Krakow who stood up for the Church's rights in the face of King Boleslaus and was martyred because of it. He knew how to connect with his people, and the message was getting out loud and clear that Pope John Paul II understood that God had called a Pole to be pope for a larger reason.

Visiting the Homeland

The year 1979 was the 900th anniversary of the martyrdom of St. Stanislaus, and Pope John Paul II made it clear that he had every intention of returning to his native Poland to take part in the festivities honoring his predecessor as Archbishop of Krakow.

Polish authorities stood in the middle of a game of tug-of-war. On one side, the Vatican and Cardinal Wyszyński were putting pressure on them to allow Pope John Paul II to visit Poland as part of the anniversary festivities, and on the other hand Moscow didn't want Pope John Paul II playing the part of a victorious warrior returning home.

What followed then were a series of blunders by the Polish government, which came out as distinct advantages for Pope John Paul II. JP2 wanted to be in Poland on May 8, 1979 (for the Feast of St. Stanislaus). Authorities fought this, seeing in it too outward a connection between the circumstances of St. Stanislaus's standing up to the state and the papal visit. They were against his coming in May and suggested the trip be the following month. Trip organizers agreed, and what was to be a two-day visit to two cities became a nine-day visit to six cities. In addition, the new dates meant that Pope John Paul II would be in Poland for the Feast of Pentecost, the traditional "birthday" of the Church, when the Holy Spirit descended upon the Apostles and empowered them to preach and teach in the name of Christ. The religious significance of that day was not lost on the people.

The next mistake on the part of the government was the offer to broadcast parts of the visit on national television. They did so for selfish reasons, hoping the ability for people to watch from their own living rooms would minimize the crowds. Not only was televising the visit ineffective in keeping the crowds away, but now the elderly and homebound were able to watch what they would never have had the chance to see, thanks to the government.

In the following sections, we look at the impact created by Pope John Paul in his pilgrimages to Poland.

The first papal visit as Pope John Paul II

In all, Pope John Paul II made eight trips (or pilgrimages, as he considered all of his apostolic journeys) to Poland. But the first visit was the one witnessed by the world and widely considered the one that began the eventual peaceful demise of Communist rule in Poland (as well as the eventual demise of the Soviet Union).

Pope John Paul II arrived in Warsaw on June 2, 1979. Warsaw had become a sea of people, as an estimated three million Poles turned out to be with the pope. Hundreds of thousands of people lined the route from the airport to the inner city just to catch a glimpse of JP2.

During the open-air Mass in Victory Square that followed, JP2 told them he came to fulfill Pope Paul VI's wish to visit Poland as a pilgrim. He told them he was there to commemorate the 900th anniversary of the martyrdom of St. Stanislaus, who was killed for standing up in the face of civil authority for the truth (something the Poles did very well). As he stood under a 50-foot cross built for the outdoor celebration of Mass, he reminded the Polish people that they had often been called to give witness to the power of the cross in the life of a Christian, and that as much as past rulers and enemies in Poland's history had tried to eliminate Christianity, Jesus Christ cannot be taken out of history.

The following day, JP2 remembered his roots as a college chaplain and celebrated a Mass for university students, before flying to the town of Gniezno to visit the relics of St. Adalbert, the first missionary to Poland back in the tenth century. The next day, he traveled to Jasna Gora, the "bright mountain," which was home to the Paulist monastery and the Polish national treasure of the icon of Our Lady of Czestochowa, followed by a meeting with the natives of the region and a meeting with the sick.

The schedule of meetings with various groups of clergy, religious, and laity continued, until he flew to Krakow for an emotional homecoming. There, he stayed in his old rooms at the Archbishop's Palace, all the while being serenaded by crowds of teens and college students who stood beneath his window and urged him to join them in singing (which he did until past midnight).

Pope John Paul II retraced his steps as a child by making a pilgrimage to Kalwaria Zebrzydowska, named for a 17th-century governor of Krakow who built a series of chapels on the side of a mountain to resemble the shrines and chapels built in Jerusalem at the places Jesus Christ walked on the way to his death on Mount Calvary. Over the years, chapels were added that took into account the traditional lore of Mary's whereabouts during her son's *Passion* (suffering).

Following this trip to Kalwaria Zebrzydowska, JP2 returned to his hometown of Wadowice, where he was met by 30,000 people. Later, he traveled to Oswiecim, the site of the Auschwitz concentration camp, where he celebrated Mass and made a trip to the cell where, in 1941, the Polish Franciscan Maximilian Kolbe had voluntarily taken the place of another man and was killed as retribution for an escaped prisoner.

On the evening of June 8, he had an emotional meeting with the young people of Krakow. The high they were feeling during the pope's visit, combined with their own natural zeal and fervor, made the situation somewhat frightening: What if these young people took matters into their own hands and started to openly and violently revolt against the government? Pope John Paul II mixed humor and paternal advice and teaching to keep them calm and nonviolent.

The last day of the pope's visit was June 10, 1979, and it began with a Mass on the Krakow commons attended by a crowd of two to three million people.

Words do not do justice to the feelings of joy and happiness that the papal visit brought to the Polish people. Thousands of people opened their homes to strangers to give travelers places to sleep. Churches remained opened around the clock for prayers and the practical necessities of the pilgrims. Homes, storefronts, and huge apartment houses were decorated as if the Holy Father were going to inspect the decorations himself.

An estimated 13 million people saw Pope John Paul II in person, and he left them with the gift of hope. For the first time, they felt there was a real opportunity to change their lives through peaceful means. The sacrifices made by so many to travel to the different places where the Holy Father would be showed them how many they were in numbers compared to the government troops. Suddenly the Polish people realized how they outnumbered those who supposedly were in the majority and in charge of the country.

Making subsequent journeys

Pope John Paul II's second trip to Poland took place from June 16 to June 23, 1983, on the occasion of the 600th anniversary of the monastery at Jasna Gora. This trip had a more somber tone to it than his first trip, because the government had imposed *martial law* (a condition that allowed them to impose a curfew, prohibit any public demonstrations, and so on) in Poland

and arrested the leaders of the Solidarity trade union. JP2 made a specific effort to give the people a feeling that he was there to comfort and encourage them. He wanted them to know that he knew how they were feeling. He visited the city of Warsaw and the St. Maximilian Kolbe shrine at Niepokalanow, met with young people at Czestochowa, and traveled to the cities of Poznań, Katowice, Wrocław, Mount St. Anne, and Krakow.

Pope John Paul II made a specific attempt to meet with Solidarity leader Lech Wałesa, and a private meeting was arranged in a cabin in the Tatra Mountains. No cameras were allowed, and Wałesa had to be flown in by helicopter in order to meet with the pope. By joining the people of Poland in their time of struggle, JP2 showed that there would be no compromise in this battle for freedom.

His third trip to Poland took place from June 8 to June 14, 1987. On this trip, he visited Warsaw, Krakow, and Gdańsk, the birthplace of the Solidarity union. (His outdoor Mass in Gdańsk attracted one million people.)

By 1987, both the Polish people and the government knew that the Solidarity union and the movement behind it was too powerful to stop. Pope John Paul II knew that freedom was soon to come to Poland, and he wanted to prepare them for the issues they soon would face as a free people.

His fourth trip to Poland came from June 1 to June 9, 1991. With the collapse of not just the Polish Communist Party but the Soviet Union, most people expected Pope John Paul II to come on this tour as their victorious leader. Instead, the pope planned to teach the Polish people of the dangers of newfound freedom and the responsibility that come with being the navigators of the future of their country. In August, he returned for the celebration of World Youth Day at Czestochowa, spending time not just with thousands of young people from around the world, but also visiting Krakow and Wadowice.

His fifth visit to Poland was a brief one — lasting only one day. It came during a pilgrimage to the Czech Republic. On May 22, 1995, JP2 crossed the border and visited the towns of Skoczów, Bielsko-Biała, and Żwiec.

The sixth visit of Pope John Paul II to Poland happened between May 31 and June 10, 1997. By that time, the Polish people had won their freedom and had begun to face the questions of how to live as free people. JP2's homilies stressed the need to remember their culture and history and not get caught up in the newfound political and economic freedom. By then it was obvious that Pope John Paul II's health was in decline, and his visits were more like time spent with your grandfather than your comrade-in-arms. The question of a Polish constitution was being debated, as well as the legalization of abortion. He visited Warsaw, Legnica, Gniezno, Poznań, Kalisz, and Zakopane.

His seventh visit to Poland took place from June 5 through June 17, 1999. On the threshold of the Jubilee Year of 2000, Pope John Paul II visited Poland to talk about the renewal of Christian life and to celebrate the 1,000th anniversary of the establishment of the hierarchy of the Roman Catholic Church in Poland. On this trip, Pope John Paul II visited 22 cities, the most of any previous papal trip, often changing details at the last minute to see the greatest number of people.

Pope John Paul II's final trip to Poland took place from August 16 to August 19, 2002. Clearly in declining health, this was among his shortest trips to Poland, involving the least amount of travel. His last trip to Poland centered on the city of Krakow.

Supporting Solidarity

In many ways, Pope John Paul II's support for the Polish trade union Solidarity began in his remote past. The men and women who bravely risked their lives to promote change in an organized and purposely nonviolent way were the generation who, as children, were taught by Father Karol Wojtyła and priests like him. Karol's election as pope and his visit to Poland in 1979 had given this generation a sense of purpose and belief that they had the ability to effect change in what was previously believed to be an unchangeable situation.

Pope John Paul II resolved to do what he could to keep his people spiritually fed and encouraged. In April 1980, the first Polish weekly edition of the Vatican newspaper, *L'Osservatore Romano,* was printed. In addition, knowing the power of radio, JP2 encouraged more programming on Vatican Radio for Polish listeners.

Supporting the strikes from afar

By July 1980, price increases of food in Poland led to strikes for increases in wages. On July 16 of that year, Polish train operators went on strike and were joined soon after by other railroad workers along with bakers and dairy employees. The strike lasted four days, and it marked the first time that striking workers articulated a list of demands based on their rights as workers (that is, the right to strike, immunity for those who went on strike, free election of their union leaders, and the right to negotiate directly with the government).

On August 14, 1980, Anna Walentynowicz was fired from her position at the Lenin Shipyards in Gdańsk for stealing. She had taken the stubs of candles from a makeshift memorial to workers who were killed in an uprising in 1970 and was planning to melt the candles down into larger candles to place back at the memorial. In protest of her firing, 17,000 shipyard workers went on strike. Their leader, Lech Wałesa, issued terms for an eight-point reconciliation that required the government to acknowledge the workers' right to organize a labor union and to allow for a permanent monument to the fallen workers killed in the 1970 strike.

Not seeing any hope for reconciliation, the government turned to the Church, which offered to try to calm the situation by providing a priestly presence to the striking workers. Instead of encouraging the workers to stop, the clergy gave the workers the spiritual strength to continue in their efforts. Soon priests began celebrating an outdoor Mass for the strikers and made themselves available for strikers to go to confession. Their cause became a spiritual struggle.

In August 1980, Pope John Paul II acknowledged the striking Gdańsk workers during his Wednesday general audience. Speaking in Polish to the Poles and the press who were present, he united himself in prayer with the workers' cause and for their safety. On August 22, 1980, the intellectuals of Polish society came to Gdańsk and offered their services to the striking workers as informal advisors. At his August 27, 1980, weekly general audience, Pope John Paul II defended the strikers' cause as a call for "peace and justice." Soon after, the Polish episcopacy came out publicly supporting the strikers' right to organize.

By August 31, 1980, the government was ready to give in and allow self-governing, independent labor unions. Buoyed by the success of the shipyard workers, Polish steelworkers, miners, and other workers followed with their own strikes. Seen as unable to control the situation, Polish Communist Party leader Edward Gierek was voted out of office on September 5 and replaced with Stanislaw Kania. Someone had to take the blame for this situation, and Gierek was the one.

By mid-September 1980, 35 labor unions gathered to organize a national union. Drawing on JP2's call for national unity amongst workers, they called the union *Solidarnośc* (Solidarity). Things did not go perfectly, though. When Wałesa followed proper procedure and went to court to legally establish the union, the government dragged its feet in granting approval for Solidarity. The union responded with a small show of strength: From noon to 1 p.m. on October 3, 1980, workers did no work. All the while, Pope John Paul II was getting briefings from people like Cardinal Wyszyński and Tadeusz Mazowiecki (one of the intellectuals who advised the Gdańsk strikers). From a distance, JP2 watched with interest what was unfolding.

On October 24, 1980, Lech Wałesa returned to court, and this time the union was finally recognized by the courts. However, even then the judge sought to add pro-Communism rhetoric to the charter of Solidarity. Wałesa announced that he and his eight million members could not accept the changes. He demanded a meeting with Polish government officials and set a date of November 12 for a national strike of all Solidarity members.

By this point, the actions of Solidarity had been making news outside of Poland, and Communist countries like Czechoslovakia and East Germany, fearful that a Solidarity success would encourage other unions to follow suit in their own countries, urged the Soviet Union to get involved. Plans were underway for a proposed December invasion of Poland from the west (East Germany), south (Czechoslovakia), and east (Soviet Union). But the invasion never happened. On November 10, 1980, the Polish Supreme Court overturned the previous judge's amendment of the Solidarity charter, taking out the objectionable amendments. But deeper than that, there was a real fear that a takeover of Poland would not be an easy prospect. The Soviet Union was already facing pressure from around the world for its invasion of Afghanistan, and this would just add another country to the list. In addition, the Soviets were fearful that Poles would not simply give in and accept that they had overstepped their bounds; there was a chance that the Poles would fight back. The Soviets didn't want to risk a negative world opinion, and at the same time, Polish leaders were assuring them they had the situation under control.

Pope John Paul II sent a letter to Leonid Brezhnev, reminding him that Poland was a sovereign nation and that he had no authority to interfere in what was essentially an internal matter for Poland. John Paul II was no fool: He knew that in 1975, the Soviets pushed for what was called the *Helsinki Final Act,* which was a strategy to keep the west from attempting to try to "liberate" any of the Warsaw Pact countries by arguing that internal conflicts within countries should be resolved by the country itself, without any interference from other nations. The Holy Father was using Brezhnev's strategy against him, and he must've had a good time doing so!

In January 1981, Lech Wałesa and Solidarity leaders traveled to Rome to meet with Pope John Paul II. He encouraged them to continue their peaceful fight for their God-given rights. By February 1981, however, rural farmers joined in the striking mood, and there didn't seem to be any sign of stopping.

By March 1981, Moscow had had enough and summoned the Polish leadership for a meeting. The U.S.S.R. told them in no uncertain terms that this uprising must end, and that martial law should be imposed to crack down on Solidarity. In mid-March, Polish police arrested and beat the leaders of Solidarity, which caused a national strike on March 27, 1981. On that one day, tens of millions of Poles did not go to work. More than that, they set a date of March 31 to begin a longer, indefinite national strike until those who arrested and beat the leaders were held accountable for their actions.

Neither side backed down, and it seemed that a larger battle was imminent. On March 28, Pope John Paul II sent a message to Cardinal Wyszyński, urging calm and expressing his hopes that the March 31 strike could be prevented. On March 30, Lech Wałesa agreed to call off the national strike scheduled for the next day. Some interpreted this as a sign of weakness on the part of Wałesa, but there was genuine fear that the government would massacre anyone who got in its way.

In April 1981, Polish Communist Party leader Kania and Premier Jaruzelski were summoned to Moscow. Once again, they were pressured to impose martial law on Poland to put an end to Solidarity, but they managed to convince Moscow that they had the situation under control and could handle it themselves. Kania and Jaruzelski knew that the Polish Communist Party was soon to lose its most visible and vocal opponent: Word was out that Cardinal Wyszyński was dying of cancer. About the same time, Pope John Paul II was shot in St. Peter's Square (on May 13, 1981). As JP2 recovered and Cardinal Wyszyński became more ill, the two spoke by telephone. Finally on May 28, 1981, Wyszyński died. Pope John Paul II spent time recuperating from his wounds and trying to decide who could replace Cardinal Wyszyński as Primate of Poland. He eventually decided upon Josef Glemp, who was a former secretary of Wyszyński and an expert in both canon law and civil law. Glemp was created a cardinal by Pope John Paul II on July 7, 1981.

On September 5, 1981, the first Solidarity Congress was held. The 900 delegates representing 9.5 million workers called for free elections in Poland, self-management in industry, and greater opportunities for non–Communist Party members to hold government positions. Pope John Paul II reinforced his commitment to stand with the Solidarity union by issuing an encyclical on the dignity of human labor, called *Laborem Exercens*. (Check out Chapter 22 for the details of this historic encyclical.)

Using the power of prayer

During the fall of 1981, things in Poland became gradually worse, with fewer goods and food available to the people. The government threatened to seek emergency powers to prevent strikes, and Solidarity threatened more strikes if they tried to pass the measures.

On December 11 and 12, 1981, Solidarity leaders met in Gdańsk to plan future strategy, and the government decided it was time to act. Sometime around midnight, all the leaders were rounded up in their hotels and arrested. Polish army troops filled Poland, drove tanks into the city, and disconnected all telephones.

Reacting to the crackdown, on December 13, Pope John Paul II held a prayer vigil in St. Peter's Square. Despite his calls for calm and peace, he made it clear whose side he was on by continually using the word *solidarity* in his address. Violence broke out all over Poland, and the Holy Father wrote to General Jaruzelski to ask him to do all he could to stop the bloodshed. Although some people saw the government's crackdown against civilian demonstrators as a sign of strength, JP2 understood that it was instead a sign of their utter weakness to stop the will of the people. They had no other choice than to use force, because they had no intellectual argument to make against the strikers. Life continued this way for the Polish people until 1988, when the Soviet empire began to crumble.

On April 25, 1988, strikes begin once again in Poland, with demonstrators demanding the reinstatement of Solidarity. Strikes in the Upper Silesia region in August 1988 could not be stopped by the government, and they turned to Lech Wałesa to intervene. The strikes ended two weeks later.

On January 18, 1989, General Jaruzelski announced that Solidarity would be reinstated as an independent, self-governing trade union. One month later, negotiations between Solidarity and the government resulted in the first free elections being scheduled for June, and in those elections, Solidarity candidates won consistently across Poland. By December 9, 1990, Lech Wałesa was elected the president of Poland. Years later, he credited Pope John Paul II with giving the Polish people the courage to rise up against the authorities: "The Pope started this chain of events that led to the end of communism," he said. "Before his pontificate the world was divided into blocs. Nobody knew how to get rid of communism. He simply said, 'Don't be afraid, change the image of this land.'"

Chapter 14

Sanctifying the Saints and Saintly of the World

Pope John Paul II reformed the whole process of *canonization,* the process of recognizing the saints that God made. The Second Vatican Council decreed that every Christian should strive to be holy, and JP2 believed that we should recognize that holiness. He recognized that sainthood happens everywhere, in every continent, among all peoples.

In this chapter, we take a look at the process of beatification and canonization. We look at how and why John Paul II streamlined the process. And, finally, we consider how he used canonization to *evangelize* (preach the Gospel and teach people about Christ and his church) and highlight examples of truly holy lives.

Quantifying the Prolific Pontiff

Pope John Paul II greatly increased the number of canonizations and saints. During the time he occupied the throne of St. Peter (1978–2004), JP2 held 51 canonizations recognizing 483 saints.

Here's how his numbers compare to previous periods in history:

▶ **16th century:** 1 canonization ceremony with 1 saint

▶ **17th century:** 10 canonization ceremonies with 24 saints

▶ **18th century:** 9 canonization ceremonies with 29 saints

- ✔ **19th century:** 8 canonization ceremonies with 80 saints
- ✔ **20th century:** Every pope canonized saints, except John Paul I who only reigned 30 days. Here's the breakdown:
  - Leo XIII (1878–1903): 18 saints
  - Pius X (1903–1914): 4 saints
  - Benedict XV (1914–1922): 3 saints
  - Pius XI (1922–1939): 34 saints
  - Pius XII (1939–1958): 33 saints
  - John XXIII (1958–1963): 10 saints
  - Paul VI (1963–1978): 80 saints

Pope John Paul II explained the increase in the number of canonizations and beatifications as a reflection of the Second Vatican Council's universal call to holiness. He believed that this holiness should be recognized among all the faithful. Holiness (sanctity) is not something rare or extraordinary — instead, it's actually common, and through Baptism, all men and women, clergy and laity, are called to be saints. What *is* uncommon is the way these ordinary people (who later became saints) carried out their call from God to be saints. In other words, Catholics believe we're all called to be saints — some just live more unique, obvious, and documented lives of holiness than others.

The great variety of gifts and personalities in the saints and blessed of John Paul II show that they come from the most diverse social and cultural backgrounds. Yet, they all invite the faithful to strive toward perfection.

All the blessed and saints share similar qualities:

- ✔ **They daily bore the cross of Christ according to their state in life — whether they were laypeople, religious people, or ordained clergy.** The "cross" is not two intersecting boards of wood on which a person is crucified, but in this case refers to any physical, emotional, or spiritual pain and suffering. They bore it with peace and even with joy. These holy men and women united their own cross (personal suffering) to the historical and spiritual cross of Christ and offered it up for others to help ease some of their suffering.

- ✔ **They were simple in their devotional lives.** In this sense, simplicity means they had an uncomplicated, direct spiritual life. For example, they had devotions to the Child Jesus, the Eucharist, the Passion, the Sacred Heart, the Blessed Mother, St. Joseph, or some other favorite saint. Through these devotions, they found the strength to bear their cross faithfully and inspirationally.

The legacy of John Paul II is that he gave us models and intercessors from different parts of the world and for all occasions. The saints and blessed are not limited to a certain part of the world or era. The faith is found throughout the world, reflecting different ethnic, cultural, and social backgrounds. Many of the saints and blessed are even contemporaries — important because it highlights the fact that JP2 believed God is still calling all His people to holiness (God's calling didn't cease in the 13th century). Therefore, Maximilian Kolbe, Sister Faustina, Padre Pio, Monsignor Jose Marie Escriva, Juan Diego, and many more have great impact on our contemporary world. (Take a look at Chapter 23 to find out more on these and other notable beatifications and canonizations of JP2.)

Revising the Process for Beatification and Canonization

Canonization is an official decree of the Catholic Church. It is the definitive judgment of the current pope that a person is now listed among the saints in heaven. Through canonization, the pope makes a formal declaration that the immortal soul of the person in question is now with God and His eternal glory. The pope orders the Church to *venerate* (honor) the holy person (in other words, to look on the person with great respect and admiration) as a saint, because the saint is in intimate connection with God. The saint is given as an example because of his or her virtues.

TECHNICAL STUFF

Identifying early milestones in the process

In the first few centuries of the Infant (early Apostolic) Church, the beatification and canonization process began spontaneously. After the person died, the people close to him or her expressed a belief in the person's holiness as expressed in his or her virtues. The first *veneration,* or honor, was given to the early martyrs (those Christians brutally killed by the Romans because they refused to renounce their faith and were subjected to violent persecution). The people would gather the relics of these innocent victims and build altars on their tombs where the priests would celebrate Holy Mass. Then the veneration had to be authenticated by the local bishop.

Around the fourth century, canonization was extended to those who were not martyrs but lived heroic lives of virtue. The process remained the same: The bishop authenticated the holiness. After the 11th century, the pope required that, for greater certitude, a general council conduct an inquiry into the virtues and miracles and then determine the beatification status of the person. Canonizations were transferred to the pope.

In 1170, beatifications and canonizations were all transferred to the pope, but, in practice, beatifications remained local until 1625, when Pope Urban VIII settled the dispute by announcing a special decree that transferred all beatifications and canonizations to the pope.

Beatification is a step in the canonization process. If a person is beatified, he has been thoroughly investigated by the Church, a miracle has been attributed to him, and he has been given the title *Blessed,* as in, Blessed Mother Teresa of Calcutta.

The Catholic Church canonizes or beatifies only those whose lives have been marked by the use of *heroic virtue* (good works that greatly outdistance those of ordinary good people). In order to be heroic, it must be done with pure and honorable motives, quickly and thoroughly. A heroic virtue is a habit of good conduct that has become second nature to the person — not just a good deed here or there, like helping an old lady across the street or shoveling your neighbor's driveway. Heroic virtue helps an ordinary person to accomplish ordinary things in an extraordinary way.

Understanding the current process

The simplest way to explain the streamlined version of beatification and canonization of Pope John Paul II is to put it into steps. Here are the current steps for opening and pursuing a *cause for sainthood* (the investigation into whether a person is qualified to be a saint):

1. **Those interested in opening the cause must wait until five years after the person's death.**

   The investigation may not open until the Vatican gives permission.

2. **A candidate's admirers persuade the local bishop that the candidate led a life of holiness.**

3. **When sufficient information has been gathered, the subject of the investigation is called a Servant of God, and the process is transferred to the Roman Curia in Rome, specifically to the Congregation for the Causes of the Saints.**

4. **Those who knew the individual are interviewed by a *postulator*.**

   A postulator examines the letters and writings of the candidate. These letters and writings are thoroughly examined and authenticated.

5. **The information is sifted by a *relator*, who prepares a position paper.**

6. **When enough information has been gathered, the congregation recommends to the pope that he make a proclamation of the Servant of God's heroic virtue.**

7. **If the pope feels the evidence proves a life of heroic virtue, then the person is given the title Venerable by the pope.**

   A Venerable has no feast day in the liturgical calendar, but prayer cards may be printed to encourage the faithful to pray for a miracle from God brought about by the Venerable's intercession.

8. **If it can be proved that a miracle was performed after the death of the candidate, as a result of someone praying to God through the intercession of the Venerable, then the Venerable is beatified and called Blessed.**

   Proven miracles are ones that neither science nor medicine can explain or refute. Usually, these miracles are healings, but they must be *complete,* irreversible, spontaneous, and instantaneous. Physicians and scientists are first consulted to determine if there are any credible medical or scientific explanations, evidence, or proof to render it a natural phenomenon. If none are obtained, then it is declared a supernatural and divine miracle.

   For a *martyr* (someone who is killed exclusively because of his Catholic faith), the pope has only to make a declaration of martyrdom, which then allows beatification, yielding the title Blessed, and a feast day in the blessed's home diocese is established. If the Venerable was not a martyr, it must be proven that a miracle took place by his or her intercession. Today these miracles are almost always miraculous cures.

9. **To be a saint, a second miracle attributable to the blessed person needs to verified.**

Sainthood does not mean a person lived a perfect or sinless life. It means that he lived a *faithful* life — in other words, he never stopped trying to do and to be better. He never gave up the daily spiritual struggle of good versus evil, despite his own mistakes and shortcomings. The point: Saints are not those who never *failed,* but those who never *gave up.*

The declaration of sainthood is considered to be an exercise of papal infallibility, while declarations of venerability and beatitude are not. A saint's feast day in the liturgical calendar is considered universal and may be celebrated anywhere within the Catholic Church. For example, St. Patrick's feast day is March 17 and St. Joseph's (husband of the Virgin Mary) is March 19. Both feast days are on the universal liturgical calendar (which contains dates of feast days and other religious solemnities) and are celebrated all over the world.

A few saints have had — in addition to the necessary post-mortem miracles — some supernatural phenomena attributed to them that can only be explained by the power of God. For instance, St. Joseph Cupertino (1603–1663) would often levitate off the ground while in prayer. St. Pio of Pietrelcina (1887–1968) was reported to have been blessed with the ability of *bilocation* (being in two places at the same time — wouldn't that come in handy in your crazy-hectic life?); he also had the *stigmata* (five wounds of Christ appearing in the body of the person) just as St. Francis of Assisi (1181–1226) did. Others, like St. Catherine of Siena (1347–1380) and St. Bernadette of Lourdes (1844–1879) had incorruptible bodies — centuries after their deaths and without any embalming, their corpses have remained intact. Most saints, however, simply lived holy lives, and a few miracles were performed by God through their intercession after they died.

Highlighting John Paul II's reforms

In 1983, John Paul II dramatically changed the process of beatification and canonization. Here's a summary of his reforms.

- ✔ **JP2 shortened the waiting period before the process can begin to five years after the death of the person.** Previously, the timeline had been 50 years. Interestingly, Pope John Paul II completely waived this time requirement in order for Mother Teresa's cause to be open, and Pope Benedict XVI did the same for JP2, but they are exceptions due to the exceptional persons involved. Normally, the five-year waiting period remains intact. The whole idea of waiting at all was to prevent a merely emotional reaction to a popular person's death. Fifty years was formerly considered enough time for hearts to "cool off," but now five years suffices. (Modern man has a shorter attention span.)

- ✔ **JP2 replaced a canonical trial with an academic-historical process, in which the key document is a biography of the candidate.** Theologians and historians now replace canon lawyers in this process. JP2 eliminated the "Devil's Advocate" (the nickname for the *Promotor Fidei,* who conducted the investigations and interrogations). The former trial was based on Church Law (also called *canon law*), which is based on Roman Law and not Anglo-Saxon (English) Common Law. (Got that straight?) Roman Law had no juries, and decisions were made by the judge or a panel of judges, whereas English Law entrusted the verdict to a jury of peers. Roman Law saw discovering the truth as the primary end; Common Law protects the rights of the accused and balances it against the common good of the public. Both have judges and lawyers, however. A canonical trial, like most Roman Law, is done by paperwork (written testimony and documentation) rather than oral interrogation. The old way (trial) took more time and sometimes became contentious, with opposing arguments getting very intense. The new way is faster and more objective.

Because the *Promotor Fidei* thoroughly and painstakingly looked for any serious moral flaw or doctrinal error to disqualify the candidate for canonization, he got the reputation of being the "Devil's Advocate" — his job was neither to defend nor promote the cause. On the contrary, the *Promotor Fidei* ensured that objective and incontrovertible proof and evidence of heroic holiness existed — otherwise, the case was closed. This process wasn't so much airing out the dirty laundry of the saint-to-be but a prudent examination into the life, writings (if any), and behavior of the candidate, as well as documented post-mortem miracles. Now, an objective historical investigation is made rather than a formal ecclesiastical trial involving canon lawyers, judges, and tribunals. This change is intended to streamline the process so as to save time and money — the trial involved using much more secretarial paperwork, meetings, and conferences. The cause takes less time and is not as rare as it was in the past.

✔ **JP2 moved much of the process out of Rome to the local diocese where the *Servant of God* (a term used to described the candidate) lived and, therefore, where the cause originated.** Before being called Blessed (after the beatification process), the Servant of God is promoted to the title of Venerable. (In other words, the process goes: servant of God → venerable → blessed → saint.) Only after being canonized by the pope is the title Saint officially ascribed to the person's name. Local bishops are now responsible for assembling the materials for judging the candidate for blessed. Because JP2 moved much of the process to the local dioceses, the process is faster, less costly, and better outfitted to produce results.

✔ **JP2 cut down the required number of miracles attributed to the holy person's intercession to one for beatification and a second one for canonization.** Formerly, two miracles were needed for beatification and two more for canonization. Because even one miracle is considered possible only by divine intervention from God, whether it is two or four or more miracles, the source is still the same. In other words, no need for multiplication of evidence when the minimum suffices.

Looking at Beatification and Canonization Ceremonies around the World

John Paul II canonized more than 480 saints, a larger number than any previous pope. These included some large groups (103 martyrs in Korea, 117 martyrs in Vietnam, and 120 martyrs in China), as well as many individuals. He canonized two French nuns who came to North America: Marguerite Bourgeoys, who worked in 17th-century Québec, and Rose-Phillipine Duchesne, who worked in 19th-century Missouri and Kansas. He canonized Katharine Drexel, an American heiress who became a nun and worked among African Americans and Native Americans. He canonized a German Carmelite nun, Edith Stein, who was killed at the Nazi death camp Auschwitz during World War II.

JP2's canonizations substantially increased the number of Catholic saints from non-European countries to reflect the diversity of the Catholic Church. Through this diversity, Pope John Paul II may have changed the course of Church history in his record setting pontificate. This diversity is now highlighted in heaven. He canonized men and women from almost every country, culture, and class — not just priests and nuns, but slaves and duchesses as well.

Pope John Paul II beatified more than 1,300 men and women. They reflect the diversity of the Church, just as the saints do. As John Paul II believed, in diversity is found unity: The qualities in the lives of these holy men and women are universal qualities. They all had a deep devotion to Jesus, were ready and willing to suffer the cross of Jesus, and were heroic even in the ordinary acts of life.

Pope John Paul II went back to the roots of the papacy in the line of St. Peter, reinstating the distinctive missionary flair of being pope. Gone are the days of the pope staying exclusively behind the walls of the Vatican, stuck in some bureaucratic office. In Pope John Paul II's philosophy, the pope shouldn't be carried on a chair with plums following as a king might be. Rather, Pope John Paul II took the role of a true shepherd. As Supreme Shepherd of the Church, he traveled to many countries, reflecting the universality of the Church. One of his chief tools of evangelization in foreign lands was to raise to the altar of sanctity men and women outstanding in holiness who could be tangible and local examples for the faithful to follow. For beatifications and canonizations, the Holy Father invited faithful from all places to gather in unity and proclaim the same faith.

Chapter 15

Giving Hope to the Young: World Youth Day

*W*orld Youth Day is a gathering of young people (ages 16 to 30) for several days during which they share their faith with one another, pray together, have some informal *catechetical* (doctrinal) instruction, sing hymns, and enjoy their religion. Protestant Christians may see similarities to their revivals, crusades, and youth camps, all rolled into one. World Youth Day invites Catholic young people to the same type of relaxed setting, to meet contemporaries from around the world and to listen to and be with the pastor of the Universal Church (the pope). Although the international locations allow for some sightseeing, the young people spend the majority of their time in prayer, song, and dialogue with each other while enjoying the scenery and background of the host nation.

World Youth Day is celebrated every year. Every two or three years, there is an international gathering. In other years, it is celebrated in the local parish or diocese.

Pilgrimages to holy places began in the Middle Ages and continue to this day. Muslims make pilgrimages to Mecca, Jews to Jerusalem, and Protestant Christians to the Holy Land, where Jesus lived and preached. Catholic Christians try to visit Rome, where St. Peter is buried and where his successor, the pope, lives and works. Pilgrimage, though, is focused on the place because of its historical and religious significance. World Youth Day is a little different in that it is not the location that matters, but the ones invited and who attend the event (young people) and the pope who comes to speak to them. If you've ever seen a Billy Graham Crusade on television, you'll know it is the message and the messenger that draw the crowds, not the place where it happens. The same is true of World Youth Day.

In this chapter, we look at how World Youth Day began. We delve into how John Paul II used it to connect with the youngest members of the flock. We explore the various themes and connect them to his ultimate message: Young people have the ability and the duty to live the Gospel. Finally, we show you how this event helped define his papacy and bring hope and faith to young Christians everywhere.

How World Youth Day Began: John Paul 2, We Love You

Seeing the youth as the future of the Church and of the world was a theme of Pope John Paul II that developed early on in his pontificate. When he traveled to different countries, JP2 was always impressed with the enthusiasm of the young people who wanted to be near him and receive a message from him. In his early days as a young cleric, he was very comfortable with the youth — they were the ones he most enjoyed interacting with. So, to coincide with the United Nations's theme of the International Youth Year, JP2 officially announced that the Church would celebrate World Youth Day annually. In his apostolic letter "To the Youth of the World," JP2 outlined the basis for this yearly celebration.

John Paul II felt that youth was a special time for people to think about their future and vocation in life. It's also a time in their lives when many institutions, people, and ideas compete for young people's attention. These are the molding years, and JP2 believed that World Youth Day gatherings could make a difference in the molding of the faith of the young people. And local and international gatherings could encourage young people, letting them see that there are many other young people interested in their faith, willing to follow Christ.

The threefold purpose of World Youth Day has been putting trust in the young, gathering together, and meeting the international world on a human level.

At these gatherings of young people, the world first heard the phrase "John Paul 2, we love you." So sincere and affectionate were those shouts of joy from the youth of the world that the pope responded: "John Paul 2, he loves you." Talk about connecting with an audience.

Identifying the Themes, Places, and Times

Depending on how you count, we've celebrated either 10 international World Youth Days with the pope or 17 annual World Youth Day celebrations (from 1986 to 2002). The discrepancy lies in the fact that Pope John Paul II did not travel to foreign countries every year for World Youth Day. The international events with JP2 took place every other year or every three years, with local celebrations in the dioceses taking place in between. The first two gatherings, in 1984 and 1985, are often not counted, because the title World Youth Day was not yet used to describe them. More than a quarter million traveled to each event to be with Pope John Paul II, so *we* count them as World Youth Days even if they weren't *officially* called that until 1986.

When celebrated locally, the bishop of the diocese gathered with the young people from all the parishes, or some countries had a national assembly of several bishops and dioceses. The big events, of course, were the international visits of JP2 to various countries specifically to meet with the youth and spend time with them in prayer.

In the following sections, we walk you through the World Youth Days from 1984 through 2002.

First World Youth Day, 1984

The year 1983 marked the 1,950th anniversary of the death of Jesus Christ according to the Gregorian calendar (based on the computation that Jesus died when he was 33 years old, which originally was thought to have been in 33 A.D.). Pope John Paul II declared it a Holy Year (March 25, 1983–April 22, 1984) and invited the youth of the world to come to Rome for an International Jubilee of Youth on Palm Sunday (April 15, 1984) in St. Peter's Square in Rome.

Three-hundred thousand young people from around the globe responded to the invitation, as did Mother Teresa of Calcutta. Stations of the cross were held in the Coliseum and daily Mass in St. Peter's Basilica. A large wooden cross to commemorate the 1,950th anniversary of the Crucifixion of Christ was entrusted to the youth of the world by JP2, because he regarded them as and reminded them that they were the future of the Church.

Second World Youth Day, 1985

The United Nations made 1985 the International Year of Youth. That proclamation encouraged another gathering of the young in the Eternal City of Rome. As before (see the preceding section), over 300,000 young people participated in this gathering. Pope John Paul II used the occasion to issue an apostolic letter, *Dilecti Amici* (Dear Friends), to all the youth of the world. In it, he encouraged them, as young as they were, to consider their futures — not just their careers, but their eternal destinies and the vocations God called them to live. At this event, JP2 announced that the following year's venue would be Buenos Aires, Argentina, and he coined the name "World Youth Day" for the first time.

March 23, 1986, was the first local celebration of World Youth Day to give the Holy Father a rest and to allow local bishops and dioceses a chance to participate in this new movement to encourage and cooperate with the youth of the Church. The theme was based on 1 Peter 3:15, "Always be ready to give an explanation to anyone who asks you for a reason for your hope."

While there was a celebration in Rome there were also simultaneous celebrations in dioceses around the world.

Some people list this as the first World Youth Day; others include the previous two World Youth Days in 1984 and 1985. Unlike the Olympics, there is no official number (like I, II or III) for World Youth Day, except the calendar year in which it occurs.

Third World Youth Day, 1987

The Third World Youth Day (and the first international one outside of Rome) was celebrated on April 11 and 12, 1987, in Buenos Aires, Argentina. The theme was based on 1 John 4:16, "We ourselves have known and put our faith in God's love toward ourselves."

One million people attended and participated in World Youth Day in 1987. JP2 told the young people from around the world:

> I would like to repeat to you what I told you on the first day of my pontificate: that you are the hope of the Holy Father, the hope of the Church. In this way you are building the civilization of life and truth, of freedom and justice, of life, reconciliation, and peace.

The following year (1988) was a local celebration of World Youth Day, with the theme: "Do whatever he tells you" (John 2:5). It took place on Palm Sunday (March 27).

Fourth World Youth Day, 1989

Santiago de Compostela, Spain, was the site for the next international World Youth Day (August 15 to August 20). The theme was John 14:6, "I am the Way, the Truth, and the Life." JP2 recognized that to be young is a special treasure. Each person discovers himself, his personality, the meaning of his existence, and the reality of good and evil. Plus, each young person discovers the whole world around them. Finally, young people discover Jesus Christ, who is the basis of the most wonderful adventure of their lives.

The famous Sanctuary of Santiago de Compostela, is an important point of reference for the celebration of World Youth Day. It has been a destination of pilgrims for centuries. The Holy Father reminded the world's youth that he would be a pilgrim like them and travel to this great place of prayer. At the tomb of the Apostle St. James, who is buried there, the pilgrim is reminded that his faith is built upon a stable foundation of the Apostles, with Christ as the cornerstone. St. James was the first to seal his witness with his own blood and, therefore, is an excellent example and teacher.

The pope also made reference to the act of the pilgrimage itself, especially along the Santiago Trail. Along the way are visible monuments to the pilgrim's faith, churches, and hospices. Indeed, he reminded the young people that the act of pilgrimage has a deep spiritual significance. It is a way of deepening your faith, strengthening a sense of communion and solidarity amongst your fellow travelers, and discovering your personal vocation in life.

JP2 posed some important questions for the youth to meditate and contemplate:

- ✔ **Have they discovered Christ, who is the Way?** Jesus is the Way that leads to the Heavenly Father. Whoever wants to reach salvation must set out along this way. JP2 cautioned that young people often find themselves at the crossroads, not knowing which path to take, which way to go. He reminded them that Christ, with the Gospel, is the finest example; the commandments are the safest way, leading to full happiness.

- ✔ **Have they discovered Christ, who is the Truth?** He reminded the young people that truth is the deepest yearning of the human spirit. The young are hungry for the truth about God and man, about life and the world. Christ is the word of truth, uttered by God himself, in response to all questioning of the human heart. Christ reveals the mystery of man and of the world.

- ✔ **Have they discovered Christ, who is the Life?** The true fullness of life is found in Christ, who died and rose from the dead. Christ alone is able to fill in depth the space of the human heart. He alone gives the strength and joy to life. To discover Christ is to encounter him over and over through prayer, participating in the sacraments, meditating on his word, *catechesis* (teaching and learning the faith), and listening to the teachings of the Church.

John Paul II reminded young people that after they have discovered Jesus — who is the Way, Truth, and Life — they must share this discovery. Young people have a special mission to be apostles and evangelizers of the world of youth. He cautioned that many young people do not know Christ. Those who do cannot remain silent and indifferent. They must get the courage to speak about Christ, to bear witness to their faith through their lifestyle and choices inspired by the Gospel.

In 1990, there was a local World Youth Day meeting on Palm Sunday (April 8) with the theme of, "I am the vine, you are the branches" (John 15:5).

Fifth World Youth Day, 1991

In 1991, over 1.5 million people came to World Youth Day in Czestochowa, Poland (August 10–15). The Iron Curtain had rusted and fallen down, and, for the first time, young people from Eastern and Central Europe had an opportunity to participate unfettered in the event. As JP2 said,

> Young people from the east and west of Europe — the old continent is counting on you to help build up this "common house" from which we expect a future of solidarity and peace. . . . For the well-being of future generations it will be necessary for the new Europe to be built on the foundations of those spiritual values that define the innermost core of her cultural tradition.

Czestochowa was the place of the Black Madonna, the icon and symbol of all Poland. This legendary picture of Mary was allegedly painted by St. Luke the Evangelist and through the centuries ended up in this ancient town. (Turn to Chapter 6 for more details about the Black Madonna and why it was important to JP2.)

The theme of the fifth World Youth Day was based on St. Paul's Letter to the Romans 8:15: "You have received a spirit of sonship." JP2 addressed the young people and asked what it meant to them to be a son or daughter of God, to be open to God's action, to be guided by him.

He reminded the young people that, in every age, the Holy Spirit raises up new men and women who live in holiness, in truth, and in justice. On the eve of the millennium, JP2 believed, the world was anxiously seeking ways of living together in greater solidarity and urgently needed to count on people who, with the help of the Holy Spirit, were capable of living as true children of God.

He reminded World Youth Day attendees that holiness is the essential heritage of being children of God. This heritage means doing the Will of God in every circumstance of their lives. Their heritage of being children of God includes fraternal love, after the example of Jesus Christ. If they call upon

God as Father, they will also recognize their neighbor as their brother or sister. So, the task of young people is to build a society where we'll have more justice and solidarity.

The Holy Father explained freedom in great detail. True freedom means liberty from sin, which is the root of all human slaveries. Freedom is not only a gift from God, but also a duty of every Christian, young or old. Exterior freedom, guaranteed by just civil law is important and necessary. JP2 took the time to honor those countries who were securing the fundamental rights of all human persons.

Then the pope reminisced that interior freedom is far more precious, to be guided by an upright and moral conscience capable of choosing what is truly good. Exterior freedom resides in interior freedom.

World Youth Day ended on the Holy Feast Day of the Assumption of Mary. (Catholic doctrine maintains that Mary was taken up to heaven, body and soul, by her son, Jesus Christ, when her life on Earth came to an end.) JP2 told the young people that even though World Youth Day had come to end for this year, their mission as disciples of the Lord Jesus were just about to begin.

He explained that understanding the Virgin Mary is the best place to learn what it means to be true sons and daughters of God. She was entrusted with the fundamental role in the history of salvation to be the Mother of God. God sent his only son, born of a woman, to redeem those who would become his adoptive sons and daughters. It's from Mary's maternal and immaculate heart that we guard the heritage of being sons and daughters of God.

A local World Youth Day took place on Palm Sunday, April 12, 1992. The theme was, "Go into all the world and preach the Gospel" (Mark 16:15).

Sixth World Youth Day, 1993

Half a million young people came to Denver, Colorado (August 10–15) for international World Youth Day with Pope John Paul II. The theme was, "I came that they might have life, and have it to the full" (John 10:10). JP2 reminded his young audience that World Youth Days are providential opportunities to enable young people to examine their deepest aspirations, to heighten their sense of belonging to the Church, and to proclaim their common faith in Jesus with increasing joy and courage. They provide opportunities to help steer the future course of history under the powerful but gentle guidance of the Holy Spirit.

The Holy Father addressed the World Youth Day attendees first by saying what a terrific success the last international celebration at the Shrine of Our Lady of Czestochowa had been. He made the comparison that the Shrine was like the Upper Room for a new Pentecost with the doors thrown open to the third millennium. He was overjoyed to see that young adults from the former Iron Curtain mingling with those from the West and Far East as well as South America and Africa. Then he homed in on the new theme, that the same Spirit that made them adoptive children of God, now compels them to evangelize: This was their true Christian vocation to be missionaries.

World Youth Day is meant to be a first step and a proposal of a new unity, a unity that transcends the political order and enlightens it. It's based on an awareness that only God can adequately satisfy their deepest desire.

The pope clarified to his young audience that human existence has its moments of crisis and weariness, despondency and gloom. Such a sense of dissatisfaction is reflected in contemporary literature, films, and lyrics. In the light of this distress, you can more easily understand the particular difficulties of adolescents and young people stepping out with uncertainty to encounter all the fascinating promises and dark uncertainties that are part of life.

Then the Holy Father changed his direction and urged his young audience to go to Jesus. He said that Jesus came to provide the ultimate answer to the yearning for life and for the infinite, which his Heavenly Father had poured into their hearts when he created them. At the apex of revelation, Jesus, who is the Word, proclaims that he is the Life. But what life, the Holy Father asks. John Paul said Jesus came to meet men and women, to heal the sick and the suffering, to free those possessed by the devil and to raise the dead. He gave himself on the cross and rose again from the dead, revealing that he is the Lord of Life, the Author and Source of life without end.

JP2 also said that life is marked by sin and threatened by death, despite the desire for good. He warned his young congregation that there are false prophets and false teachers of how to live. Specifically, he warned against

> ✔ **Those who teach people to leave the body, time, and space in order to be able to enter into what they call "true life":** They condemn Creation and lead thousands of young people along the paths of an impossible liberation, which leaves them even more isolated, victims of their own illusions and of the evil in their lives. This concept is based on the false idea that the physical and material world is evil and only the spiritual and immaterial world is good. The first book of the Bible, Genesis, says otherwise; it states that God created the world in six days and saw that it was "good." Christianity also teaches the doctrine of the *incarnation* (God becoming flesh), when Jesus united his divine nature with a human nature through his conception and birth. The false teaching, however, distorts the intrinsic goodness of Creation. It fools people into thinking that only an invisible, intangible, and ethereal world is worth our attention. Transcending the material world through esoteric philosophies (like New Age) is not the answer, according to Pope John Paul II.

> ✔ **The teachers of fleeting moments:** They invite people to give free rein to every instinctive urge or longing, with the result that individuals are left with a sense of anguish and anxiety, leading them to seek refuge in false, artificial paradises, such as drugs.

> ✔ **Those who teach that the meaning of life lies solely in the quest for success, the accumulation of wealth, the development of personal abilities, without regard for the needs of others or respect for values:** These last two are on the extreme opposite end of the spectrum of the false prophets who deny the basic goodness of the material world and the human body. They exaggerate the physical and ignore or deny the spiritual, which results in a denial of sin and moral responsibility. This philosophy of life spawns selfishness, materialism, hedonism, and so on as it accentuates the individual and ignores social responsibility.

Pope John Paul II expressed the truth that only God can satisfy the expectations that he himself placed in their hearts upon Creation. JP2 said that God draws near to each person and announces a hope that will never disappoint, because he is the pathway into life. In the mystery of his cross and resurrection, JP2 said, Christ destroyed death and sin and bridged the infinite distance that separates all people from new life in him. Christ achieves all this by pouring out his Holy Spirit, the giver of life, in the sacraments, especially Baptism. Catholics believe that this sacrament ensures that those who receive them are not destined to end in death, but rather to a path toward eternity.

The same world of young people is a mission land for the Church today. He specifically reminded them of the problems that plague the environment, in which they live, the collapse of values, doubt, consumerism, drugs, crime, and eroticism. At the same time, he told them that every young person has a great thirst for God, even if at times this thirst is hidden behind an attitude of indifference or hostility. He reminisced on how many young people — lost and dissatisfied — went to Czestochowa to find deeper meaning in their lives. How many of them came from a distance, not only geographically, but also spiritually. Czestochowa was a form of pre-evangelization; it marked the turning point in their ongoing conversion.

He reminded them that the harvest is abundant, but that there are many young people seeking Christ and few laborers to proclaim him in a credible way. He reminded the attendees of the need for vocations to the priesthood and religious life, teachers in the faith, and a need for young people to join in.

John Paul II recognized the tremendous opportunity with the collapse of Marxism and Communism in the countries of Eastern and Central Europe. The opening of these countries to the proclamation of Christ was a new sign of the times to which the Church was called to give a response. JP2 believed that the enthusiasm that the young people could offer the Church was indispensable.

Proclaiming Christ means giving witness to him with your life. It's the simplest form of preaching the Gospel and at the same time the most effective way. It consists in showing the visible presence of Christ in your life by a daily commitment and making every concrete decision in conformity to the Gospel. The world today needs credible witnesses and youth need to be clear witnesses to Christ. A disciple of Christ is never a passive observer. Rather, a disciple is compelled to transform society, politics, economics, and culture.

He warned the young crowds that much ignorance exists about the Christian faith at the same time that there is a deep desire to hear the Word of God. When a person hears the Truth, he must make a positive response. JP2 urged young people to speak about Christ in their families and in places where they study, work, or play. These places are where they can, alone, bring the seed of God's word.

With this message, he told them the very familiar "Be not afraid." JP2 believed that Christ was the true answer to all the questions that concern humanity. Therefore, he asked the young people to have courage to present Christ. This was not going to be an easy task, so he told them not to be discouraged and to remember that they are never alone. He reminded them that local parishes are faith communities and are dynamic and fertile fields for increasing and spreading the gifts of the Holy Spirit.

Seventh World Youth Day, 1995

Local celebrations of World Youth Day on Palm Sunday, March 27, 1994, and the international celebration in Manila, Philippines (January 10–15, 1995), had the same theme: "As the Father sent me, so am I sending you" (John 20:21).

It was the largest gathering ever. Four million people cheered JP2 as he asked, "Are you capable of giving yourselves, your time, your energy, and your talent to the well-being of others? Are you capable of love? If you are, Church and society can expect great things of each one of you."

He spoke to the young people about their vocation in life to be missionaries. After Jesus's resurrection, he returned to his own disciples. The Apostles were filled with happiness and joy. They could see with their own eyes that Jesus's message was not false. The meeting with Jesus was, therefore, the event that gives meaning to human life and profoundly alters it.

The pope told his young audience that the virtue of hope becomes a certainty: If Jesus conquered death, then they too could triumph one day. JP2 believed that this message of hope had to be communicated. The missionary vocation summons every Christian; it becomes the very essence of every testimony of concrete and living faith. It's a mission that traces its origins from God's plan of salvation through the power of the Holy Spirit. It enables disciples to carry out the mission of Jesus.

He reminded the young people that they were especially called to become missionaries of the New Evangelization, by daily witnessing to Jesus. Knowing that they have anxieties and doubts, and that they can lose their way to Christ, the Lord offers his Church to be the traveling companion. As faithful guardian and representative of the wealth of faith transmitted to her by Christ, the Church is ready to enter into a dialogue with the new generations, in order to answer their needs and expectations and be the path to salvation.

Local celebration of World Youth Day took place on Palm Sunday, March 31, 1996, with the theme: "Lord, to whom we shall go? You have the words of eternal life" (John 6:68).

Eighth World Youth Day, 1997

From August 19 through August 24, 1997, 1.2 million young people gathered in Paris, France, for international World Youth Day. The theme was: "Teacher, where are you staying? Come and see" (John 1:38–39). JP2's health was beginning to decline, but at each World Youth Day he became revitalized and reenergized by the vim and vigor present in the young attendees. In Paris, he began to unveil his plan to prepare for the third millennium.

While the secular world feared and trembled over what havoc Y2K would cause, Pope John Paul II saw the end of the 20th century and the advent of the 21st in terms of the life of Christianity and, therefore, as a reason for joy and hope. The Church was two millennia old and about to begin its third.

JP2 spoke about Paris as the crossroads for people for centuries, being a place for art and culture. The focus of this World Youth Day was to search for and encounter Jesus. The fundamental dimension of the encounter is not dealing with some*thing,* but with some*one,* and that someone is Jesus.

The year 1997 was also the 100th anniversary of the death of St. Therese of Lisieux, or the "Little Flower" as she is often called. Pope John Paul II used this figure as a source of inspiration for the young pilgrims. Her spirituality centered on being, living, and acting as a child of God. She constantly sought to be childlike without becoming childish. Therese formulated a simple relationship with Jesus, similar to the friendship between two children. Her goal was to become "little" by acts of humility (not humiliation, however). She would often say that little things, done well, done often, and done with love mean more to God than anything else. Whether it was doing the laundry, scrubbing the floor, tending the animals, washing the dishes, or her daily prayer and scripture reading — she did all these things lovingly, attentively, and diligently. JP2 reminded the young people to imitate St. Therese in her "little way" of holiness. Fame, fortune, and power may be appealing in a world that glorifies such things, but John Paul asked his young audience to seek the things of heaven instead.

The local World Youth Day celebration took place on Palm Sunday (April 5, 1998), and the theme was: "The Holy Spirit will teach you all things" (John 14:26). One year later, another local celebration of World Youth Day occurred on Palm Sunday (March 28, 1999); the theme was, "The Father loves you" (John 16:27).

Pope John Paul II had named 1997 the Year of God the Son, 1998 the Year of God the Holy Spirit, and 1999 the Year of God the Father. This series was to prepare the world for the year 2000, which would mark the advent of the third millennium of Christianity and the Catholic Church.

Ninth World Youth Day, 2000

The year 2000 ushered in the ninth World Youth Day and the big celebration of the Jubilee Year. Two and half million young people crowded the streets and squares of Rome during its hottest and most humid month of the year. Italians tell a local joke: In August, the only ones who visit Rome are the *cani e Americani* (dogs and Americans). Even the numerous cats of Rome get out of town in August due to the sweltering heat. Popes often moved to their summer residence (Castel Gondolfo), south of Rome, in August, to avoid the oppressive humidity.

Yet, 2.5 million young people flocked to the Eternal City to see and to listen to an 80-year-old celibate man in the month of August. Who would have believed it? JP2 was much more than an elderly unmarried cleric — and the youth who came from all over the world knew that.

The theme of the Jubilee Year World Youth Day was, "The Word became flesh and dwelt among us" (John 1:14).

Jubilee years go back to the year 1300, when Pope Boniface VIII inaugurated the first one. Having its roots in the Hebrew Jubilee celebration every 50 years since the time of Moses, the Catholic celebration of the Jubilee Year took place every 50 years from 1300 to 1900. The 20th century shortened the span to 25-year intervals so that 1925, 1950, 1975, and 2000 were all Jubilee years. Large bronze doors in each of the major basilicas of Rome (St. Peter's, St. John Lateran, St. Mary Major, and St. Paul's Outside the Walls) are closed except for the Jubilee Year, when pilgrims from around the world walk through them. Many of the 2.5 million young people who attended World Youth Day went through those Holy Doors as a symbol of being a pilgrim, hoping one day to walk through the pearly gates of Paradise.

John Paul II told the young pilgrims, "I mention, too, the young people of other Churches . . . who are here this evening . . . may the World Youth Day be another occasion for us to know each other and to implore together from the Spirit of the Lord the gift of the perfect unity of all Christians!"

JP2 asked his audience to seek and pursue personal holiness; to be attentive to the needs of others, especially those who are in need. Sanctity and service go hand in hand, he reminded them. Feeding the hungry, giving drink to the thirsty, clothing the naked, sheltering the homeless, visiting the sick and the imprisoned are not only corporal works of mercy but acts of love. Rather than isolated incidents, Christian charity and love connect the one being served with the one serving and together with God. Seeing Christ in the poor, the homeless, the unemployed, the refugee, the migrant, the foreigner, and so on is only possible when one "sees" Christ in personal prayer.

The local celebration of World Youth Day took place on Palm Sunday, April 8, 2001, and the theme was, "If any want to become my followers, let them deny themselves and take up their cross daily and follow me" (Luke 9:23).

Tenth World Youth Day, 2002

More than 800,000 people came to international World Youth Day in Toronto, Canada, July 23–28, 2002. The theme was: "You are the salt of the earth . . . you are the light of the world" (Matthew 5:13–14). That image of being "salt" and "light" permeated all the talks of Pope John Paul II during this gathering.

Salt preserves and gives flavor and so, too, does the 2,000-year-old faith Pope John Paul II personally represented. This faith, which is shared by more than a billion believers around the world, is designed to preserve the truth of revelation and to give the flavor and taste of God's mercy and love.

Light is essential for life, for growth, for safety. As Jesus reminded his audience two millennia beforehand, "One does not light a lamp and then place it under a bushel-basket. One puts it on a stand for all in the house to able to see" (Matthew 5:15). JP2 urged the young people to shine the light of truth and grace into the darkness of sin, prejudice, pride, envy, lust, anger, greed, and so on.

Evil abhors the light — hence, the need for criminals and terrorists to plan and do things at night when it is hard to recognize them. Faith gives light to the mind to be able to see what God has revealed. JP2 wanted his young people to never stop hungering for the truth. Leading others to the light of faith is the best help anyone can give.

We can't help but think of the perverse evil engaged by Hitler when he conducted his nightly Nuremburg rallies where torch-bearing followers formed a huge swastika. At those rallies, the darkness of hatred, anti-Semitism, bigotry, prejudice, violence, terror, and lies were cultivated like a bacteria in a Petri dish. On the opposite end of the spectrum, the daily gathering of hundreds of thousands of young people in Rome with the pope for World Youth Day expressed joy, hope, love, mercy, forgiveness, peace, and truth.

John Paul II warned the young people, however, of the darkness of false doctrines and manmade evils. War, crime, abortion, euthanasia, violence, terrorism, racism, hedonism, materialism, atheism, and the like threaten to spread, but the light of truth and grace, which come from Christ and are found in his Church, can dispel the shadows of fear and evil.

No one knew, but many suspected, that JP2 might not see many more World Youth Days. His Parkinson's disease and health complications from pneumonia and the flu had begun to weaken his body and often confined him to bed. Toronto was the last international World Youth Day that JP2 attended. But his successor, Benedict XVI, committed himself to continue and promote these wonderful gatherings. John Paul II lived until 2005. The local celebration of World Youth Day took place on Palm Sunday, 2003 (April 13) and the theme was: "Behold, your mother" (John 19:27).

JP2's last encounter with the young people would be the local World Youth Day celebration in 2004, the theme of which was, "We wish to see Jesus" (John 12:21). Poignantly, that would be JP2's dying thought before he left this world on April 2, 2005. He was ready — after 26 years of being Pope, 47 years as a bishop, and 59 years as a priest — "to see Jesus." His entire papacy, however, was centered on helping others to see Jesus. To see Jesus in each other, in one's neighbor, in the stranger, in the poor, in the Church, and most of all in the Holy and Blessed Sacrament (Holy Eucharist) — that is what JP2 taught and showed the youth of the world.

Entrusting the Future: Giving Confidence to Youth

Consistently, through every World Youth Day, John Paul II empowered youth, spoke to their concerns, and encouraged them to evangelize, spreading the faith to all. He acknowledged their state as one of searching and discovery. He spoke to their hearts and touched their souls.

Most importantly he charged them with a duty: a duty to live the life that God wanted them to live, a life rooted in the Gospel, using Christ as the ultimate example. He knew that they could touch those searching for the Word and the Truth in places others could not. They could bring other youth hungry for God to the eternal Word. Not only could they do it, he reminded them, but they must do it. Through their daily lives, their choices of vocation, and their personal choices, they must walk with God.

Part IV
Embracing Modernity and Looking to the Future

The 5th Wave   By Rich Tennant

"Your Holiness is still popular with the young people. According to a poll of high school students, when asked to name one person who has done the most to rid the world of evil, you came in just behind Buffy the Vampire Slayer."

In this part . . .

We investigate the groundwork JP2 left for his predecessors — not just his immediate one (Pope Benedict XVI), but all the future popes who would follow in the 21st century. In this part, we look at his use of technology, from a Vatican Web site to using satellite and cable television and radio to flying around the world in jet planes for pastoral visits. Although he preserved the best of the past in terms of maintaining doctrinal orthodoxy, Pope John Paul II was also the first pontiff to adapt the tools of the modern time and use them for *evangelization* (spreading the faith) and *catechesis* (teaching the faith).

Chapter 16

The Epic Visits of a Traveling Pope

*F*erdinand Magellan was the first sailor to circumnavigate the globe in 1522. Four hundred and forty years later, in 1962, John Glenn was the first astronaut to orbit the Earth in space. Although Pope John Paul II did not make one continuous trip around the world, he did travel 721,052 miles (1,243,757 km), which is the equivalent of 31 times around the planet.

In this chapter, we look at how far and how often JP2 traveled. And we examine how these visits changed lives, bringing hope, love, and unity to all who saw him, heard him, or even knew he was there.

Understanding the Scope of His Travels

Sometimes called the "papal globetrotter," Pope John Paul II made these spiritual road trips because he saw himself as the pastor of the Universal Church. Just as a pastor tries to visit as many parishioners within his parish as he can over the course of his assignment, bishops try to visit as many parishes in their diocese as they can during their pastoral ministries. The pope, as the Supreme Pastor of the entire Church, has a right to visit any and as many parts of the worldwide Catholic Church as he feels is necessary.

Here's a look at some travel facts for JP2 during his 26-year pontificate:

- ✔ He made 143 pastoral visits inside Italy.

- ✔ He made 104 international trips to 129 countries.

- ✔ He visited a total of 876 cities.

- ✔ He gave approximately 3,288 speeches.

- ✔ He spent 18.75 percent of his papacy traveling.

Being a traveling terrorist target

Al Qaeda, the terrorist group responsible for the September 11, 2001, attack in the United States, had planned an assassination of Pope John Paul II in 1995 during his pastoral visit to Manila. Disguised as a priest, an Al Qaeda operative was supposed to get close to JP2 and detonate a bomb hidden on his body. This would be followed by several airplane bombings involving flights to or from the United States and on various airlines in America. The codename was "Project Bojinka" and originally was aimed at assassinating President Bill Clinton during a trip to the Philippines in November 1994 but became too difficult to accomplish. The plot to kill Pope John Paul II was foiled a few weeks before the pontiff landed in Manila when the laptop computer of Ramzi Ahmed Yousef (the mastermind of the first World Trade Center terrorist attack in 1993), containing all the details of the nefarious plan, was found at the scene of an apartment fire.

The figure shows the pope in his bulletproof vehicle, visiting Lithuania in 1993.

© Reuters/CORBIS

JP2 was received by heads of state as a visiting head of state himself, because Vatican City is a sovereign, independent nation, having diplomatic relations around the world and sharing embassies and ambassadors with numerous countries. Unlike a formal state visit by Queen Elizabeth II or Prince Charles of England, Pope John Paul II did not spend most of his time with civilian, military, industrial, political leaders representing his homeland; instead, he came as a shepherd to visit his flock.

Even so, he was welcomed on arrival with a red carpet, a band playing the national anthem of Vatican City, papal flags flying, and a president or prime minister to welcome him. After the formal greetings, however, JP2 would press on to his first spiritual meeting, usually at the local cathedral, often with the local clergy, and many times with invited representatives of other denominations and religions. Because thousands and thousands of people wanted to attend a papal Mass, no building could accommodate such large crowds, so during these papal pastoral visits, outdoor ceremonies and liturgies were often celebrated in civic centers and sports arenas.

While visiting a country, JP2 often beatified or canonized men and women outstanding in faith. Many were martyrs for the faith who lost their lives as recently as the 20th century, either as a result of the world wars or oppressive regimes, be it Nazi, Communist, or anti-Catholic.

Identifying Some Key Visits

The papal visits of Pope John Paul II can be divided into three phases. The first phase runs from 1979 to 1981; during this period, the major theme was evangelization, which he addressed to the hierarchy of each country he visited. The years of 1981 to 1989 are the second phase; the major subject he dealt with was Communism and the support of *Solidarity* (a Polish labor union founded in 1980 by Lech Walesa, which eventually lead to the demise of Communist rule in Poland). In the final phase, from 1989 to 2004, JP2 dealt with the dangers of yielding to materialism. He also outlined and highlighted themes leading up to the Jubilee Year of Jesus's birth, the millennium.

Focusing on Evangelism (1979–1981)

As a newly elected pope, John Paul II embarked on a bold campaign to *evangelize* (spread the Gospel to) a very secular world. At 58 years of age, he was one of the youngest popes in recent history and certainly the most athletic as an avid swimmer, skier, and hiker. His relative youth and good health gave him the strength to take the papacy on the road. At the time of the nearly fatal assassination attempt on his life in May 1981, JP2 had visited 21 nations in just two years and had been to five continents.

Mexico was his first international pilgrimage, and it was an epic one, because the country had officially been anticlerical since the Revolution of 1910, yet the population remained 90 percent Catholic. With no diplomatic relations between Vatican City and the United Mexican States, a papal visit would not be treated like the state visit of a foreign sovereign. John Paul II would be just another tourist and need a visa like everyone else. Fortunately, the sisters and mother of President José López Portillo were devout Catholics, and they persuaded him to formally invite the pope who had planned to visit months before.

At Puebla, JP2 cautioned and warned the bishops of Latin America who were meeting in Mexico to beware of the efforts by some to assimilate Marxist ideology with Christianity. The phenomenon known as *liberation theology* was becoming popular among some of the intelligentsia. This philosophy was a hybrid of Catholicism and Communism, developed to convince the common folk they needed to "liberate" private property and business by empowering the state to nationalize companies and seize land from foreign ownership. Christianity teaches the social imperative to care for the poor and disadvantaged and to share with one another. Marxism reduces everything to political struggles between the proletariat and bourgeoisie. Christianity finds true spiritual liberation from sin in divine grace gained by Jesus's death and resurrection. Marxism finds political and economic liberation by revolution and state control by the political party.

Next, JP2 traveled to Cuilapan, Mexico, to speak to 500,000 native Indians. There, he denounced the exploitation of the poor and indigenous peoples. He repudiated those who abused Latin America for their own profit. Pope John Paul II showed that he did not favor capitalism over Marxism; he pointed out that the Gospel of Jesus Christ is not confined or constrained by any political or economic system.

Pope John Paul II recognized a significant paradox at work in the world. On the one hand, old-world Europe and her "younger sister," North America, were becoming more and more secular and less and less religious. On the other hand, third-world places like South America, Africa, and the Orient were spreading their newfound faith. Centuries ago, Europe and North America sent missionaries to South America, Africa, and Asia. Now, because of the secularism of the industrialized nations, those former missionary lands were sending their own missionaries to Europe and North America. Vocations to the priesthood and consecrated life of religious sisters and brothers were booming in Africa, while on a decline in the United States and Canada.

In June 1979, JP2 visited his native Poland and in October of that same year, he came to the United States. While in Poland, he encouraged peaceful political freedom; in the United States, he preached moral responsibility of superpowers and their citizens not to abuse their freedom to help others in need. In both cases, Pope John Paul II sought to evangelize both the Old World and the New World. He showed concern that neither democracy nor Communism had answers to life and the human condition and what constituted a just society. But, according to JP2, religion would show us who did (Jesus).

Opposing Communism (1981–1989)

John Paul II visited his native Poland seven times as pope. (Take a look at Chapter 13 for the details of these trips and their significance in helping to end Communism in Poland and Eastern Europe.) Soviet General Secretary Leonid Brezhnev tried to talk Polish First Secretary Edward Gierek out of inviting JP2 to Poland after his election as pope in 1978. He warned the Polish Communist leader that it would undermine the authority of the state to flirt with the Catholic Church in such an obvious way. Gierek replied that it would be more dangerous to incite the population by not inviting their favorite native son to his homeland for a visit.

The 1979 papal visit (within the first year of JP2's pontificate) was allowed by the Communist-controlled government of Poland. That decision, however, was not appreciated back in Moscow at the Kremlin, and KGB Chief Yuri Andropov developed a secret plan to take care of the new Polish pope. Bulgarian agents recruited the help of a Turk, Mehmet Ali Agca, to assassinate John Paul II. The failed attempt took place on May 13, 1981, during an outdoor papal audience in Rome.

Although he seriously injured the pope, Agca did not succeed in killing him. When the Polish people — especially the labor union leaders of Solidarity, like Lech Walesa — learned of this Soviet skullduggery, public disdain for the imposed regime grew exponentially. Later in 1981, Polish General and Prime Minister Wojciech Witold Jaruzelski declared *martial law* in Poland. Martial law is the law applied in an occupied territory by the military authority of the occupying power. In essence, martial reduces some personal rights of citizens and prescribes more severe penalties than ordinary law. Whenever Pope John Paul II visited Poland, he never advocated a violent revolution, but he did consistently speak of defending human rights, especially the freedom of a nation to self-determination.

As a Warsaw Pact country, Poland had been a satellite nation of the U.S.S.R. since the end of World War II. The Communist government, which was forced upon the Polish people after the Soviets had liberated them from the German Nazis, was officially and essentially atheistic. Yet, Poland was 95 percent Catholic and now had a fellow Pole on the throne of St. Peter.

During the Cold War, the Soviet Union created an agreement with the countries in Eastern Europe that they occupied or controlled. An attack on one of these countries would be considered an attack on all, most especially the U.S.S.R. The Western nations responded with their agreement among the nations of Western Europe and called it the North Atlantic Treaty Organization (NATO). The Eastern European Alliance, equivalent to NATO, was called the Warsaw Pact.

A Polish pope was problematic enough, but one who came home to visit regularly would be the greatest threat to the oppressive regime second only to Solidarity, the Polish labor union. Each papal visit to Poland produced great crowds, enthusiastic for their Catholic faith and Polish heritage. They were not political rallies but religious pilgrimages and, because of that, Poland eventually rid itself of foreign control and abandoned its Communist overlords, but in a peaceful manner.

That is not to say things did not get tense before the regime dissolved. Martial law was not a pleasant experience and having Soviet-made tanks rolling through Polish streets reminded people too much of the short-lived Hungarian uprising of 1956. Nevertheless, those several visits to Poland by the Polish pope and his words of peaceful resistance and diligent perseverance for political, economic, and religious freedom did act as a catalyst for change without the need for bloodshed.

Resisting materialism (1989–2004)

Although his message to the world was "Resist materialism," Pope John Paul II also had two historic encounters with icons of Communism, the premier of the U.S.S.R., Mikhail Gorbachev, and Fidel Castro, the dictator of Cuba. Both men epitomized the power of Soviet influence, showing the world that capitalism was not the only ideology that could put too much importance on things of the world. Whereas the *first world* (all the industrialized non-Communist countries) bled the world dry seeking profit, the *second world* (all the Communist nations and their satellite countries) abused the world seeking political domination. Neither capitalism nor Communism was a perfect system. Both had the defect of relying too heavily on the things or materials (means of production labor and capital) of the world. Religion, on the other hand, transcended materialism. Christianity in particular, did not demonize the material world, as did the dualists of the past; instead, it kept the proper relation and priority of material and spiritual (body and soul), because both were created by God.

In December 1989, the Soviet leader Mikhail Gorbachev and his wife made a very significant visit to the Vatican, the first and last in history. No one could have imagined that Gorbachev would, in fact, be the last Communist ruler of the U.S.S.R. before it dissolved in December 1991. No one envisioned an independent Russia emerging with Boris Yeltsin as President of the Russian Republic in place of the defunct Soviet Union. U.S. President Ronald Reagan had called upon Mr. Gorbachev to "tear down" the Berlin Wall. It's anyone's guess what Gorbachev's real intention was for facilitating the disintegration of the Warsaw Pact. What was evident was that the infamous Iron Curtain had finally rusted through.

Stalin once quipped "How many divisions has the pope?" when he learned that FDR and Churchill were about to ask Pope Pius XII to participate in postwar discussions on how to rebuild Europe. Gorbachev would later remark, "What has happened in Eastern Europe in recent years would not have been possible without the presence of this pope, without the great role, even political, that he has played on the world scene." But before he lost his office and the Soviet Empire, Gorbachev first paid a visit to JP2 in 1989. The leader of an atheistic Communist superpower came to see the spiritual leader of a billion Catholic Christians.

This trip was not a specific trip to the Vatican — Communist First Secretary General Gorbachev was primarily in Rome for a summit meeting with President George Herbert Walker Bush. Yet, the fact that he made a point to bring his wife, Raisa, and make a courtesy call on St. Peter's is still significant because he was the first and last leader of the U.S.S.R. to do so.

At the time, Gorbachev had been informed that his government had no connection to the assassination attempt on Pope John Paul II in 1981. Ironically, it was after the Soviet Union disintegrated that secret KGB files were discovered that proved otherwise. The operation was kept secret even from the Secretary General and only known by high-ranking KGB officials, initially to maintain credible deniability should the plot fail, which thankfully it did. Even the mafia and Al Qaeda tried to assassinate this pope at some time, so it is no surprise that the infamous KGB had its own botched plan as well.

John Paul II's turn to visit a heartland of Communism came in 1998 when he went to Cuba and met with Fidel Castro. Both Castro and JP2 were in their seventies. Even though JP2 was in declining health, he still led one billion believers around the world. Castro, strong as an ox, was the last vestige in the Western world of the old Soviet satellite system.

When confronting Communism or fascism, Pope John Paul II consistently spoke about political freedom, whether it was Solidarity in Poland or Catholicism in China. When confronting secular humanism, he spoke equally as strong about spiritual and moral freedom instead of enslavement by worldly values that violate God's laws, dishonor the human person, attack the sanctity of marriage and the family, and threaten innocent human life. As Mother Teresa of Calcutta, a dear friend to JP2, often said, while there is a material poverty in many parts of the world, there is a spiritual and moral poverty in Europe and the United States. The pope realized that Communism was not the answer — and neither was moral indifference.

Making a Jubilee Pilgrimage to the Holy Land in 2000

Pope John Paul II's visit to Jerusalem, Israel, was the first time any pope since St. Peter himself, set foot in the Holy Land. The year 2000 marked the advent of the third millennium of Christianity, and JP2 wanted to celebrate the momentous occasion by visiting the land where Jesus Christ was born, was raised, lived, preached, was crucified, died, and according to Christian faith, rose from the dead and ascended into heaven.

JP2's trip began with a visit to the Kingdom of Jordan in March 2000, where he went to Mount Nebo, the place where Moses is buried. From there, he went to Israel to visit the towns of Bethlehem (where Jesus was born), Nazareth (where Jesus grew up), and Jerusalem (where Jesus died and, Christians believe, was resurrected). He met with Palestinian Chairman Yasser Arafat and with Israeli Prime Minister Ehud Barak.

JP2 walked a political tightrope and balanced his support for both the Palestinians and the Jews. He reiterated his consistent position by saying, "The Holy See has always recognized that the Palestinian people have the natural right to a homeland." Yet, he also took time to visit Yah Vashem Holocaust Memorial, which honors and remembers the six million Jews killed in the *Shoah* (the Nazi Holocaust). During the millennium celebrations, on March 23, 2000, the pope made a statement at Yah Vashem Memorial:

> As Bishop of Rome and Successor of the Apostle Peter, I assure the Jewish people that the Catholic Church, motivated by the Gospel law of truth and love and by no political considerations, is deeply saddened by the hatred, acts of persecution, and displays of anti-Semitism directed against the Jews by Christians at any time and in any place. The Church rejects racism in any form as a denial of the image of the Creator inherent in every human being.

John Paul II was not apologizing for anything that the Church as a whole said, did, or did not do. But he did explicitly apologize for the sins and mistakes made by individuals in the Church, whether clergy or laity.

The most poignant part of the papal trip to the Holy Land, however, was the visit to the Wailing Wall in Jerusalem. The Wailing Wall is the remnant of the second temple that the Romans destroyed in 70 A.D. Faithful Jews have inserted pieces of paper containing personal prayers in between the cracks of the stones for centuries. Pope John Paul II went up to the Wailing Wall, prayed, and stuck the following note in a crevice:

> God of our fathers, you chose Abraham and his descendants to bring your Name to the Nations. We are deeply saddened by the behavior of those who in the course of history have caused these children of yours to suffer and, asking your forgiveness, we wish to commit ourselves to genuine brotherhood with the people of the Covenant.

John Paul II grew up in a Polish neighborhood where Catholics and Jews lived and worked together, and he had several Jewish friends who were sent to the Nazi extermination camps of Belzic, Chelmno, Sobibor, Majdanek, Treblinka, and the infamous Auschwitz-Birkenau. Anti-Semitism was not something he grew up with, nor was it something practiced by his father or brother. He respected Judaism as the parent religion of Christianity, because Jesus Christ himself was a Jew; because of that, JP2 held every Jew in high regard and loved them with the same brotherly love he had for his fellow Christians, whether they were Catholic, Protestant, or Eastern Orthodox.

Despite his health problems, John Paul felt it absolutely necessary for the leader of the Catholic Church to visit the Holy Land as the world prepared for the 21st century and walk the same earth traveled by the feet of Christ two millennia before. The year 2000 not only marked the beginning of a new century, but the advent of the third millennium of Christianity, because the calendar year was based on the year of the Lord (*A.D.* stands for *Anno Domini,* or "in the year of the Lord").

JP2 came to Israel not so much as a leader of a billion Catholic Christians or the ruler of a Christian nation (Vatican City), but as the spiritual representative of a fellow monotheistic religion. He prayed and asked for peace and justice among Palestinians and Israelis; among Jews, Muslims, and Christians. He asked forgiveness for the evils done in the name of religion to members of other religions. John Paul II saw the new millennium as an opportunity for reconciliation and cooperation, and his visit to the Holy Land was essential to laying the groundwork for that epic and ongoing project.

A few of his critics claimed he did not say or do enough to repair the damage and division caused between Catholicism (and Christianity, in general) and Judaism in light of the historical persecution of Jews during the first two millennia. Many others, however, were grateful that the first Catholic pope since St. Peter (a Jewish fisherman) to visit a Jewish Synagogue in Rome (on April 13, 1986) would also be the first pope to visit the Holy City of Jerusalem and the nation of Israel. JP2 himself had aggressively worked for the establishment of diplomatic relations between the state of Israel and Vatican City (finally achieved on December 20, 1993). Much of the delay centered on the issue of his support for an independent and sovereign Palestinian homeland, but in the mind of JP2, he regarded both peoples with equal dignity and respect and denounced acts of terrorism, violence, and injustice committed on both sides.

His global travel made John Paul II, the Catholic papacy, and Catholicism itself better known around the world and, indeed, reflected the universality of the religion. By canonizing saints from every corner of the Earth, by creating cardinals from almost every nation who would elect the next pope and be eligible for election themselves, and by visiting as many countries on Earth as he could, JP2 showed the world that the Catholic Church was truly *catholic* (universal). Though the headquarters and leader were located in Rome, the scope, vision, and experience would forever be global.

Chapter 17

A Media-Savvy Pope

. . . .

. . . .

During John Paul II's papacy (1978–2005), the world saw an explosion in technology — instead of having just one or two means of communicating with one another, people could get their messages out in a myriad of ways, and JP2 was no exception. From personal computers and cell phones, to the Internet and wireless devices, modern technology crept into every facet of people's daily lives. Today, you don't have to own stock in Microsoft or love your motherboard more than your mom to use technology to your advantage. Around the world, people of every age range, socioeconomic group, and experience level have technology at their fingertips.

John Paul II saw these ever-present and ever-growing tools as a way to bring the message of the Catholic Church and the Gospel of Jesus Christ to people everywhere, in many more formats and through more delivery systems than any pope before him could have ever imagined.

In this chapter, we show you how JP2 viewed technology's role in spreading the message and the faith. We look at how he used more traditional media, like TV and radio, to deliver teachings of the Catholic Church. And we explore the development of the papal Web site as a 24/7 portal to centuries of Catholic doctrine.

Can You Hear Me Now? Using the Communications Tools at His Disposal

The Second Vatican Council, in a decree on social communications called *Inter Mirifica,* specifically identified the press, cinema, radio, and television as "means of communication which of their nature can reach and influence not merely single individuals but the very masses and even the whole of human society." *Inter Mirifica* gives very specific direction for each member of the Church —laypeople and members of the clergy alike — to participate in spreading the Gospel message of Jesus Christ through the media. It also outlines the duties and obligations like writing and producing programming, praying, and donating funds to support the effort.

Pope John Paul II saw this decree as part of his mandate to spread the Gospel of Jesus Christ. And he executed that decree to its fullest extent during his time as pope, using all kinds of tools to do so.

Within the Vatican's *Curia* (central administrative government), the pope's eyes and ears in the world of social communications is the appropriately named Pontifical Council for Social Communications. The roots of the Council actually go back to the 1940s, when Pope Pius XII established an office in the Vatican to examine the morality and soundness of the new presence of motion pictures. Through the years, the Council developed and became the means of acting upon Vatican II's decree on social communications. Since 1984, an American, Archbishop John P. Foley of Philadelphia, has headed the Council.

Read all about it! The Vatican newspaper and Vatican Information Service

The Vatican's oldest means of communications with the outside world is the newspaper *L'Osservatore Romano* (The Roman Observer). Begun on July 1, 1861, the paper began as a means to defend the Papal States as the pope's temporal power was gradually reduced. In 1870, the paper became the voice of opposition when troops of the Kingdom of Italy declared war against the Papal States in their efforts to unite the country. In 1885, Pope Leo XIII officially became the "owner" of the newspaper and made it the official source of information for the Holy See. Besides the daily Italian edition, *L'Osservatore Romano* also prints weekly editions in French, English, Spanish, Portuguese, German, and (beginning in 1980) Polish.

In 1991, the Vatican Information Service was created within the Holy See Press Office. The service makes available — in English, Italian, Spanish, and French — a daily bulletin of the activities of the pope; his homilies, speeches, and nominations; and announcements made by Vatican congregations and the Holy See Press Office itself.

You can read these daily bulletins online at `www.vatican.va/ news_services/index.htm`.

The world press

With Pope John Paul II's election in 1978, he made it clear that he would have no problem speaking to the people in any way he could find — including the press. From his first appearance on the central balcony of St. Peter's Basilica following his election, Pope John Paul II broke precedent by addressing the crowd rather than simply pronouncing the Apostolic Blessing. Five days later, on October 21, 1978, Pope John Paul II again broke new ground and met with journalists who had been in Rome since the death of Pope John Paul I. (His successor, Pope Benedict XVI, followed suit after John Paul II's death.)

Before Pope John Paul II, popes did not speak to the press. Like royalty, it was considered unthinkable for a reporter to "grill" a pope in the same way that a political figure or an actor would be questioned. Even the Vatican newspaper and Vatican Radio simply reported the official meetings and printed official statements from the Holy Father. Because of this, no papal spokesman was ever really considered necessary. In 1984, about the same time that the 24-hour news cycle began to emerge, Pope John Paul II appointed a layman, Dr. Joaquin Navarro-Valls, as papal spokesman and director of the Holy See Press Office. A Spaniard, Dr. Navarro-Valls is a trained medical doctor and psychiatrist (something he often jokes about in his assignment of dealing with the press).

Vatican Radio

Vatican Radio is impressive not only for the global transmissions that extend from the antenna located on the highest point of Vatican City's 108 acres, but for the founder, Guglielmo Marconi, the Father of Radio himself!

In 1925, the Holy See's Director of Communications began plans for the establishment of a wireless transmission station within Vatican walls. By 1927, the Vatican contacted Guglielmo Marconi (the Father of Radio, who sent the first radio signal in 1895) and asked him, on Pope Pius XI's behalf, to take on the task. Following the 1929 signing of the Lateran Treaty, which recognized the Vatican city-state as a sovereign nation, Marconi received permission from Pius XI to begin construction. On February 12, 1931, at 4:49 p.m., Pope Pius made the first transmission of Vatican Radio to the world. Catholics in London stood for hours in Westminster Cathedral in London, waiting for the transmission. *The New York Herald* wrote that the pope having the ability to speak directly to the people of the world was "a miracle of science, and no less a miracle of faith."

Pope John Paul II certainly knew the value of Vatican Radio. From 1962 to 1965, Bishop Wojtyła used Vatican Radio to broadcast the happenings of the Second Vatican Council back to Poland. On August 19, 1978, Cardinal Wojtyła shared his memories of Pope Paul VI in a broadcast. As pope, in 1979, JP2 began the tradition of broadcasting the recitation of the Rosary on the first Saturday of each month. And during the Cold War, Pope John Paul II knew that Vatican Radio was one of the few ways that he could communicate directly with Poles without fear of censorship.

Today, Vatican Radio programs are beamed around the world on a daily basis in 47 different languages on short wave, medium wave, and satellite. The most recent addition to the Vatican Radio arsenal is "One-O-Five Live", 105.1 FM (hence the name), which broadcasts on mainstream FM radio throughout Italy.

You can access Vatican Radio over the Internet at www.vatican.va/ news_services/radio/index.htm or www.vaticanradio.org.

Vatican TV

The Vatican Television Center (in Italian, *Centro Televisivo Vaticano,* or CTV for short) was created in 1983. It officially exists to both record Vatican cere- monies for historical purposes, as well as provide world media with a video transmission that they can use in their reporting. But it also serves the pur- pose of assisting the pope in spreading the Gospel by televising events in the day-to-day activities of the Vatican for broadcast around the world. Catholic cable stations around the world, such as the U.S.'s Eternal Word Television Network (EWTN) and Italy's Telepace, often broadcast excerpts from the feed.

CTV televises about 130 live broadcasts each year, ranging from the pope's Wednesday general audiences to his weekly appearances at his apartment window on Sundays at noon to pray the Angelus prayers to the Holy Father's foreign trips to large liturgical ceremonies such as beatifications and canon- izations to Masses and ceremonies on the major feast days on the Catholic Church's calendar. The most well-known products of Vatican Television are the broadcasts of Christmas Midnight Mass from St. Peter's Basilica, as well as the Pope's *Urbi et Orbi* (to the city [of Rome] and to the world) on Christmas Day and Easter Sunday. These transmissions are available, via satellite, to television networks around the world.

In addition, CTV follows the day-to-day events of the pope and the Holy See for historical purposes. Not only do these events get put into the Vatican archives, but the footage is also made available to press agencies that request the footage (for example, when the Grand Duke of Luxembourg visits the Vatican, Luxembourg nightly news can show the moment when the Grand Duke and the pope shake hands). CTV also produces a weekly news TV show called *Octava Dies* (Eighth Day), which shows the events of the past week at the Vatican. The show is played on Catholic television stations throughout Italy and can be watched over the Internet. When they're not doing everything else, CTV also produces documentaries on the Vatican and other historic churches of Rome in several languages.

Have you ever met the pope? Do you know someone who was at a special event at the Vatican? CTV will provide you with a video of the event (for a small charge, of course). You can access the Vatican Television Center over the Internet at www.vatican.va/news_services/television.htm. You can e-mail them for information on the video at ctv@ctv.va.

Author, author: JP2 breaks new ground

In 1993, to coincide with the 15th anniversary of his election, Pope John Paul II agreed to sit for a television interview to be broadcast on Italian television. The interviewer, veteran journalist Vittorio Messori, submitted suggested questions to the pope. As it turned out, the pope's busy schedule made it impossible for the interview to take place, but he was intrigued by the questions and wrote out answers to each one. His responses became the first book ever written by a reigning pope, called *Crossing the Threshold of Hope*, published in 1994.

In September 1995, the Congregation for the Clergy held a meeting to celebrate the 30th anniversary of the Second Vatican Council's decree on the priesthood. During the meeting, several priests told their vocation stories and, moved by this, JP2 wrote *Gift and Mystery* to coincide with the 50th anniversary of his ordination to the priesthood in 1997. The worldwide acclaim of this book and the 45th anniversary of his consecration as a bishop caused him to write the "sequel," *Rise, Let Us Be On Our Way,* in 2004.

In 2003, *Roman Triptych: Meditations* was published. This book was a collection of poetry written by Pope John Paul II. A *triptych* is a three-paneled icon, and, in the book, the Holy Father includes three poems ranging from God's gift of nature, to God's Creation as seen in the works of Michelangelo on the ceiling of the Sistine Chapel, to God's love in the sacrifice of Jesus Christ as foreshadowed by God's command to Abraham to sacrifice his son, Isaac.

The final book written by Pope John Paul II was *Memory and Identity,* published just before his death in 2005. This book flows from the seminars held each summer at the papal summer retreat Castel Gandolfo. JP2 says that, in looking at the "memory" of past experiences, humanity can better understand our "identity" as we embark on the 21st century.

The Vatican Goes Live: Development of the Papal Web Site

In 1995, Sister Judith Zoebelein, a Franciscan Sister of the Eucharist, was asked to create a Web site for the Holy See. Archbishop Foley of the Pontifical Council for Social Communications had already registered the top-level domain suffix of .va for the exclusive use of the Holy See (.va is the two-letter country code for the Vatican City-State, as .ca is for Canada and .uk is for the United Kingdom). The Internet was still relatively new, but already the word *Vatican* was turning up on Web sites having nothing to do with the Holy See. Archbishop Foley wanted to assure people around the world that anything with the .va suffix was official and reliable.

The Vatican Web site (www.vatican.va) has been online since Christmas 1995, available for those seeking information about the pope, Church history, or documents, or those simply wanting a glimpse of the artistic treasures of the Vatican. The Web site is maintained by a multilingual staff, including Sister Judith and sisters from her congregation, in offices down the street from St. Peter's Basilica. The Web site itself is visited literally millions of times each day by Internet users around the world.

Pope John Paul II had six different e-mail boxes set up within the Web site (based on the language the e-mailer used), and the Web servers were quickly overloaded with e-mails written by people wanting to correspond with the pope. In reality, though, the e-mail addresses were never actually checked by JP2 himself. Nowadays, for Pope Benedict XVI as it was for Pope John Paul II, the pope's e-mail address is only accessible on special occasions, such as his birthday or significant anniversaries in his life, and during those times a sampling of e-mails are printed out and forwarded to the Apostolic Palace to be shown to the Holy Father. These e-mail addresses were meant to be another means for people to write letters to the pope, as generations before had done the "good, old-fashioned way."

JP2 was a big supporter of the Vatican Web site and saw tremendous potential in the Internet. In 2001, he transmitted by Internet for the first time an apostolic letter to the bishops of Australia and New Zealand following the Synod of Bishops on the topic of the Church in Oceania. Instead of simply sending the letter the old-fashioned way, by regular mail, the 81-year-old JP2 was making a point of being seen (and photographed) clicking a mouse to instantly send the document "down under."

Interestingly enough, the last apostolic letter ever issued by Pope John Paul II was "The Rapid Development" (written on January 24, 2005, and released four weeks later on February 21), written for the 40th anniversary of the Vatican II document *Inter Mirifica*. In it, JP2 spoke of the potential of the Internet when he wrote,

> New technologies, in particular, create further opportunities for communication understood as a service to the pastoral government and organization of the different tasks of the Christian community. One clear example today is how the Internet not only provides resources for more information, but habituates persons to interactive communication. . . . Do not be afraid of new technologies! These rank among the marvelous things — *inter mirifica* — which God has placed at our disposal to discover, to use and to make known the truth, also the truth about our dignity and about our destiny as his children, heirs of his eternal kingdom.

Pope John Paul II may not have understood *how* these new advances in communications worked, but he certainly saw the potential for their use in evangelization.

The Vatican Web site is housed on three main servers, named "Michael," "Gabriel," and "Raphael" for the archangels. Because the word *angel* literally means "messenger," it seemed appropriate to name the three tools for the Vatican's outreach into cyberspace after God's three main messengers.

During the period between JP2's death and the conclave that elected his successor, the staff of the Web site worked around the clock heroically to keep these servers from crashing. Why would they crash, you ask? During that time (April 2005), it's estimated that the Vatican Web site received around 50 million hits (or visitors) each day from people worldwide seeking official information.

Chapter 18

Exploring Sainthood

The funeral of Pope John Paul II on April 8, 2005, will be remembered not just because of the estimated crowd of 300,000 attendees filling St. Peter's Square and overflowing into the neighboring streets (in all it's estimated that Rome was filled with four million additional pilgrims from the time of the Pope's death to his funeral), but because of the many handmade signs held by pilgrims, which read *Santo Subito* (A Saint Soon).

In this chapter, we explore the current state of the cause for sainthood for John Paul II. We look at how his life and teachings mesh with the process of declaring a saint. And we speculate on whether (okay, *when*) John Paul II will be declared a saint.

Santo Subito: The Fast Track for Sainthood

Through John Paul II's funeral, the world got to see a throwback to the Catholic Church's historical past: The early Church had no official "process" for declaring a saint — no one ever investigated St. Joseph, the Apostles, and so on. Even today, the choice of who will be added to the list (or *canon*) of recognized saints rests more with the laity than the hierarchy of the Church. True, the Church has the structure to examine the life of the person, but a person being considered for possible sainthood is being considered because ordinary people hold them up as someone holy whom they feel they can pray to for intercession on their behalf. In short, although the *how* rests with the Church's administration, the *who* rests with the Church's lay faithful.

Take a look at Chapter 14 for details on the process involved in making someone a saint.

Standing the test of time

The cause for Pope John Paul II's beatification and canonization is unique compared to most other causes dealt with by the Congregation for the Causes of Saints. In most cases, the person being examined for possible canonization is largely unknown to the rest of the world, except for a small group of people wherever the person lived and worked. So the person's life story, his writings, and the like, need to be thoroughly examined and investigated before the Church will accept the cause for consideration. Pope John Paul II was certainly not an unknown person, so it could be argued that much of the investigation into his life, his writings, and his sanctity had already begun. Allowing time to pass also tests whether any momentum is building amongst the people for the Church to acknowledge the sanctity of the person.

The Catholic Church has never bought into "instant gratification" — the Church doesn't do anything quickly. Nor does the Church see any need to move quickly. Roman Catholics believe that those men and women who lived lives of holiness on Earth gain entrance into heaven, into the presence of God, Jesus, the Virgin Mary, and all the angels and saints. To quote St. Bernard of Clairvaux (1090–1153):

> The saints have no need of honor from us; neither does our devotion add the slightest thing to what is theirs. Clearly, if we venerate their memory, it serves us, not them.

Saints have no seniority in heaven; the ones we know about have no prestige or special privileges that other saints do not. They've made it — they're in! Recognizing them as saints is meant to help us more than them.

Removing the five-year waiting period

This is one of those times when "it's good to be the pope." Canon 331 of the Church's *Code of Canon Law* states that the pope, "in virtue of his office enjoys supreme, full, immediate, and universal ordinary power in the Church, which he can always freely exercise."

On May 9, 2005, the Congregation for the Causes of Saints announced that in a meeting on the previous April 28, Pope Benedict XVI met with Cardinal Camillo Ruini, the Vicar General of His Holiness for the Diocese of Rome. At the meeting, Pope Benedict XVI agreed to dispense with the normal five-year waiting period, allowing the cause of beatification and canonization of John Paul II to begin immediately. This announcement was made in a meeting of Pope Benedict XVI with the clergy of the Diocese of Rome at the Basilica of

St. John Lateran on May 13, 2005 (which happened to be the 24th anniversary of the assassination attempt of Pope John Paul II), and those present showed their approval by a lengthy standing ovation.

What Pope Benedict XVI did in waiving the five-year rule wasn't radical or unique — as recently as 1998, Pope John Paul II himself dispensed with the five-year waiting period for the cause of Mother Teresa of Calcutta (whom he later *beatified,* or declared "Blessed," in 2003).

John Paul the Great

As early as 1997, the Catholic magazine *Crisis* featured a cover story that included a photograph of Pope John Paul II and the caption "John Paul the Great." The magazine was celebrating 15 years of publication at the same time that JP2 was celebrating 50 years of priestly ordination, and the issue included a series of essays by Catholic clergy and laity assessing the long-range impact of JP2's pontificate. Though he may not, as of yet, have the title of saint, he certainly has begun to be called "great."

In Catholic circles, posthumous surnames are nothing new. One of the earliest was the fourth-century Bishop of Constantinople and Doctor of the Church, St. John Chrysostom, whose surname means "golden-mouthed." The fifth-century Bishop of Ravenna St. Peter Chrysologos (which means "golden word") was known for his zeal and oratory.

With regards to those labeled "the Great," the Roman Catholic Church commonly held four until Pope John Paul II (five if you include the Apostle St. James the Greater, though his "greatness" was more of an identifier for being older or taller than the other Apostle, St. James the Less).

- ✔ **St. Basil the Great (329–379)** was a bishop and Doctor of the Church who fought early heresies that disputed the nature of Jesus Christ.

- ✔ **Pope Leo the Great** reigned from 440 to 461 and fought to preserve the unity of the Church from forces outside as well as within the Church.

- ✔ **Pope Gregory the Great** reigned from 590 to 604 and brought great spiritual renewal to the Church.

- ✔ **St. Albert the Great (1206–1280)** was a Dominican friar known to be a brilliant scientist, philosopher, and theologian.

What arguments could be made for "John Paul the Great"? Deal W. Hudson, the editor and publisher of *Crisis* magazine's special "John Paul the Great" issue (published almost prophetically in 1997), explained it this way:

"Be not afraid," he told us at the beginning of his reign, and fearlessness has characterized his . . . pontificate. John Paul II has shown us that courage combined with wisdom can move what seems immovable. . . . He has taught Catholics once again to think beyond the headlines, to retain their confidence in the restless heart of mankind, and to serve the deepest needs of the human heart rather than the manipulators of popular opinion. In doing so, John Paul II has given us the agenda for the next century, and strong and effective tools to implement it. . . . The Holy Father's papacy has strengthened the visibility of the invisible Church. The Catechism, the Code of Canon Law, his unmatched series of letters and encyclicals: all these great gifts to the Church will continue to bear fruit.

Peggy Noonan, in her 2005 book, *John Paul the Great: Remembering a Spiritual Father*, wrote that

Great men lift us up. They tell us by their presence that everything is possible, that as children of God we are a part of God, and as a part of God we can, with him, accomplish anything. *Anything.* He was an obscure Polish boy with no connections, no standing, without even, by the time he was of college age, a family. He worked in a factory and ate potatoes in water for dinner during a war. He went on to become the most famous man of his age, and famous for that finest of reasons; a life well lived.

Living a Life of Heroic Virtue

The first step in the long road to recognizing Pope John Paul II as a saint of the Roman Catholic Church began with an investigation of how, over a period of time, he lived the cardinal virtues as well as the theological virtues.

The cardinal virtues are

- **Prudence:** The virtue that disposes a person to discern the good and choose the correct means to accomplish it. In other words, how did he live according to the law of Christ?

- **Justice:** The virtue that consists in the constant and firm will to give what is due to God and to neighbor. In other words, how did he respect the rights that were due to his neighbors and to God?

- **Fortitude:** The virtue that demonstrates firmness in difficulties and constancy in the pursuit of the good. In other words, did he overcome temptations? Did he conquer fear?

- **Temperance:** The virtue that provides balance in the use of created goods and moderates the attractions of pleasures. In other words, did he live an upright, godly life in this world?

The theological virtues, which help a person adapt to his life in relationship with God, are

- **Faith:** The virtue by which the person believed in God and all that God revealed to him, including the things revealed to him through the Church.

- **Hope:** The virtue by which he desired the kingdom of heaven and eternal life, trusting in the promises made to him by Christ.

- **Charity:** The virtue by which the person loved God above all things and his neighbors because they, too, are creations of God.

Receiving the title "Servant of God"

When a bishop asks the Congregation for the Causes of Saints whether he can begin examining the cause of a person for consideration for beatification and canonization, he sends to the congregation preliminary information about the person, including a detailed biography, basic evidence of his living of "heroic virtue," and any details surrounding his martyrdom if that was the case. The congregation then gives a preliminary approval for the bishop to begin the research. When that approval to proceed with the research is given, the person is considered a *Servant of God.* When Pope Benedict XVI, asked by the Diocese of Rome to dispense with the five-year wait, granted the dispensation from the rule so that the investigation could begin, Pope John Paul II became known as a Servant of God.

As of the writing of this book, the cause of the Servant of God Pope John Paul II stands at this stage.

Verifying that he's "Venerable"

Living the cardinal and theological virtues is important, but it's only the first step of a long process. The next step in the process involves an investigation of the published writings of the candidate, to see whether those writings are theologically sound. For Pope John Paul II, this review includes thousands of pages of written text (encyclicals, apostolic letters, homilies, and books such as *Love and Responsibility* and *Crossing the Threshold of Hope.*)

After the published works are investigated, any unpublished works are also researched and investigated (this would include writings like diaries and personal letters). Pope John Paul II's last will and testament said, "My personal notes are to be burned." However, Archbishop Stanislaw Dziwisz, the pope's longtime private secretary, has indicated that he has not done so, stating that "Nothing is fit for burning, everything should be preserved and kept for history. . . . These are great riches that should gradually be made available to the public." Archbishop Dziwisz also knew that some of the papers would be useful in the cause for beatification.

Interviewing witnesses

At the same time that written works are being examined, a list of witnesses is prepared by the Postulator of the Cause. In the case of Pope John Paul II, the witnesses would include those who worked closely with him. Obvious names on the list would include

- Stanislaw Cardinal Dziwisz (now the Archbishop of Krakow)
- Other past secretaries of Pope John Paul II
- Members of the Sister Servants of the Most Sacred Heart (a Polish religious women's order that served in the papal household)
- Vatican curial officials such as Secretary of State Angelo Cardinal Sodano

Other people will likely also be interviewed as witnesses. These people will all be interviewed to give their own testimony on the sanctity of Pope John Paul II.

At the end of this process, copies of the published and unpublished works, as well as transcripts of the witnesses' testimony will be forwarded to the Congregation for the Causes of Saints. A *relator* (a person who examines these documents) will be assigned the case and will see to it that the writings, testimony, and any other submitted information are sent to appropriate experts for their comments and/or criticisms.

When all these have been examined and discussed by the College of Relators, a vote is taken whether to send the cause to the cardinals and bishops who make up the membership of the Congregation for the Causes of Saints. These men will then discuss the matter amongst themselves and vote whether to recommend the person's cause to the pope. If the pope officially "recognizes" the heroic virtues of the person, this recognition is published, and the person is now called "Venerable," meaning his virtues are worthy of being venerated by the lay faithful.

Beatifying John Paul II

The next step on the road to canonization (and indeed the last step before it) is to be declared "Blessed" (*beatus* in Latin, hence the term *beatification*). The most necessary requirement for beatification is that a miracle is attributed to the candidate in question.

Looking for a miracle

The *Catechism of the Catholic Church* defines a *miracle* as "a sign or wonder, such as a healing or the control of nature, which can only be attributed to divine power." Miracles are understood to be contrary to the natural order of things, and evidence of supernatural "interference" in the normal course of events. In short, something happened that should not have happened, and no one can figure out why.

Evaluating the evidence

When something considered "miraculous" has occurred, the investigation of the miracle always begins in the diocese in which the miracle took place (this may or may not be the same diocese that first proposed the person's cause for canonization). After the Postulator of the Cause petitions the local bishop to investigate the alleged miracle and includes a "brief but accurate" report about it, the bishop asks the help of experts in the field pertaining to the miracle (a bodily healing would involve the expertise of a physician, while a miracle of nature might involve a geologist or meteorologist). The experts examine the evidence and report back to the bishop whether the alleged miracle can by explained by any natural cause.

The investigators will also seek to determine whether the alleged miracle can be attributed to the Venerable Servant of God alone. In other words, the other question being asked is "Whodunit?" In the case of a bodily healing, did the person healed make it known she was praying for the intercession of this Servant of God? Was a piece of the Servant of God's clothing or an item used by the person in this life "touched" to the affected area? Is it possible that the person was healed by another saint or blessed besides the one whose cause is being considered?

After receiving the testimony of his experts, the local bishop discusses the matter with his local theological commission. If it is determined that (1) there is no other explanation except for a "miracle", and, (2) that miracle can be directly attributed to prayers directed specifically to a particular Servant of God by asking his intercession with the Lord, then a report of the findings is sent to the Congregation for the Causes of Saints in Rome.

Something else that works in the favor of the cause of a Servant of God is universal appeal. In the past, universal appeal was done very simply and very low-key through the printing of prayer cards. A small card was printed with a photograph of the person on one side and a prayer approved by the local bishop on the other side. In small print would have been written something like, "Any testimonies should be forwarded to the Postulator of the Cause at the following address. . . ."

In the case of Pope John Paul II, a public notice (called an *edict*) was published by the Vicariate of Rome, notifying anyone and everyone to come forward if they have information either for or against the cause of the Servant of God. The edict gave an address and telephone number for interested persons to contact; the edict was posted not only on the doors of the headquarters of the Vicariate of Rome, but also on the doors of the headquarters of the Archdiocese of Krakow. (This public posting of an edict at the location where the cause originated, as well as places where the candidate lived and worked, is a standard practice.)

Today, thanks to the Internet, not only can information about the cause be sent around the world, but testimony about any possible miracles can be easily sent back to the postulator via e-mail. The Web site for the case of JP2 opened on June 19, 2005, and since then has had hundreds of thousands of Web visitors. These visitors can leave testimony, prayer intentions, remembrances of personal meetings with Pope John Paul II, as well as freewill donations to be used to further the cause. You can visit the site at www.vicariatusurbis.org/beatificazione.

Receiving the title "Blessed"

When these testimonies lead to the discovery of a possible miracle, and when the report of the findings of the local diocese is sent to the Congregation for the Causes of Saints, commissions are established to look at the scientific as well as theological explanations. If these commissions vote to accept the findings of the reports, then the reports are passed along to the cardinals and bishops who make up the congregation. If they vote to approve the report supporting the alleged miracle, it is sent on to the pope.

Here we should note that, if the person whose cause is being considered was martyred for the faith, then the miracle needed for beatification can be waived by the pope. When Pope John Paul II first died, rumors circulated that his very public suffering leading up to his death might cause him to be classified as a martyr, thereby eliminating the need for a miracle before beatification. However Cardinal José Saraiva Martins, the current Prefect for the Congregation for the Causes of Saints, has publicly said that this is not the case for Pope John Paul II's cause: "Only those may be considered martyrs who have shed their blood voluntarily," the cardinal said, "those who were killed 'in odium fidei' — out of hatred for the faith." If a person's cause is the result of his martyrdom, then a report detailing the events of the death would be prepared by the local diocese, the Congregation for the Causes of Saints would vote to certify it as a true martyrdom, and the pope would issue a Decree of Martyrdom.

When the pope accepts the report and approves the miracle, the person can be beatified. With beatification comes some privileges. The blessed can now be honored through the liturgical life of the Roman Catholic Church. A feast day is assigned to honor the blessed (usually the day the person died). Special prayers may be written for the Mass to be celebrated in honor of the blessed, although they may simply be allowed to use the "common" prayers already written for pastors, martyrs, virgins, and so on.

The beatification ceremony itself is done in the context of the Holy Sacrifice of the Mass. During the Mass, the celebrant reads the decree of the pope declaring the person a blessed. An extremely moving moment of the ceremony is when a huge image of the newly beatified is unveiled for the public to see.

Taking the Next Steps for Sainthood

Following the beatification, the next step is the final one: the canonization of the person. As you might expect, a miracle is involved in order for a person to be canonized.

Witnessing a second miracle

What is needed, again, is a miraculous happening. But here's the catch: To prove that the blessed is at work in heaven actively interceding for people, the miracle has to have taken place *after* the beatification ceremony. No miracles from the past can be used for consideration for canonization; they must be recent.

If a miracle takes place, the same rules apply as before: The diocese in which the miracle takes place conducts a local investigation and, if they agree it is extraordinary, they pass their findings on to the Congregation for the Causes of Saints. The congregation's experts "investigate the investigation," and if they approve, they pass their findings on to the members of the congregation. The congregation members discuss it and vote on it, and if they approve, it is passed along to the pope for his final approval. At any stage along the way, a *no* vote (providing there's a good reason), can cause the whole process to stop until another miracle comes along. That may be soon, or it may be years away.

The findings of the congregation are submitted to the pope, and if he approves their findings, he certifies the miracle. This step sets the stage for a canonization ceremony.

Receiving the title "Saint"

Under Pope John Paul II, beatifications and canonizations closely resembled each other, the only real difference being the wording of the declaration formula pronounced by the pope.

Pope Benedict XVI has restored the tradition of only presiding at canonization Masses, while normally allowing the Prefect for the Congregation for the Causes of Saints to preside at beatification Masses. This revival of tradition also reminds the faithful that, although a beatification is a necessary step in the process, it is not the "end of the road." A beatification allows the public veneration of a Servant of God in specific areas, such as the dioceses where he lived, or in specific geographic boundaries. A canonization makes the veneration of the blessed obligatory for the whole Church, and although different regions of the world may have stronger devotions to some saints more than others, Catholics everywhere must acknowledge the person as a saint of the Roman Catholic Church. Pope Benedict XVI also wants to remind the faithful that canonization invokes papal infallibility, whereas beatification does not — hence, from now on, the pope will limit himself to canonizing saints while allowing local bishops or cardinals to beatify the blessed.

In an interview on the first anniversary of Pope John Paul II's election following his death, Archbishop Stanislaw Dziwisz indicated that he was hopeful that the beatification of Pope John Paul II could take place in Poland as early as 2006. During Pope Benedict's visit to Poland in the spring of 2006, no beatification occurred, though the Holy Father made a specific point, in address to the crowd at the Polish Shrine of Kalwaria Zebrzydowska, of saying, "I would like to say, as dear Cardinal Stanislaw Dziwisz' said, that I hope Divine Providence will soon concede the beatification and canonization of our beloved Pope John Paul II."

If Pope John Paul II is declared a saint someday, that declaration would undoubtedly be done in Rome. In the meantime, the postulator for JP2's cause is actively investigating the case of a religious sister in France who claims to have been cured of Parkinson's disease (the same ailment that afflicted Pope John Paul II) after praying to him on nine consecutive days (called a *novena*).

Chapter 19

Concerning the Future of the Papacy

*A*t one time in history, every pope was a schoolboy, a student, and a son. Through intervention from God, their own ceaseless faith, and struggle through the many obstacles in life, each of them rose to the office of Supreme Pontiff. No matter what circumstances the boy began his life in, the path was a difficult one.

In this chapter, we look at the College of Cardinals, the group of men who elect a new pope from within their own ranks. We take a look at the papal election process and its most recent result, the election of Pope Benedict XVI. And finally, we consider what the future holds for the Catholic Church under his leadership.

Identifying the College of Cardinals

Church law (called *canon law*) says, "The cardinals of the Holy Roman Church constitute a special college whose responsibility is to provide for the election of the Roman Pontiff. . . ." We refer to this process of choosing a pontiff as a *conclave,* which is a secret meeting. In reality, the meeting itself isn't secret (everyone knows when and where it takes place), but the proceedings are private. (Check out the "Understanding Conclave: The Papal Election Process" section later in this chapter for details on what happens during a conclave.)

In the beginning, there was the bird . . .

Where does the term *cardinal* come from? Not from the red bird. In fact, it's the other way around: The red birds were named after the red-robed cardinals of the Roman Catholic Church (just as a cappuccino with the light brown liquid on the bottom and the white foam on top was named because it looked like a little, light-brown-robed, gray-headed Cappucin monk, but that's another story).

The word *cardinal* comes from the Latin word *cardo,* meaning literally a "hinge" on a door. Just as a hinge connects the door to the rest of the house, so in the early days of the Catholic Church the pope (in his capacity as Bishop of Rome) gave the title to leaders of Church communities that were on the outskirts of the city,

far enough to prevent them from easily coming to Rome for religious services. These people were the "hinges" that connected these communities to the Bishop of Rome.

Having local representatives for faraway officials wasn't such an odd thing in Roman society. At about the same time, Romans had a position in government called *proconsul,* which was an assistant to a leader in government or society (for example, a senator). It was understood that when the proconsul spoke, it was with the authority of his boss. So, just as in other things, as the Church came out of hiding for fear of persecution and began to establish an organizational structure, the patterns and style mimicked the Roman rule of the day.

The College of Cardinals has two roles for the Church:

- ✔ **To participate in the election of the pope when the Holy See is vacant.**

- ✔ **To advise the Roman Pontiff (the pope) about Church matters when he summons them to a consistory.** A *consistory* is a formal meeting of the College of Cardinals and is held in Rome for taking care of the business of the college and advising the pope on important matters. The pope creates new cardinals in the presence of the college; the consistory is the meeting where this takes place. A *conclave* is also a consistory with the purpose of electing a new pope upon the death of the former pope.

The College of Cardinals includes 192 cardinals, of whom 120 are currently eligible (being under the age of 80) to vote to elect a pope. One hundred are from Europe (40 from Italy alone), 31 from Latin America, 20 from North America (15 from the United States), 20 from Asia, 17 from Africa, and 4 from Oceania. When a cardinal dies or turns 80, the current pope can create a new cardinal. Normally, the limit is 120 voting eligible cardinals, but any pope can create more if he so chooses. For centuries, the number never went above 70, to mirror the 70 elders who advised Moses as he led the Hebrew people after the Exodus. Pope Paul VI and, later, Pope John Paul II saw the need to internationalize the College of Cardinals, so they raised the limit on the number of voting members.

Over time, the title "cardinal" grew from its meaning of an office with territorial jurisdiction to become a title of esteem for someone who was a close advisor to the pope for the sake of the Church. Eventually, the term *cardinal* became synonymous with importance, and theological terms like the *cardinal virtues* (meaning the most important virtues) began to take hold.

By the 800s, within the College of Cardinals, a structure-within-the-structure had developed: The cardinals of the Catholic Church had evolved into the different levels of cardinal-bishops, cardinal-priests, and cardinal-deacons. These levels of rank still exist today within the College of Cardinals:

- ✔ **Cardinal-bishops** are those cardinals who hold the most important offices such as Vatican Secretary of State, heads of major Vatican congregations, or the Dean or Vice-Dean of the College of Cardinals.

- ✔ **Cardinal-priests** are those cardinals who head large archdioceses around the world like those in New York, London, Sydney, and Paris.

- ✔ **Cardinal-deacons** are those cardinals who assist the pope in the central governance of the Church, as well as those who are honored after years of service to the Church.

Regardless of their rank within the College itself, all cardinals assist the pope through their work as members of the many congregations, pontifical councils, commissions, and institutions connected with the Vatican. These organizations are usually assigned to them just after the consistory, during which the pope officially makes them cardinals of the Roman Catholic Church by an official declaration.

When most people think of cardinals, they think of the color red. Not just any red, but bright, scarlet red. Cardinals wear the color red for one obvious and one not-so-obvious reason. The obvious reason is that the red they wear reminds them of the possibility that, one day, because of their special relationship to the pope and the Universal Church, they may have to defend the Catholic faith even to the point of shedding their own blood. The not-so-obvious reason is the privilege they have to wear the same color as the pope wore, thus showing the world their unique relationship to the pope.

Popes did not always wear white, and even today you still see the color red in the pope's shoes, in the *mozzetta* (the shoulder cape that buttons down the front; see Figure 19-1) that the pope wears on formal occasions, and even in the red cloak worn outdoors by the pope on cold days. Pope Benedict XVI has, in fact, brought back the papal fur-trimmed (faux fur nowadays) winter mozzetta and *camauro* (a fur cap not seen since it was regularly worn by Pope John XXIII [1958–1963]). Today, cardinals are usually seen in either a black cassock trimmed with a scarlet *fascia* (sash) and *zucchetto* (skullcap; see Figure 19-2). On more formal occasions, they may be seen in all-scarlet cassocks, either with a white surplice and matching scarlet mozzetta in what is called *choir dress,* or under their vestments when celebrating Mass.

Figure 19-1:
Pope John
Paul II
wearing his
mozzetta, a
shoulder
cape.

© David Turnley/CORBIS

The symbol of the dignity of a cardinal is the scarlet *biretta,* a stiff square cap with three or four ridges across the crown (see Figure 19-3 for a photograph of then-Cardinal Wojtyła wearing his biretta in Vatican City). The hat itself, which is the forerunner of the academic mortarboard worn by thousands of graduates each year, is not unique to cardinals; technically, it can be worn by any clergyman in the Church in the color proper to his dignity (black for priests, violet for bishops, and scarlet for cardinals).

Figure 19-2:
Then-Cardinal Wojtyła wearing the cardinal's skullcap and holding in his hand the cardinal's biretta.

© Vittoriano Rastelli/CORBIS

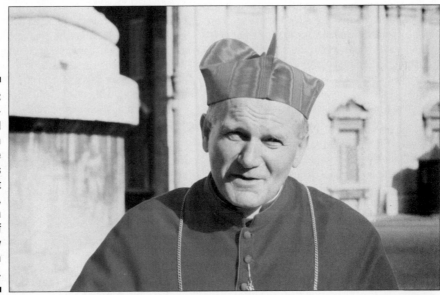

Figure 19-3:
Then-Cardinal Wojtyła wearing the cardinal's scarlet biretta, which is a symbol of the dignity of a cardinal.

© Bettmann/CORBIS

How cardinals are chosen

The pope alone is the one who can promote someone to a cardinal. Church law says, "Those promoted as cardinals are men freely selected by the Roman Pontiff, who are at least in the order of the *presbyterate* [meaning they are ordained priests]. . . ." Other than that one condition, it's entirely up to the pope who he gives the honor to.

Church law does say that those priests who are named cardinals "must receive Episcopal consecration," meaning they should normally be ordained a bishop if they aren't so already, although the pope has allowed them to decline being ordained a bishop. Because there are currently two members of the College of Cardinals not ordained bishops (Avery Cardinal Dulles of the United States and Albert Cardinal Vanhoye of France, both Jesuits), we can say that not all bishops are cardinals, and not all cardinals are bishops.

A person is "created" a cardinal, not "ordained," which means that being a cardinal does not give a person any abilities beyond the office to which he was ordained. For example, when Pope John Paul II named American theologian Father Avery Dulles a cardinal in 2001, he was not named a bishop. So although Cardinal Dulles wears the vestments proper to a cardinal (which are indistinguishable from a bishop), he cannot ordain anyone a priest, as a bishop has the ability to do.

During his pontificate, Pope John Paul II made several cardinals from amongst those who gave the Church years of service, either as a theologian (such as Cardinal Dulles in 2001 or French theologian Henri Cardinal De Lubac in 1983) or in service to the Vatican (such as former Prefect of the Papal Household Dino Cardinal Monduzzi

in 1998 or Roberto Cardinal Tucci, the organizer of most of JP2's apostolic pilgrimages, in 2001).

Occasionally, the pope names someone a cardinal whom he is not ready to announce to the world. When he does so, it's said that he makes the decision to create someone a cardinal *in pectore* (meaning "in his chest," not publicly). The naming of an *in pectore* cardinal takes very specific form and makes for great speculation in Church circles. The most obvious circumstance in which the pope creates "secret" cardinals is when announcing the person's identity could put them in danger. In 1979, Pope John Paul II announced that he had created a cardinal *in pectore.* In 1991, the pope announced that cardinal as Ignatius Kung Pin-Mei, the Archbishop of Shanghai, who was arrested by the Chinese government in 1955 and sentenced to life imprisonment. After he was released and emigrated to the United States in 1988, there was no longer any danger of harm coming to Cardinal Kung, so JP2 publicly announced his elevation.

Pope John Paul II similarly named two cardinals *in pectore* in 1998 (whom he announced in 2001 as Cardinal Marian Jaworski and Cardinal Janis Pujats), and one in 2003 whom he never announced before his death. In this case, when the pope dies without publicly announcing a cardinal created *in pectore,* nothing happens, and the person may never know he was a cardinal until he gets to heaven!

No matter when an *in pectore* cardinal is publicly announced, he enters the College of Cardinals in the place of seniority when he was secretly named.

In the ceremony in which the pope installs new cardinals (called a *consistory*), the newly created cardinal kneels in front of the pope, who places the biretta on the cardinal's head and hands him a scroll, which elevates him to the College of Cardinals. The biretta has replaced the more ancient tradition of a *gallero,* a broad-brimmed hat that was carried behind the cardinal in processions but now is only seen in ecclesial heraldry or hanging from the rooftops of cathedrals where deceased cardinals are buried. The tradition is that the hat will stay in place until the cord connecting it to the ceiling breaks, at which time the deceased cardinal has been released from purgatory and has made it to heaven. The problem is that, today, many of these galleros are hung on steel cables, which take considerably longer to decay!

Understanding Conclave: The Papal Election Process

The conclave has gone through several changes in the past 2,000 years. The most recent revisions came on February 22, 1996, when Pope John Paul II issued the Apostolic Constitution *Universi Domenici Gregis,* on "the vacancy of the apostolic see and the election of the Roman Pontiff." These are the procedures that were followed after the death of Pope John Paul II on April 2, 2005.

According to the current rules, upon the death of the pope the cardinals become the caretakers of the Roman Catholic Church. They don't become a bunch of "mini-popes" — if they did, the temptation would be to not elect anyone! Upon the death of a pope, the heads of almost every Vatican institution and congregation lose their offices (they're usually reinstated upon the election of the new pope). The cardinals continue in this trusteeship of the Church until the moment a successor is elected, at which time they go back to their previous (and not-too-shabby) positions.

During the time between popes, the cardinals are required to meet each day in a *general congregation* to discuss the important matters of state, while lesser questions are handled by *particular congregations,* which are made up of cardinals chosen by lottery of the three ranks of cardinal-bishops, cardinal-priests, and cardinal-deacons. At the same time, the cardinals participate in nine days of funeral rites for the deceased pope. On the last of the nine days, the pope is buried.

Following the burial of the pope, preparations begin for the conclave that will elect his successor. The conclave must take place within Vatican City, with the actual balloting taking place in the Sistine Chapel. Pope John Paul II changed part of the conclave procedures. Per his decree, cardinals are no longer housed in makeshift lodgings within the Apostolic Palace. Cardinals reside at the Domus Sanctae Marthae, a residence built in the 1990s especially for the housing of cardinals during a conclave. Even with this innovation, the cardinals are still cut off from the outside world — meaning no telephones, no Internet, no newspapers, and no contact with anyone else (although the constitution allows for priests to be available to hear the cardinals' confessions; medical doctors to be available for emergencies; and other staff such as cooks and housekeepers, all of whom must take a specific oath of secrecy included in the constitution). In addition, the Sistine Chapel as well as any other place where the cardinals will be assembled are to be checked for any electronic listening devices.

Between 15 and 20 days after the death of the pope, the conclave begins. The cardinals assemble in St. Peter's Basilica to participate in a Mass for the intention of the election of a new pope. In the afternoon of the same day, those cardinals who are able to vote (those under the age of 80) assemble in the Pauline Chapel of the Apostolic Palace (down the hall from the Sistine Chapel). There, after invoking the Holy Spirit by singing the Latin hymn _Veni Creator Spiritus,_ the cardinals go into the Sistine Chapel to start the conclave.

At this point, the cardinals together make a public oath to "observe faithfully and scrupulously the prescriptions contained in the Apostolic Constitution of the Supreme Pontiff John Paul II," as well as promise that whichever one of them is elected will "not fail to affirm and defend strenuously the spiritual and temporal rights of the Holy See." Furthermore they "swear to observe with the greatest fidelity and with all persons . . . secrecy regarding everything that in any way relates to the election of the Roman Pontiff and regarding what occurs in the place of the election, directly or indirectly related to the results of the voting. . . ." Finally, each individual cardinal, in order of seniority, completes the oath by placing his hands on a Book of the Gospels, asking God to help him to keep the oath he has just made. Following the last of the cardinals' oaths, the Master of Papal Ceremonies announces _"Extra omnes!",_ basically telling everyone other than the cardinals to get out, because the voting is about to begin.

Balloting takes place once on the first day of the conclave (after the concelebrated Mass in the morning and the procession into the Sistine Chapel in the afternoon). Following that first day, two ballots are to be held each morning, and two ballots each afternoon.

The Apostolic Constitution outlines the balloting in three phases: the pre-scrutiny, the scrutiny, and the post-scrutiny. In the pre-scrutiny, the following steps take place:

1. **Ballots are distributed to the cardinal electors.**

2. **Nine cardinals are selected by random lottery.**

   Three cardinals are to be _scrutineers_ (who will count the votes and record the tally), three cardinals are to be _infirmarii_ (if a cardinal is so sick as to not make it into the Sistine Chapel, these cardinals collect the sick cardinal's vote from his sickbed and transfer it to the Sistine Chapel), and three cardinals serve as _revisers_ (those who check the work of the scrutineers).

3. **If any of the nine originally chosen cardinals is unable to fulfill the task for whatever reason (poor eyesight or weak legs, for example), new names are chosen by lottery.**

In the scrutiny phase, the cardinals proceed with three more steps:

1. **The cardinals vote.**

   Each cardinal writes his candidate on a paper ballot, folds the ballot twice (yes, this is *specifically* called for in the constitution), and brings it up to the Sistine Chapel altar (all the while holding it in plain view of everyone else — again, specifically called for in the constitution) under the watchful eyes of the previously chosen scrutineers. Each cardinal makes the oath, "I call as my witness Christ the Lord who will be my judge, that my vote is given to the one who before God I think should be elected." He then drops the ballot onto a plate, tilts the plate so the ballot drops into the receptacle (in other words, no one's hand is in the ballot box), bows, and returns to his seat.

2. **The chosen infirmarii travel to the Domus Sanctae Marthae to collect the votes of any ill cardinals, if necessary.**

3. **The number of ballots are counted (to ensure the number of ballots equals the number of electors) and then the three scrutineers, separately, tabulate the votes received by each candidate.**

   The first scrutineer unfolds the ballot, records the name, and passes it to the second scrutineer. The second scrutineer reads the name to himself, records the name, and passes it along to the third scrutineer. The third scrutineer reads the name on the ballot aloud so that all the cardinals can record the vote tally for themselves. After each name has been read, the third scrutineer pierces the ballot with a needle and thread (so that the same ballots can't be counted again).

And finally, in the post-scrutiny — no big shock — they follow three more steps:

1. **Each of the scrutineers who counted votes checks his totals on his own before comparing results with the other scrutineers.**

   If a cardinal has received two-thirds of the votes, then the new pope has been elected. If not, then an election has not taken place.

2. **Whether or not a new pope has been elected, the revisers now come in and check the math of the scrutineers.**

   If no one has received two-thirds majority, then the whole process begins again with Step 1 of the scrutiny.

3. **Whether or not a new pope has been elected, the ballots *along with any notes taken during the voting or counting of the votes* (specifically included in the constitution) are burned.**

   If no majority is reached, the ballots are burned with wet straw, making the smoke that flows out of the Sistine Chapel black. If a majority has been reached, the ballots are burned without the straw, causing white smoke (and telling the waiting world that a new pope has been elected).

If someone has received a two-thirds majority of the cardinals' votes, then the Secretary of the College of Cardinals and the Papal Master of Ceremonies are called into the Sistine Chapel. The Dean of the College of Cardinals (or, if it was the dean who was chosen, the first cardinal in order of seniority) asks the electee in Latin, "Do you accept your canonical election as Supreme Pontiff?" When the candidate responds in the affirmative, the question is asked, "By what name do you wish to be called?" Just as Christ changed Simon's name to Peter (Matthew 16:19), popes have traditionally followed suit by changing their own names to signify the new office they've entered.

At that moment, standing at his desk surrounded by fellow cardinals, this person becomes the pope (even if he is still dressed as a cardinal). With that consent, the conclave officially ends. The new pope is escorted to a small room adjacent to the Sistine Chapel called the Room of Tears (because it is while he is alone in this room that reality sets in for the new pope). In the room are white papal cassocks in three sizes. The pope puts on the one that best fits him (and his measurements are taken so that work can immediately begin on custom-fitted clothing) and gets ready for his first appearance on the central balcony of St. Peter's Basilica. In the meantime, the senior cardinal-deacon appears on the balcony and makes the announcement, *"Habemus Papam!"* ("We have a pope!") and tells the crowd who the new pope is and by what name he wants to be known. Following the announcement, the new pope comes out on the balcony and gives his first apostolic blessing *urbi et orbi* (to the city and the world), after first saying a few words if he chooses (as did Pope John Paul II and Pope Benedict XVI).

Meeting the New Pope, Benedict XVI

By all accounts, Pope Benedict XVI is a brilliant intellectual. He brings renewed energy to the papacy and a dogged devotion to doctrine. In the following sections, we give you a brief summary of Benedict's life.

If you want more information on Pope Benedict XVI, check out works such as Aiden Nichols's *The Thought of Benedict XVI* (2005) or an anthology titled *Pilgrim Fellowship of Faith* (2005). Interviews with then-Cardinal Ratzinger are contained in *The Ratzinger Report* (1985) and *Salt of the Earth* (1997). The only memoir ever written by Pope Benedict XVI is *Milestones: Memoirs 1927–1977*.

Looking at his childhood

Josef Alois Ratzinger was born on April 16, 1927, in the town of Marktl am Inn, in the heavily Catholic region of Bavaria in southern Germany. He was the third child of Georg and Maria Ratzinger (their other children, a son and daughter, were named for their parents). The future pope's father was a civil servant, a constable for the town, and his mother was a professional cook before she married.

In 1929, the Ratzinger family moved to Tittmoning, a town that bordered on Austria. Young Josef crossed the border to make pilgrimages to Catholic shrines in Austria. They lived in a house on the town square. Although it looked impressive on the outside, inside it had cracked floors, steep steps, and crooked rooms. The Ratzingers weren't alone: Following World War I, Germany was full of unemployment and hostility toward the rest of the world. With the rise of Adolph Hitler and the National Socialists, many Germans were led to believe that they could rise above their misery and gain jobs and a better lifestyle.

Experiencing the Nazis firsthand

By 1932, Georg Ratzinger, Sr., had seen enough of the Nazis to know that he didn't agree with them. He saw the rise of Hitler to lead Germany as an inevitability, so he transferred his family to the smaller village of Aschau am Inn. Aschau was a rural village whose people spent more time worrying about crops than politics. By 1933, Hitler was Chancellor of Germany, and things grew steadily worse. Boys' and girls' clubs (religious and secular) were abolished, and young men were required by law to join the Hitler Youth. Like all the other boys at the time, young Josef Ratzinger and his brother, Georg, attended compulsory meetings, but neither one of them ever joined the Nazi Party. He was fortunate to find a sympathetic person who obtained a dispensation for Ratzinger, excusing him from attending further Hitler Youth activities due to his seminary studies.

His father was uneasy about the Nazi persecution of clergy. Georg, Sr., would have no active hand in it (the orders were usually carried out by a pro-Nazi deputy he had been assigned), and would usually tip off the clergy about what was soon to happen. In 1937, Georg Ratzinger, Sr., turned 60 (the mandatory retirement age for policemen); upon his retirement, he moved the family into a farmhouse in the town of Traunstein. Of all the places he lived growing up, Pope Benedict XVI regards Traunstein as his true home. He entered the school at Traunstein and excelled in his studies, especially classes like Latin and Greek.

On Easter in 1939, Josef Ratzinger entered the seminary. That September, Germany invaded Poland, and World War II began. By 1940, the German army has defeated France, Holland, Belgium, and Luxembourg, and established occupying armies in Norway and Denmark. At the time, Germans rejoiced in the military victories, and a surge of patriotism ran across the once-conquered Germany.

Serving time in the German army

In 1942, Georg Ratzinger, Jr. (Josef's older brother), was drafted into military service. In 1943, at the age of 16, Josef and his seminary classmates were drafted into service as members of an antiaircraft unit in Munich. In 1944, Josef was drafted into service at a military labor camp and endured what he called "mockery and verbal abuse" when he told them it was his intention to become a Catholic priest. He ended up on labor details that dug antitank trenches, actually ending up near the family home in Traunstein.

Finally, in April or May 1945, with the war a lost cause, Josef decided he had had enough and returned home, deserting the German army. Here he faced a delicate situation, because there were still Nazis unwilling to concede the war was lost who could have shot Josef as a deserter. He was, in fact, once stopped by a patrol and questioned, but with his arm in a sling because of a recent injury, he was allowed to pass and continue on his way.

His time at home did not last long. When Allied soldiers arrived in his home-town, Josef was mistaken for a soldier and brought to a prisoner-of-war camp. In June 1945, he was released by the Allies and returned to Traunstein, where, a month later, Georg, Jr., returned home to complete the family reunion.

Joining the priesthood

By late 1945, the Ratzinger brothers entered the seminary at Freising. In 1947, after completing the two-year course of studies in philosophy, Josef continued his seminary studies in Munich. On June 29, 1951, Josef and Georg Ratzinger were ordained to the priesthood at the cathedral in Freising. After a brief time as a parish priest at the Parish of the Precious Blood in Munich, Josef was assigned to the seminary faculty in Freising on October 1, 1952, and earned his doctorate in theology in July 1953.

In April 1959, Father Ratzinger was named Chairman of Fundamental Theology at the University of Bonn. Here, the Archbishop of Cologne, Josef Cardinal Frings, attends one of his lectures. The cardinal asked Father Ratzinger to serve as an advisor for the upcoming Second Vatican Council, which Pope John XXIII had recently called for. Each fall from 1962 through 1965, Father

Ratzinger traveled to Rome to watch the events of the council, and to advise Cardinal Frings. He was named a *Peritus,* an official Council theologian, and quickly became noticed as an astute mind, getting the attention of other prelates besides Frings.

At the same time, his academic career continued to progress. In the summer of 1963, he became a professor of the University of Münster. In the summer of 1966, he became a professor of theology at the University of Tübingen. And in 1967, he became a professor at the University of Regensburg, where he remained for ten years.

Moving up the ranks

With the death of Julius Cardinal Döpfner in July 1976, Pope Paul VI appointed Father Josef Ratzinger as Archbishop of Munich and Freising, and he was ordained a bishop on March 24, 1977. In a consistory on June 27, 1977, Pope Paul VI created Archbishop Ratzinger a cardinal. Here he remained until 1981, when Pope John Paul II named Cardinal Ratzinger Prefect of the Congregation for the Doctrine of the Faith. He held this position until the death of Pope John Paul II (when, upon the death of the pope, all prefects of congregations lose their office — see "Understanding Conclave: The Papal Election Process" for more information).

As Dean of the College of Cardinals (having been elected so in November 2002), Ratzinger played a major role in the ceremonies surrounding the funeral of Pope John Paul II. When the cardinals entered the conclave of April 2005, certainly everyone in the room knew who Cardinal Ratzinger was, but many felt his reputation was too large for the cardinals to elect him pope. Yet, on Tuesday, April 19, 2005, after less than two days in conclave, Josef Ratzinger was elected the 265th successor of St. Peter and took the name Pope Benedict XVI.

Discovering his reputation

Perhaps no one in the history of the Catholic Church has had such a turn-around in his reputation as Pope Benedict XVI. Newspaper headlines the day after his election used words such as *conservative, hardliner,* and the always-popular *God's Rottweiler.* However, in the 1960s, he was considered one of the avant-garde theologians who was going to usher in a new understanding of the Church, and his name was often used amidst other more liberal theologians such as Karl Rahner, Hans Küng, and Edward Schillebeeckx.

Ratzinger's "transformation" seemed to take place in the years following the close of the Second Vatican Council in 1965. He saw that the writings of some theologians who were disappointed that the Council did not do what they had hoped, plus the general student unrest and distrust of authority figures that prevailed amongst young people in the mid-1960s, had led to a revisionist attitude within the Church. Angry that the Council had not changed the Church into what they wanted, the movement began to act as if it had happened that way. This sentiment was compounded by a new wave of interest in Marxism (teaching about the futility of religion), which swept Germany and found a receptive ear among university students. At the time, Pope Benedict XVI was a professor at the University of Tübingen, where student protests were especially fierce. Students disrupted classes and meetings of the faculty, at times shouting down professors trying to teach their classes. He began to see that what the fathers of the Second Vatican Council intended and what was being implemented were becoming more and more unrecognizable to each other. When his home region of Bavaria opened a new university in Regensburg in 1967, he saw it as a chance to return to his home, spend more time with his brother and sister, and escape the confrontational climate that had become more of a steady rain than a passing storm.

However you feel about Pope Benedict XVI, there is no arguing the intellectual genius of the man. He is the kid you knew in high school who everyone knew was the smartest in the room but who never showed off or made himself the center of attention because of it. From his earliest days, he has been an academic, finding his service to the Church in the study of theology. He has written essays, homilies, instructions, articles, and books too numerous to count. A priest who worked with him at the Congregation for the Doctrine of the Faith said he could write "as if possessed . . . twelve or thirteen hours without eating." In a burst of creativity, he could dictate 20 pages to a transcribing secretary without any grammatical errors.

But there is another, more personal side to the man. He loves cats. He has a weakness for cookies (anything sweet, actually). He loves music and enjoys playing the piano for relaxation, especially the works of Mozart, Bach, and Palestrina. During his summer holiday in the Italian Alps and at Castel Gandolfo, he asked that a piano be installed. He is also a family man, inasmuch as a celibate priest can be. His sister, Maria, came to live with him in Rome and managed his residence until her death in 1991. His brother, Georg, now retired and living in Regensburg, has spent holidays and summer vacations with his brother, who also owned a home in Regensburg. The Christmas before his election as pope, the Ratzinger brothers spoke about the day when Josef could retire and spend more time with Georg, "finishing", according to Georg, "all the talks they've started through the years." Many times he offered his resignation to Pope John Paul II, and each time the pope refused it. But as he watched the pope continue in his ministry even in the face of great suffering, he knew he could hardly ask to retire in order to relax. Rupert Hofbauer, who acts as caretaker for Pope Benedict XVI's home in Regensburg, said that the Holy Father "thought it sounded nice, to retire, to take it easy. That's not how it worked out though, is it?"

Identifying his goals

Pope Benedict XVI's first identifiable goal was given away by the Holy Father's choice of a name. Benedict is not only the father of monasticism in the west (and a co-patron of Europe, thanks to Pope John Paul II), but also the name of the pope who tried his best to save Europe from the horrors of World War I. Clearly, Pope Benedict XVI sees the re-evangelization of Europe as his first area of concern.

The homily delivered by then-Cardinal Ratzinger on the morning of the start of the conclave gives us another hint at an area Pope Benedict XVI may concentrate his attention on:

> How many winds of doctrine have we known in recent decades, how many ideological currents, how many ways of thinking. We [popular culture] are building a dictatorship of relativism that does not recognize anything as definitive and whose ultimate goal consists solely of one's own ego and desires.

The answer, to Pope Benedict XVI, is possession of a mature, adult faith. "An 'adult' faith," the Holy Father said, "is not a faith that follows the trends of fashion and the latest novelty; a mature adult faith is deeply rooted in friendship with Christ. . . . The Lord calls us friends, He makes us friends, He gives us His friendship. . . . The more we love Jesus, the more we know Him, the more our true freedom develops and our joy in being redeemed flourishes."

Figuring Out Where We're Going from Here

The future is hard to predict. Popes may technically be "elected," but there is no set term to the office. Although the Church's canon law does allow for the possibility that a pope may resign (and even then his absolute authority in the Catholic Church means that he "resigns" to himself), Pope Benedict XVI, like his predecessor, knows that this is the last job he'll ever have. Because of this, he has no reelection to concern himself with, as do other elected leaders.

In the homilies and speeches following his election, Pope Benedict XVI repeated over and over his understanding that the *Petrine* office (meaning related to St. Peter, the one we recognize as the first pope) was one of service. "My real program of governance is not to do my own will, not to pursue my own ideas," he said during the April 24, 2005, homily at the inauguration of his pontificate, "but to listen, together with the whole Church, to the word and to the will of the Lord, to be guided by Him, so that he himself will lead the Church at this hour of our history." On January 25, 2006, Pope Benedict XVI issued his first papal encyclical, a reflection on Christian love titled *Deus Caritas Est* (God Is Love), which was warmly received by the world. In addition, he held his first consistory on March 24, 2006, naming new members of the College of Cardinals.

At the close of the Great Jubilee Year 2000, Pope John Paul II told the Church in his apostolic letter *Novo Millennio Ineunte* to *"Duc in altum!"* (Put out into the deep!). As Pope Benedict XVI takes over command of the ship from John Paul the Great, Roman Catholics trust that he is the one God has chosen to take the Church on the course laid out for it.

Part V
The Part of Tens

The 5th Wave   By Rich Tennant

"Sorry, but I don't understand your 'Ecclesiastical Latin'.
Could you repeat that using 'Classical' pronunciation?"

In this part . . .

We use the familiar *For Dummies* feature of the Part of Tens to zero in on some interesting aspects of the life and legacy of Pope John Paul II. From the most popular or influential papal documents to the great number of men and women he beatified and canonized, this part looks at the other accomplishments of this pope besides his role in the fall of Communism, the renewal of Catholicism, and the global exposure and influence of the modern papacy. Plus, we throw in some fun and interesting tidbits as well.

Chapter 20

Ten (Or So) Reasons That Pope John Paul II Was Truly the "People's Pope"

Popularity is a fickle thing. Winston Churchill was popular during World War II for rallying the British people while Hitler's Luftwaffe dropped bombs on London night after night. After the war, the famous prime minister was voted out of office in 1945 by the same people to whom he brought victory.

John Paul II was more than famous, and his popularity was not fleeting. He has been called "the People's Pope" by Catholics and non-Catholics alike, not just since his death, but also during his life.

Ironically, Karol Wojtyła didn't become pope by popular ballot. Popes are not elected by the people as prime ministers or presidents are. Instead, cardinals elect him. So, if the people didn't directly choose or elect him, how did this guy from Poland endear himself to so many around the world?

He Was Visible and Accessible

JP2 traveled more than any other pope, making 104 pastoral visits to 129 foreign countries (plus 143 trips within Italy), and flew more than 700,000 miles (more than 1.1 million km), the equivalent of circling the globe 28 times. (Bet he had a good frequent-flier program with Alitalia!) He brought himself, the papacy, and the Catholic Church to the four corners of the Earth. People appreciate it when you visit their homeland. Whenever JP2 made these papal visits, millions attended the outdoor Masses and ceremonies, but even millions more watched on TV and listened by radio from their own local and national networks.

Pope Paul VI (1963–1978) was the first pope to visit the United States, but he didn't woo the crowds like John Paul II did when he came to America. Coming back again and again also endeared JP2 to the people. Frequency is a sign of affection, and so the pastoral visits were not just historical dates but a series of encounters with someone who loved to spend time with the flock he was asked to shepherd. He made seven trips to the United States, three trips to Canada, five to Mexico, and nine to his native Poland. (For more on his pastoral visits, check out Chapter 16.)

Television and radio have been around for a while, and previous popes were "on the air" before JP2, but he used the electronic medium more (and more effectively) than any other pontiff. His weekly Wednesday audiences to pilgrims in Rome were broadcast regularly around the world. Vatican Radio and Television and EWTN (Eternal Word Television Network) send signals around the globe in many languages, and many of their programs included speeches and sermons given by Pope John Paul II at home and abroad. Besides traditional media (cable and wireless), he was also seen and heard by millions on the Internet, satellite television, radio, and short-wave. So his image and voice were transmitted globally, and he himself traveled around the world, which made the man and his message accessible to everyone.

He fluently spoke nearly a dozen languages, including English, French, German, Italian, Polish, Portuguese, Russian, Slovak, Spanish, and Ukrainian. This linguistic talent also helped him read and speak another two dozen languages so that he could give talks in the native tongue wherever he visited. (Speaking the local language always makes a deep impression on the home crowd.) So, he was not only seen and/or heard by millions, but he was also *understood* by millions.

Previous popes were often aloof, distant, and unapproachable due to primitive means of communication and travel. The papacy was seen as another aristocratic monarchy among several others (which had unraveled or was beginning to unravel), so it seemed removed from the people. Without compromising his office as Supreme Pastor of the Universal Church, JP2 was still able to get close to his audience and have them feel that nearness. He always wore his official papal clothing (the white *cassock* [gown] and white *zucchetto* [skull cap]) or he wore Mass vestments. He didn't feel the need to dress down and wear blue jeans and go casual. Despite the ancient uniform, the pope could nevertheless bridge gaps and forge ties between various ages, cultures, and backgrounds. Although he was born a Pole and later became the visible head of the Roman

Catholic Church, JP2 could and did appeal to many people, no matter how he dressed. He maintained the dignity of his office while bringing a humanness and warmth to his role as Supreme Pastor of the Universal Church.

He Was Born a Common Man

Many previous popes had come from aristocratic backgrounds, and they had an appearance of nobility, as in the case of Pius XII. Other popes came from more humble beginnings. Karol Wojtyła worked in a stone quarry and in a chemical factory before being ordained a priest. His family lived a modest life; tragedy struck soon and often as his mother and brother died (three years apart) while he was a boy, and his dad died nine years afterward. At the age of 21, Karol was alone in the world.

His early history was like a forge that purified the iron into steel: It strengthened John Paul's faith and would always remind him of the sufferings of others. His humble background tempered his pride and ego, so he never came off as patronizing or condescending, as a priest, bishop, cardinal, or pope. Yet, Wojtyła never felt nor acted like a victim despite the personal family tragedies and the horrible experience of Nazi occupation followed by Soviet control of his homeland. Because he didn't have a privileged upbringing, many common people could readily identify with JP2 — which was another source of his popularity.

He Was Sincere

Pope John Paul II was not a politician in the sense of needing to be popular. He did not say things to placate the crowds, and he often risked ridicule and dissent from his audience — yet he consistently spoke what he believed was the honest truth. He was famous for telling it like it is.

Not only was he visible and accessible to the world, he also did not abuse his status and bask in his popularity. He was willing to say and do difficult things when he knew they were necessary. When he consistently denounced abortion, contraception, euthanasia, and other controversial subjects, he knew some people disagreed with him. But he could not lie or ignore what had to be said: the truth, no matter how unpopular, no matter how painful.

JP2 spoke to his flock as a teacher, as a shepherd, and as a loving fellow Christian. This sincerity won him admiration and respect. Had he merely reiterated what opinion polls showed, no one would have seen the strength of his convictions, nor would they have detected any sincerity in his voice or writings. JP2 also passionately believed what he preached, so he spoke with credibility. Even those who disagreed with him could never accuse him of being a phony.

He Loved His Job — and It Showed

The underlying basis for JP2's authenticity as pope was that he saw his role as the Vicar of Christ as the servant of the servants of God. What we mean by this title of the papacy, is the fact that, by baptism, all are called to serve the Lord. The pope, then, is the chief of the servants ministering to others by uniting them in one belief code and mission.

Though a leader of a nation (Vatican City is the smallest country in the world, comprising only 0.17 square miles, one-third the size of Central Park in New York City), Pope John Paul II saw himself not only as the leader of one billion faithful around the world, but as the representative of Christ whose bride is the Church. Therefore, he looked at everyone in the Church as his beloved spouse. He loved the Church as a whole and each individual member as his beloved spouse, because they were de facto the beloved spouse of Christ.

When the young people at a World Youth Day would chant, "John Paul 2, we love you," he would often reply, "John Paul 2, he loves you." So when his flock was at their best, he was proud and happy. But when some of the fold were not trying hard enough, when they became apathetic, indifferent, or mesmerized by the glitz and glamour of materialism or lured by political ideologies, he was very disappointed. Even his attempts to get Catholics to abandon immoral behavior or to reject false doctrine were motivated by love — he desperately tried to show the true and the good, even to an audience that, at times, chose to close its eyes and cover its ears.

He Was Respectful

As an actor and poet, JP2 knew the value of symbolic gestures. Not only was he a linguist, philosopher, and theologian who knew the value of choosing words wisely, but he could also use the right type of nonverbal communication when needed. The best example of this occurred whenever he visited a country for the first time.

Just the papal visit alone would have been enough for most people. JP2 visited places whose people had never seen the Bishop of Rome set foot upon their soil. When he arrived in a foreign nation for the first time as pope, he dramatically got down on his knees and kissed the ground. It was a silent gesture that spoke loudly and clearly: This ground was holy because the people who live here are children of God. Every human being — male or female, young or old, rich or poor, regardless of religion — is made in the image and likeness of God. JP2 wanted to show them that they were special to him and special to God, as was the very land where they lived and worked.

When his frailty made it difficult for the pope to kneel down and kiss the Earth, the Vatican aides and assistants who travel with the pope came up with the idea of offering John Paul a bowl of local soil that he could symbolically kiss. When he visited Israel in 2000, he went to the Western Wailing Wall in Jerusalem and prayed privately before placing a written prayer in a crevice, just as any local Jewish resident would have done. The piece of paper contained these words:

> God of our fathers, you chose Abraham and his descendants to bring your Name to the Nations. We are deeply saddened by the behavior of those who in the course of history have caused these children of yours to suffer and, asking your forgiveness, we wish to commit ourselves to genuine brotherhood with the people of the Covenant.

It was a gesture of contrition and reconciliation for the evils done by Christians or in the name of Christianity to individual Jews and Judaism as a whole. He also personally visited Jewish synagogues and Islamic mosques as a sign of respect for these houses of worship and for the religions they represent. In fact, he was the first pope, after St. Peter, to visit a synagogue, and the first pope ever to visit a mosque.

He Had Courage

John Paul II showed courage and fortitude when he spoke to foreign leaders and heads of state, especially when he met them on their own turf. People were endeared by knowing that the pope had no problem being grateful for the invitation of a foreign ruler to make a papal visit to the ruler's homeland, and at the same time JP2 had the chutzpah to challenge those same leaders to defend human rights and religious freedom.

He did not flinch in reminding Ferdinand Marcos in the Philippines or Fidel Castro in Cuba about their need to improve their governments' treatment of human rights. He spoke with equal vigor to presidents Carter and Clinton on the issue of defending human life, for the born and unborn, and he challenged President George W. Bush and British Prime Minister Tony Blair on the use of war. Whether it was a Communist or fascist dictator or a democratically elected prime minister or president, liberal or conservative, Republican or Democrat, JP2 had the courage to say what had to be said — not to embarrass the leaders themselves but to remind them that they govern God's people.

He Loved Young People

No one can deny that John Paul II loved the youth, as evidenced by his World Youth Days, where anywhere from 300,000 to 5 million young people gathered in one place and at one time to see and hear the pope. But his love for youth went back to the time before he was pope, to his early first days as a newly ordained priest. As a young priest, he went hiking, mountain climbing, kayaking, and skiing, as well as took camping trips, with young adults whom he considered the future of the Polish nation and of the Catholic Church. While in these situations — relaxed and far from school, family, and work — JP2 could still speak openly about faith, religion, morality, and spirituality.

By showing an interest, a love, and indeed a trust and confidence in the youth of today, JP2 gave them the encouragement they needed to commit themselves to making their faith a priority. Any pastor or bishop who shows interest in the youth wins the hearts of the young people's parents, too. Pope John Paul II was beloved by the youth he loved, as well as by their parents, who appreciated such concern.

He Practiced What He Preached

John Paul II is beloved not only because he taught what the Catholic Church and Gospel have consistently taught for 2,000 years, but also because he followed his own words with actual deeds. He, like any religious leader, preached often about forgiveness. What separated JP2 from the rest was that he himself did it. His actions and deeds corresponded with his words. He didn't just talk the talk — he walked the walk.

He demonstrated this consistency between word and deed many, many times, but two instances stand out:

✔ **His forgiveness of the man who tried to kill him:** Early in his pontificate, after he was shot by Ali Agca on May 13, 1981 (and after seven hours of surgery and months of therapy and recuperation), Pope John Paul II visited the prison of his would-be assassin and forgave him. "Easier said than done," goes the saying. Well, JP2 not only talked about forgiveness, he practiced it personally. That act of mercy touched the heart of many people, Catholic and non-Catholic alike.

✔ **His unwavering defense of life, even as his own health deteriorated:** Toward the end of his papacy, his several years of battling Parkinson's disease began to take its toll on JP2. Known as a staunch defender of life, from the first moment of conception to the last breath of old age, John

Paul II denounced not only abortion but also euthanasia. When age, disease, and medical complications ganged up on him, he did not retreat from his papal teachings on life-and-death issues.

A year and two weeks prior to his death, while in reasonably stable health, JP2 issued a statement on the moral obligation to provide nutrition and hydration to terminally ill and dying patients, even those in a persistent vegetative state. (Artificial nutrition and hydration is the use of medical means to deliver food and water to a patient who is unable to eat or drink on his or her own.) The document John Paul II wrote on this topic considers such procedures as normal "care" as opposed to "treatment." According to JP2, a sick person who is either in the process of recovery or preparing for a natural death, has the right to receive basic health care, like "nutrition, hydration, cleanliness, warmth," and so on. The withholding or removal of nutrition and hydration, which would cause the sick person to die, was considered by John Paul II (and, thus, the Catholic Church) to be euthanasia and immoral.

Ironically, less than a week before his death, Pope John Paul II's physicians inserted a feeding tube to help maintain nutrition. A month earlier, he had a temporary *tracheotomy* (a procedure in which a tube is inserted into the neck to help breathing). Beginning with the flu in January 2005, the pontiff then succumbed to septic shock, caused by a urinary tract infection and the collapse of his cardio-circulatory system. Despite his frail condition, his doctors were instructed to follow the moral-ethical norms John Paul II himself elucidated a year earlier — namely, that nutrition, hydration, and other normal care be given until natural death. By taking his own medicine, so to speak, JP2 again showed the world that he lived the words he spoke and practiced what he preached.

He Was a Man of Hope

One of the most sublime aspects of John Paul II's papacy was his ability to inspire others to aspire and to never lose hope. His unofficial motto inaugurating his pontificate was the phrase "Be not afraid." John Paul survived World War II and Nazi and Soviet invasions; endured the sadness of losing his mother while he was still a boy; buried his only brother and his father before he turned 22 years old; barely escaped death after an assassin's bullet pierced him in the side; and suffered the humiliation of a terrible disease that robbed him of much of his dignity. All that and he could still say to the world, "Be not afraid."

John Paul II came along when the Catholic Church was in desperate need of some solid hope. Pope Paul VI had closed and implemented the Second Vatican Council, but he also witnessed the mass exodus of priests and nuns giving up their vocational commitments in order to get married, or pursue other goals. Vocations dropped, seminary and convent enrollment declined, Mass attendance fell to all-time lows, and overall morale among the clergy, religious, and general faithful was virtually rock-bottom.

A small spark was ignited when Albino Luciani was elected Pope John Paul I. His extremely brief (one-month) papacy is remembered mostly for his smile. But his short reign further exasperated the rank-and-file members of the Catholic Church. One month? Is that all we get?

John Paul I's successor, however, fanned the flames and set the Church ablaze. Karol Wojtyła was young (58 years old), athletic, intelligent, linguistically fluent, and a philosopher-theologian, who was also a poet, actor, and playwright in his early days. He was a man who had survived Nazis and Communists alike and who had felt the full chill of the Cold War in his native Poland.

Paul VI had lingered in bad health for a while before his death in August 1978. John Paul I lived one month in the Vatican. Then the crowd in St. Peter's Square saw the white smoke from the papal conclave and wondered, who was the new pope?

Annuntio vobis gaudium magnum; habemus Papam: Eminentissimum ac Reverendissimum Dominum Carolum Sanctae Romanae Ecclesiae Cardinalem Wojtyła, qui sibi nomen imposuit Johannes Paul Secundum. This Latin sentence translates "I announce to you with great joy, we have a Pope, Karol Wojtyła, who has taken the name John Paul II." You could have heard a pin drop for a second. Wojtyła? Without subtitles, the crowd just heard a name that sure didn't sound Italian. Only when JP2 appeared on the balcony and started to speak in fluent Italian did they realize that, not only did they have a Polish pope, but he spoke their language. If it were possible for a non-Italian — a Pole, no less — to become Bishop of Rome and Supreme Pastor of the Universal Church, then anything was possible. Hope sprang once again in the hearts of the faithful.

No caretaker pope who would just fill in for a few years, this healthy specimen of an athletic outdoorsman gave every indication that he would be around for a long time. He also showed he had his own mind and intellect. Advisors would still be needed, but *he* would make decisions, not them.

Karol Wojtyła was elected pope while the Cold War was still in full bloom. Later, it was revealed that JP2 and President Ronald Reagan both helped dismantle and dissolve the evil empire once known as the Soviet Union. Before the Berlin Wall came down however, Polish workers had renewed hope in a newly elected Polish pope. That encouragement kept *Solidarity* (the Polish labor union that aided in the breakup of the Communist government in Poland) alive.

JP2's World Youth Days and more than a hundred papal visits around the globe spread hope among Catholics everywhere. Vocations to the priesthood and religious life began to increase. All three of us authors attribute our vocation and perseverance in it to the papacy of Pope John Paul II, who reminded us to be proud of our Catholic heritage and identity. He loved being pope, but he also loved being Catholic.

JP2 calmed the sea of theological dissent and deceit by promulgating the first universal catechism in almost 500 years. The *Catechism of the Catholic Church* entered the world in 1992 and, once and for all, defined in black and white what Catholics believe. Church doctrine would not be changed but defended, albeit perhaps presented in different wrapping paper than before.

The current pope (Benedict XVI) or future ones are the only people authorized to canonize John Paul II a saint. But history and the will of the people decide whether the title "The Great" is bestowed on any pope. A grass-roots effort to give such an honor to this man because of the hope he engendered as well as his accomplishments has been growing among the faithful clergy and religious. We believe JP2 deserves both distinctions, and one more. Some historical figures of Church history have the distinction of being named "Doctor of the Church." This doctor has nothing to do with antibiotics, pain relievers, or prescriptions. This type of doctorate deals with wisdom and learning, like an academic doctorate as opposed to a medical degree.

Besides revising the *Catechism of the Catholic Church* in 1992 and the *Code of Canon Law* in 1983 (no minor feats, mind you), JP2 also wrote numerous and profound papal encyclicals. He added five new mysteries to the Rosary in 2002. They are called the Luminous Mysteries or the Mysteries of Light and are meant to complement the preexisting Joyful, Sorrowful, and Glorious Mysteries.

Because of these new Luminous Mysteries and thanks to the learned wisdom contained in his papal documents, we feel soon (God willing) "St." John Paul "the Great" will also be given the moniker "Doctor of Light." *Veritatis Splendor* (Splendor of Truth — on the Natural Moral Law), *Fides et Ratio* (Faith and Reason), and *Evangelium Vitae* (Gospel of Life) are the indispensable letters that John Paul gave to the Church and that in turn shed the light of hope and truth into the minds of millions. Take a look at Chapter 22 to get a detailed account of these and other world-changing encyclicals written by John Paul II.

Chapter 21

Ten Fun Facts about Pope John Paul II

. . . .

In This Chapter

▶ Uncovering Pope John Paul II's past

▶ Finding out about JP2 the athlete

. . . .

Pope John Paul II was the spiritual leader for a billion people for almost three decades. But he was also a man — a man of great intellect, great passion for his interests, and great love for all humanity. In this chapter, we share some little-known anecdotes and details about John Paul II that made him the complex man he was.

Soccer Papa

From his early days in Wadowice, Poland, Pope John Paul II had a love for the game of soccer — he usually played goalkeeper — and lifelong friends often reminisce about young Lolek (his Polish nickname) and his athletic ability. But apparently not everyone was a fan: According to one story, young Karol was chastised by the parish priest for repeatedly kicking a soccer ball against the wall of the parish church!

When he was installed as pope on Sunday, October 22, 1978, he scheduled the Mass to take place in the morning, so that everyone (himself included) could watch the afternoon's soccer matches on TV. Many commentators have remarked that his papacy was like that of a goalkeeper: He was someone who protected, and he understood the value of being a team player. Once he was overheard chastising a bishop: "If you're going to be in the choir, you've got to learn to sing in harmony."

Shoes of the Fisherman

During a papal *conclave* (the election of a pope by the cardinals), after each ballot, the votes are burned, and chemicals are added so that the crowds of faithful waiting outside in St. Peter's Square know if a pope has been chosen. Black smoke means no decision; white means we have a new pope; and gray smoke (as seen most recently during the 2005 conclave) means, "Something is wrong with the centuries-old stove, so keep watching!"

When white smoke poured out of the chimney of the Sistine Chapel on October 16, 1978, the world anxiously awaited the announcement of who the next pope would be. The faithful wondered, "Which cardinal was elected? What name is he taking?"

In addition to the cardinals who were in the room, one other person knew something unexpected was about to happen. At the end of the conclave, shoemaker Telesforo Carboni received an emergency call to make a pair of red papal shoes in size 11. Carboni knew that most Italian men wear shoes in size 8 or 9, so the new pope was likely not an Italian. John Paul II was the first non-Italian pope in 455 years.

JP2's Summer School

As if he didn't have enough reading and writing to do in his everyday duties, in 1983 Pope John Paul II began the tradition of an annual "summer school" during his vacation at Castel Gandolfo, the papal residence on Lake Albano outside of Rome. The Holy Father would choose the topic himself (the first topic was "Man in the Modern Sciences") and then invite historians, scientists, and academics who were experts in the field to attend and make presentations. The experts were men and women, Catholics and non-Catholics, and even a few atheists. Pope John Paul II would sit off to the side and listen in. At the end of the event, he would give a discourse that summed up the discussions at the seminar.

Papal Threads

Popes have not always worn all white. In the past, they kept a lot of the red clothing they were accustomed to as cardinals before their election as pope. The custom of wearing white began after the election of Michele Ghislieri in 1566, who took the name Pope Pius V. Ghislieri was a member of the

Dominican Order, whose religious habit is white. As pope, Pius V continued to wear his white religious habit, and the tradition was born that popes would wear white.

The task of dressing JP2 belonged to the Gammarelli family, whose tailor shop is open to anyone walking in the neighborhood behind the Pantheon in Rome. (Don't expect to see the pope there — for him, they make house calls.) The papal *simar* (a fancy cassock [full-length robe whose color designates the rank of the person wearing it: white for the pope, red for cardinals, purple for bishops, black for priests] with a shoulder cape) is always custom-fitted to the pontiff, along with extras like his coat-of-arms embroidered on the white silk *fascia* (sash), Velcro to keep the shoulder cape in place, and a small band of felt on the inside of the *zucchetto* (pronounced zuh-*keh*-to; the skullcap) to prevent slippage. In later years, as John Paul II's gait became more hunched over, the Gammarellis tapered the simar in the front so that, when he was standing, the garment flowed perfectly to the ground.

Before the conclave, no one knows who will be elected pope, so they keep an off-the-rack white simar ready for the newly elected pope to change into from his former cardinal red one. Small, medium, and large samples are on hand. After the new pope gives his first blessing from the balcony, tailors measure the pontiff for his new outfit, which is made from scratch within a few hours.

The Pope's Pool

Shortly after his election, Pope John Paul II asked that a modest swimming pool be installed at Castel Gandolfo for exercise. An aide asked him if he was concerned about how much it would cost. Mindful of the sudden, unexpected death of his predecessor, John Paul I (who only lived one month as pope), JP2 allegedly responded, "It'll be cheaper than the cost of another conclave!" A pool would also be less expensive than installing a ski slope — he was an avid skier as well as a swimmer.

Actually, several sources claim the pool was paid for by a group of Polish Americans who gave it as a gift. John Paul II swam until 2002 (even if just for physical therapy), when his deteriorating health no longer permitted him. When elected, JP2 was only 58 years old, in excellent health, and a good athlete and sportsman besides. He enjoyed hiking and kayaking in addition to swimming and skiing.

The Actor Pope and the Pope Actor

Morris West's 1963 novel *The Shoes of the Fisherman*, which described the fictional election of Kiril Lakota, a Slavic pope who experienced Soviet domination while a priest, was made into a 1968 movie starring actor Anthony Quinn. In his memoir, *One Man Tango*, Quinn recounted the story of a vacation in Italy. Walking on his own one evening around Lake Albano underneath Castel Gandolfo, he was approached by security guards who recognized him but nonetheless told him he needed to leave the area, because Pope John Paul II was out for a walk and heading in Quinn's direction. Quinn, being in a mischievous mood, told the guard, "You tell your pope that I was pope long before he was, and that I will walk around this lake any time I choose!" Quinn and the guards laughed. The irony was that before he was pope, John Paul II was an actor, and Anthony Quinn as an actor played the role of pope.

Pope on a Slope

John Paul II's love for skiing goes back to his childhood; most of his recorded reminiscences of Poland recall his love for skiing. If you visit his boyhood home in Wadowice or the museum created by the Archdiocese of Krakow, which froze his rooms in time, you'll find the sets of skis that he used. The first 15 years of his pontificate included an annual skiing vacation, usually in the Italian Alps.

The most often told skiing story about JP2 took place while he was still Cardinal Wojtyła. While cross-country skiing in the Tatra Mountains, he lost his way and ended up crossing the border into present-day Czech Republic (then called Czechoslovakia). Border guards stopped this man dressed in a stocking cap, tattered sweater, and old skis. They asked for his identification papers, and found out he wasn't carrying any. When he identified himself as the Cardinal-Archbishop of Krakow, a guard sarcastically responded, "Sure, and I am the pope." Wojtyła was soon identified and quickly released.

Speaking in Tongues?

Pope John Paul's linguistic abilities were legendary. Those who had interactions with him recount the ease in which he flowed from one language to another, whether addressing large crowds at rallies or greeting the guests after his daily Mass. Though it has never been officially recorded, we can say that, at the very least, besides his native Polish, Pope John Paul II was fluent in eight languages including Italian, Spanish, German, English, and French, and he had a working knowledge of several others and knew the classical languages of Ancient Greek, Latin, and some Hebrew. He quickly learned Spanish soon after his election as pope, because nearly 400 million Catholics (40 percent of the one billion members of the Catholic Church) speak Spanish. On Easter Sunday of 2004 his *Urbi et Orbi* (Latin for "To the City and to the World") message included Easter greetings in 62 languages!

Walking the Walk

Shortly after he became a bishop in 1958, Pope John Paul II made a pilgrimage to the Holy Land with other Polish bishops and priests. On the trip, he lamented that much of Jerusalem had become so modernized that he was unable to find Christ amidst modern buildings and the noise associated with tourists and tourism.

Finally, one night, Bishop Wojtyła was determined to find Christ on the streets of Jerusalem. Alone, dressed in a robe he bought at an Arab market, and without his shoes, he began to walk the streets of old Jerusalem. "I walked by myself from holy place to holy place in the depth of the night, where silence reigned. . . .", Pope John Paul II later said. "My feet hurt me terribly, my heart bled, but I was with the real Christ. I stopped at the place where He prayed on the road to Golgotha . . . and prayed. . . . My hands hurt me; my shoulders hurt, my heart was beating so fast I thought it would leave me. Most of all, I felt my bleeding feet . . . but I was happy that I could talk to Jesus Christ man to man."

It's Good to Be Pope

Vatican City-State is an independent nation separate from Italy, thanks to the 1929 Lateran Treaty between Italy and the Roman Catholic Church, which recognized the sovereignty of the Vatican as an autonomous country. Not only was Pope John Paul II the spiritual leader of one billion believers, but he was also the head of state like any other president or prime minister. World leaders often paid official visits to the Vatican to see John Paul whenever they visited the country of Italy.

As the legal head of this nation and according to the Fundamental Law of the Vatican City-State, the Holy Father "has the fullness of legislative, executive, and judicial powers." What this means is that he has the power to create a law, to enact that law, and to interpret whether that law is fair and just, all without having a conversation with another person!

Now you may be wondering how the pope runs the Universal Church and still concerns himself with whether the grass will get cut in the Vatican gardens. Not to worry. In the Vatican *Curia* (government), a President of the Pontifical Commission for the State of Vatican City and the Governorate of the State of Vatican City is named by the pope and oversees the day-to-day operations.

The Vatican City-State is, technically, a 108.5-acre tract of land (compared to the 485 acres of the Principality of Monaco or the 843 acres of New York's Central Park), plus other churches and buildings outside its walls. Their currency is the Euro, and the Vatican mints its own coins and stamps. It has its own newspaper, postal system, radio and television stations, and railroad. Although there is no Vatican army, the Swiss Guards have been protecting the person of the pope since 1506. The Vatican Observatory is the oldest astronomical institute in the world.

Like other countries of the world, Vatican City has its own flag and national anthem and issues its own passports and citizenships. It also has the oldest diplomatic corps in the world, with embassies in 179 countries. Those diplomatic relations allowed John Paul II to visit many nations during his pontificate. The president of the United States flies on a plane called *Air Force One,* and Catholic journalists coined the phrase "Shepherd One" for the papal jet that Pope John Paul II used to travel around the globe to visit his flock.

Alitalia Airlines flew JP2 from Rome to his many pilgrimage destinations around the world. But for the return trip, an airline native to the visited country would fly the pope back home. Within Italy, the Italian military provided a helicopter for the pope's travels.

Although elected for life by the cardinals, the pope may freely resign whenever he feels it necessary, but most popes stay in office until they die. The first pope to resign was St. Pontian in 235 A.D. and the last one so far was Gregory XII in 1415. John Paul believed it was his mission as pope to lead by his teaching authority in what he said and wrote but also by his example — so he did not retire when Parkinson's disease and other medical ailments greatly slowed him in his final years. For the good of the nation, secular heads of state often abdicate when their health impedes their office, but Pope John Paul II was head of state of the world's smallest country.

Besides, papal representatives handle the practical matters of running Vatican City. It was JP2's role as spiritual leader and as the father of the Catholic family of faith from which he could step down. Instead, he saw his patient endurance of pain and suffering as a mirror of the local human family where elderly parents often are burdened with the weight of illness and disease.

Chapter 22

Ten Important Papal Encyclicals of John Paul II

In This Chapter

▶ Figuring out what an encyclical is

▶ Understanding John Paul II's point of view on timely topics

▶ Applying Catholic doctrine to everyday situations

*A*n *encyclical* is an official letter of the pope sent around the world to all the bishops and the faithful. Encyclicals are the primary way that popes exercise their teaching authority on matters of doctrine or morality.

Generically, any official document of the pope meant to exercise his universal teaching authority is an encyclical. Some documents written by a pope are called *apostolic letters, apostolic exhortations,* or *apostolic constitutions.* Formerly, great emphasis was placed on the levels of papal authority each document contained, so a different name was given to each level. Since the Second Vatican Council (1962–1965), most Catholics classify all official teaching letters of a pope as encyclicals.

Most of the time, papal encyclicals are pastoral in nature, so they address a contemporary concern as it relates to the Christian religion. For example, Pope John XXIII wrote an encyclical in 1963 titled *Pacem in Terris,* which is Latin for "Peace on Earth"; this encyclical focused on the issues of world peace and human rights. An ancient custom is to name an encyclical after the first two or three words of the original Latin version of the text. Sometimes, that's enough to figure out what the letter is about, but sometimes it's just enough to pique your curiosity. *Centesimus Annus* (One Hundredth Year) written by Pope John Paul II in 1991 concerns the centenary of Pope Leo XIII's *Rerum Novarum* (Of New Things) in 1891. In this case, neither title gives you a clue that the encyclical is about working conditions, labor unions, and the economy.

Traditionally, a pope would write an encyclical to all the bishops of the world, and they, in turn, would spread the teachings to their priests who as local pastors would share the information with the faithful of their parish.

Now that we have instantaneous access via radio, television, and the Internet, the actual text of a papal encyclical is made available to the global public at the same moment. The Vatican's Web site (www.vatican.va) has become the first source in recent times, whereas before, the Catholic world had to wait for the official publication in print by Vatican Press in the official Latin newspaper *Acta Apostolica Sedes* (Acts of the Apostolic See) then in the vernacular Italian edition of *L'Osservatore Romano* (The Roman Observer). Although both papers still print the hard-copy edition of an encyclical, the computer savvy geeks can get their fill at the Vatican homepage or through Catholic media like EWTN (www.ewtn.com).

In this chapter, we look at the ten most important papal letters of John Paul II. Even though he is best known by the huge number of frequent-flier miles he racked up making pastoral visits all over the world, JP2 was also a top-notch scholar. He used the vehicle of the encyclical to teach. It's in those papal letters that you can find the mind and thought of the man himself. Beginning with Jesus Christ (*Redemptor Hominis,* 1979) and the Virgin Mary (*Redemptoris Mater,* 1987), John Paul II not only dealt with doctrinal concerns but also tackled the social issues of employment (*Laborem Exercens,* 1981), the family (*Familiaris Consortio,* 1981), and abortion and the death penalty (*Evangelium Vitae,* 1995). (You can find these documents online at www.ewtn.com/johnpaul2/writings/pontifical.htm or www.papalencyclicals.net.)

Redemptor Hominis (1979): On the Dignity of the Human Race and Its Redemption by Jesus Christ

The first two words of this encyclical mean "redeemer of man." The encyclical is about Jesus Christ, who John Paul II reiterated is the "center of the universe and of history." This was JP2's very first encyclical as pope, and it sets the tone of his style of teaching. In it, he said that, a year earlier (1978), when he was elected by the cardinals, the question was put to him, "Do you accept?" He replied, "With obedience in faith to Christ, my Lord, and with trust in the Mother of Christ and of the Church, in spite of the great difficulties, I accept."

The key goals of the encyclical

Although not explicitly stated in this document, the theme of John Paul II's papacy punctuated everything he said and did. "Be not afraid," he told the crowds at a general audience one afternoon shortly after he became pope.

In his first encyclical, he wanted to begin his papacy by reminding his flock of some key elements of the faith, including the following:

- ✔ **The link between Jesus Christ and the Bishop of Rome as the head of the Roman Catholic Church:** JP2 saw his role as that of the Vicar of Christ on Earth. It wasn't "his" church, but Christ's church, and he was simply God's representative. He was a steward who cared for, protected, defended, and served the spiritual needs of one billion members around the globe.

- ✔ **The centrality of the doctrine in the Christian religion that Christ is the Son of God:** He reaffirmed that Catholics are indeed Christian (just like their fellow Christians the Protestants and Eastern Orthodox).

- ✔ **His belief in the second coming of Christ at the end of the world, which he called the** *New Advent:* JP2 did not fear the second coming, nor did he think the end of the world was near or imminent just because the year 2000 was around the corner.

Redemptor Hominis is meant to give a ray of hope to a world that became cynical, skeptical, and fearful. Knowing that previous generations endured war, crime, disease, and persecution by faith in God's grace, JP2 used this encyclical to encourage and to rally the troops. The cosmic battle is between good and evil (grace and sin), but it isn't a war of religions, in which one faith fights another, as has happened, sadly, throughout the course of human history.

The essential parts of the encyclical

The document is divided into four parts identified as the inheritance, the mystery of redemption, redeemed man and his situation in the modern world, and the Church's mission and man's final destiny.

Inheritance

John Paul stated his intention to maintain continuity by taking the names of his immediate predecessors Pope John Paul I, Pope Paul VI, and Pope John XXIII. As John Paul II, he wanted to continue the work begun by these previous popes who were the ones who initiated the reforms of the Second Vatican Council. (For more details on the Second Vatican Council, or Vatican II as it's often called, check out Chapter 7.)

Though no new dogmas were defined and no previous ones altered, the purpose of Vatican II was more pastoral than doctrinal. The same teachings of the Church would be presented in a new way.

Some have claimed Vatican II was meant to update the Church. In fact, the truths of faith are revealed by God and, therefore, are eternal — no pope can change the content of what has been taught through the centuries. However, the pope — and the bishops united with him — can and must adapt the way the message is presented. For example, ancient disciplines like celibacy were not going to be up for discussion, but archaic customs that lost their original meaning (like the rule that required all women to wear a hat or veil over their head whenever inside a Catholic church or like the theological premise of limbo to explain where infants who die before baptism go) would have to be replaced with newer expressions to address contemporary concerns. Tradition would still be preserved and respected while modern adaptations, where appropriate, would be introduced, because the Church does not exist in a vacuum.

John Paul II gave no revolutionary teaching in *Redemptor Hominis.* He quoted former popes, Sacred Scripture (the Bible), St. Thomas Aquinas (13th-century theologian and philosopher), and documents from Vatican II. Being the good steward, he protected and preserved the heritage of what the Church has formally and officially believed and taught about Jesus, from his divinity to his humanity.

The mystery of the redemption

This section of the encyclical focuses on the central reason and purpose of the *incarnation* (the Christian doctrine that God became man and, in Christ, there is both a true human nature and a true divine nature). JP2 answered the question of why? What was the mission of Jesus Christ? Simply put, it's to be the redeemer and savior of the human race. Humanity sinned against God, and only divinity could fix the mess.

Redemption (to recover what was lost) in theological terms means to rescue what is wounded. Sin wounded human nature by breaking the bond of grace God gave us, but it didn't destroy or corrupt us completely. Humankind was in a sense lost, in that we no longer knew the way to heaven because of sin, but we were not hopelessly lost. We're salvageable, so to speak. A wound can be healed. But a corpse is too late to be saved. Though infected by sin, a human being can be redeemed by one who has the power to save. JP2 reminded us that forgiveness and mercy is what Jesus brought from heaven to share with us on Earth.

John Paul II saw the Church as the living extension of Christ on Earth. This is based on the Catholic belief that Jesus instituted the Church to continue his work after his death, resurrection, and ascension. Rather than a mere organization, the Church is seen as the Mystical Body of Christ (the spiritual union of believers united in doctrine, discipline, and worship). Therefore, the Church has the same mission as Christ: the work of redemption. As Christ came to save us from our sins, so, too, JP2 considered the primary work of the Church to save souls. Teaching the truth of revelation and faithfully celebrating divine worship are essential duties of the Church, but even these are seen as tools to achieve the end result: salvation through Christ. The other necessary mission of the Church is to participate in the work of redemption by calling sinners to conversion and seeking the mercy and forgiveness of God.

Redeemed man and his situation in the modern world

John Paul II pointed out in this section of the encyclical that the true human nature of Christ, which was united to his true divine nature, was also united to humanity as a whole. In other words, Christ is united to every man and woman who ever lived or will live. He was not just one of us, but by sharing in our human nature and uniting it with his divinity, Christ sanctified and made holy every human being no matter what the person's religion, race, or creed.

The human nature of Christ will forever be united to his divine nature. JP2 said that this unity means that the human race has been, in the words of St. John Chrysostom, "divinized." We are a holy people as a human race, having been made in the image and likeness of God, and having been redeemed by Jesus Christ his son.

This divine connection between God and man makes the human race a family of faith so that we are truly sons and daughters of God. When any one person or group of people is mistreated, abused, persecuted, or injured, we all suffer in the long run, because we are united in Christ. John Paul said that human rights are not just an individual matter but a matter of social justice. Society has an obligation to protect and defend human rights of all people, individually and collectively.

The Church's mission and man's destiny

JP2 concluded the encyclical by explaining the mission of the Church to teach the truths necessary for the salvation of all men and women. The reason the Church has this mission is to help human beings achieve their destiny, which is eternal life with God. We were created to share in the divine life of heaven after we live this earthly life.

Transmitting the truth is essential. Like a doctor who gives a life-saving medication to a critically ill patient, the Church provides the sacraments that give the divine grace needed by the soul. Yet, physicians don't just give medicine, they give instructions (prescriptions) on how to take the medicine. Both are important. Similarly, the Church not only provides the sacraments that give grace, but the Church also gives the needed instructions (teachings or doctrines) to know what is good and to be done and what is evil and to be avoided.

Laborem Exercens (1981): On the Spiritual Purpose and Sanctity of Human Labor

In this encyclical, John Paul II wanted to honor the 90th anniversary of Pope Leo XIII's encyclical *Rerum Novarum,* which addressed the issues of labor and management, especially the working conditions as they applied during the industrial revolution. His letter expanded on the idea of the nature of human work in itself and the conditions of labor in the last quarter of the 20th century. This document is often called "On Human Labor."

On the one hand, he condemned the exploitation of the worker to increase profit. Unrestricted and uncontrolled capitalism and materialistic consumerism deny or threaten the dignity of the laborer who makes the product being sold or purchased. On the other hand, JP2 also condemned the denial of private property espoused by Marxist Socialists and Communist governments. Persons can own property, and the state should only appropriate it when absolutely necessary for the common good with just compensation.

The key goals of the encyclical

This encyclical seeks to explain the relationship between the human person and human work. John Paul II wanted to show that like the Creator who worked, man and woman also work because both are made in the image and likeness of God. The encyclical also wants to differentiate humankind from labor, because human dignity is based not on what man does but on who he is (that is, a human person).

Pope John Paul II used this letter to reaffirm a constant and traditional teaching that human work is different from what animals do and because of the immortal human soul, human work has a natural but also supernatural purpose. In other words, he wants to show that holiness and sanctity can be and must be found in ordinary daily work and not just in exclusively religious acts such as praying and going to church. He also wants to warn of the abuses and distortions of human work, whether from the far right or the far left of the political and economic perspectives.

The essential parts of the encyclical

The encyclical is divided into four parts:

- **The connection between work and man:** John Paul II made it clear that only man can work. Animals and machines can perform tasks, but only a rational and moral creature like man can actually work because it involves purpose.

- **The conflict between labor and capital:** Fallen human nature is such that since the time of Cain and Abel (the sons of Adam and Eve) human beings have had conflicts with one another and very often over material things and possessions. Owners of land or of the means of production have historically had conflicts with the hired help (the laborers who worked the fields or factories). The economic, social, and political ideologies like Communism and capitalism are addressed.

- **The rights of workers:** Neither a Communist nor a capitalist, John Paul nevertheless explained the rights of workers and the duties of management and owners.

- **The spirituality of work:** He concluded with a teaching on the holiness of daily work, from the mundane to the sublime.

Establishing an essential connection between work and man

Even though *work* is technically a four-letter word, it doesn't have to have a negative connotation. Though some people hate their jobs and dread the work they do, work in and of itself is not an enemy to man, nor is it a consequence of sin (as Catholics believe death and illness are).

Work was a holy thing for John Paul II because it imitates the Creator. God himself worked for six days during Creation and rested on the seventh day. The way JP2 saw it, work can't be evil or a consequence of sin if God engaged in work. Jesus, the Son of God, worked in the carpenter shop with his foster father Joseph (the husband of Mary, the mother of Jesus) before his public ministry as a rabbi. The Apostles called by Christ to begin his church were mostly fishermen who worked long and hard.

According to JP2, unlike animals who do things to survive and stay alive, only human beings actually work. Man alone is the only creature on Earth whose tasks have both an objective and subjective meaning, which we call *work*. In other words, not only is there purpose in work (such as providing food and shelter for yourself and your family), but there is meaning in work as well. Man defines himself by his work because it involves a conscious, deliberate, and free act of the will. Human work involves the community of man so that men and women work together doing different tasks but serving the one family of mankind. This belief is why protecting the dignity of human work was so important to John Paul II.

Slave labor is not work because it isn't done freely or willingly but imposed by force on the human person and because his human dignity is not recognized, protected, or enhanced.

Science and technology should help serve the human race, not deprive us of the opportunity to work. A life of complete leisure and no physical or mental work is not a human life according to JP2. Technology should make work easier but not eliminate the need for human workers. Advances in science have made the workplace safer, more efficient, and less onerous than in the days of coal mines, sweat shops, and labor camps.

Human work not only transforms nature according to the plan of God to "fill the earth and subdue it" (Genesis 1:28), but it also defines man. The first man, Adam, even before he was expelled from the Garden of Eden, was given the work of cultivating and caring for it (Genesis 2:15). It was not a punishment but part of his nature to do work and to take pride in one's work.

John Paul II also reminded his readers of the need for workers to protect themselves and to work together as a community. The medieval guilds were the first example of worker solidarity and labor and trade unions, which JP2 saw as being of invaluable worth.

Identifying today's conflict between labor and capital

Historically, there has been tension between labor and capital, between the workers and management. This struggle isn't intrinsic or essential as Karl Marx (19th-century German philosopher and father of the ideology of Communism, in which he reduced everything to a class struggle between the *bourgeoisie* [those who own the means of production and capital] and the *proletariat* [those who work and labor]) proposed. Instead, according to John Paul II, the struggle is a sad consequence of original sin. Greed can tempt owners to pay their workers less than they deserve, give them more work for less pay, or tempt workers to demand more than they produce or to work less for what they are paid. Just and fair wages for just and fair work is part of the Natural Moral Law, just as the consumer should expect a fair price for decent products. High prices and low wages are obviously not good for workers, but neither are unfair and unreasonable discounts and pay raises that threaten not just the owners but the very existence of the companies who employ the workers.

John Paul II insists in this encyclical that the dignity of the worker is more valuable than the profits gained. Unrestricted capitalism that puts profits before employee or consumer safety is as bad as Communist governments that seize private property, land, and business in the name of the state just to exploit the workers for the sake of the political party.

Emphasizing the rights of workers

In this encyclical, JP2 spelled out that workers retain their innate and inalienable human rights at all times. Being employed does not rob them of their human nature, which was made in the image and likeness of God. Therefore, every single employee, worker, staff member, or office personnel must be treated with respect and dignity.

Workers are neither biological machines nor organic tools; rather, they are human beings who have rights and require nonnegotiable necessities including:

- ✔ Just and fair wages for just and fair work

- ✔ Reasonable safety and security from injury and danger

- ✔ Necessary days off and vacation days for rest and relaxation

- ✔ Decent working conditions

- ✔ The right to address their bosses and the owners of the companies when their rights are being ignored or violated

John Paul II also encouraged certain other labor principles, including:

- ✔ **Equal pay for equal work:** Women shouldn't be unfairly underpaid for doing the same work as their male colleagues.

- ✔ **The rights of women who have chosen to become mothers:** They should never be forced out of the home away from their children just because there are not adequate wages for her husband to provide for the family.

- ✔ **Not denying someone work based on his race or nationality.**

- ✔ **Equal pay and fair employment for those with disabilities:** All human beings have a right to work to the extent that they are mentally and physically capable.

- ✔ **Not exploiting foreigners because of their lack of knowledge or skills, and not paying unfair wages to undocumented non-citizens:** Employers should not try to make bigger profits by keeping employment costs down.

- ✔ **The right to strike or work stoppage as a last resort:** The right to strike can be abused, and the consequences are usually disastrous for both labor and management, so JP2 believed it should be a last resort.

- ✔ **Not prohibiting unions, and not requiring membership in unions in most places of employment.**

- ✔ **Providing adequate and just wages and safe working conditions, and (when possible) assisting in the ongoing education and training of employees so they can advance professionally and improve personally.**

Defining a spirituality of work

John Paul II concluded this encyclical with the teaching of the Church on the spirituality of work. Christians are to bring their faith into the workplace, not by proselytizing and preaching, but by living according to their religious convictions and values. Acting and behaving in a Christian manner at all times — but especially in the workplace — is the vocation of all the laity, because they live and work in the world.

Just as St. Joseph worked in the carpenter's shop and the Virgin Mary worked in the home, both showed the example of *consecrating* (making a voluntary spiritual dedication of a human activity for the greater honor and glory of God) his or her daily work. Doing one's work well pleases God, even if the boss doesn't notice it. Working diligently, honestly, and in accord with common morality is the mandate of all men and women, whether they're labor or management, blue collar or white collar, employee or owner. Taking pride in your work, not for the sake of raises and promotion but because it's the right thing to do, makes your work a holy task even if what you do isn't directly connected to anything religious.

Catholics believe that any occupation — farmhand, cashier, truck or bus driver, waitress, receptionist, doctor or nurse, teacher, stock broker, whatever — can provide the opportunity to consecrate your work by doing it well, just as if God himself had hired you. Therefore, the Church has an obligation to remind employers and employees to maintain fairness, justice, dignity, and respect in the workplace. Any human work, be it manual or intellectual, can be offered to God.

Familiaris Consortio (1981): On the Value of the Christian Family in the Modern World

Pope John Paul II convened a *synod* (a temporary gathering of some bishops representing many nations whose purpose is to discuss specific matters and to advise the pope) in 1980 on the family. Only two years into his papacy, JP2 wanted to prioritize his agenda by explaining to the Church and to the world that the human family was the cornerstone of civilization, of society, of government and of the Church. He also wanted to warn families of the dangers lurking in the world that threatened the health and well-being of the very institution of family. This papal letter is a response to the Synod on the Family.

The key goals of the encyclical

John Paul II wanted to teach about the sanctity, dignity, and necessity of the human family. A primary component of both religion and civil society (church and state), the family is the nucleus of culture and civilization itself. He wants to show that it is part of God's plan that human beings come from, develop in, and live within a family context. The pope also wants to underscore that it was no accident, nor was it merely incidental that Jesus, the Savior and Redeemer, was born and raised in a human family. This letter also tries to encourage both individuals and society itself to promote, defend, and sustain the family and provide assistance and healing where there are broken or wounded families.

The essential parts of the encyclical

Familaris Consortio is composed of four parts:

- **The bright spots and shadows of the modern family:** John Paul II defined the family as a community of persons and not just a biological, legal, or social grouping of individuals.
- **God's plan for marriage and the family**
- **The role of the Christian family in today's world**
- **The pastoral and spiritual care of the family**

John Paul II saw the family as the fundamental and essential building block to all society, for both the church and the state. Even though each individual person is made separately by God, the intent of the Creator is that we are born, raised, and live within the context of a family. Families are the best place for individuals to realize their full potential because they profit from the gifts and talents of each member and compensate for respective weaknesses.

John Paul II saw good and bad elements affecting modern families today:

> **On the one hand,** in fact, there is a more lively awareness of personal freedom and greater attention to the quality of interpersonal relationships in marriage, to promoting the dignity of women, to responsible procreation, to the education of children. . . .

> **On the other hand,** . . . a mistaken . . . concept of the independence of the spouses in relation to each other; serious misconceptions regarding the relationship of authority between parents and children; . . . the growing number of divorces; the scourge of abortion; the ever more frequent recourse to sterilization; the appearance of a truly contraceptive mentality.

Addressing these concerns, JP2 reminded his readers that it was not an accident or whim that the Savior, the Son of God, was born and raised within a human family. Jesus had a human mother who lived with her husband. The three of them formed what is typically called the Holy Family, but all human families can be rightfully called the *domestic church* or *the seminary of life.* Both of these terms reinforce the fact that in the family:

- ✔ Parents have a primary responsibility to teach their children the Christian faith, even if they send their kids to formal religious education.

- ✔ Sons and daughters learn about being brothers and sisters, how to cooperate and coexist with one another.

- ✔ People learn firsthand about the love of God and the necessity to worship and communicate with Him through prayer.

In other words, families that never pray or go to Church are setting as poor an example as families that don't eat their fruits and vegetables or brush their teeth and wash behind their ears.

John Paul II reminded his audience that even though there are examples of good single parents, being a single parent shouldn't be anyone's first choice or desire, because every child deserves the chance and opportunity to grow up in a complete and safe family situation; even more importantly, each child deserves a father and a mother. The best scenario is a loving mother and father who are also a loving husband and wife, to care for their sons and daughters. Just as it may be a medical necessity to amputate a leg or even both legs to save the life of a sick or injured person, ordinarily it's a preferred and better thing to keep both limbs for your entire life. Likewise, married couples who stay married and who raise their children to believe, to worship, and to obey God should be the norm and not the exception or mere alternative, according to JP2.

John Paul II reminded married couples that Christian marriage is the foundation of the Christian family. Just as Christ loved his bride, the Church, husbands and wives are to love and serve each other. Their sacrificial love often will lead to the birth of new life and family members. A happy family is not one free of suffering but one that can endure any hardship because each member is willing to sacrifice for the sake of the others. The bottom line: Good families are built on good marriages.

The family is a reflection of the Holy Trinity (God the Father, God the Son, and God the Holy Spirit), which is a community of persons but still one God. Likewise, the family is a community of persons (mother and father, son and daughter, brother and sister) but still one family. The mutual love of husband and wife — as intense as it can get — is still built on the principle of self-sacrificing love: surrendering your own wants and desires for the needs of others.

John Paul II reiterated the essential duty of the state to protect marriage and the family because both contribute to the health and welfare of society. Laws should protect, defend, and assist families — especially in cultures that glorify the individual to such extremes that haven't been seen in centuries. JP2 spoke clearly on the dignity of all women, both married and single, mothers and childless. He denounces the evils of pornography, prostitution, and discrimination, which offend the dignity of every woman.

Salvifici Doloris (1984): On the Christian Meaning of Suffering

This papal letter has its origin in Karol Wojtyła the man, who personally knew suffering in his own life and in that of his family, friends, and fellow countrymen during World War II and the Cold War. It also reflects the response of Father Wojtyła the priest and John Paul II the pope, who wanted to give encouragement and comfort to the many innocent victims of suffering.

The key goals of the encyclical

Pope John Paul II wanted to address the mystery of why there is evil in the world — specifically, why innocent people suffer. He sought to address the question not only of why there is human suffering but also of what the Christian response to it is. Because he was no stranger to suffering — having lost his mother, his brother, and his father before he became a priest; having endured Nazi occupation and Soviet Communist control of his native Poland; having survived an assassin's bullet; and bearing the cross of Parkinson's disease — JP2 could and did speak not only with authority but from experience in this document.

He wanted to teach about the solidarity of suffering (that human beings are intimately connected to one another by sharing their grief, anguish, and pain with another human being). The old notion that only the evil suffer and the good have a charmed life is not based on real human experience, nor is it verified in the Bible. John Paul II wanted those who suffer in body, mind, or soul to know that they are not being punished; instead, they are being embraced by the crucified Lord.

The essential parts of the encyclical

The first part of the letter is on the world of human suffering. Pain, misery, and disappointment, death and disease, do not discriminate. They affect men and women, boys and girls, young and old, rich and poor, of any race, creed, religion, nationality, or ethnic background. The second part of the encyclical is the quest for the answer to the question of what is the meaning (or purpose) of human suffering. The third part is on how Jesus Christ conquered suffering by divine love. The fourth segment deals with the very Catholic doctrine of *salvific suffering* (how the believer can share in the sufferings of Christ by uniting his own personal suffering with the cross of Christ). The fifth segment is on the Gospel of Suffering. And the sixth segment is on the Good Samaritan parable that Jesus preached to encourage the helping of others — even strangers — who suffer.

Pope John Paul II wrote this encyclical titled "Salvific Suffering" three years after he was shot in an attempted assassination that nearly killed him, well *before* he contracted Parkinson's disease. He opened his letter with the mysterious and profound words of St. Paul in his epistle: "In my flesh I complete what is lacking in Christ's afflictions for the sake of his body, that is, the Church" (Colossians 1:24).

Christians believe that Jesus suffered and died for our sins. Was St. Paul saying that Christ did not suffer enough, so we have to compensate? No, Christ's suffering was sufficient to save the world — however, Christ mysteriously chose to leave room for us to unite our sufferings with his and, thus, make it *salvific* (having the ability to save or redeem). Rather than saying Jesus did not suffer enough, Paul was actually saying that Christ allowed us to join him on the cross, not out of necessity but by choice. Jesus wanted us to voluntarily surrender as he did.

When animals suffer pain, we instinctively have pity for them and put them out of their misery. Because they have no rational intellect and no free will, an animal is incapable of voluntarily, consciously, and deliberately offering up its suffering for its fellow beings. Human beings, however, have a free will and are able to reason. Unavoidable and untreatable pain and suffering can be made useful in men and women when they freely unite their "cross" with the sufferings endured by Christ 2,000 years ago. Even though his Passion (scourging and crucifixion) and death occurred long ago, because Christians believe Jesus is both God and man, divine and human, what Christ endured had an effect on all humanity for all time.

Christ's suffering conquered death and opened the way to heaven for humankind. Pain and death were not eliminated from human experience, but their power over us was removed because, after death, they have no effect whatsoever. Though no human being is immune or exempt from physical, mental, or emotional suffering, there is a limit to what suffering we are allowed to bear and that limit is called *Divine Mercy*. Christians believe that their deceased loved ones who are with the Lord experience no more pain and no more tears, only joy without end. Heaven is the state of total blessedness where there is never any suffering.

The extreme suffering of Christ is not just an incident of the past, John Paul II reminded us. Like a mother who willingly endures the pain of labor for the sake of her newborn child, Jesus embraced his suffering in order to save us because we could not save ourselves. Although no one can ever approach — let alone equal — the suffering experienced by the Savior, as St. Paul alludes in Colossians 1:24, we can unite our sufferings in the present with Christ's sufferings in the past.

John Paul II did not advocate a sadistic or masochistic perspective where pain is enjoyed or sought. In fact, alleviating as much pain and suffering as possible using moral methods and means is permissible and necessary. From aspirin to morphine, modern medicine has developed marvelous drugs to reduce or eliminate pain, which is a good thing as long as the treatment itself does not cause or hasten death.

JP2 used the gospel parable of the Good Samaritan (Luke 10:29–37), in which a stranger meets a man who was brutally attacked by robbers. The stranger rescues the victim, tends to his wounds, and brings him to safety. Therefore, taking care of the sick, wounded, and victims of violence and abuse is not only a good thing to do — for Christians, it is a gospel *mandate*. Had the Samaritan "put the man out of his misery" as some would do today by using so-called "mercy killing," that would not have been morally acceptable.

John Paul II also used the example of the Virgin Mary as one who suffered by helplessly watching her son Jesus suffer excruciating pain before his death on the cross. There was nothing Jesus's mother could do to stop or even reduce the pain on that first *Good Friday* (what Christians call the day Christ was crucified and died), but she nevertheless lovingly and, for her, painfully stood by. Her presence was helpful to Jesus, but it was equally painful for him to see his own mother suffering emotionally because he was suffering physically. Mary united her suffering as a grieving and sorrowful mother with the suffering of her son — and God gave her the grace to endure. John Paul II said that we, too, can get the strength and courage to endure by the same grace from the same God. Being present with someone who is suffering and dying is not pleasant and is extremely difficult for family and friends, but it's helpful for the patient emotionally and spiritually.

Redemptoris Mater (1987): On the Virgin Mary as Mother of the Redeemer (Jesus Christ) and Her Role in Salvation

Pope John Paul II, like most popes, took a motto as well as a new name when he was elected Bishop of Rome by the Cardinals in 1978 after the untimely death of Pope John Paul I, one month after his election. JP2's motto was *totus tuus,* which is Latin for "totally yours." It is based on the spirituality of St. Louis de Montfort, a 17th-century French priest, who promoted a strong devotion to the Virgin Mary. Part of that spirituality focused on being "totally yours" — that is, being totally committed to following the holy example of Mary, the mother of Jesus, especially in her humility and in her obedient discipleship to that same son of hers. This papal letter was written to show and explain the bond and the significance of the relationship between God and the human race.

The key goals of the encyclical

Since the time of the Protestant Reformation in the early 16th-century and especially in the aftermath of the Second Vatican Council (1962–1965), some Catholics and many non-Catholics have misunderstood how the Church sees the role of the Virgin Mary in the work of redemption. John Paul II wanted to use this encyclical to reaffirm the consistent Catholic teaching on Mary and her participation in salvation. He wanted to make sure that no one would distort this principle that every Christian church — from Protestant to Catholic to Eastern Orthodox — maintains: that Jesus Christ is the one and only Savior and Redeemer of mankind. The document goes on to show the fact that it is not by necessity but by divine choice that God allows any human being to participate in salvation history. While upholding the unique and singular role of Christ as Mediator between God and man (because Jesus is both human and divine himself), JP2 also pointed out that God freely chose to use the cooperation of certain human persons to accomplish his divine plan. The Virgin Mary was totally human while her son was true God and true man (not a hybrid 50/50 — half-god/half-man — but one divine person with a full human nature and a full divine nature).

Mary's role, as this letter explains, was auxiliary and by God's design (that is, in accord with his will). She could not replace or duplicate what her son did as the Savior and Redeemer. Her participation was by divine invitation. She was asked to assist just as are all children of God. JP2 knew that many misconstrue *Marian devotion* (devotion to Mary) as idolatry. He wanted this letter to show that Catholic Christianity does not give, and has never given, Mary worship and adoration that belong to God alone. At the same time, he used this encyclical to define what Catholicism does in fact say and teach about Mary, the woman, the person, and the mother of the Redeemer.

The essential parts of the encyclical

The title of this encyclical is "Mother of the Redeemer," and it's about Mary, the mother of Jesus. John Paul II had a strong devotion to Mary throughout his priesthood and especially during his entire pontificate.

The encyclical is divided into three parts. The first part is Mary in the mystery of Christ. This section connects the life of Mary with the life of her son, Jesus. The second part is Mary at the center of the pilgrim church. This section goes into the area of Mary being an integral part of the infant church. The third part is Mary's maternal intercession. This final section relates Mary to the believer of today.

If you're not a Catholic, you may initially be uncomfortable with such deep devotion to Mary — you may wonder if such devotion takes away from the worship and love that Catholics must also have for Christ. JP2 never diluted his enormous and intense love of Jesus for one moment, before or after becoming pope. He knew well the First Commandment, to love the Lord God with all your heart, all your mind, and all your strength (Deuteronomy 6:5). But he also knew equally well the commandment to honor your mother and father (Exodus 20:12). Although he never *worshipped* Mary — because that would have been sinful idolatry — he always honored her with great affection just as he had great affection for his own earthly mother. The reasoning is that all human beings are adopted children of God and as such Christians can say they are brothers and sisters in Christ. The human mother of Christ by way of the same adoption becomes spiritual mother to the faithful. Because Christ honored his human mother in accord with the commandments, so, too, the believer honors not only the mother of the Redeemer but also the believer's spiritual mother by spiritual adoption.

John Paul II grew up in a time and place where showing honor and respect to your friend's mother was not just common but normal. Honoring and respecting your friend's mother was considered the highest compliment and a sign of fraternal love for a friend. In JP2's mind — and in the minds of Catholic and Eastern Orthodox Christians — devotion to Mary was not worship or adoration (which is forbidden); it's giving the greatest honor and respect to the human being who was literally the mother of the Savior. Though Christians believe Jesus was the Son of God, he was also the son of Mary. He is considered both human and divine. Mary had to worship him in his divinity but in his humanity, Jesus deeply loved and honored his mother like any other son or daughter.

In this encyclical, JP2 explained true and healthy Marian devotion and its place in a Christian life. Here are the main points he makes in *Redemptoris Mater:*

> ✔ **Your faith must be *Christocentric*, or always centered on Christ.** Mary is no substitute for Jesus because he is the one and only Savior, Redeemer, and Mediator between God and man. Jesus is the second person of the Holy Trinity, and the Son of God is to be given the same worship and adoration proper to God alone.

> ✔ **Proper devotion to Mary is never equivalent to worship.** Although not in competition with the worship of Christ, Marian devotion is meant to enhance Catholics worship of God because Mary herself was a faithful and obedient servant of the Lord.

In this encyclical, John Paul II looks at what the Sacred Scriptures tell us about Mary to cultivate good Marian devotion. When the angel Gabriel appeared to Mary and announced that she would become the mother of the Savior, he addressed her as "full of grace" (Luke 1:28). Soon afterward, when Mary visited her cousin Elizabeth, who was six months' pregnant with John the Baptist, she got this greeting: "Blessed art thou among women and blessed is the fruit of thy womb" (Luke 1:42). These two passages from the Gospel have been combined to form the prayer that Catholics know as the Hail Mary, or *Ave Maria* (in Latin).

Why the accolades to this poor peasant girl? What did she do to merit such lofty salutations from an angel? She did nothing. Mary didn't earn her condition. God chose her, and she freely and willingly accepted the invitation. The grace she was given came from God — as does all grace. She didn't win a reality show to become the mother of Jesus — but what she did after she conceived and gave birth to the Savior is why she is given such praise. She herself said "all generations shall call me blessed" (Luke 1:48). Was she tooting her own horn? Was it pride popping out? No. In fact, JP2 pointed out that Mary showed great humility at all times. She also showed complete acceptance of the Will of God: "I am the handmaiden of the Lord, be it done unto me according to your word" (Luke 1:38). Humility, however, recognizes and accepts the truth, positive or negative, talent or flaw. It owns up to mistakes made and acknowledges that all talent and gifts come from God.

Although Christ is the Mediator, his mother Mary and others in the Gospel, took on the role of *intercessors* (those who ask favors for another). As the Son of God, Jesus knew what people needed before they asked; yet, he told people to ask, and they shall receive. Not only are individuals to ask for spiritual assistance themselves, but it is a Christian virtue to pray for others. Asking God to help someone else is considered a wonderful thing. Christians have been praying for one another for millennia and not only for family and friends, but for enemies and persecutors as well. Praying for another person is, in essence, intercession.

It was not by necessity that the Virgin Mary interceded for anyone but by divine choice that she was allowed to make intercession, as she does in the Gospel of John. The first public miracle of Jesus, the son of Mary, is performed at a wedding feast in Cana. When the wine ran out, Mary mentions it to her son, and Jesus changes water into wine (John 2:1–11). Mary intercedes on behalf of the bride and groom and goes to her son, the Mediator, the Savior, and Redeemer, Jesus Christ.

Others interceded to Jesus on behalf of their family and friends. Jesus never rebuked them and said that the sick person himself had to come to Jesus directly. He allowed a Canaanite woman to intercede for the recovery of her daughter in Matthew 15:22. Jesus allowed the Roman Centurion to intercede on behalf of his sick servant boy in Luke 7:1–10. John Paul II concluded that human intercession is part of God's plan, as the intercessor still goes to the one Mediator, Christ, and it is Christ who performs the miraculous cures and healing, not the intercessor. Likewise, Mary's intercession, whether at the wedding feast of Cana or from her place in heaven, is based on the same principle. She goes to her son and asks a favor for someone else. If I ask you to pray for my mother's recovery after she broke her shoulder, I am asking you to intercede to God for my mom. When Catholics pray to Mary, it is the same idea: She is being asked to ask her son, Jesus, to help someone on Earth.

Because it is not by necessity, Protestant Christians may see no need to seek such intercession. Likewise, no one really needs to ask anyone for prayer because the person can always go to God directly and ask on his own behalf. Yet, the beauty of intercessory prayer is that it affirms that we are a spiritual family, and the Bible exhorts us to pray for each other (James 5:16). Mary's prayers are just the same.

Also in this encyclical, JP2 pointed out that in the Gospel of John, we see the heart of Jesus and the heart of Mary at the foot of the cross (John 19:26–27). With John next to her, Mary is told by her son, Jesus, just before he dies, "Behold your son," and he says to John, "Behold your mother." If Jesus had sibling brothers and sisters, Jewish custom and law would have ensured that those siblings would have taken care of Mary. With no brothers or sisters, the widow Mary would have been all alone after her only son Jesus died, so Jesus entrusted her to his best friend, John. JP2 reiterated the ancient Catholic tradition that John represents all of us: We are brothers and sisters in Christ, and we share the same mother on the spiritual level. She becomes our spiritual mother by adoption, and her function is to help up get closer to her son. John Paul II said that's why there is Marian devotion: to follow Mary's example of being close to Jesus.

He concluded his letter with an idea posed at the Second Vatican Council, in which Mary was given the title "Mother of the Church." Just as the phrase the "Mother of God" is okay because it is used analogously (Mary is the mother of Christ and because Chris is the Son of God, Mary is the Mother of God), likewise, Mary is the mother of the church because she is the mother of Christ, and the church is the Mystical Body of Christ.

St. Paul used the analogy of a body to describe the Christian church in Ephesians 4:4–13. Christ is the head of the body, and the baptized are members of the body (like arms, hands, legs, feet, and so on). Mary gave birth to the physical body of Jesus, and by way of analogy she is considered the spiritual mother of the mystical body of that very same son of hers. The church then is an organic union of all the faithful members, just as a human body has many parts that work in unison.

In this encyclical, John Paul II declared 1988 to be a Marian year to honor her role as mother of the Redeemer and as faithful servant of the Lord. It was also the same Marian year two of us authors were ordained. JP2 wanted to prepare for the super-duper celebration of the new millennium when 2,000 years of Christianity would be honored.

Ex Corde Ecclesiae (1990): On the Nature, Purpose, and Duties of a Catholic University

"The Catholic University was born from the heart of the Church," said John Paul II in this papal letter. As a philosopher, theologian, and former college professor in Poland, a man of great intelligence, wisdom, and stamina, JP2 valued the treasure of a solid education founded on the truth, be it of faith or of reason. He used this encyclical to address Catholic academia, as well as parents and students.

The key goals of the encyclical

This letter is meant to clarify once and for all what defines a Catholic college or university and what obligations and duties accompany that designation. John Paul II was painfully aware that many Catholic institutions of higher learning had lost their Catholic identity over time, and many of them were no different than their secular or public or nondenominational equivalent. JP2 issued *Ex Corde Ecclesiae* to encourage those schools that never abandoned or diluted their Catholic Christian identity, values, and atmosphere. It was also issued to enforce the Church law that required any school that used the name *Catholic* to teach sound doctrine in the theology department and to insist that Catholic faith and morals were protected and defended on campus.

The essential parts of the encyclical

This document is divided into three parts. The first part is the identity of a Catholic university; the second is its mission as a Catholic university; and the third concerns general and transitional norms to implement the document.

This document, literally titled "From the Heart of the Church," is about Catholic education (specifically, Catholic colleges and universities). It caused some controversy because John Paul II expressed concerned that, over time, many

Catholic institutions of higher education had lost, forgotten, abandoned, or watered down their Catholicity for the sake of pluralism and academic freedom.

Universities were originally all religious institutions from the time of their creation in the Middle Ages. The pursuit of truth — be it theological, philosophical, or scientific — was the objective of these centers of higher learning. The medieval scholar was expected to know religion (theology) but also to be trained in the classic disciplines — often called the *seven liberal arts:* grammar, rhetoric, logic, math, geometry, astronomy, and music. Sacred sciences included Sacred Scripture (Bible), dogmatic theology, moral theology, Church history, and sacramental theology. They were called *sacred sciences* because, unlike the liberal arts, these disciplines had unique and precise methods and were very systematic as well as explicitly defined as they came under the jurisdiction of the *Magisterium* (the teaching authority of the Church).

Because God is the author of truth and the Creator of the universe, there is no conflict in studying both the sacred and the *profane* (or nonreligious) sciences. Catholic universities taught both for centuries. Only in recent modern times have their Catholic identities been hidden or compromised. JP2's goal in *Ex Corde Ecclesiae* was to reinforce the need for accountability in the religious realm.

Imagine a math teacher telling his students that he is personally opposed to $2 + 2 = 4$ and he prefers to believe that $2 + 2 = 5$. He may think and believe that — but if he taught it, he'd probably lose his job. Ironically, theologians began to express dissent about defined Church teachings and give their own opinions, which contradicted the official doctrines of the Catholic Church. That was tantamount to saying $2 + 2 = 5$ — but none of these theologians lost their jobs. The divinity of Christ, the inerrancy of scripture (that is, the concept that there are no errors in the Bible), and other doctrines were being disputed right and left in numerous Catholic universities and colleges, and no one was being disciplined. For example, moral theologians openly defied Pope Paul VI when he issued his encyclical *Humanae Vitae* (1968), in which he condemned artificial contraception and abortion.

Natural and physical sciences ascertain the truth by observation and experimentation. Philosophy learns the truth by using reason and logic. Theology is the only discipline that gets the answers directly from God, through revelation. Unlike the other two sciences, theology does not depend on the world or on man himself for the answers — instead, the answers are given to him, and he must accept them on faith. Theologians cannot prove that there are three persons in one God, but the Christian doctrine of the Triune God (the Father, the Son, and the Holy Spirit) is not up for debate among Christians any more than mathematicians would consider $2 + 2 = 4$ as untrue.

John Paul II didn't want to tell scientists, historians, or philosophers how to do their jobs, but as Supreme Pastor and Supreme Teacher of the Catholic Church, he used his authority over Catholic theologians as was his right. *Ex Corde Ecclesiae* required theologians to have a mandate, which is equivalent to an authorized license. Doctors who graduate from medical school get a degree, but they can't practice medicine without a license from the proper authority. When they don't practice orthodox medicine, their license can be revoked. Similarly, John Paul II wanted to license, through the local bishops, theologians who teach in Catholic colleges and universities, having them pledge their allegiance to what is officially taught and not give opinion or dissent an equal footing.

In addition to ensuring doctrinal orthodoxy at Catholic universities, John Paul II also called for promoting a religious and moral environment on campus. Unlike secular colleges — which are often prohibited from public display of faith — JP2 believed that Catholic schools should not be ashamed of their heritage, which can be done without attacking or ridiculing other religions. Instead of imitating the secular universities in every way, Catholic colleges can still have sports teams and other extracurricular activities, but JP2 believed that there should be a closer watch on what activities are being done after hours. Religious schools are not filled with perfect people, and so no one should expect there never to be mistakes or that no sins would be committed on campus. At the same time, parents and students need to be reassured that the campus is safe and promotes family values and faith values. Acting morally and learning the truth should go hand in hand.

Veritatis Splendor (1993): On the Basis and Foundation of Christian Morality and Ethics

JP2 the philosopher and the theologian manifests his identity in this papal encyclical where he addresses the crisis in modern civilization — namely, the loss of moral responsibility and accountability among many people in our modern world. The Ten Commandments and the Bible tell us *how* to live (do good and avoid evil). *Veritatis Splendor* seeks to explain why this is a good, necessary, and urgent priority.

The key goals of the encyclical

This encyclical wants to explain the foundation of Catholic morality and Christian ethics. Using both Sacred Scripture and the Natural Moral Law, John Paul II synthesized both faith and reason in terms of knowing and living the moral life God has called every human person to live. JP2 also wanted to expose the errors of false doctrines and the dangers of ideologies and philosophies not based on reality and on the innate goodness of human nature and the human person, but that distort values and principles and endanger civilization itself.

The essential parts of the encyclical

This epic work is contained in three chapters. The first chapter deals with the first moral principle (namely, "Do good and avoid evil"). The second chapter describes how to discern the errors of present-day so-called morality. The final chapter concerns the purpose or reason for being and doing good (that is, the attainment of real happiness and the reward of everlasting life). John Paul II used this encyclical to show the natural reasonableness of seeking and living a virtuous and morally good life; at the same time, for the believer, it is but a building block upon which a supernatural life of grace and holiness are to be pursued.

The "Splendor of Truth" is the title of this encyclical letter. In this piece, John Paul II showed his expertise as a philosopher and moral theologian — especially in explaining the perennial teaching of the Church on the existence, importance, and necessity of the *Natural Moral Law:* "Do good and avoid evil." Every human being who has the ability to reason is expected to know the basic tenets of the moral law. When World War II ended, Nazis who committed heinous atrocities like the Holocaust, were put on trial in Nuremberg in 1945. They were found guilty of murdering innocent men, women, and children not on biblical grounds (that it violated the Ten Commandments) but on *moral* grounds (that murder is wrong).

A religious person may do good and avoid evil merely because God said so. But what about nonreligious people? Are they exempt from obeying moral laws if they don't believe in the Church, in the commandments, or even in God? The Nazi war criminals were tried and punished not on religious reasons but on moral ones. Legally, they didn't break the civil law — the Nazis had enacted legislation authorizing them to seize property and deport Jews. The soldiers tried to say, "We only followed orders," but because there is a universal Natural Moral Law, that trumps everything else. In other words, if you're in the army, and you're ordered to do something immoral, you're obligated according to Natural Moral Law *not* to obey the orders. As JP2 points out in this encyclical, if there is no Natural Moral Law, we may be victims of future acts of genocide and all other unspeakable evils just because somewhere someone has declared them "legal."

His springboard for this encyclical was the scene in Matthew 19 where a rich man asked Jesus, "Teacher, what good must I do to have eternal life?" In the very question, the young, rich man shows wisdom. He knows he *must* do good. Doing good and avoiding evil aren't optional — they're mandatory. In addition, good is to be *done,* not just desired. The young man asked what good must he *do?* You can think about and talk about doing good, but actually *doing* it is another matter. So the man realized he had a duty to do good. The purpose of doing good is to obtain eternal life. It isn't to be recognized by the world as a hero or to seek awards or rewards. Doing good just because it is the right thing to do is the goal.

John Paul II reminded his readers that Jesus clearly says that how to "do good" is explicitly stated in the commandments: Love God, love your neighbor, honor God, honor your neighbor, honor God's name and his day, honor your neighbor, honor your neighbor's safety, honor your neighbor's wife, honor your neighbor's reputation and his property. The young man said he had kept all these commandments. Now what? Jesus told him that being good means keeping the commandments (basically, following the Natural Moral Law). If the young man wanted to go beyond goodness and seek personal holiness, then, in this man's case, because he was attached to his worldly possessions, Jesus told him to sell what he had and give it to the poor. The man went away sad, because he had many things and couldn't part with them.

The pope used basic ethics and moral theology to reiterate that only conscious, deliberate, and voluntary acts can be moral acts. If there is no work of the free will, it is not a moral act. When you laugh, that is an act of man, because it is something a human being can do. When you lie or steal, that is a human act, because it involves deliberate free will. Any act that is deliberately and freely done is a moral act. Moral acts are either good or evil.

Animals act on instinct and computers are programmed, but only human beings can invoke their free will and, thus, make moral acts that are either morally good or morally evil. An animal or machine cannot sin, but human beings can. Our free will is not absolute. I cannot do anything I want if it results in others being harmed. I cannot make up my own morality any more than I can make up my own reality. Whether I like or understand the laws of gravity or not, they still affect me. The moral law applies to us 24/7.

Freedom is not the ability to do anything I want; instead, JP2 said that freedom is the ability to do what I *ought* to do or doing the right thing for the right reason. I can freely choose to tell the truth, but if my motives are bad (I hate this person and want to ruin his reputation), then revealing embarrassing secrets, true though they may be, is considered the sin of detraction. If they were false rumors, I would be committing slander. If I tell an embarrassing secret in order to keep an alcoholic from drinking and driving and endanger himself and others, that's a good thing.

Freedom to do what I *ought* to do is true moral freedom. Because I act freely, doing good for the right reason makes me a better person. Today, many people believe that they should just follow their own consciences without any examination of whether their consciences are well and properly formed — and JP2 pointed out in this encyclical that this isn't good. Prayer, study (Bible and catechism), and solid advice from trusted friends are the best sources of examination. Otherwise, one man's vice is another man's virtue. One person could say he has no objection to slavery, but that doesn't make it moral. An act is either morally good or evil — it has nothing to do with whether the person committing the act *thinks* the act is good or evil.

Veritatis Splendor does not advocate imposing a morality but merely a defense and implementation of the already always existing: Natural Moral Law. If I see a crime and do nothing to stop it, I can be considered an accomplice or guilty of criminal negligence when I refuse to help someone who is in urgent serious need. I would also be guilty of the sin of omission. John Paul II said that society must promote good and discourage evil if it is to endure and have any legitimacy. When evil is tolerated and condoned or, worse yet, encouraged, then that society and culture is sick and will die.

JP2 concluded this encyclical with very traditional philosophy and theology — namely, that the human intellect (the mind) was designed by God to seek the truth and the human free will was made to seek the good. Only the supreme good and supreme truth will ever bring humankind real and lasting happiness. That is what heaven is all about: knowing truth itself and goodness itself (in other words, God). The splendor of truth is that not only do we seek to know the truth, but when we find it and possess it, we will be happy forever.

Evangelium Vitae (1995): On the Value and Inviolability of Each and Every Human Life

Witnessing the horrors of the Nazi atrocities during World War II and the brutal regime of the Soviet-controlled Communist regime during the Cold War in Poland, JP2 was no stranger to unjust attacks on innocent life. He saw the consequences when society created a "culture of death" and saw the need to address the attacks on innocent human life in all its stages of development.

The key goals of the encyclical

John Paul II wanted, in this encyclical, to explain why every human life is sacred, precious, and deserving of protection, regardless of age, gender, race, creed, religion, nationality, political affiliation, economic status, and so on. This encyclical tries to show the believer that it is God's will and command that all innocent human life, from the moment of conception to the last breath, be given every reasonable means of protection and defense, especially those most vulnerable to attack (the unborn in the womb and the terminally ill and disabled). JP2 also used Natural Moral Law arguments to convince those of other faiths or of no faith that it is an ethical imperative for all human beings to show respect and make efforts to protect innocent human life. Whereas the person of faith has the revelation of Scripture to inform her of the Will of God by means of the Word of God, the person of no or of uncertain faith has his human reason to guide him in doing what is morally right for the common good.

The essential parts of the encyclical

John Paul II divided this letter into four parts. The first part deals with present-day threats to human life such as violence and murder. He included in this section abortion and euthanasia as being threats to innocent life, even though they may be done without deliberate malice, as in the case of violent murder. The terms *culture of death* and *culture of life* are first mentioned in this chapter of the encyclical. The second part deals with the Christian meaning of life, especially that in Jesus Christ, the God-made man, is found the author and source of life (divinity) and the fullness of life (Savior and Redeemer of mankind). The third part focuses on the law of God, both the Divine Law (the Ten Commandments) and the Natural Moral Law (ethical norms knowable by any human being with the ability to reason). Finally, in the last section, John Paul II dealt with the Christian response to a "culture of death" (namely, to defend and promote a "culture of life"). This is done not only by defending and protecting all innocent human life but also by improving the quality of life of each human person and praying and working for the conversion of sinners, especially those who deliberately seek to threaten innocent human life.

This encyclical is called the "Gospel of Life." John Paul II often referred to the modern era as having a culture of death, where life is cheap and treated with disrespect. The best way to counter the culture of death is to return to the Gospel of Life.

JP2 began with the familiar story of Cain and Abel from Genesis 4:8. Cain and Abel were the sons of Adam and Eve. Cain was envious of his brother Abel and murdered him. Cain had no excuse. Even though the Ten Commandments (with one of them saying "Thou shalt not kill") didn't appear until centuries later, Cain couldn't say he didn't know it was wrong to murder his brother. Even without a written commandment, as we know from *Veritatis Splendor,* written two years before *Evangelium Vitae,* the Natural Moral Law is known by any human being who can reason. All sane and rational people know: "Do good and avoid evil." They also know innately and intuitively by that same Natural Moral Law that murder is wrong even before anyone verbally tells them. Cain knew he did evil.

The Gospel of Life looks at all threats to innocent life — abortion, euthanasia, genocide, terrorism, and the conditions that make these evils prevalent, like poverty, violence, exploitation, slavery, prostitution, and so on. Human life is sacred because it is made in the image and likeness of God. Human beings have immortal souls, and directly killing an innocent life is always wrong and immoral. Because the ends never justify the means (Romans 3:8), not even one innocent life can be deliberately taken — even to save hundreds, thousands, or millions of others. No evil can be intentionally done no matter how much good may come from it. Any exception would open the door to more exceptions in the future. We cannot kill even one innocent life to save another or several others. If one innocent life is allowed to be murdered, then it can easily deteriorate into a numbers game (kill a few to save many). The danger then becomes who decides how many innocent can or must die in order to save how many others? Who determines what is the viable and credible threat? As soon as you allow just one innocent life to be taken, you open the door of death to many down the line.

Whenever the culture, society, or government attempts to justify the killing of innocent life, John Paul II reminded us of what the Apostles said: "We must obey God rather than men" (Acts 5:29). When the Nazis enacted anti-Semitic laws that allowed them to incarcerate and exterminate six million Jews, it may have been legal, but it was inherently and always immoral and evil, and those who followed orders or just obeyed the law should have known and done better.

Whether abortion and euthanasia are legal or not, John Paul II said that the criteria is not the legality but the *morality.* Directly taking an innocent life by causing death or intentionally withholding normal, ordinary, life-saving treatment is murder. But JP2 also ventured into the water of non-innocent life as well. Even though the Church has consistently taught that the state has the right to execute criminals, the right of capital punishment (or the death penalty) is not an absolute right. For it to be morally permissible, it must be done as a last resort — justly, fairly, and humanely. JP2 in theory upheld the right of the state to impose the death penalty, but in practice he did not see how in today's world it is truly ever necessary or done justly.

Within the United States alone, some, but not all, states have capital punishment. Some crimes of murder get death sentences; others do not. It all depends on what state the crime was committed in and what kind of lawyer the defendant can afford. Because the death penalty isn't done uniformly across the board and because there are other means to protect society, like life imprisonment with no parole, John Paul II didn't believe the moral criteria existed for a moral application of the death penalty.

Fides et Ratio (1998): On the Connection between Faith and Reason

Knowing that religion and science are not innate enemies, JP2 continued to show his ability to use solid philosophy and theology as tools to explain and defend the Catholic faith when ridiculed or persecuted. This letter is an intellectual response to the false attacks made on the Church as being irrelevant to the modern, technological world we live in.

The key goals of the encyclical

John Paul II wanted to show that faith and reason do not contradict one another and are not in competition. He showed the historical problem of going to extremes whenever someone would propose to exclude either faith or reason and attempt to limit human knowledge to only one source. The encyclical tried to convince the reader that science and religion are not natural enemies — they're just two perspectives looking at and understanding the world from two different but valid viewpoints.

The essential parts of the encyclical

Fides et Ratio is divided into seven chapters. The first chapter concerns Jesus as the revelation of God's wisdom and the fact that the Creator endowed man with reason from the beginning. The second part deals with wisdom as distinct from knowledge. The third part is on the pursuit of truth in and of itself. The fourth part is on the relationship of faith and reason and how they complement one another. The fifth part concerns the Church's teaching authority and its interest in human philosophies. The sixth part is on the interaction of philosophy and theology. Finally, the seventh part is on the current needs and direction of theology in general.

This encyclical is titled "Faith and Reason." In it, JP2 again showed his talent as a philosopher as well as a theologian. In previous centuries, there were two extreme positions: the fideists and the rationalists. *Fideism* is the belief that faith alone is the only true and valuable knowledge man needs. It rejects the truths known by empirical science or philosophical reasoning. The opposite ideology is known as *Rationalism*, which only counts the value of human science and sees no merit or worth in anything known by faith. It denies the existence of divine revelation.

Christianity sits between the two extremes. Science and religion are not natural enemies — faith and reason look at the same reality, just from two different perspectives. Faith believes what is divinely revealed by God, whereas reason ponders what is observed by the senses and known through reason. These philosophies are not different worlds — they just come from different directions looking at the same location.

Natural revelation is what is known merely by observing creation. Reasonable people have concluded that someone, some intelligent design, was behind Creation. Something cannot come from nothing on its own — otherwise, it would have always been here. The fact that the universe has an age means it has a beginning. What was there before there was anything? Nothing. Well, nothing begets nothing. Only a Supreme Being who is not confined to time and space can create something out of nothing.

Believing in a Creator doesn't violate science. If God is the one who set off the Big Bang, so what? Someone or something initiated the explosion. What keeps things in existence? Why is there order in the universe? Why is our planet far enough from the Sun not to burn up the atmosphere but close enough for us not to freeze to death?

God gave us an intellect to seek the truth — be it scientific, philosophic, or theological truth. Faith and reason are not competing forces but two sides of the same coin. When modern man realizes that he needs both a natural and a supernatural wisdom, and that earthly knowledge is not contradicted by spiritual knowledge, then he is on the road to fulfillment.

JP2 warned of these false philosophies:

- ✔ **Eclecticism:** A hodge-podge of thought borrowing from here and there with no regard to integrity.

- ✔ **Historicism:** A point of view that erroneously maintains that only the present and future have valid knowledge, and that what is in past is out of date and useless; in other words, newer is always better.

- ✔ **Scientism:** A system of thought that only accepts what is empirically verifiable and, therefore, denies any supernatural, spiritual reality; a form of materialism.

- ✔ **Pragmatism:** The notion that whatever works is ethical. If it can be done, then it ought to be done with no regard to consequences or the use of immoral means to obtain the end.

John Paul II believed that only an objective realism that embraces the full scope of human existence, body and soul, faith and reason, will provide the human race with the wisdom and knowledge it needs to survive.

Ecclesia de Eucharistia (2003): On the Eucharist and Its Relationship to the Church

The heart and soul of the Catholic Christian faith is the Holy Eucharist (the consecrated bread and wine used at Mass). It is also the heart of the papacy of JP2, as he spent a minimum of one hour of prayer each day in the presence of the Holy Eucharist.

The key goals of the encyclical

This is the very last letter John Paul II wrote before his death and appropriately enough it is on the most important and precious treasure of the Catholic faith, the Holy Eucharist. He wanted to show the essential and necessary connection between the Church and the *Eucharist* (the consecrated bread and wine that Catholics believe are really the body and blood of Christ, only under the appearances of bread and wine).

This encyclical not only closes the papacy of John Paul II but it underscores his very soul in that he was totally and completely dedicated as a man, as a priest, as a bishop, and then as pope to the Church and to the Holy Eucharist. He wanted to dispel any lingering doubts among Catholic Christians that the Eucharist is only symbolic. JP2 reaffirmed the consistent teaching in what is referred to as the *Real Presence* (the doctrine that Jesus Christ is really, truly, and substantially present in the Holy Eucharist, during and after the Mass. John Paul II hoped to show that the Church and the Eucharist are intimately united and can never be divided. The Church is considered the Mystical Body of Christ (the union of all baptized believers), and the Eucharist is considered the sacrament of the body of Christ (spiritual food for the soul and object of adoration because it is regarded as being the real presence of Christ himself).

The essential parts of the encyclical

The letter is composed of six parts. The first part concerns the Eucharist as the mystery of faith. How the consecrated bread and wine can become and remain the body and blood, soul and divinity of Christ is one of the most profound mysteries of Catholicism. The second part deals with the Eucharist as the foundation of the Church. The third part looks at the Eucharist as *apostolic* (being historically connected to what the Twelve Apostles themselves did). The fourth part talks about being in communion as a requirement to receive Communion. The fifth part explains the proper dignity, respect, and reverence demanded of this holy celebration. The sixth and last part is used to explain the role of the Virgin Mary and the Eucharist.

This final encyclical of John Paul II is titled the "The Church of the Eucharist." In it, he wanted to expound on the centrality of the *Holy Eucharist* (the consecrated wafer of bread that Catholics believe is miraculously transformed into the real body and blood, soul and divinity of Christ whenever the priest at Mass speaks the words of Christ, "This is my body" and over the cup of wine, "This is my blood). For JP2, the Eucharist and the Church are inseparable. The Eucharist exists to spiritually feed the members of the Church, and the Church exists to make present the Eucharist by ordaining priests.

JP2 affirmed the mystical presence of Christ when two or three are gathered in his name; when the sacraments are celebrated; whenever the inspired word of God is read; and in the person of the ordained minister. JP2 also affirmed the real, true, and substantial presence of Christ in the Holy Eucharist; of all the possible ways he is present, this one is par excellence. Only the Holy Eucharist is called the "Real Presence", and it alone is given the worship and adoration due to God, because it is considered to be the real, true, and substantial body and blood of Christ himself. The other ways are mystical and spiritual but not substantial and not considered sacraments in and of themselves.

The word used for the real presence of Christ is *Eucharist* from the Greek word for thanksgiving. John Paul said it was named this way because the faithful were extremely thankful and grateful for the awesome gift of being able to receive the body and blood of Christ. It is also called Holy Communion. Communion comes from the Latin *cum* (with) + *unio* (united) = *communio* (being united together). This phrase came about to describe the intimate union established between the believer and God when the believer receives Holy Communion. They are united with Christ by eating his body and drinking his blood.

The communion is not limited to the vertical dimension of the individual and God. It is also horizontal, because it expresses the unity of the person with the faith community who share the same beliefs. This belief is the reason a believer must be *in communion* to receive Communion in the Catholic Church. When a person is *in communion,* it means that he accepts everything that the Church teaches, obeys all the laws and disciplines of the Church, and follows the leadership of the pope and bishops united to him. A unity of doctrine, worship, and authority is necessary to be in communion. When the believer is united with the Church, the believer can physically partake of Holy Communion.

John Paul II reminded his readers of the teachings of Trent and Vatican II that the Holy Eucharist is, above all else, a sacrifice. It is the unbloody sacrifice of Christ on Calvary — his body broken and his blood poured for the remission of sins. It is not a new or duplicated sacrifice, but the one and same sacrifice of Holy Thursday and Good Friday. A sacrifice because it is the Son offering himself, his very life, to the Father on behalf of the human race. At Mass, the priest separately consecrates the bread and then the wine, symbolizing the separation of body and blood, which causes death. This is considered the unbloody sacrifice of Calvary on the altar at every Mass where the body and blood of Jesus are sacrificed for the sins of the world. Christ the Son offers his body and blood to the Father in atonement for the sins of mankind.

The Eucharist is also a sacred banquet or meal, but John Paul II cautioned those who take that out of context and neglect the primacy of the sacrificial nature of the Holy Eucharist. Yes, it is sacred food for the spiritual journey from Earth to heaven, but always *sacred*. And finally it's a sacrament, the Blessed Sacrament that is kept in tabernacles around the world. People come and visit the Eucharistic Presence because they are in the presence of God himself in a way not like any other.

Devotion and reverence to the Eucharistic Presence of Christ will only enhance and vitalize the Church, increase the Church's membership, encourage vocations, and reinvigorate the faithful. When the Blessed Sacrament is taken for granted, ignored, or treated irreverently, then the faith is weakened, if not poisoned.

JP2 encouraged

- ✔ **Frequent visits to the Blessed Sacrament:** When the faithful see their priests and deacons showing reverential love to the Holy Eucharist, they will learn and imitate the priests' pious example. Sometimes called Eucharistic devotions, any and all public adoration of the Holy Eucharist is considered Sacred Liturgy, which means it is a public (not private) act of worship of God by the Church.

- ✔ **Holy Hours of Adoration:** Holy Hours are 60 minutes spent in a church or chapel where the Blessed Sacrament is placed in the gold container called a *monstrance* (often resembling a sunburst on a stand with a glass container revealing the Host inside).

- ✔ **Exposition and benediction:** Exposition and benediction are when the consecrated Host are placed in the monstrance, which allows the Holy Eucharist to be seen behind a glass. The faithful look at the Host and, because they believe it is the Real Presence of Christ, they kneel before it and worship Jesus, whom they believe is there before their eyes. After being exposed in this fancy manner, the priest or deacon blesses the people with the consecrated Host, and that is called *benediction*.

✔ **Corpus Christi processions:** *Corpus Christi* is Latin for the "body of Christ," which Catholics believe is the consecrated Host. It is also an official liturgical feast that affirms the doctrine of the Real Presence. Traditionally, there are outside processions on this day with a priest or deacon carrying the monstrance containing the Blessed Sacrament and walking the street with the faithful marching along in procession.

✔ **Perpetual Adoration chapels:** Perpetual Adoration chapels are small places of worship where the Blessed Sacrament is exposed in a monstrance 24 hours a day. Catholics usually commit themselves to signing up for an hour of prayer so that in any one day, there are at least one or two people in the chapel praying before the Holy Eucharist. You'll find someone in prayer in one of these Perpetual Adoration chapels throughout the day and night, even after midnight and into the wee hours of morning.

✔ **Masses celebrated with reverence and decorum proper to the Sacred Mysteries being celebrated:** The Holy Eucharist is the expression of unity among the believers of Christ who not only believe in His real presence but share their beliefs in His church, and the church's doctrines, disciplines, and leaders. Every Mass is an ecclesial celebration that unites the people and priest, their local bishop, and the pope in one sacred action of worship.

As wheat is ground to make flour to be baked into bread and grapes are crushed so they can be fermented into wine, these two elements were chosen by Christ to become His body and blood in the Holy Eucharist. Likewise, the believer must be willing to be crushed and broken in his ego in order to become more like Christ. The Eucharistic sacrifice centers on divine love. It inspires those who partake of it to surrender themselves totally and completely to the Will of God and to offer up all that they have and all that they are for the sake of the kingdom of heaven. More than a mere symbolic reminder of what happened 2,000 years ago at the Last Supper, the Holy Eucharist at Mass is the reenactment of those Sacred Mysteries. In taking part in the Eucharist, we become part of the mystery ourselves and not just spectators.

Chapter 23

Ten Notable Beatifications and Canonizations of Pope John Paul II

In This Chapter

▶ Getting to know a few of the saints recognized by John Paul II

▶ Finding role models for your own life

Here, we highlight some of the 484 men and women Pope John Paul II canonized as saints and some of the 1,337 people he beatified. Catholics believe that anyone and everyone in heaven are considered *saints.* Canonization does not make someone a saint — that is done by God's grace. The formal process of *canonization* is an official recognition that a particular person, who is now deceased, lived a virtuous and holy life worthy of imitation, and after an elaborate investigation, has had his or her sanctity verified.

After a good person dies, if a miracle has happened by the power of God through that person's intercession, then the case can be opened for consideration. Initially, the title *Servant of God* is given to someone of heroic virtue or who was martyred for the faith. The next level is the title of *Venerable.* This is conferred by the Vatican Congregation for the Causes of Saints if the Servant of God lived a virtuous life and his or her writings are judged to be *orthodox* (that is, in conformity with the official teachings and doctrines of the Church). When a miracle has been discovered after death (or if the person was martyred), the person is called *Blessed,* hence the name of the process, *beatification* (from the Latin word *beatus,* meaning "blessed"). If two miracles have been established, and if the pope chooses, he can declare that the title *Saint* be publicly attributed to that person in the process called *canonization* (which is an authorized recognition). Some of the people JP2 beatified early in his 26-year pontificate he later canonized after the required second miracle had been found. We explain the whole process in more detail in *Catholicism For Dummies* (Wiley).

JP2 made significant changes to the processes of canonization and beatification. To see the details, check out Chapter 14. And to get the lowdown on the status of JP2's own sanctification, take a look at Chapter 18.

St. Pio of Pietrelcina

Francesco Forgione born in Pietrelcina, Italy, in 1887, was a priest. He joined the Franciscan Order of the Friars Minor Capuchin. His professed name was Pio, and he became known simply as Padre Pio. After his ordination he came to live in San Giovanni Rotundo in Italy. He was responsible for building a famous hospital, Casa Sollievo della Sofferenza, open to all the sick; the hospital opened in 1956. Even today, this hospital is known throughout Italy as being one of the best equipped and best staffed, with some of Italy's brightest doctors. Being treated at this hospital is absolutely free.

St. Pio had the *stigmata* for many years. The wounds of Padre Pio would bleed profusely during the Holy Sacrifice of the Mass.

The stigmata is a miraculous phenomenon where a person receives wounds identical to those inflicted on Jesus during his crucifixion — namely, the nail marks in the hands and feet, wound in the side of the abdomen (where the lance of the Roman soldier pierced the heart of Christ), and/or head wounds (from the crown of thorns). These wounds are not self-inflicted, and there is no evidence of any internal or external cause, yet the wounds appear and will often bleed during time of prayer. Antibiotics will not heal the wounds; they do not become infected and they don't become worse. No one is born with the stigmata and no one dies from it.

The most notable saint who had the stigmata was St. Francis of Assisi, who received them in 1224. St. Francis is the founder of the Order of Friars Minor, also known as the Franciscans, from which the Capuchins became a separate branch in 1525 A.D., when they sought to reform the original order. So, both the founder of the original Franciscans, St. Francis of Assisi, and later St. Pio, a Franciscan Capuchin, were blessed with the stigmata.

The fact that Padre Pio's wounds bled during Mass is most important because Catholics believe that the Mass is the unbloody sacrifice of Christ on the cross. It is not a new sacrifice, a different sacrifice — it's the same sacrifice brought through the centuries. The ordained priest is, therefore, a mere instrument of God's grace, so when the priest says the words of Christ — "This is my body" and "This is my blood" — over the bread and wine, the priest is speaking in the person of Christ (*in persona Christi,* the Latin equivalent). Though the priest says "my" body and "my" blood, it is not the priest's own body and blood, but that of Christ. Catholics believe that, every Mass, the priest and victim is Jesus

Christ Himself, using the ministry of the priesthood. When Padre Pio bled during the Mass, it called to mind the actual wounds of Christ on *Calvary* (the place in Jerusalem where Jesus was crucified and died on what Christians call the first Good Friday).

Pio became known during his life as a miracle worker. In addition to Padre Pio having the stigmata, people believed that he *bi-located.* Bi-location is a supernatural act of appearing in two or more places simultaneously. It was reported during his life that he would be at prayer in San Giovanni Rotundo while at the same time appearing to some distressed soul in New York who was praying to God through the intercession of Padre Pio.

In the course of a day, Padre Pio would hear hours and hours of confessions and absolve men and women of their sins. God gave Pio the ability to read hearts. This charisma enabled him to know when someone was being deceitful in confession or simply had forgotten serious sins. (To deliberately leave a mortal sin out of a confession invalidates the confession and makes a mockery of the sacrament. However, if you honestly forget a sin, you're exonerated.) Padre Pio also was able to tell the penitent exactly what they did and when. This drew many hundreds a day to him. Padre Pio would guide them through the wisdom of God in the spiritual life and most of all to correct their errant ways.

St. Pio bore the cross of Christ, meaning he suffered — emotionally and spiritually — by the many detractors he had. In 1922, those who were his enemies even had the Holy Office for the Doctrine of the Faith (formerly known as the Inquisition) suspend him from publicly exercising his priestly duties (preaching and teaching). In 1931, due to the controversy of his stigmata, Padre Pio was ordered to celebrate Mass in private. In 1933, Pope Pius XI ordered the Holy Office to reverse its ban on Pio's public celebration of Mass. By 1934, Pio's ability to hear confessions was restored. He offered all these humiliations in total obedience to his legitimate superiors and never disobeyed a single rule, even when in his heart he must have thought they were unjust.

During Padre Pio's lifetime, he enjoyed a vast reputation for sanctity because of his virtues, spirit of prayer, sacrifice, and total dedication to the good of people's souls. In the years following his death, his reputation for sanctity and miracles grew steadily and became established in the Church, all over the world.

In 1982, his archdiocese and the archbishop opened the cause for sainthood for Padre Pio. In December 1998, Pope John Paul II approved a miracle attributed to the Venerable Pio. In May 1999, before the largest crowd in recent history ever assembled in St. Peter's Square for a beatification ceremony, Pope John Paul II declared him Blessed Pio of Pietrelcina. In June 2002, Blessed Pio was solemnly canonized by Pope John Paul II as a saint.

St. Josemaria Escriva

St. Josemaria Escriva was born on January 9, 1902, in Spain. He was ordained a priest in 1925 and soon after founded the Prelature of the Holy Cross and Opus Dei. (*Opus Dei* is Latin for "work of God.") The institute is headed by a *personal prelature,* who is a member of the clergy and has ordinary jurisdiction over the group; much like a bishop has over his people in a particular diocese. The organization is composed of secular priests and laypeople, all of whose aim is to contribute to the evangelizing mission of the Church, by spreading the message of the Gospel and the message that everyone is called to holiness and, therefore, to be saints.

A *secular priest* is the opposite of a *regular priest.* The term *secular* means "without a rule," whereas *regular* means "with a rule." The regular priests are commonly known as religious priests in that they belong to religious orders (Dominican, Franciscan, Benedictine, Augustinian, and so on), which follow a "rule" (or *regula* in Latin) that tells them how to live in community (in a monastery or friary). Priests of the Personal Prelature of Opus Dei are not religious (regular) but secular. As secular priests, they do not have a "rule," do not wear a religious habit (but wear the garb of a secular priest), and do not live in community (but live in rectories or private residences).

Opus Dei was radical in 1925 in the fact that there were no provisions for its format in the *Code of Canon Law* of 1917. It wasn't until Pope John Paul II in 1983 added the canonical status of the personal prelature that clergy and laity could be formally constituted together without being either a religious community or a diocesan association. Opus Dei was founded over 50 years before the Second Vatican Council, which reiterated the same theme of universal holiness of all people.

Here are the chief teachings of Josemaria Escriva, all of which fit well with Pope John Paul II's own evangelization:

- ✔ **Ordinary life:** Having become a member of God's family through Baptism, all Christians are called to a life of holiness according to their particular vocation.

- ✔ **Sanctifying work:** A Christian's work becomes a fitting offering to God. The majority of Christians sanctify themselves by their ordinary work.

- ✔ **Love for freedom:** Christians should love freedom because the Second Person of the Trinity (Jesus Christ) took flesh and, therefore, took on human freedom, freely obeying His Father's will throughout His life.

- ✔ **Prayer and mortification:** The center of sanctity and Christian service is nurtured by constant simple trust and prayer, including devotion to the Eucharist, confession, the Sacred Scriptures, and the Virgin Mary.

Opus Dei: A secret society?

Ninety-five percent or more of Opus Dei are laypeople who live normal, ordinary lives as husbands and wives, teachers, doctors, nurses, lawyers, secretaries, blue-collar and white-collar workers, labor and management, and so on; only a small minority of Opus Dei are clergy. That means the majority of members dress, look, and act like any other ordinary layperson and are not visibly recognizable as priests, monks, or nuns in their proper garb. Their *apostolate* (spiritual and corporal works of mercy) are done discreetly, humbly, and without fanfare. And because of this (and because they don't wear any kind of religious habit), some people have unfairly accused them of being "secretive."

Members of Opus Dei merely seek to sanctify their ordinary lives — at home, at work, in school, in the office, privately, and publicly. They don't advertise or brag about their private efforts to grow in holiness, and their detractors unjustly accuse them of covert activities. In reality, their behavior is nothing more than prudent discretion and humility. Recent references to Opus Dei being some kind of right-wing conspiracy or a super-secret Catholic version of the CIA, MI6, or KGB for the Vatican are sheer fantasy and fiction and nothing more.

Mortifications are practices that try to control the body, passions, and wills. For example, Christians often fast in order to counteract the vice of gluttony. Mortifications help to control vices and make room for the virtues.

✔ **Charity and apostolate:** Christians are to give the highest importance to the virtue of charity. *Charity* means loving kindness toward others.

✔ **Unity of life:** A Christian who practices these teachings has no double life. Rather, he has a profound union with Jesus Christ. A Christian's work should be God's work — hence, the term *Opus Dei.* A Christian strives to be another Christ in the world.

On October 6, 2002, Pope John Paul II canonized Josemaria Escriva giving him the title of the Saint of Ordinary Life.

St. Faustina

St. Maria Faustina Kowalska of the Most Blessed Sacrament was born on August 25, 1905, in Glogowiec, Poland. She was the third of ten children. Her baptismal name was Helena. Very early on in her life she pondered a call to become a nun. Early on, she began her devotion to the Sacred Heart of Jesus and His Mother Mary. Because of her family's poverty, she did not have the customary dowry to enter the convent. Young Helena took work as a domestic servant to earn the funds she needed to pursue her religious calling.

She tried several convents to see if they would accept her, but she was turned away from all of them. Despite her discouragement, she kept searching until she was finally accepted by the Sisters of Our Lady of Mercy. In 1926, she took the name of Maria Faustina. Soon after she entered the convent, she began to receive apparitions of Jesus Christ as the King of Divine Mercy. The famous image that Catholics have today of the Divine Mercy of the white garment with one hand raised in a sign of blessing is what greeted Faustina.

Faustina spoke to Jesus and Mary several times. Jesus asked Faustina to have this image painted, but when she relayed this message to her superiors, they were skeptical. They wanted to be sure that this was an authentic apparition and not just a fantasy of an overzealous and pious young nun. Through the aid of a spiritual directory, Father Sopocko, she wrote a spiritual diary that later became a book, *Divine Mercy in My Soul: The Diary of St. Faustina.*

In the beginning, like St. Margaret Mary, who also received visions of Christ (in the 17th century), Faustina was ridiculed by her fellow sisters. Yet, Jesus would appear to her and comfort her. At the same time, her health began to weaken. The other nuns — out of spiritual jealousy — didn't believe her illnesses and made her work even harder.

Eventually, the superior of the convent transferred her from the hard labor of the gardens to the role of gatekeeper. It was at this assignment that she came in daily contact with the poor of the city. She listened to their stories and helped them in their needs.

One of the apparitions of Jesus was in disguise. Jesus came as a humble beggar to Sister Faustina. Of course she did not recognize him. Yet, she bestowed upon this beggar the same kindness and attentiveness that she did everyone else. Then Christ revealed to her who he really was. His message to her was that the Lord comes to people in many different ways and we should not lose any opportunities of serving him.

One of the messages of Jesus was to establish a religious community to promote his Divine Mercy. When Faustina went to her superiors, she found many obstacles:

- She was in *final vows* (the last stage of becoming a permanent member of a religious order) and, therefore, could not easily be released.

- They were still skeptical of her apparitions and probably did not believe her. *Remember:* She was a poor peasant girl, and some of the other nuns were more educated and felt they were better qualified to receive messages from the Lord. Yet, as in many of apparitions of the Lord to pious people, he often comes to the poor and the weak in order to prove his might and power.

Catholics believe that obedience is the hallmark of humility and that submission to the Will of God ultimately leads to holiness. Faustina remained obedient to her superiors, the legitimate voice of God's will for her. She knew that if God wanted her to establish this special order, he would find the way. Sister Faustina, however, became so ill that she never did establish this order, but the Divine Mercy devotion did thrive, partly due to her diary.

As she approached the end of her life, it was filled with much physical pain and suffering due to her illnesses. During this time, she prayed the Chaplet of Divine Mercy, a devotion that Jesus gave to her in one of his apparitions.

The Chaplet of Divine Mercy is a set of prayers that are prayed on ordinary Rosary beads. The prayers are the sign of the cross, Our Father, Hail Mary, and Apostles' Creed. Then for each of the five decades of the Rosary on the large bead, a special prayer is said, which was revealed to her by Jesus. The prayer was, "Eternal Father, I offer You the Body and Blood, Soul, and Divinity of Your Dearly Beloved Son, Our Lord Jesus Christ, in atonement for our sins and those of the whole world." Then on the smaller ten Hail Mary beads, another revealed prayer is said: "For the sake of His sorrowful Passion, have mercy on us and on the whole world." The Chaplet concludes by praying three times, "Holy God, Holy Mighty One, Holy Immortal One, have mercy on us and on the whole world." Jesus gave special emphasis to Sister Faustina to pray this chaplet at 3 p.m. This is the hour of His Divine Mercy, the hour Jesus died on the wood of the cross.

Sister Faustina died on October 5, 1938. The task entrusted to her to spread the devotion to the Divine Mercy continued under her spiritual director, Father Sopocko. Due to the simple nun's poor grammar and the confusion that resulted in understanding her diary, her message was nearly halted in 1958. It wasn't until the intervention of the Archbishop of Krakow (the future JP2), where the convent existed, that a new investigation into the message and prayers of Sister Faustina took place. When Karol Wojtyła became pope, he soon brought this devotion to the forefront of Catholic piety. Sister Faustina was beatified in April 1993 on the Feast of the Divine Mercy and later canonized a saint in 2000. John Paul II himself died shortly after the liturgical celebration of Divine Mercy began in Rome (Saturday evening before Divine Mercy Sunday).

St. Teresa Benedicta of the Cross

Edith Stein was born on October 12, 1891, into a Jewish family in Germany. In 1904, she renounced her faith and became an atheist. She studied philosophy at the University of Freiburg, received a doctorate in 1916, and became a member of the faculty. During the course of teaching, she began to read the life of the mystic St. Theresa of Avila, which had a profound effect on her — she converted to Catholicism in 1922. She then started to teach at a Catholic girls' school and continued her studies in philosophy. She read St. Thomas Aquinas, the famous 12th-century scholastic philosopher, and started to translate his works.

In 1934, she entered the Carmelite convent at Cologne. This order is the same one that St. Theresa of Avila reformed in the 16th century. Edith Stein took the name of Sister Teresa Benedicta of the Cross. In the convent, she continued her philosophical development and wrote on the philosophy of metaphysics.

To avoid the Nazis, who were persecuting anyone from Jewish descent, St. Teresa transferred to a convent in the Netherlands. There she wrote a mystical piece based on another great Carmelite mystic and contemporary of St. Theresa of Avila, St. John of the Cross.

As the war raged on, Sister Teresa was not safe in the Netherlands, and it all came to a head when the Catholic bishops denounced Nazi racism. As a result, Adolf Hitler ordered the arrest of Jewish converts. Sister Teresa and her sister Rosa, who also converted to Catholicism, were sent to Auschwitz. They both died in the gas chambers on August 9, 1942.

Six million Jews were killed in the Holocaust, and roughly five million non-Jews lost their lives in concentration camps as a result of the Nazi oppressions. Edith Stein — Sister Teresa Benedicta of the Cross — and her sister Rosa are living witnesses of what happens in a corrupt and evil system, organization, or government. Yet, they are also testimonies to faith in the cross of salvation. Her meditation of the cross that she did years before on the theology of St. John of the Cross influenced her spiritual strength as she became a martyr to truth. She died not only because she was of Jewish descent, but also because the Dutch Catholic hierarch took a public stance against Nazi racism. She died to uphold the moral position of the Church and, therefore, she was declared a martyr.

In 1987, Pope John Paul II beatified her, and on October 11, 1998, she was canonized a saint. She is the patron saint of orphans, Europe, and martyrs.

St. Katharine Drexel

Katharine Drexel was born on November 26, 1858, to the wealthy Drexel banking family. Though they had money, Mr. and Mrs. Francis Drexel taught their children early on about the importance of their civic duty to the less fortunate. Often, from their City-Line mansion in Philadelphia, the Drexel family would open their doors and give new clothing, shoes, and other necessities to the city poor. No one was ever turned away from their home.

As a youth, Katharine traveled widely in the United States and even in Europe. Early on, she became aware of the plight of Native Americans and African Americans. In 1891, she founded the Sisters of the Blessed Sacrament for Indians and Colored People. She inherited a vast fortune from her father and dedicated it to the mission of her newly established order. Soon she opened mission schools for Native Americans. In New Orleans, she opened Xavier University for African Americans. At the time of her death, more than 500 sisters were teaching in 63 mission schools throughout the country.

She was beatified on November 20, 1988, and canonized on October 1, 2000.

St. Maximilian Kolbe

Maximilian Kolbe was born in 1894 in Poland and was given the baptismal name of Raymond. Both of his parents were devout Catholics, and they had specific devotion to the Blessed Virgin Mary.

As a child, he had a mystical experience that changed him forever. Being a normal boy, he was into mischief, which led to scolding by his mother. This discipline had a profound effect on the young boy. When he prayed to the Blessed Mother, she appeared to him in a dream holding two crowns, one white and the other red. Mary explained that the white is for purity and the red for martyrdom, and she asked him whether he was willing to accept them. Indeed, he did accept the crowns.

Kolbe entered the junior seminary of the Franciscan Order in 1907. He studied the sciences and was quite smart. In 1910, he became a novice and received the habit of St. Francis. He changed his name to Maximilian Rome during World War I, and was ordained a priest in 1918.

Among the chief enemies of the Church at the time were the Freemasons. Along with six companions, in 1916, he founded the Crusade of Mary Immaculate with the aim of converting sinners, especially the Freemasons. Unfortunately, he contracted tuberculosis.

He returned to Poland in 1919 and taught history at the seminary in Krakow. Due to his tuberculosis, he had to go on medical leave for eight years. Yet, Maximilian did not waste any time. Soon he founded a publication titled *Knight of the Immaculate,* to fight religious indifference.

In 1927, Maximilian founded his own monastery, which housed a junior seminary and printing press for his magazine. Soon he started to publish a daily Catholic newspaper. In 1930, Maximilian, along with four friars, went to Nagasaki, Japan, to establish a new monastery. Miraculously, the monastery survived the war and nuclear bomb and exists to this day.

Because of his poor health, he returned to Poland, only to open a Catholic radio station. By 1939, the monastery he founded totaled 800 men. The year 1939 also saw persecution of his community by the Nazis, who wanted to control the press and radio. The monastery became a refuge for 3,000 Poles who were displaced; among them was a significant Jewish population. Then the Nazis shut down the presses, suppressed the congregation, and dispersed the brothers. Maximilian was imprisoned in Auschwitz.

At Auschwitz, some of the prisoners were going to be put to death to teach a lesson to other prisoners. A family man with young children was chosen to die. Maximilian volunteered to take his place. He was always at peace with God and himself; the nurse who was going to administer the lethal poison remarked that he gave her his Rosary beads, forgave her, and asked what a nice person like she was doing in a place like this. She was a fallen-away Catholic. After his death, she had a conversion, all based on her witnessing a saint dying and entering heaven before her eyes.

Pope Paul VI beatified him in 1971. Pope John Paul II canonized him a saint in 1982. He is the patron saint of drug addicts, imprisoned people, journalists, political prisoners, and the pro-life movement.

St. Rose Philippine Duchesne

Rose was born in France in 1769 to a wealthy family. She was educated by the Visitation nuns and entered the order in 1788 during the French Revolution. Because of the revolution, the convent was confiscated by the government, and Rose returned to her family. However, she continued to practice the virtues, especially charity, by caring for the sick, the poor, and refugees; she also taught children and visited the imprisoned. After the revolution, with the unsuccessful attempt to reestablish the Visitation Sisters, Rose entered a new religious community, the Society of the Sacred Heart. At the time, the former French colony of Louisiana asked the nuns for help in the diocese. Rose came to the United States, arriving in New Orleans in 1818.

Along with four other nuns, she was sent to St. Charles, Missouri, where she opened a school in 1820. Soon afterward, she built convents, orphanages, schools for the French and Native Americans, a boarding school, and a *novitiate* (a place where nuns live before they take their final vows) for her order. In 1827, she went to St. Louis where she founded another orphanage, more convents, and additional schools. Even at the age of 72, she was still establishing missions for Indian girls in Kansas.

In the final years of her life, she lived in St. Charles, Missouri. She was a model of charity to all around her. She died on November 18, 1852, at the age 83. Pope John Paul II canonized her a saint in 1988, calling her a true American pioneer.

Blessed Kateri Tekakwitha

Kateri Tekawitha was born into an Indian tribe in 1656 in a section of New France. Her mother was a Christian Algonquin Indian who had been captured by the Iroquois and saved by the father of Tekakwitha. When she was 4 years old, her parents died of smallpox and she was adopted by her aunts and uncle. She also contracted smallpox but was healed from it. As a result of the illness, however, she was left with marks on her face and severely impaired vision.

In 1667, the Jesuit missionaries spent three days with Tekakwitha's tribe. From them she received her first knowledge of Christianity. She was not allowed by the tribal chiefs to convert — only in her heart did she give herself to Jesus. When the tribe moved, it was mixed with others who lived an extremely immoral life. All through it, Tekakwitha was able to remain virtuous. She had consecrated herself and her virginity to Christ even before she was baptized. Finally, at the age of 18, she was baptized.

From her Baptism forward, she was a devout Catholic, practicing the virtues even in the midst of persecution from her own tribe. She was kicked out of her tribe because of her Catholicism and rescued by some Christian Indians. Later, she escaped to Caughnawaga on the St. Lawrence River. There she lived with another Christian Indian woman. Her sanctity impressed not only her own people but also the French missionaries. She practiced mortifications in order to attain a spiritual union with God in prayer. Upon her death in 1680, devotion to her began immediately. Within 15 minutes of her passing, Father Pierre Cholenec personally witnessed the transformation of her scarred and disfigured face into one of youthful beauty. Pilgrims visited her grave.

She was beatified by Pope John Paul II on June 22, 1980.

Blessed Mother Teresa of Calcutta

Mother Teresa was born in Albania in 1910 and baptized Agnes. Her father was a successful businessman, and she was one of three children. Very early in her life she felt God called her to be a sister. It wasn't until the age of 18 that she entered the Sisters of Loreto, an Irish community, and left for Calcutta. She chose this community because she wanted to be a teacher of girls. In 1931, she made her profession of faith and took the name Mary Teresa. In her early years, she taught at the girls' school in Calcutta and eventually became principal. However, the extreme poverty outside the convent wall impressed her deeply. Sister Mary Teresa felt called to serve these poor.

In 1948, she received permission from Pope Pius XII to leave her community and begin life as an independent nun. In 1950, Teresa received permission from the Holy See to start her own order, the Missionaries of Charity. The special missions of these sisters were to:

- Feed the hungry
- Clothe the naked
- Give shelter to the homeless
- Help the handicapped, blind, and lepers
- Give care to all the unwanted and unloved in society

Shortly after the establishment of her order, she established a hospice for the dying in an abandoned temple. Many young girls were attracted to Mother Teresa's simple spirituality and works of charity, and by the 1960s she had opened hospices, orphanages, sanitariums for lepers, and convents throughout India.

Pope Paul VI in 1965 granted Mother Teresa the permission to expand her order to other countries. She went to Venezuela, Italy, and Tanzania, as well as other countries in Asia, Africa, and Europe. She came to the United States and opened a convent and mission in one of the most depressed sections of the country, the South Bronx in New York.

In 1963, she founded the Missionaries of Charity Brothers and a contemplative branch of the sisters in 1976. Lay Catholics enrolled in the Co-Workers of Mother Teresa, known as the Sick and Suffering Co-Workers and Lay Missionaries of Charity. In 1981, Mother Teresa began an association for priests, the Corpus Christi Movement for Priests.

In 1971, Pope Paul VI awarded her the first Pope John XXIII Peace Prize. She received the Albert Schweitzer International Prize, the United States Presidential Medal of Freedom, the Congressional Gold Medal, and the Nobel Peace Prize.

In 1997, Mother Teresa fell and broke her collarbone. In August of that year, she suffered malaria and heart failure. She died on September 5, 1997, at the age of 87. At the time of her death, the Missionaries of Charity totaled 4,000 sisters, 300 brothers, and 100,000 lay volunteers operating 610 missions in 123 countries.

Following her death, the Holy See began the process of beatification. Normally, under the revised rules for beatification, the Vatican would wait five years, but Pope John Paul II dispensed this, noting her holiness and works that serve to prove this fact. In 2002, the Vatican recognized a miracle attributed to her intercession. She was beatified by Pope John Paul II on October 19, 2003, with the title of Blessed Teresa of Calcutta. Figure 23-1 shows Mother Teresa with Pope John Paul II.

Figure 23-1:
Pope John
Paul II and
Mother
Teresa,
during the
pope's visit
to India in
February
1986.

St. Juan Diego

This modest man of Aztec descent was born Cuauhtlatoatzin in 1474 in Mexico. He was of humble means, considered a peasant in comparison to the Spaniards who occupied and controlled his country at the time. When he converted to the Catholic faith in 1524 or 1525, he was baptized Juan Diego. His wife, Maria Lucia, was baptized at the same time. She died in 1529, and he moved in with his uncle Bernadino, who lived in Tulpetlac.

Daily, he walked barefoot for 15 miles to attend Mass. On December 9, 1531, on his way to Mass, he encountered an apparition of the Virgin Mary. She appeared, however, dressed in the attire of an Aztek princess with Hispanic facial features. She instructed him to tell the local bishop (an aristocrat from Spain) to build a church in her honor on that spot.

The bishop asked for a sign to verify the apparition. On the way back, Juan learned that his uncle Bernadino was dying, so instead of going to the place where he met the Virgin Mary, he headed for a local priest to bring home instead. The Virgin Mary intercepted him on the way and said that God had cured his uncle; she asked him to go back to Tepeyac Hill, the place they first met. When he arrived, he found gorgeous roses, which were out of season and not indigenous to the region. He gathered them in his *tilma* (cloak) and brought them to the bishop.

At the Episcopal residence, the bishop was flabbergasted to see Castilian roses, as he himself was a horticulturalist of sorts. More amazing, however, was the image of the Virgin Mary found on the inside of Juan Diego's tilma, which had protected and carried the roses. The image showed Mary wearing the attire of an Aztek princess and having Hispanic features while obviously pregnant and wearing a crown of 12 stars on her head, with the moon under her feet. This image depicted verbatim the passage of scripture found in the last book of the Bible, Revelation 12:1.

A cathedral was built on Tepeyac Hill and dedicated to Our Lady of Guadalupe, the name she herself used when she appeared to Juan Diego. Millions of native Indians in Mexico converted to Catholic Christianity because of that shrine. In that church, the tilma is displayed. The image remains visible and scientists cannot explain how it got on the tilma. Almost like the Shroud of Turin, the tilma of Juan Diego of Guadalupe remains a mystery. No paint, dye, or coloring can be detected, yet the image remains after 500 years.

Juan Diego died in 1548 and was canonized by Pope John Paul II in 2002.

Part VI
Appendixes

The 5th Wave   By Rich Tennant

Spiritually, I believe I can manifest many good things in my life. But right now, I'd settle for being able to manifest a cab.

In this part . . .

We bring you a few resources that you may find handy while you read this book. In particular, we give you a timeline of John Paul II's life, including all the important dates. We also include a separate appendix that gives you the details of JP2's travel itinerary throughout his amazing pontificate. Use these as you need them (or as they interest you) to put the text into chronological context.

Appendix A

A Brief Chronology of Pope John Paul II's Life and Times

· ·

May 18, 1920   Karol Josef Wojtyła is born in Wadowice, Poland, to Karol Wojtyła and Emilia Kaczorowska.

June 20, 1920   Karol is baptized at St. Mary Church by Father Francizek Zak, a military chaplain.

April 13, 1929   Karol's mother dies from kidney failure and heart disease.

May 1929   Karol receives his First Holy Communion.

December 5, 1932   Karol's brother, Dr. Edmund Wojtyła, dies from scarlet fever, which he contracted while treating a patient.

May 3, 1938   Karol receives the Sacrament of Confirmation.

May 27, 1938   Karol graduates from secondary school as class valedictorian.

August 1938   Karol and his father move to Krakow, where the younger Karol begins studies at Jagiellonian University.

September 1, 1939   Germany invades Poland.

September 1940   Karol begins work as a laborer at Zakrzowek stone quarry, part of the Solvay Chemical Works.

February 18, 1941   Karol's father dies.

February 1942	Karol is accepted as a secret seminarian by Archbishop Adam Sapieha. He continues to live at home and work at the chemical plant.
February 29, 1944	Karol is hit by a truck on his way home from work. He is brought to a hospital and spends weeks recovering.
August 6, 1944	After the Nazis begin arresting Polish men in retribution for the Warsaw Uprising, Archbishop Sapieha decides that all his "secret" seminarians should move into his residence, including Karol.
January 18, 1945	The German army retreats from the city of Krakow.
November 1, 1946	Karol is ordained to the priesthood by then Cardinal Sapieha.
November 15, 1946	Father Wojtyła leaves for graduate studies at the Pontifical University of St. Thomas Aquinas in Rome.
June 15, 1948	Father Wojtyła returns to Poland from Rome with the degree of Doctor of Sacred Theology.
July 28, 1948	Father Wojtyła is assigned as curate at the Church of the Assumption of Our Lady in Niegowić.
March 17, 1949	Father Wojtyła is transferred to St. Florian's Church in Krakow. He begins working with university students.
October 1953	Father Wojtyła begins to lecture at Jagiellonian University.
October 1954	Father Wojtyła is appointed to the philosophy department at the Catholic University of Lublin.
July 4, 1958	Father Karol Wojtyła is named an auxiliary bishop of Krakow by Pope Pius XII.
September 28, 1958	Bishop-Elect Wojtyła is consecrated bishop in Wawel Cathedral, Krakow.
January 28, 1959	Pope John XXIII announces his decision to call the Second Vatican Council. The Council meets annually from 1962 through 1965.

December 30, 1963	Bishop Wojtyła is named Archbishop of Krakow by Pope John XXIII.
March 7–13, 1976	Archbishop Wojtyła is created a cardinal by Pope Paul VI.
	Cardinal Wojtyła preaches the annual Lenten retreat of Pope Paul VI, giving him exposure to the Roman Curia.

December 30, 1963 Bishop Wojtyła is named Archbishop of Krakow by Pope John XXIII.

June 28, 1967 Archbishop Wojtyła is created a cardinal by Pope Paul VI.

March 7–13, 1976 Cardinal Wojtyła preaches the annual Lenten retreat of Pope Paul VI, giving him exposure to the Roman Curia.

August 25, 1978 Cardinal Wojtyła participates in the conclave that elects Pope John Paul I.

September 28, 1978 Pope John Paul I dies.

October 16, 1978 Cardinal Wojtyła is elected the 263rd successor of St. Peter and chooses the name Pope John Paul II.

March 4, 1979 Pope John Paul II publishes the first of his 14 papal encyclicals, *Redemptor Hominis.*

June 10, 1979 Pope John Paul II makes his first pilgrimage to Poland. He will make a total of eight such visits during his papacy.

May 13, 1981 Pope John Paul II is shot by Mehmet Ali Agca during an outdoor audience in St. Peter's Square.

June 20, 1981 Pope John Paul II returns to Gemelli Hospital with a virus two and half weeks after being discharged for gunshot wounds.

May 13, 1982 One year after the attempt on his life, Pope John Paul II makes a pilgrimage to Fatima, Portugal.

December 27, 1983 Pope John Paul II meets Mehmet Ali Agca in Rebibbia Prison.

April 15, 1984 On Palm Sunday, Pope John Paul II holds the first World Youth Day in Rome.

August 19, 1985 Pope John Paul II meets with Muslims at an outdoor rally in Casablanca, Morocco.

April 13, 1986 Pope John Paul II visits Rome's Jewish community at the Synagogue of Rome.

October 27, 1986	World religious leaders meet at the World Day of Prayer for Peace in Assisi.
July 15, 1992	Pope John Paul II has a benign tumor removed from his intestines.
November 11, 1993	During an audience, Pope John Paul II falls down steps and breaks his shoulder.
April 28, 1994	Pope John Paul II falls and breaks his hip. An artificial hip is implanted.
October 19, 1994	*Crossing the Threshold of Hope,* Pope John Paul II's written responses to an interviewer's questions, is published.
October 8, 1996	Pope John Paul II's appendix is removed at Gemelli Hospital.
November 1996	Pope John Paul II celebrates 50 years of priesthood by inviting fellow golden jubilarians from around the world to join him in Rome. He publishes *Gift and Mystery,* a reflection on his priesthood.
April 1, 1997	The Vatican Web site goes live.
October 18, 1998	Pope John Paul II celebrates the 20th anniversary of his pontificate with an outdoor Mass.
December 25, 1999	Pope John Paul II begins the celebrations for the Great Jubilee of 2000 with the opening of the Holy Year Doors.
February 26, 2000	Pope John Paul II makes a pilgrimage to Mount Sinai.
March 12, 2000	On the first Sunday of Lent, Pope John Paul II acknowledges past sins committed by members of the Church and asks for forgiveness at a Day of Pardon at St. Peter's Basilica.
March 21, 2000	Pope John Paul II makes a pilgrimage to the Holy Land.
January 6, 2001	Closing of the Jubilee Year.

May 4, 2001	Pope John Paul II makes a pilgrimage to Greece, Syria, and Malta, in the "footsteps of St. Paul."
October 16, 2002	Pope John Paul II calls for a Year of the Rosary and introduces new Luminous Mysteries.
April 17, 2003	Pope John Paul II calls for a Year of the Eucharist.
February 1, 2005	Pope John Paul II enters Gemelli Hospital with the flu and spasms of the throat.
February 24, 2005	Pope John Paul II reenters Gemelli Hospital with breathing difficulties, and a tracheotomy is performed on him. Doctors later insert a feeding tube for nutrition and hydration.
March 27, 2005	Pope John Paul II makes his last public appearance at his apartment window. Unable to speak, he gives a silent blessing.
April 2, 2005	Pope John Paul II dies at 9:37 p.m.
April 8, 2005	Pope John Paul II is buried in St. Peter's Basilica after his body is viewed by millions of mourners from around the world. The largest gathering of the world's heads of state as well as four million pilgrims attend the funeral Mass. An estimated two billion people — one-third of the planet's population — watch on television.

Appendix B

Travel Itinerary for John Paul II's Papacy

The official statistics from the Vatican Information Service (VIS) list the places, dates, length, and distance traveled for each papal visit abroad from 1979 to 2003. We've provided them for you in the following table.

Number of Visit	Place(s) Visited	Date	Length of Visit	Number of Speeches Made	Distance Traveled
1	Dominican Republic, Mexico, Bahamas	Jan. 1979	7 days	36	14,733 miles (23,710 km)
2	Poland	June 1979	8 days	36	1,979 miles (3,185 km)
3	Ireland, United States	Sept. 1979	9 days	76	11,243 miles (18,093 km)
4	Turkey	Nov. 1979	2 days	12	2,352 miles (3,785 km)
5	Zaire, Congo, Kenya, Ghana, Upper Volta (now Burkina Faso), Ivory Coast	May 1980	10 days	72	11,753 miles (18,914 km)
6	France	May 1980	3 days	30	1,559 miles (2,509 km)
7	Brazil	June 1980	12 days	51	17,195 miles (27,673 km)
8	Germany	Nov. 1980	4 days	29	1,790 miles (2,880 km)
9	Pakistan, Philippines, Guam, Japan, United States	Feb. 1981	11 days	60	21,823 miles (35,120 km)
10	Nigeria, Benin, Gabon, Equatorial Guinea	Feb. 1982	7 days	44	9,155 miles (14,734 km)
11	Portugal	May 1982	3 days	22	2,755 miles (4,433 km)
12	Great Britain	May 1982	5 days	27	3,032 miles (4,880 km)
13	Brazil, Argentina	June 1982	2 days	8	16,717 miles (26,904 km)
14	Switzerland	June 1982	15 hours	10	877 miles (1,412 km)
15	San Marino	Aug. 1982	5 hours	3	146 miles (235 km)
16	Spain	Oct. 1982	9 days	48	4,517 miles (7,269 km)
17	Portugal, Costa Rica, Nicaragua, Panama, El Salvador, Guatemala, Honduras, Belize, Haiti	Mar. 1983	8 days	44	14,919 miles (24,009 km)
18	Poland	June 1983	7 days	23	2,235 miles (3,597 km)

Number of Visit	Place(s) Visited	Date	Length of Visit	Number of Speeches Made	Distance Traveled
19	France	Aug. 1983	2 days	14	1,302 miles (2,096 km)
20	Austria	Sept. 1983	3 days	20	1,078 miles (1,735 km)
21	United States, Republic of Korea, Papua New Guinea, Solomon Islands, Thailand	May 1984	9 days	46	23,886 miles (38,441 km)
22	Switzerland	June 1984	5 days	36	1,378 miles (2,218 km)
23	Canada	Sept. 1984	11 days	50	16,680 miles (26,843 km)
24	Spain, Dominican Republic, Puerto Rico	Oct. 1984	4 days	10	10,456 miles (16,827 km)
25	Venezuela, Ecuador, Peru, Trinidad and Tobago	Jan. 1985	11 days	50	18,530 miles (29,821 km)
26	The Netherlands, Luxembourg, Belgium	May 1985	10 days	59	2,934 miles (4,721 km)
27	Togo, Ivory Coast, Cameroon, Central African Republic, Zaire, Kenya, Morocco	Aug. 1985	11 days	44	15,802 miles (25,431 km)
28	Switzerland, Lichtenstein	Sept. 1985	15 hours	8	982 miles (1,580 km)
29	India	Jan. 1986	10 days	41	12,584 miles (20,252 km)
30	Colombia, Saint Lucia	July 1986	7 days	35	13,128 miles (21,127 km)
31	France	Oct. 1986	3 days	27	1,262 miles (2,031 km)
32	Bangladesh, Singapore, Fiji, New Zealand, Australia, The Seychelles	Nov. 1986	13 days	57	30,431 miles (48,974 km)
33	Uruguay, Chile, Argentina	Mar. 1987	13 days	63	22,750 miles (36,613 km)
34	Germany	Apr. 1987	4 days	22	1,969 miles (3,169 km)
35	Poland	June 1987	6 days	27	2,833 miles (4,559 km)

(continued)

Number of Visit	Place(s) Visited	Date	Length of Visit	Number of Speeches Made	Distance Traveled
36	United States, Canada	Sept. 1987	11 days	48	18,930 miles (30,465 km)
37	Uruguay, Bolivia, Peru, Paraguay	May 1988	12 days	54	21,388 miles (34,420 km)
38	Austria	June 1988	4 days	20	1,555 miles (2,503 km)
39	Zimbabwe, Botswana, Lesotho, Swaziland, Mozambique	Sept. 1988	9 days	43	12,775 miles (20,559 km)
40	France	Oct. 1988	3 days	2	1,381 miles (2,222 km)
41	Madagascar, La Reunion, Zambia, Malawi	Apr. 1989	9 days	36	13,491 miles (21,712 km)
42	Norway, Iceland, Finland, Denmark, Sweden	June 1989	9 days	38	7,448 miles (11,986 km)
43	Spain	Aug. 1989	2 days	9	2,428 miles (3,908 km)
44	Republic of Korea, Indonesia, East Timor, Mauritius	Oct. 1989	10 days	28	24,263 miles (39,047 km)
45	Cape Verde, Guinea-Bissau, Mali, Burkina Faso, Chad	Jan. 1990	7 days	36	8,938 miles (14,384 km)
46	Czechoslovakia	Apr. 1990	1 day	10	1,325 miles (2,133 km)
47	Mexico, Curacao	May 1990	8 days	26	18,165 miles (29,233 km)
48	Malta	May 1990	2 days	12	955 miles (1,537 km)
49	Malta, Tanzania, Burundi, Rwanda, Ivory Coast	Sept. 1990	9 days	41	11,643 miles (18,737 km)
50	Portugal	May 1991	3 days	12	5,566 miles (8,957 km)
51	Poland	June 1991	8 days	39	2,847 miles (4,581 km)
52	Poland, Hungary	Aug. 1991	7 days	28	2,788 miles (4,487 km)
53	Brazil	Oct. 1991	9 days	31	12,800 miles (20,599 km)

Number of Visit	Place(s) Visited	Date	Length of Visit	Number of Speeches Made	Distance Traveled
54	Senegal, Gambia, Guinea	Feb. 1992	8 days	26	6,220 miles (10,010 km)
55	Angola, São Tomé e Principe	June 1992	6 days	2	10,427 miles (16,780 km)
56	Dominican Republic	Oct. 1992	5 days	16	9,391 miles (15,114 km)
57	Benin, Uganda, Sudan	Feb. 1993	7 days	28	9,526 miles (15,331 km)
58	Albania	Apr. 1993	14 hours	4	871 miles (1,402 km)
59	Spain	June 1993	5 days	17	2,136 miles (3,438 km)
60	Jamaica, Mexico, United States	Aug. 1993	7 days	22	12,876 miles (20,722 km)
61	Lithuania, Latvia, Estonia	Sept. 1993	6 days	30	3,330 miles (5,359 km)
62	Croatia	Sept. 1994	2 days	5	817 miles (1,314 km)
63	Philippines, Papua New Guinea, Australia, Sri Lanka	Jan. 1995	10 days	30	20,763 miles (33,415 km)
64	Czech Republic, Poland	May 1995	2 days	11	1,439 miles (2,315 km)
65	Belgium	June 1995	2 days	7	1,468 miles (2,362 km)
66	Slovak Republic	June 1995	3 days	11	1,642 miles (2,642 km)
67	Cameroon, Republic of South Africa, Kenya	Sept. 1995	6 days	13	10,428 miles (16,782 km)
68	United States	Oct. 1995	4 days	15	9,002 miles (14,488 km)
69	Guatemala, Nicaragua, El Salvador, Venezuela	Feb. 1996	6 days	22	14,951 miles (24,061 km)
70	Tunisia	Apr. 1996	12 hours	6	797 miles (1,282 km)
71	Slovenia	May 1996	2 days	8	1,065 miles (1,714 km)

(continued)

Number of Visit	Place(s) Visited	Date	Length of Visit	Number of Speeches Made	Distance Traveled
72	Germany	June 1996	2 days	9	1,599 miles (2,573 km)
73	Hungary	Sept. 1996	2 days	7	1,175 miles (1,891 km)
74	France	Sept. 1996	3 days	12	2,307 miles (3,712 km)
75	Bosnia-Herzegovina	Apr. 1997	2 days	11	660 miles (1,062 km)
76	Czech Republic	Apr. 1997	2 days	8	1,301 miles (2,093 km)
77	Lebanon	May 1997	2 days	5	2,789 miles (4,489 km)
78	Poland	May 1997	10 days	26	2,410 miles (3,878 km)
79	France	Aug. 1997	3 days	11	1,522 miles (2,449 km)
80	Brazil	Oct. 1997	4 days	8	11,430 miles (18,394 km)
81	Cuba	Jan. 1998	5 days	12	11,543 miles (18,576 km)
82	Nigeria	Mar. 1998	2 days	7	5,451 miles (8,772 km)
83	Austria	June 1998	2 days	10	1,275 miles (2,052 km)
84	Croatia	Oct. 1998	2 days	9	826 miles (1,330 km)
85	Mexico, United States	Jan. 1999	6 days	13	13,361 miles (21,502 km)
86	Romania	May 1999	3 days	9	1,640 miles (2,640 km)
87	Poland	June 1999	12 days	30	3,408 miles (5,484 km)
88	Slovenia	Sept. 1999	1 day	3	932 miles (1,500 km)
89	India, Georgia	Nov. 1999	5 days	10	7,842 miles (12,621 km)

Number of Visit	Place(s) Visited	Date	Length of Visit	Number of Speeches Made	Distance Traveled
90	Egypt (Jubilee Pilgrimage to Mount Sinai)	Feb. 2000	3 days	4	3,052 miles (4,912 km)
91	Israel, Palestine, Jordan (Jubilee Pilgrimage to the Holy Land)	Mar. 2000	7 days	14	3,496 miles (5,626 km)
92	Portugal	May 2000	2 days	1 speech	2,594 miles (4,174 km)
93	Greece, Syria, Malta	May 2001	5 days	19	3,245 miles (5,223 km)
94	Ukraine	June 2001	5 days	11	2,499 miles (4,022 km)
95	Kazakhstan, Armenia	Sept. 2001	6 days	13	6,072 miles (9,772 km)
96	Azerbaijan, Bulgaria	May 2002	5 days	11	4,046 miles (6,511 km)
97	Canada, Guatemala, Mexico	July–Aug. 2002	8 days	11	13,811 miles (22,226 km)
98	Poland	Aug. 2002	4 days	6	1,649 miles (2,653 km)
99	Spain	May 2003	2 days	3	1,693 miles (2,724 km)
100	Croatia	June 2003	5 days	6	1,486 miles (2,392 km)
101	Bosnia-Herzegovina	June 2003	1 day	3	619 miles (996 km)
102	Slovak Republic	Sept. 2003	4 days	7	1,713 miles (2,756 km)
103	Switzerland	June 2004	2 days	5	*
104	France	Aug. 2004	2 days	6	*

Unable to determine.

Index

• W •